Jesus

The Rock of Offense

Edgar Jones

Logos Press

P.O. Box 23
Southaven, MS 38671

Scripture quotations, other than the author's, are from the *Revised Standard Version* of the Bible.

The quotations from Jesus are inset and italicized. Other quotations from the Bible are blended into the text.

To all the faithful witnesses,
beginning with Stephen,
who loved not their lives unto death.

Something quite definite I have to say:

I have something upon my conscience as a writer. Let me indicated precisely how I feel about it. There is something quite definite I have to say, and I have it so much upon my conscience that (as I feel) I dare not die without having uttered it. For the instant I die and so leave this world (so I understand it) I shall in the very same second (so frightfully fast it goes!), in the very same second I shall be infinitely far away, in a different place, where, still within the same second (frightful speed!), the question will be put to me: "Hast thou uttered the definite message *quite definitely?*" And if I have not done so, what then?

— Soren Kierkegaard
From *The Journal*, 1853

PREFACE

H*e will become ... a rock of offense and a stone of stumbling to both houses of Israel, a trap and a snare to the inhabitants of Jerusalem* (Isaiah 8:14). This verse is the source of our subtitle, *The Rock of Offense*. Both Paul (Romans 9:33) and Peter (1 Peter 2:8) interpreted this to be a prophetic description of the Messiah. Jesus, the Messiah, also knew that he would be a rock of offense to the whole world, and he pronounced a blessing on "whosoever shall not be offended in me" (Matthew 11:6). In the Greek New Testament this idea is rendered by "skandalon," which we generally translate into "stumbling block." The English "scandal" also derives from the same Greek word, so that we could just as accurately transliterate the New Testament expression as "scandal." Jesus then becomes a scandal to the world, and he pronounces his blessing upon whoever is not scandalized by him.

He is most definitely a rock of offense, a stumbling block, and a scandal to the world. Paul pointed to the cross as the focus of the scandal (Galatians 5:11), and Christendom has generally understood this to reflect the hateful nature of the cross, that despised instrument of execution of despised men, on which the righteous one suffered so incongruously, and on which he is considered to have become sin for us. But I have discovered that the cross was a most appropriate instrument for the execution of Jesus. Contrary to popular belief, Jesus' life and the doctrine that personifies that life scandalizes the world, including Christendom, when it is rightly perceived. The whole person of Jesus is a stumbling block, not just the cross on which he died. Jesus is a scandal to the world, not because he became sin for us on the cross, but because his doctrine interdicts humanity's supreme love — the love of life (John 12:25). The cross is a locus of

v

that scandal because on it Jesus illustrated the ultimate expression of life hatred. The blessing of Jesus comes only to those who are not scandalized by this, and so he said, "Blessed is whosoever shall not be offended in me." This thesis underlies the work found in these pages.

Having already stated my thesis, I hope I have not lost you. What you are about to read contradicts Christendom's universal creed, the belief in the crucifixion as a sacrifice for our sins, and so I do not expect many persons to be positively inclined. There must be a few scattered about who are truly hungry for Truth, however, and it is for you that this book is written. These pages contain unusual material that may be offensive, and simple honesty demands candor at the outset.

Perhaps it will help if I give you some preliminary information about me, and how this book came to be. Hiroshima started it. I was a Navy V-5 student at the University of the South when the news came. My first reaction, like that of my fellow students, was one of great joy and satisfaction. Pearl Harbor was avenged! They would not send us unto combat! The festive mood continued through our victory celebration on the Eve of VJ Day, but it was not unmixed. This triumph of technology had shaken the foundation of the life I planned to live. Technology was my future, or so I had thought. Then, suddenly, Hiroshima and Nagasaki! So ... this is where it leads!

The months following VJ Day were an uncertain time as I reevaluated career plans. Then, in July of 1947, I became a disciple of Jesus of Nazareth and joined the Walnut Grove Baptist Church in Gibson County, TN, the church of my childhood, from which I transferred to Second Ponce de Leon Baptist Church in Atlanta, GA. By the following spring my feeling for Him was so strong that I could no longer continue planing for a career in engineering. After graduating from Georgia Tech with a degree in chemical engineering, I entered the Southern Baptist Theological Seminary as a foreign missions candidate. Southern awarded me a B.D. degree in the Spring of 1952, and there I met and married Nellie Ruth Harmon.

This was the beginning of a long and fruitful career for most of our fellow graduates, but not for us. My confidence in the church was often challenged at Southern. While studying the Gospels, I could not fail to compare the Lord's words to the practices of the church, and my professors were unable to resolve the apparent contradictions. The comparison left me with many more questions than answers, but I plunged boldly on. I am the problem, I thought. The church is surely right. How can I be correct and all Christendom in error? Some day, I thought, I will see the light. So, when Fortune Baptist Church, a congregation near Parkin, Arkansas, that Nellie and I had founded, told us one evening in 1955 that I could no longer be pastor, it became one of the saddest days of my life. Everyone was hurting that night: Nellie, me, and every member of the church. They loved us. They did not want to sever us, but they felt compelled to do so. The issue was whether we were to continue ministering to both blacks and whites without discrimination, a practice they were unable to support.

With the encouragement of a few local friends, and by invitation from persons in an adjoining community, we moved down the road a few miles and set up shop again. There we founded Boatrun Community Church, which now exists as Trinity Baptist Church. This was always a small congregation. In the early years there were hopeful signs, but the membership stabilized at about twenty persons, and there it stayed. The Baptists would never accept the congregation while we were there. This Boatrun period lasted twelve years, from 1955 until November 1967. By 1959 our family had grown to include four young children and the wolf was always at the door. Despairing of a making a living in the ministry, I found it expedient to dust off my engineering skills. Near the end of that year, I was employed in Memphis as a chemical engineer.

I remember the next seven years, until November 1, 1967, with mixed feelings. There were many happy times. Our daughter and three sons were healthy and doing well. My engineering work was going well. We had a good home in Memphis. But I entered a different world in the evenings when I settled down to prepare for weekends with the church. How could I succeed with this congregation, small and dwindling? How could some semblance of a career as a minister be salvaged? What was to happen, spiritually, to the members of my church? How could I continue in the ministry and maintain the integrity of my faith? Must I abandon the Lord as I knew him, and did I not know him aright? I was blind to the answers. To quit was to give up on the church — in my heart to condemn it, and this I was never prepared to do. Not to quit seemed to be condemning me. Many happy days of work and family life were closed not only by the shades of night, but also by the darker shades of frustration and fading hope.

Once, during pastoral visitations in Boatrun community, I approached a home only to be attacked by a small, feisty dog that attached itself to my heel and would not let go. I tried to shake it off by swinging my foot, kicking at it and dashing it against the ground. Even when its master appeared with loud commands to cease and desist, it remained firmly attached until I finally knocked it loose. So it was with me. I was hanging on to the church, doggedly persistent, determined, and resolved, although I was being shaken, kicked, and abused every step of the way. What is worse, I now know my Master was there, all the time telling me in words that should have been loud and clear, "Let go! Let go!"

November 1, 1967, was the day that knocked me loose. That morning I blacked out at work. Thus began my breakdown, and thus ended my ordeal with the church. There was no question of continuing that ministry, for it was many months before I could function normally. The first days were especially dark and there were times when I was a great danger to myself and to others.

A particular experience from that illness stands out boldly. You see, one type of the periodic attacks to which I was subject differed from the others. They all came from within me, from maladies in my system, but this one came from without. There was no doubt about that. I could feel it approaching before it arrived, and my practice was to suspend all activity. Then I would clamp my jaws and hang on, like a roller coaster rider as the car tops the crest and begins its descent. Yes, this was different, and the longer I endured it, the more I began to wonder ... can it be? Then, sometime in the summer of 1968 I felt strong enough to journey alone to visit a Christian commune near Durham, N.C. It was a Sunday afternoon and I was to speak to the community that evening, so I went out into a nearby woods seeking solitude to collect my thoughts. Hardly had I settled under a large tree when I felt "it" descending on me again, through the trees, like a great eagle alighting on its prey. Without premeditation, suddenly believing and without any doubt, I found myself lifting my face to the leaves above and crying out, "Satan, in the name of Jesus I command you to be gone and never to return!"

Instantly there was what seemed a great "swish" as the dread shadow reversed itself and shot up beyond the trees. It was gone, and it has never returned! Peace enveloped me, and I was ecstatic. It is true! It is true exactly as he announced when he told his disciples after his resurrection, "All authority, in heaven and on earth, has been given unto me." The problem was not in me, it was in the church! I could no longer deny it. I need no longer deny it. That afternoon, in profound peace, I knew the Lord and I knew that I knew him! At last, I was free to follow him, free from the shackles of institutional religion. I was free to receive and believe what I already knew in my heart. Best of all, the Lord was with me.

The seventies found me with a confident faith in Jesus. Many doors were opening after that liberation in the Carolina woods. The mind was free to entertain new and unusual thoughts. The most important change in thinking began early in this period. One day, while reading from Chapter 17 of John's Gospel, my mind focused on the verses referring to the Word of God. Speaking to the Father, of the Apostles, Jesus said, " ... I have given them the words that thou gavest me ... ". Then a little further and he said again, "I have given them thy word ... ". And yet a little further and he said " ... thy word is truth." Suppose, I pondered, suppose the truth is to be found only in the utterances of Jesus? They are the words of which he spoke here, which the Father gave to him, and which he delivered to the disciples. And they are the words he defined as "truth." The church had always taught me, and until that day I never questioned it, that the whole Bible is the inspired word of God. In consequence all of us have been sorting out the truth from the entire Bible. We search the Hebrew prophets, the New Testament epistles, and even sometimes listen to Jesus. But we arrive at different conceptions of truth. What would result if I were to start over, wiping the slate clean and listening *only* to Jesus — to his very words as recorded in the Four Gospels?

Reading a little further I heard him saying, "I do not pray for these only, but also for those who believe in me through *their word*, that they may all be one; even as thou, Father, art in me, and I in thee, that they also may be in us, so that the world may believe that thou hast sent me." Here, it appears that the word of the Apostles is also a basis of truth. Yes, but what is this "word of the Apostles?" Why, look, I thought, "their word" must be their repetition of the words he had delivered to them. When he said to the Father, "…thy word is truth," he immediately added, "As thou didst send me into the world (to deliver the words), so I have sent them into the world." Excitedly I thought, the very words I am reading are the words of Jesus delivered by the Apostles and recorded in the Gospels. Jesus knew we would be divided if we did not adhere exclusively to his very utterances as the word of truth. He knew, as I have since learned, that the only basis of our unity in him must be in our common devotion to his utterances as delivered by the Apostles. His utterances must be the exclusive well of truth. Not Moses, not the prophets, not even the apostolic commentary in the New Testament epistles — just his very words!

The pilgrimage changed its direction as I began to look at the utterances of Jesus in this new light. Today I understand that not only are his very words the exclusive source of the Father's Truth, but the words *are* Jesus! To receive him is to receive his Word; to receive his Word is to receive him! To abide in his Spirit is to abide in his Word; to abide in his Word is to abide in his Spirit. To have his Spirit within is to have his Word within; to have his Word within is to have his Spirit within. There is no difference between the Lord, the Spirit, and the Word. Jesus is alive in the world because his Word is alive in the world. Take a quick journey through John's Gospel and you should see that he said all of this, and more. Yet after a seminary degree and twenty-five years in the church, no one among all their scholars, pastors, and professors had ever told me this, and I had never guessed! When he said, "I am with you always, even to the end of the world," he meant that his *very word* is with us. Did he not also say, "Heaven and earth will pass away, but my word will not pass away?"

Everything did not clear up overnight. The pure ideas of Jesus kept bumping into obstructions planted in my mind by the years in the church. "Wipe the slate clean" is much easier said than done. In addition, I always studied under the conviction that the Truth of God must be simple. If we require scholars to define and explain it, then the ignorant and unlettered are condemned simply because they are ignorant and unlettered. No, if God is just, then it must be so simple that even a child can understand. Why couldn't I? Then slowly, surely, I began to draw the first buckets of pure, living water from his well.

I know now that I was a slow learner because the Truth, while simple, is hard! For example, I kept reading, "Do not resist one who is evil." and saying to myself, "He can't really mean that." Finally I quit doing that and said to myself, "Look, Ed — what it says is clear and simple. Perhaps he does mean exactly what he says." Then understanding came. Prior study of the entire Bible and the learned works of scholars was only teaching me that he did *not* mean exactly what he said. Only one thing was needful ... that I hear the voice of Jesus speaking the words of the Father ... and that I listen like a child to receive the simple Truth.

It turns out his Truth is a product for which there is little demand. The one thing I could do was write, and through the last twenty years, I have defined and recorded the faith, posed and answered questions, sought and found. This book is the fruit of that labor. I was constantly looking about for a church or fellowship or individuals that knew Jesus as I was learning him, but with little success. Have there been no prominent persons since the Apostles who knew Jesus after this fashion? I am persuaded that they are numerous, though it is hard to find them recorded in history. Had I lived in their times and places, I must have met many of them among the Hutterites, the Mennonites, the Quakers, the Amish, the Waldenses, the Anabaptists, and wherever the children of God gave up their lives for Jesus. There must be many redeemed persons in the churches this day who are frustrated and hungry for the Living Bread, supposing, as I did, that the problem is in them, not in the church.

More recently, I see Leo Tolstoy, during the later years of his life and in his work, "The Kingdom of God is Within You." Then, a hundred and fifty years ago there was in Denmark the most remarkable brother, Soren Kierkegaard, whose "Attack on Christendom" is, I believe, the boldest and most accurate evaluation of the maladies of Christendom to have ever been written. Everything he said is, in principle, fully as applicable to modern American Christianity as to the state church in Denmark in 1855, when he left this world. Kierkegaard addressed himself to a state church, but on the absolute principles of Jesus. He helped me greatly during the lonely times. I could always turn to his later writings and find a friend who understood.

I honor all the persons, organizations, and sects listed above because I believe that they took the utterances of Jesus seriously as he intended. Frequently they reached conclusions that differ from mine, and I regret that. The differences are easily explained. In every case I see that they went astray due to their consuming interest in the injustice of their times and by their compassion for its victims. Tolstoy's heart bled for the poor peasants; Kierkegaard's for the multitudes of the Danes buried under the deathly shroud of the state church. The radical reformers were overwhelmed by the brutality of medieval Catholicism with its Inquisition. I was sorely tempted to toss in my lot with that of the civil rights activists of the fifties and sixties. Certainly Jesus grieves for the victims of injustice. His solution to their problem is, however, the absolute one, and it differs from all those attempted by the world. When, like Tolstoy (or later, Martin Luther King) we attempt to make the Gospel "relevant" to the needs of our times, we take the heart out of it and render it impotent and powerless to accomplish the aims we seek. I will say again in the following chapters that the words of Jesus are the very words of God and are the *absolute Truth*. His message was absolutely unconditioned by the circumstances of his time, or by those of any time. They cannot be made relevant to any time or place, or to any set of historical circumstances.

I went through five employers during the seventies. My last employer released me from a position as manager of a clay mineral processing plant in Tippah County, MS in 1983. I was 57 years of age and unemployed, so Nellie and I purchased a laundromat in Memphis and "went into business." This was our livelihood for the next eleven years, and we prospered. We purchased a second store in 1991, and by the spring of 1993 we owned two great stores and had no debt. There was great satisfaction in the humble work of taking in laundry, and ample time to study the Word and to write. By 1994 most of my questions were answered and this book was complete. In the spring we sold the stores and I retired from business to resume the foreign mission that began misguided, and was aborted, forty years ago.

CONTENTS

Blessed is whosoever shall
not be offended in me.

Jesus, Matthew 11:6

INTRODUCTION

Christendom is the realm of contradictions. It is the place where those who speak in the name of the Lord contradict the words of the Lord, and where those who act in the name of the Lord contradict the deeds of the Lord. This results in a general mental disposition that accedes to unrealistic fantasies when thinking of Jesus and his times. For example, according to a popular Christmas carol, "O Little Town of Bethlehem," the little town of Bethlehem is quiet and peaceful throughout the night. The silent stars drift across the sky while the villagers rest in deep and dreamless sleep. The angels keep the quiet peace while watching through the night; then morning stars sing out praises to God and peace to men on earth. It is the night of the Savior's birth. Such is the fantasy of Christendom.

Here is the reality, according to the testimony of the Gospels: the tyrant, King Herod, was enraged because the wise men had deceived him. He sent and killed all the male children in Bethlehem and in all that region who were not more than two years old. It was to insure that he would destroy the infant Messiah (Matthew 2:16). Jeremiah foretold this awful crime when he wrote, "A voice was heard in Ramah, wailing and loud lamentation, Rachel weeping for her children; she refused to be consoled, because they were no more (Jeremiah 31:15)." This happened to Bethlehem and its children because Jesus had been born there!

The birth of Jesus in Bethlehem therefore cast a dark shadow of terror, death, and grief over the town and its whole territory. Can you imagine the horror of Herod's soldiers pounding on doors, searching, dragging out mothers clutching infant sons? Snatching the infants out of the wailing mother's arms and putting them to the sword before their eyes?

Silent stars? Dreamless sleep? This is typical of the contradictions of Christendom. There are so many, so gross and inexcusable, that anyone who reads the Gospels with an open mind must conclude that the whole of Christendom is a contradiction. Bethlehem may have been quiet and peaceful on the night Jesus was born. The slaughter was later. Still, the contradiction stands because the carol depicts Bethlehem as a place greatly blessed by the birth of the Savior. It suggests that peace and quietness will follow the infant and spread throughout the earth — that he is to bring peace not only to Bethlehem, but to all the world. Well, we have seen the consequences for poor Bethlehem and, for two millennia, we have been witnessing the consequences for the world.

Mary is another example of contradiction. She foretold that "All generations will call me Blessed" (Luke 1:48), and Christendom has fulfilled her prophecy by placing her upon a pedestal of joy and exaltation. Everywhere one hears her called "The Blessed Virgin" or "blessed among women," but the picture takes on a different hue when you put yourself in her shoes. First, there was a tense situation when she became pregnant out of wedlock. She was, according to the law, subject to death by stoning (Deuteronomy 22:13-21). Who knows how she managed to survive? Later, after the birth of Jesus, her husband took them on the hard journey to Egypt. They trudged across more than 200 miles of desert with no more justification than a dream (Matthew 2:13-15). There, during many months of hardship, they dwelt in the midst of strangers speaking a strange tongue. Then it repeated, another dream and another journey, from Egypt all the way back to Nazareth in Galilee (Matthew 2:19-22).

Mary probably had never heard of the massacre at Bethlehem. Such news traveled slowly in those days, if at all; we know that they did not learn of the death of King Herod until it was revealed to Joseph in the second dream, and I visualize their return to home and kindred as a very mixed blessing. The long trek is ending as they pass the gates of Nazareth and approach the home of Mary's parents. Someone has just rushed ahead of them with the good news of their arrival, and her mother bursts out of the door to meet them. Running to Mary and embracing her, she weeps for joy and cries out, "Oh, Mary! How happy I am! We thought you had all perished in the slaughter of the innocents!"

"Slaughter? Mother, what slaughter?"

"Mary, where have you been? Have you not heard how Herod put all the baby boys of Bethlehem to the sword because he thought the Messiah had been born there?"

Mary stiffened. She pushed her mother away as a look of agony and shock passed across her young face. She turned her head slowly toward Joseph, who was holding the boy in his arms. The child was so safe, so secure. There was a long silence. Then, a low moan began to issue from her mouth. Misery and grief took hold of her and she fell face down to the ground and clawed at the earth. Suddenly, all the sorrow of the mothers of Ramah exploded in Mary's heart. She cried out repeatedly, "My God, Oh, my God, why have you chosen me? My God, Oh, my God, why have you chosen me?"

Perhaps it was thus that the prophecy of Simeon began to be fulfilled, which he spoke to Mary saying, " ... and a sword will pierce through your soul also" (Luke 2:35).

The Bethlehem contradiction is bad; the Mary contradiction is worse; worse yet is the Jesus contradiction. The Jesus of Christendom is a direct contradiction of the Jesus of history. If the Apostles and other founders of the church, knowing Jesus well, had deliberately and falsely proclaimed a Jesus having characteristics exactly opposite to the true ones, the Jesus of Christendom would not have been a greater contradiction than the one now proclaimed. This Jesus, the Jesus of Christendom, applies his perfect love to bring peace to the earth and to heal relationships — for example, to mend broken homes; but what did the Jesus of history say?

> *Do you think that I have come to give peace on earth? No, I tell you, but rather division; for henceforth in one house there will be five divided, three against two and two against three; they will be divided, father against son and son against father, mother against daughter and daughter against her mother, mother-in-law against her daughter-in-law and daughter-in-law against her mother-in-law* (Luke 12: 51-53).

Again, the Jesus of history called upon the prophet Hosea to support him in teaching that God requires mercy and not sacrifice.

Christendom presents a Jesus who makes himself a sacrifice to God. The "Christians" everywhere call their male progenitor "Father," and certain churchmen, who claim to represent Christ on earth, encourage their parishioners to call them the same. What did the Jesus of history say about this?

Call no man on earth "Father," for you have one Father, who is in heaven (Matthew 23:9).

The Jesus of history taught that all righteousness springs from the hatred of life (John 12: 25). The clerics, who are the experts in such matters, praise a Jesus who would have us love life. They extol, in funeral orations, the departed sister or brother because she or he "loved life," but to the Jesus of history, this is condemnation.

This last contradiction, the "life contradiction," is fundamental to all the others. The "attitude to life" is the key to the comprehension of the Word of Christ and, paradoxically, also the stumbling block to acknowledgment and acceptance of the Truth. It is therefore one of the major themes of this book, which focuses on the Jesus of history and consequently exposes the "Christendom Contradiction."

The Jesus of history *can* be known. The quest of the historical Jesus begins and ends with the consideration of his words — the very words of Jesus of Nazareth. There is no other way to know him. Only by abiding in his utterances is it possible to see him face-to-face. He himself said it:

If you abide in my words, you will know the Truth (John 8:31-32).

I am ... the Truth (John 14:6).

Therefore, the book begins with a chapter devoted to examining the utterances of Jesus and, in particular, what Jesus said about what he said. The latter chapters are also founded on his utterances with little consideration given to other sources. His words are so simple and plain that no other sources are necessary.

Chapters 2 - 6 focus on relationships and identity, beginning with close personal family relationships and then extending out to the nation and to the world. I have examined these first because his teachings about relatives and relationships are fundamental to his message. On this subject also the light of Jesus' words and example readily exposes the "Christendom Contradiction." These chapters will prompt questions that begin to be answered in the next chapters (chapters 7 and 8), dealing with Life and Will. There we discover why Jesus' utterances on relationships and identity are so radical.

The latter chapters (chapters 9-13) examine some major doctrines of Christendom, including salvation, the Kingdom of God, eschatology, and ethics. There one sees how all things come together to form a consistent whole only in the light of Jesus' doctrine of the hatred of life. This imparts meaning and purpose, not only to the ministry of Jesus, but, through him, to the whole world and to our lives in the world. The final chapter (chapter 14) deals with the general application of the Principles of Christ to the living of life in this world.

The key utterances of the Lord, those that are fundamental to his message, are the ones the clerics are prone to call "the hard sayings." These are the words that, according to the mentors of my youth, are "better left alone." This goes a long way toward explaining the contradictory nature of Christendom, with its complex ethical and theological formulations. When one takes the backbone from a body, one must inevitably resort to cumbersome external support structures. The "flying buttresses" of Christendom's cathedrals symbolize this most appropriately.

Churchmen have therefore neglected these "keys to the kingdom" that are also the keys to the comprehension of his Truth. They call them "hard sayings" because they are offensive. They offend because we are sinners, and the essential nature of our sin forestalls serious consideration of their portent. Only after you have dealt with your sinfulness can you consider the hard sayings. I hope that you have done this and that their presentation in the pages that follow will not offend you.

I fervently hope you will agree with me, for I firmly believe what I have written, being fully persuaded that it is the Truth. Yet your response to *my* words is not really important. It is your response to the words of Jesus that *is* important for your eternal salvation. Hear him:

> *If I tell you the truth, why do you not believe me? He who is*

of God hears the words of God; the reason you do not hear them is that you are not of God (John 8:46-47).

Truly, truly, I say to you, if anyone keeps my word, he will never see death (John 8:51).

Freedom is one of the results of receiving the message of Jesus. It is only through dwelling on his words that anyone can know the truth that "shall make you free." This freedom is so profound that it is beyond words. I have mentioned it herein often, but no one can possibly describe or define it adequately. For me, it is enough to exult inwardly in it, to be amazed at its beauty and its glory and its liberating power. This book is also my effort to share this freedom with you.

There are two facets to freedom that I mention here because I hope that you will find yourself realizing them as you read. One is the revelation of the purpose of life and of the universe that serves as its container. The other is liberation from the very oppressive threats and anxieties that characterize life in this world — especially those that emanate from death to that life. The despair that fills the faces of many elderly people can, in your case, be exchanged for the joyful, eager expectancy characteristic of any young scholar contemplating graduation. The approach of death should inspire in you joyful anticipation, not morbid dread. It is precisely as Jesus said:

If you abide in my word, you shall know the truth, and the truth will make you free (John 8:31-32).

The primary interpretative tools have been science and common sense. By "common sense," I mean the sense that acknowledges that a lord, or commander, expects his words to be heard and taken seriously, and his instructions to be obeyed. According to common sense, a teacher is truly a teacher only when the students listen and respond appropriately. To say one is your teacher or lord while you ignore his or her words defies all common sense. So, if I say that Jesus is my teacher and lord, the statement is sensible only if I receive his words and obey his commandments. To ignore his words would render my assertions of his lordship contrary to common sense.

Science is another matter. It is the leading edge of the attack on ignorance. In particular, I mean the attack on ignorance about the fundamental nature of the universe. No world view can be tenable that is formulated without reference to the attributes of the natural world. For example, only in this Twentieth Century has cosmology parted the curtain of darkness to enlighten our perceptions of the origin and destiny of the material order. This, in turn, enlightens our perceptions of its purpose. It has shown convincingly that the cosmos has both a beginning and an end, fully compatible with the biblical revelation. This cosmos, once highly ordered and compact, has, since the beginning, been accelerating toward random disorder and dissolution. We have evolved to our present state due to a local "order enhancement," which came at the expense of greater disorder in the environs, in accord with the Second Law of Thermodynamics. This also confirms the biblical testimony to the ultimate futility of this age (Matthew 6:19, 24:35; Romans 8:20-22).

Science has also focused on the fundamental nature of human personality so that here, too, some light has penetrated a previously dark window. Now we can perceive the individual as legitimately motivated by the pursuit of happiness, the will to power, the lust for unending (eternal) life and the thirst for glory. We also can see how the creative process has harnessed that individual incongruously to the futile cosmic order that is his or her temporal home. The result is history — a perpetual frustration that issues in despair, greed, war, crime, tyranny and oppression. It has just enough gratification to fuel the incessant, but hopeless, drive for a temporal fulfillment. It promises, but does not deliver.

Now, in the dawning of this new, scientific understanding of ourselves and the world we inhabit, we have all we need to derive the true significance of our existence. But there are so many pitfalls! There are so many lies, deceptions, delusions, and false messiahs! We are exposed to them from infancy so that our understanding is darkened and confused. How can we ever chart our course around these shoals to arrive at the goal of true understanding?

We need a way-shower, a pioneer, whose testimony and example confirm us in rectitude and correct us in error. Such a guide is not just helpful; one is necessary. It is human to err, and it is also human to persist in error. Therefore we require an authority to over-rule us and by whom we may prove all things. It is my contention that only Jesus of Nazareth can fill that position. This, again, is a contention formed by the tools of common sense and science. The testimony of

Jesus meets all tests, being thoroughly consistent with the nature of man and the cosmos. He thus affirms his cosmos, as his cosmos affirms its Lord and Creator. The Psalmist said it well when he wrote, "The heavens are telling the glory of God, and the firmament displays his handiwork (Psalm 19:1).

Some have sought to formulate world views from purely human investigations, rejecting the deity as a lingering, primitive superstition. Others have attempted the opposite, by acknowledging only divine revelation as authoritative for Truth. But what if God, desiring both to make his glory known and to glorify his children, has ordered reality so that no one can realize the Truth apart from the application of human reason to divine revelation? What if God has revealed himself in Christ such that only through Christ can we correctly interpret the results of our science? It is not sensible to suppose that we can grasp a true view of the cosmos without reference to its Lord and Master. Neither is it sensible to suppose that we, the creatures, can draw a true picture of the Creator without reference to the creation that reveals him. Therefore science and religion, knowledge and faith, are co-workers in the building of understanding, and in the writing of this book.

I make no claims to unique divine revelations or inspiration of the Holy Spirit. Neither do I disclaim divine revelation, for I believe that the Holy Spirit acts through the normal tools of human reason that are available to almost everyone, and these are the tools I have used. I do disclaim any supernatural visions, insights, or hot-lines to God. The claim of such special gifts is the device of deceivers who have founded many of today's religious institutions. My view is that if people have not responded to the plain and simple words of Jesus, they have no basis whatever for the conception of Truth. His words *are* plain and simple! They are so simple that anyone can understand them, if they will, without the need of any special teaching or inspiration of the Holy Spirit. The Father has spoken through the Son; if one refuses to hear his words so plainly discerned in the Gospels, why should the Holy Spirit impose doctrine by supernatural means?

No, we do not require visions, visits of angels, or any supernatural revelation other than the one provided long ago when the only begotten Son of God became incarnate and spoke words of God to men. We do not need superior intellect, higher education or seminary degrees. What do we need? A copy of the Gospels containing the Words of our Lord, our fair share of common sense, coupled with the love of Truth, and a disposition to believe.

I have not spoken on my own authority; the Father who sent me has himself given me commandment what to say and what to speak.

Jesus, John 12:49

1

THE WORD

Matthew, Mark, Luke and John recorded the crucial words of Jesus. Their records, though incomplete, are adequate both to disclose the man and to define his doctrine. Therefore I have relied almost exclusively on their accounts of his sayings. The Gospel of John has an editorial flavor that sets it apart from the Synoptics, but the quoted words are the words of Jesus. His words from all the Gospels consistently testify to the TRUTH that no man could conceive by himself. Why? Because it is, I believe, a thing inconceivable to mere humans. Therefore only the Eternal Son could have uttered such words.

What did Jesus say about the origin of his words? John's Gospel repeatedly answers this question, and the quotation on the previous page is typical. With strong emphasis and by much repetition Jesus makes this one thing unmistakable: the words are from the Father. Jesus is only the messenger.

These assertions about the origin of his words eliminate the option of indifference and confront us with a compelling choice. If his words are the very words of God, of God who can neither lie nor err, then Jesus must be the eternal Son whom they reveal. Or, if they are only the words of the man Jesus, he is of necessity a liar and a deceiver for having attributed them to God.

He absolutely must be one or the other, and there are no reasonable grounds for other views. For example, the view that he was only one good religious leader among many cannot be correct. If that were so, the words were his alone since he then could not have heard them from his Father during a unique prior heavenly existence. Thus he must have lied when he said he did — but then, as a liar, he

1

was not good! Or, could he simply have been mistaken? Perhaps he was an ordinary man who honestly believed *his* words were directly from God? Of course—but then he was deluded, self-deceived, and a deceiver of many others. So, again, in this case as in the others, he was not good!

Many seemingly intelligent people have viewed him thusly, as a good man among many and as a true prophet among many, but to do so they must ignore his words — especially those that attribute all his words to God. Being thus ignorant of his utterances, their views of him can be nothing more than the fruits of fertile imaginations.

It is clear in retrospect that he deliberately presented himself in this way. He means to compel all who hear him to respond according to one of these two extremes: he *is* the eternal Word of the only righteous God, or he *was* a liar and/or a deceiver. One should decide between these only after careful consideration of the message the words convey, applying this simple test: is it of God, or is it of man? If it is of man, then its human, temporal, earthly origins will be evident in the formulation of its underlying principles. If it is of God, we will find it impossible to make such connections. As for me, having devoted much of my lifetime to the consideration of his utterances, I am confident his message is of God just as he consistently maintained.

Many things have confirmed this persuasion. I emphasize two of them here: the perception of the transcendent quality of his message, and the reception of the marvelous freedom that the message conveys. This is the freedom he promised when he said:

> *If you abide in my word, you will know the truth, and the truth will make you free* (John 8:32).

This is not an empty promise! It really happens! Whenever anyone opens his or her heart to Jesus' words and abides in them, the fundamental ideas of Jesus come to mind. One also understands then that no mortal could have conceived them. It is the Truth, and it yields a supernatural freedom that is beyond mere human conception. I do not mean to imply that the words are beyond human understanding. On the contrary, they are very simple and easy to comprehend. Children and simple-minded persons are competent to fathom them. But they are *hard to receive* because of the perceptual barriers characteristic of all mere human thought. They cut across the grain of all that men value, and therefore are unthinkable from within.

The Truth communicated by the words that the Father gave to Jesus and that the latter announced in the world is, like God himself, changeless and eternal. It is ABSOLUTE TRUTH, and the ancient world that first heard it absolutely did not condition it. Thus, having its origin in the eternal Father, it confronts every temporal human condition with equal force. Any effort to explain it in terms of Jesus' historical setting is utterly inappropriate.

This in no way contradicts the human origins of Jesus. On the contrary, I readily affirm his full humanity. He was born of woman, and grew to maturity in a Jewish home, village, and nation then under Roman rule. He experienced the Jewish traditions and first addressed himself to Jews. He applied his teachings using ideas already familiar to them, including the precepts of their revered prophetic scriptures. The Jewish culture therefore flavored the message, but only to relate it to those who immediately heard it. Never did it have any effect on the underlying principles.

The expression "Kingdom of God," which lies at the heart of his message, is a prime example of the ideas familiar to his hearers. To the Jews, its *coming* signified the restoration of the Jewish kingdom under a new David, but Jesus knew it to be something else. To him, it was to be the effective inception, on earth, of the Father's unique will. He did not impart new definitions to such terms. Instead, he restored the original meaning of the inspired prophets, which the Jews had adulterated. Since he did not present them with a new dictionary, people usually misunderstood him at first hearing and followed him due to fundamental misconceptions. Then, as time passed and he refused to respond to their expectations, they took offense and turned against him.

He consistently maintained that God is his father and that the Father had sent him down to earth from heaven with words to relay to the world. He was God's messenger, whose primary purpose on earth was to deliver the words of God to men. He was never mistaken, never changed his mind, and never altered the meaning of his words. He could not, because God had endowed them with meaning from eternity, where Jesus had received them in full realization of their eternal significance.

Given that he was born of Mary in the usual way and that he was reared as the eldest son of Joseph and Mary, also in the usual way, how are we to account for his clear recollection of heavenly pre-existence? (John 8:42). This question has a simple answer: He was the same person here as there, and his memory was very good. Yes, it was perfect!

The Temple incident, when he was twelve, illustrates this. Mary scolded him saying, "Son, why have you treated us so? Behold, your father and I have been looking for you anxiously (Luke 2:48).

Mary referred to Joseph as his father, even though the gospels testify to a virgin birth. We can reasonably conclude that this was her usual practice. If she were inclined to make exceptions she would have done so here, when they were in God's house. It is unlikely that she had ever instructed him about his unique birth. Yet at this early age he clearly understood that God, and not Joseph, was his father. He therefore felt a strong compulsion to be in his Father's house, as befits a twelve-year-old child. So, when the time came for him to return home, it was to God's house, not Joseph's, that he resorted. He understood his heavenly parentage because he remembered it. Also, no one on earth instructed Jesus what to say. Not Mary, for his message left her dumbfounded. Not any man, for his word communicated ideas such as no mortal can devise. Think of the amazed teachers in the Temple! (Luke 2:47). He had such uniquely peculiar and powerful words because, and only because, he recalled hearing them from his Father in heaven, just as he remembered that God *is* his father.

Jesus is undoubtedly unique in his early recognition and continued awareness of his heavenly origin, eternal character, and glorious destiny. This uniqueness is compatible with the virgin birth and helps to convince me of its validity, although it is not essential to his message. Jesus never mentioned such a birth, and must have considered it to be a minor "technical detail" of his sojourn on this planet. We can ignore it as a point of interpretation, just as Mary ignored it when she spoke of Joseph as his father.

So the Father delivered certain words to the Son in Heaven, then sent him to earth to repeat the message in the hearing of men. The Son entered the world through the door of human reproduction exactly as did you and I. Then he grew up in the midst of his people as a man among men. At some point in his early years he began to recall the words of God and to realize his heavenly origin and identity as Son of God. Then he accepted his unique commission to utter God's words on earth as he had heard them in heaven. This was the "work" his Father had sent him to do.

After completing his work, he addressed himself to the Father in the prayer of John 17, saying:

> *I glorified you on earth, having accomplished the work which you gave me to do* (John 17:4).

Then he proceeded to define the work in three parts as follows:

> *(1) I have manifested your name to the men whom you gave me out of the world* (John 17:6).

> *(2) Now they know that everything that you have given me is from you, for I have given them the words which you gave me* (John 17:7-8).

> *(3) While I was with them, I kept them in your name which you have given me* (John 17:12).

He then went on to say that he had sent these men into the world as the Father had sent him — to be bearers of the words of the Father to the people of the world. The only difference was that Jesus had received the words directly from the Father, whereas they had the words relayed to them through Jesus as intermediary.

Finally, he extended his prayer to succeeding generations of hearers and believers:

> *... that they may all be one, ... so that the world may believe that you have sent me* (John 17:21).

Thus his work consisted totally of the introduction and perpetuation of the words of God in the world, and he uttered them without regard for consequences.

It was typical at first hearing that the multitudes were favorably impressed by the wonderful words proceeding out of his mouth.

Then, suddenly, he would shock them with some very offensive statement, which turned them into bitter enemies on the spot. He explained this hostile response by saying:

> *The world ... hates me because I testify of it that its works*
> *are evil* (John 7:7).

His address to the congregation in the home synagogue at Nazareth is a good example (Luke 4:16-30). The initial response was good, and he had their rapt attention as they listened and marveled at the wisdom of this native son. Then, suddenly, he confronted them with two biblical events in which the Father seemed to favor non-Jews: Elijah's ministry to Zarephath the Sidonian woman (1 Kings 17:9-24), and Elisha's ministry to Naaman the Syrian (2 Kings 5:1-27). Just as suddenly, the temper of the congregation changed. Enraged, they rushed him to the brow of a nearby hill in an attempt to kill him by casting him over it.

Another time he gained the favorable attention of a large group of Jews such that many believed in him. Then he threw his verbal punch again, saying:

> *If you continue in my word, you are truly my disciples, and*
> *you will know the truth, and the truth will make you free*
> (John 8:32).

Their mood immediately changed to hatred. They took offense at this implication that they were subject to bondage, and they ended the speech with an attempt to stone him to death.

He sometimes gained the people's admiring attention by wondrous acts in addition to words, but then rejected their appeals. When great multitudes came out to hear him and became hungry, he fed them all by the multiplication of a few loaves and fishes. This finally convinced them that "This is indeed the prophet who is to come into the world." They then sought to force the kingship upon him but he withdrew from them (John 6:1-21).

These incidents illustrate the power of his words to separate the children of God from the children of this world. This effect can be compared to the operation of a sieve, which admits the few while repelling the many. He said:

He who is of God hears the words of God. The reason you do not hear them is that you are not of God (John 8:47).

Our responses to his words therefore establish our eternal destiny. Prefacing his statement with the words, "Amen, amen," or "truly, truly," he said:

If anyone keeps my word, he will never see death (John 8:51).

Yet again he said:

Truly, truly, I say to you, he who hears my word and believes him who sent me, has eternal life; he does not come into judgment, but has passed from death to life (John 5:24).

The Synoptics present Jesus' "Parable of the Sower" (Matthew 13:3-9; Mark 4:2-9; Luke 8:4-8) which summarizes the effect of the Word in the world. In the parable, the seed is the Word, and some fall along the path. The birds, which immediately take it away, correspond to Satan who takes away the Word. Some seeds fall on rocky ground, where they take root for only a short time, for the soil is shallow. This corresponds to those who gladly receive the Word, but fall away in a time of persecution. Some seeds fall among thorns. This corresponds to those who receive the Word, but the love of riches and such things choke it. Finally there is the good soil, where hearers receive the word and accept it and are fruitful.

Absolutely everything depends upon our responses to his words. Most persons, in and out of churches, hate his words and cannot bear to hear them. Church people tend to be selective. They focus on the words they like to hear and ignore the rest. Only a few listen with love and appreciation ... and fewer yet endure until the end of their earthly captivity.

The Parable of the Builders (Matthew 7:24-27; Luke 6:46-49) at the conclusion to the Sermon on the Mount illustrates this responsiveness, or lack of same, and its consequences. Those who hear "these words of mine" and "do them" are building, on rock foundations, houses destined to endure; but those who hear and "do not do them" are building, without foundations, houses doomed to fall.

It is very simple! He will sort us for eternity according to our responses to his words. So we hear him say elsewhere:

> *He who rejects me and does not receive my sayings has a judge; The word that I have spoken will be his judge on the last day* (John 12:48).

He said of those who hear:

> *My sheep hear my voice, and I know them, and they follow me. A stranger they will not follow, but they will flee from him, for they do not know the voice of strangers* (John 10:4-5, 27).

John's Gospel presents a teaching of Jesus in which he asserts that it is essential to life that his hearers eat his flesh and drink his blood. What did he mean? The discourse began when some Jews asked him for a sign, and spoke of the sign of the manna, or "bread from heaven" that their fathers ate in the wilderness. Jesus responded by saying that he himself is the true bread that came down from heaven. Their fathers all died, but anyone who eats of this bread will not die. Then he added:

> *The bread which I shall give for the life of the world is my flesh* (John 6:51).

As the Jews disputed how he might give them his flesh to eat, he rephrased the statement for emphasis and cast the following words at them:

> *Truly, truly, unless you eat the flesh of the son of man and drink his blood, you have no life in you. ... he who eats me will live because of me. This is the bread which came down from heaven, not such as the fathers ate and died; he who eats this bread will live forever* (John 6:53-58).

This strange, cannibalistic statement also offended his closest disciples, so Jesus explained:

> *It is the spirit that gives life. The words that I have spoken to you are spirit and life* (John 6:63).

He finally explained it! His words are what must be eaten. They are so intimately identified with the medium that brought them into the world — that is, his flesh — that he speaks of them interchangeably. There is here a sequence of metaphors beginning with the manna, which is the bread of life, which is the flesh and blood of Jesus, which is his Word, which is the Spirit. It should not surprise us to learn that he was really speaking of his words all along. Had he not earlier stated that anyone who hears and believes his Word has eternal life?

Jesus explained with metaphors, parables, and bold statements that the words he uttered mediate eternal life to the world. They are the Bread of Life that comes down from Heaven and gives life to the world. Those who receive it and believe have eternal life, but those who refuse to "eat" the Word are forever dead. He announced these words to the world through the exclusive medium of his voice. They are the true manna that came down from Heaven!

What of the voices of those other ancient and venerated spokesmen of God? Surely someone else has mediated words of life? What of Moses? No, not Moses. Jesus expressly stated that all those who ate of the bread of Moses died — every one of them! (John 6:49). No, there are no others — neither prophet, apostle, priest, nor preacher!

"Surely" you say, "surely some more recent voice has something to add to the revelations of the Christ?"

Absolutely not! The utterances of Jesus are the perfect WORD OF GOD. They lack nothing except hearers to take them seriously. Jesus stated all this. Thus he automatically ruled out all such considerations within the context of his perfect word. Dear reader, if you are entertaining such notions, that very fact is conclusive evidence that you have not yet heard him! Listen:

No man comes to the Father but by me (John 14:6).

Only Jesus is "The Life," and his voice first uttered the words of life in the world. He even said:

Truly, truly, I say to you, the hour is coming and now is, when the dead will hear the voice of the Son of God, and those who hear will live (John 5:25).

Jesus said something else that should clear the confusion from the minds of those who are inclined to listen to a later prophet:

Heaven and earth will pass away, but my word will not pass away (Matthew 24:35; Mark 13:31; Luke 21:33).

If this isn't a firm statement concerning whose is the last word, what would we need to hear? If the Word of Jesus were incomplete, we would have need of someone else to come later to add what was lacking. The word of the later prophet would then become the last word, and the Word of Jesus would pass away; it would become obsolete. When the new has come, the old is ready to pass away. Or, if the Word of Jesus were erroneous, then of course we would need someone to correct or condemn it and to replace the lie with the truth. The Word of Jesus would then pass away! Yet again, if the Word of Jesus lacked power, the lies of the world would overcome it, and it would pass away. Yet it stands today, two thousand years after its utterance in the world, as firm and immovable as on the day Jesus uttered it. Therefore we have good reason to believe that Jesus uttered Truth when he said his Word would survive heaven and earth. Other prophets of similar antiquity, whose words endure to this day, are very few, and none have had as much impact on the world.

Of course, two thousand years are a very small time in the full span of creation. No one can be certain whose word will reign two thousand years from now ... or two million ... or two billion. Yet history is busily applying progressively finer screens to the words of the prophets and pretenders. As time passes, fewer words survive. The words of Jesus are among the very few from antiquity that have survived. His Word is therefore a top contender for the last and final word. I believe it will surely remain when all others have fallen silent, exactly as he prophesied by the "pass away" utterance.

Some later pretenders have incorporated Jesus into their systems of belief by teaching their followers that he was a good man and a great prophet of God. Then they go on to propagate their unique ideas as if there were something they could say to make up what was lacking in the Word of Jesus. I have always seen this as terrible inconsistency: to call a man who professed to have the *last* word a great man and a prophet of God, then to add their words to his. If he were a good man and a true prophet of God, he would not pretend to have the last word unless that were precisely so. These later prophets involve themselves in a contradiction in which they cannot accept Jesus and also add their words to his. His words forbid it! He was either the true prophet of God with the last word for the world … or he is a deceiver for having professed to have the last word, that Word that will outlast the heavens and the earth! Such pretenders will eventually silence themselves as their followers become aware of their contradictions.

Now, it would be normal for any subsequent "disciple" who sought to impose a new "truth" on the world to look in the recorded utterances of Jesus for his authority. Those who do this find what they seek in the following verses:

> *I have yet many things to say to you, but you cannot bear them now. When the Spirit of truth comes, he will guide you into all the truth; for he will not speak on his own authority, but whatever he hears he will speak, and he will declare to you the things that are to come. He will glorify me, for he will take what is mine and declare it to you. All that the Father has is mine; therefore I said that he will take what is mine and declare it to you* (John 16: 12-15).

This is taken to mean that there were many words that Jesus left unsaid because the world was not ready for them, or more specifically, the disciples were not ready and were unable to hear. Later, any prophet, preacher, or priest would present new ideas as "truth" and claim that his were the words of Jesus that the world was then unable to hear, but that now are proclaimed in his name. There seems no way to prove such a person in error, and so persuasive individuals can, and have, deceived many people, causing them to believe that theirs are the very words of Jesus (and of God) previously unspoken in the world. But is it reasonable to suppose that Jesus would have left so strong a basis of deception to plague all of us who follow? I do not think so; furthermore, this interpretation contradicts another utterance of Jesus as follows:

> … *I have given them the words which thou gavest me, and they have received them and know in truth that I came from thee; and they have believed that thou didst send me* (John 17:8).

... All that I have heard from my Father I have made known to you (John 15:15).

No holding back here! This after he had just said the following:

I glorified thee on earth, having accomplished the work which thou gavest me to do ... (John 17:4).

So, did he give them *all* the Words of God, and did they receive them, or did he hold some back because they were not able to receive them? In the first passage, he "has yet many things to say, but you cannot bear them now." In the second, he has "accomplished the work" and asserts, "I have given them the words which thou gavest me, and they *have received them,*" and again "All that I have heard from my Father I have made known to you." This does look like he contradicted himself—yet I am assured that he did not. To reconcile these statements we need only refer to another utterance from the same context:

These things I have spoken to you, while I am still with you. But the Counselor, the Holy Spirit, whom the Father will send in my name, he will teach you all things, and bring to your remembrance all that I have said to you (John 14:25-26).

I conclude that Jesus had given them everything. The words were in memory, but they had not absorbed them. They did not understand and would not be qualified to do so until the Holy Spirit came. Then, he "would bring to their remembrance" all the words that Jesus had spoken, and "teach them" to understand. There is absolutely no justification, within the context of these utterances, for the expectation that later "teachers," under the influence of the Holy Spirit, would come to provide additional "truth" not addressed by Jesus while he was here.

Jesus is the Good Shepherd (John 10:11,14). All who preceded him were thieves and robbers, and after him there is no need of another. Those whom God gives to him are his sheep, and they hear his voice and believe (John 10:4, 16, 26-27).Others react with hostility to the Word, because they cannot bear to hear it (John 8:42-47). They do not hear because they are not of God — just as Jesus explained.

By this means the Word is the judge: those who hear and believe are of God, all others are not of God. Just so, everyone's eternal destiny depends only on this one thing: the response to the divine words uttered by that one man — Jesus!

A prophet is not without
honor, except in his
own country and his
own house.

Jesus, Matthew 13:57

2
THE FAMILY

The preachers say that Jesus will mend our broken homes and strengthen family ties. Jesus says otherwise. Here is his word:

> *Do not think that I have come to bring peace on earth; I have not come to bring peace, but a sword. For I have come to set a man against his father, and a daughter against her mother, and a daughter-in-law against her mother-in-law; and a man's foes will be those of his own household. He who loves father or mother more than me is not worthy of me; and he who loves son or daughter more than me is not worthy of me; and he who does not take his cross and follow me is not worthy of me* (Matthew 10:34-38).

> *If any one comes to me and does not hate his own father and mother and wife and children and brothers and sisters, yes, and even his own life, he cannot be my disciple* (Luke 14:26).

> *There is no one who has left house or brothers or sisters or mother or father or children or lands for my name's sake and for the Gospel, who will not receive a hundred fold now in this time ... and in the age to come eternal life* (Mathew 19:29; Mark 10: 29-30).

> *Brother will deliver up brother to death, and the father his child, and children will rise against parents and have them put to death, and you will be hated by all for my name's sake.*

But he who endures to the end will be saved (Matthew 10: 21-22).

You will be delivered up even by parents and brothers and kinsmen and friends, and some of you they will put to death; you will be hated by all for my name's sake (Luke 21:16-17).

These utterances are simple. It is difficult to misunderstand them, as they do not include exceptions or qualifications and there are no contrary utterances. When one searches the Gospels in quest of other words that place top priority on the maintenance and healing of family relationships, the quest is vain. One finds instead that family ties are inimical to discipleship. One's closest relatives can be expected to react with hostility to the word. Yes, with severe hostility that may result in the death of the disciple. Jesus foretold this when he said, "Brother will deliver up brother to death, and the father his child, and children will rise up against parents and have them put to death." Therefore, all who would become disciples must decide beforehand to deny, and yes, to "hate" (I use Jesus' word), the close relatives. It is a condition of discipleship. Jesus saw no end to this state of things, even to the end of the world. It was to be so in the experience of his first and immediate disciples (and it was), and it is to be thus in the last days. The world is then not subject to change in this regard. From the beginning to the end, it makes enemies of a disciple's closest relatives.

Jesus understood that one's family is normally one's first love, so he met this competition directly with the assertion that "he who loves father or mother more than me is not worthy of me; and he who loves son or daughter more than me is not worthy of me" (Matthew 10:37). Anyone must therefore pay a heavy price to become a disciple, as he specified in the following utterance:

For which of you, desiring to build a tower, does not first sit down and count the cost, whether he has enough to complete it? Otherwise, when he has laid a foundation and is not able to finish, all who see it begin to mock him, saying, "This man began to build and was not able to finish." Or what king, going to encounter another king in war, will not sit down first

*and take counsel whether he is able with ten thousand to
meet him who comes against him with twenty thousand?
And if not, he sends an embassy and asks terms of peace. So
therefore, whoever of you does not renounce all that he has
cannot be my disciple* (Luke 14: 28-33).

I have heard some assert that this applies only to the original twelve
apostles, but they err. We only need to examine the context to
determine that he addressed the above words to "great multitudes,"
and that he began by saying, "If anyone comes to me and does not
hate ...

Will you now say that the words, "If anyone ... ," addressed to
"great multitudes," applies only to twelve disciples? Of course it
applied to them, but only as the earliest of a continuing succession.
See how James and John, the sons of Zebedee, were in their boat
mending their nets when Jesus called them. "They left their father
Zebedee in the boat with the hired servants, and followed him"
(Mark 1:20). Later, when he said that it is easier for a camel to go
through the eye of a needle than for a rich man to enter the Kingdom
of God, Peter responded, "Lo, we have left everything and followed
you. What then shall we have?"

Jesus answered,

*Truly I say to you, in the new age, when the Son of Man shall
sit on his glorious throne, you who have followed me will
also sit on twelve thrones, judging the twelve tribes of Israel.
And every one who has left houses or brothers or sisters or
father or mother or children or lands for my name's sake,
will receive a hundredfold, and inherit eternal life* (Matthew
19:28-29).

So the twelve, who left everything to follow Jesus, will have a regal
reward in the new age. All others who have participated in a similar
forsaking also will receive wondrous rewards. We have then a general
teaching of universal application allowing no exceptions!

Jesus said that he had come to send — not peace, but a sword, and
he immediately applied the sword to the family unit, with the words,

*For I have come to set a man against his father; and a
daughter against her mother, and a daughter-in-law against*

her mother-in-law; and a man's foes will be those of his own household (Matthew 10: 35-36).

The family unit is where it begins, and it begins there for all who follow him in Truth. Anyone who would qualify for discipleship must endure a very difficult situation. Such a person has made potential enemies of those of his or her household — yet without losing one whit of affection for them. One must reckon with this at the start, while "counting the cost." Otherwise, after having made a good beginning, one may fall away for lack of endurance. Jesus has assured us that what we stand to gain is much greater than anything we might lose. He has promised us "a hundredfold" in this age, and in the age to come, "eternal life." When making such promises, Jesus accepts and caters to our highest self interest. It will cost you — oh how it will cost you — and so you will be wise to reckon the cost beforehand. But consider also the promise of reward — here, in this time, a hundredfold! That is only the beginning, for in the age to come one receives ... eternal life!

So we have this dual promise: the hundredfold, and eternal life. Jesus cannot accept anyone into discipleship who does not hate his father, mother, wife, children, brothers, and sisters. Therefore it is correct to conclude that his promises to his disciples are only to those who conform to this utterance. Apart from this there is no promise of salvation and eternal life, or of the hundredfold.

What is the significance of the hundredfold promise? I have asked the question only to answer it with the assertion: "Jesus meant exactly what he said!" The words are simple and require no clarification. Look, for example, at Matthew's version:

> *And everyone who has left houses or brothers or sisters or Father or mother or children or lands, for my name's sake, will receive a hundredfold, and inherit eternal life* (Matthew 19:29).

Now consider Luke's rendition:

> *There is no man who has left house or wife or brothers or parents or children, for the sake of the Kingdom of God, who will not receive manifold more in this time, and in the age to come, eternal life* (Luke 18:29-30).

Finally, compare these with Mark's version:

There is no one who has left house or brothers or sisters or mother or father or children or lands, for my sake and for the gospel, who will not receive a hundredfold now in this time, houses and brothers and sisters and mothers and children and lands, with persecutions, and in the age to come eternal life (Mark 10: 29-30).

Mark includes something the others omitted — that the hundred-fold promise comes with persecutions. He also details the promise completely, applying it to every family member forsaken, except two — the spouse and the father. There were very important reasons for these omissions, which I will discuss later in separate chapters devoted to each.

We are, at this point, in need of some enlightenment about how the hundredfold promise is to be realized as a practical matter. This Jesus provides in association with an incident that involves his particular relatives and the definition of his relatives. I will include it in the consideration of his personal example regarding family ties. To this I now turn.

Jesus' unusual conduct and the resulting great uproar among the people troubled Mary. She went to see him, accompanied by his unbelieving brothers. When they found him he was in the midst of a crowd that pressed so tightly they could not get to him. They conveyed a message through the crowd to him, "Your mother and your brothers are standing outside, desiring to see you" (Matthew 12:47). He replied,

Who is my mother, and who are my brothers?

Then, stretching out his hands toward his disciples, he said:

Here are my mother and my brothers! For whoever does the will of my Father in heaven is my brother, and sister, and mother (Matthew 12:49-50).

These words radically redefined his personal family relationships. He did not intend this to be a definition of "spiritual" relatives as distinguished from physical ones. The newly defined relationships displaced the ones that Mary and his siblings represented. The circumstances make his intent clear. Mary is not necessarily his mother, and her sons are not necessarily his brothers. His only family, consisting specifically of brothers, sisters, and mother, was related to him by the single common bond of doing the will of his Father in heaven. He did not affirm carnal relationships. He also taught elsewhere, saying,

The flesh profits nothing (John 6:63).

Now we have new insight into his meaning. If the flesh profits nothing, then those relationships arising out of it are nothing!

Please remember now and always that when Jesus spoke, he uttered not his words but the words of God that he heard from his Father in heaven. Therefore this definition of his relatives is of God. It was uttered from the perspective of eternity by him through whose word the world and all things in it have their being. Those relationships that men commonly acknowledge among themselves have no existence before God — except as obstructions to realizing the true and genuine relationships.

He denied that these physical relationships are what we think, yet he acknowledged them as serving the function of reproduction. Speaking elsewhere to the Jews on the subject of fatherhood, he said, "I know that you are Abraham's seed [Greek, *sperma*]" (John 8:37). Mary gave birth to him, but that did not make her his mother. Neither were her other children his brothers and sisters. His radical redefinition of these terms, given as it is from the perspective of eternity, reveals the Truth as it has been "from the beginning."

It is not difficult to see how our worldly view came about. Men and women are created in the likeness of God. Therefore we have places in the heart of each individual that can be occupied only by relationships characterized by mutual love and acceptance. This constitutes a need that must be satisfied. Because we are in God's likeness, we are at heart and in essence spiritual beings, and these places can be truly satisfied only by spiritual relationships. But the men and women of the world are blind to the spiritual; therefore we have sought to satisfy this need by means of counterfeit substitutes based on carnal associations. These counterfeit relatives are continually failing us in that they can never satisfy our inner, eternal needs nor can they fill the empty spaces in our hearts. Those spaces have the shape and size of eternity and the temporal things never fit.

Progenitors, siblings, and progeny serve vital functions and are obviously essential, but one commits a great error by admitting them to the spiritual inner sanctum. Consequently, Jesus totally rejected Mary as his mother, and his siblings as brothers and sisters. She and her other offspring did not by nature belong in those relationships, where they were counterfeit pretenders. He acknowledged only his genuine mother, brothers, and sisters — those related to him by a common inner spiritual disposition. They are the ones who heard the Word of God and did it and thus showed that they were his true relatives.

It is not possible to acknowledge both types of relationships and hold them side by side. The nature of things is such that they simply will not fit together in that way. Therefore, if we are ever to realize the genuine we must divest ourselves of the spurious, and so Jesus said:

> *If any one comes to me and does not hate his own father and mother and wife and children and brothers and sisters … He cannot be my disciple* (Luke 14:26).

This incident redefined his true relatives. It also exemplified what he means by hating one's own mother and brothers, for that is what he did that day. Now we can understand what he meant by his "hundredfold" promise. Our genuine relatives are all who hear the Word of God and do it. Therefore whoever forsakes the counterfeit stands to receive a hundredfold of the genuine. Jesus absolutely rejected those relationships commonly associated with the earthly progenitors, and replaced them with other relationships arising from a shared association with the Father in Heaven. We establish this by the reception of the words of the Father that Jesus uttered. He gave these relationships the same names as those associated with the earthly relatives. It is his intent to replace the latter with the former in the hearts and minds of his disciples, just as he did for himself. He does not merely amend the old relationships with new ones. His intent is to dispose of the old entirely by displacing them with the new!

Perhaps you are objecting at this point, as many do, and saying, "Surely not! Jesus referred only to special cases where mothers, brothers, and sisters oppose us because we have become his disciples."

Consider this position on its merits. It hinges on a certain sequence of events: first, one becomes a disciple, then one's relatives oppose the discipleship. Finally, one has to disavow one's relatives because of their opposition. How does this sequence correspond to the words of Jesus already quoted?

> *If any one comes to me and does not hate his own father and mother and wife and children and brothers and sisters, yes, and even his own life, he cannot be my disciple* (Luke 14:26).

A similar scrutiny of this utterance shows the following sequence of events: first, one hates ones' relatives, and then one becomes a disciple. This position contradicts Jesus. Far from being a consequence of discipleship, the hatred of these relationships is a condition of discipleship! No amount of equivocation can make the Word mean other than it unequivocally does: the hatred comes first, as a qualification. Later, having qualified, comes the discipleship!

Surely there are many exceptions? No, there are none. Look at his words:

> *If any one comes to me ...* (Luke 14:26).

Is any term more comprehensive than "any one?" Where is the basis for an exception — for even a single one? Jesus definitely included himself, and now he commands all would-be disciples:

> *Follow me* (Matthew 16:24).

> *For I have come to set a man against his father, and a daughter against her mother, and a daughter-in-law against her mother-in-law, and a man's foes will be those of his own household* (Matthew 10: 35-36).

Was Jesus' personal example consistent with the application of this doctrine? Yes! There is a limited amount of relevant material in the Gospels, but it is sufficient. If the significance of his teaching is as I have said, then to be consistent he must never have addressed Mary as "Mother." Did he?

Jesus addressed Mary directly only three times in the Gospels. The first is the temple incident already discussed in another context, in which he responded to her with the words:

> *How is it that you sought me? Did you not know that I must be in my Father's house?* (Luke 2:49).

We see immediately that he was consistent in not calling Joseph his father, and he used no special term to designate Mary. The wedding at Cana is the setting for the second incident. When Mary said to him, "They have no wine," he responded:

> *O, woman, what have you to do with me?* (John 2:4).

He did not say "mother." Instead he used the same term as when addressing the woman encountered at Jacob's Well, the Canaanite woman, Mary Magdalene, and the woman taken in adultery. "Woman" was appropriate for addressing strangers, adulteresses ... and the one who bore him.

The quotation concludes with " ... what have you to do with me?" This suggests rejection, even hostility. It is illuminating to examine other biblical incidents using these or similar words. First, there is the example of Elijah and the widow of Zarephath. The prophet was lodging with Zarephath when her son became ill and either died or was at the point of death. Knowing that Elijah was a man of God with unusual powers, she assumed that God was using him to punish her for her sins. She said to him, "*What have I to do with you,* O thou man of God? Have you come to me to call my sin to remembrance and to slay my son?" Then Elijah took the son, prayed for him, and he revived (1 Kings 17:9-24).

When Jesus was teaching in the synagogue in Capernaum, there was a man with an unclean spirit who cried out, "*What have you to do with us,* Jesus of Nazareth? Have you come to destroy us? I know who you are, the holy one of God." Then Jesus rebuked him and cast out the evil spirit (Mark 1:24).

Another time, in the country of the Gerasenes, Jesus encountered a demoniac who, on seeing Jesus, cried out, *"What have you to do with me,"* Jesus, Son of the most high God? I adjure you by God, do not torment me." Then Jesus cast a legion of demons out of him and into a herd of swine (Mark 5:7).

The similarities in these cases, including the wedding at Cana, are too much for mere coincidence. The speaker in each case recognized the other party as an adversary. In each case the godly party proceeded to work a miracle for the other, as did Jesus at Cana, though his oral response was tantamount to rejection.

Lastly, when Jesus was hanging from the cross he saw Mary standing near "the disciple whom he loved," and he called out to her:

"Woman, behold your son."

Then, addressing the disciple, he said,

"Behold your mother."

From that hour, the disciple took her into his home. Making this provision of a home for Mary was next to the last thing he did, but he did not call her "Mother." Instead, he used again that distant, impersonal word for strangers, and then called her someone else's mother (John 19:25-27).

Since Jesus had said, "A man's foes shall be they of his own household," it is reasonable to infer that his personal experience was consistent with this statement. Of all the accounts of Jesus' transactions with members of his immediate family, and with the people of Nazareth, not one fails to be accompanied by stress, anxiety, hostility, conflict, or grief. There was Joseph's troubled state of mind on learning of Mary's pregnancy (Matthew 1:19-21). There were the difficult circumstances of Jesus' birth, far from home and with poor accommodations (Luke 2:7, 8). There was the fearful flight to Egypt. There was the parental anxiety before finding him in the temple (Luke 2:48). There was the murderous riot following his speech at the home synagogue (Luke 4:16-30). There was the hostile crowd that assembled at Nazareth when his friends sought to seize him in the conviction that he was out of his mind (Mark 3:20-21). There was the rejection of Mary and her sons when they sought to reach him in the crowd only to hear him cry out to all:

Who is my mother, and who are my brothers? (Matthew 12:48).

Then there was the time his brothers urged him to go to Jerusalem where they knew the Jews were seeking to kill him (John 7:1-8).

Finally, there was Mary's ultimate grief as she witnessed his horrible execution as a rebel outlaw and a scandal to the world (John 19:25). On the other hand, when we search the record for incidents suggesting a close relationship, such as moments of family pride in their son and brother, joyful reunions, or pleasant hours together ... we search in vain. There is not one such event in all the New Testament record!

But from the beginning of
creation God made them
male and female. For this
reason a man shall leave
his father and mother and
be joined to his wife, and the
two shall become one flesh.
So, they are no longer two
but one flesh. What therefore
God has joined together, let
not man put asunder.

Jesus, Mark 10:6-9

3
THE JOINING

Mark 10:6-9 is packed with information. Since it is an utterance of Jesus, the words are the words of the Father and are therefore final and eternally authoritative. Jesus delivered it in response to the Pharisees' question, "Is it lawful for a man to divorce his wife?" Therefore it directly addresses the topic of divorce. It also defines the essence of marriage, which we must realize if we are to comprehend Jesus' doctrine about divorce. This utterance is the source of the insights that follow.

What constitutes a marriage? Jesus did not elaborate on this question, but the answer is implicit. First, marriage is the *joining* of a man and a woman (hence the title of this chapter). Jesus said,

> *What therefore God has joined together, let not man put asunder.*

Next, who performs this joining? Only God. Is it not clear in the phrase,

> "What God has joined together ..."

Again, what is the binder that cements this joining? It is the sexual differentiation, and God is the joiner because he alone is responsible for the sexual differentiation. As Jesus said,

> *But from the beginning of creation God made them male and female, wherefore a man shall leave his father and mother and be joined to his wife ...*

What is the essence of this joining? It is the flesh. The flesh is the essence because the sexual differentiation enables the joining. When

27

two people have thus consummated the joining, the result is "one flesh." Therefore, the flesh is the essence.

Is this a loose confederation, or is it a tightly bound unit? It is a unit. The word is "one," in the phrase,

> *They two shall be one flesh.*

They are no longer two, but one flesh. Where there were two, there is one. That which was a pair suddenly constitutes a unit. As a unit, it is more than the mere alliance of two distinct entities.

Can any man divide this unit? No. Again, Jesus said it so clearly:

> *What God has joined together, let not man put asunder.*

God alone is responsible for the joining. It is not possible for man to break it. This includes, of course, the parties to the joining.

Can God divide them? Yes. As God alone has joined them, only God can divide them. He not only can do so, but he does. He *always* divides them. Jesus revealed this in the passage about the resurrection when he said,

> *The sons of this age marry and are given in marriage; but those who are accounted worthy to attain to that age and to the resurrection from the dead neither marry nor are given in marriage, for they cannot die any more, because they are equal to angels and are sons of God, being sons of the resurrection* (Luke 20:34-36).

God has set a limit to the duration of the flesh. Men call this limit "death" because it separates us from the world of men. It is the dissolving of the flesh. Therefore it is also the dissolving of that union of the flesh that God has ordained by the sexual distinction that men call marriage. When either party to a marriage dies, the other is delivered from the bond of flesh that joined them because that bond no longer exists. One gender has been dispersed, therefore the bond has split and the one who remains is free to seek a new mate.

This resurrection passage was a response of Jesus to the Pharisees. They had approached him with a question involving a woman whose husband died, after which she had married his brother. This began a cycle that they repeated six times, for there were seven brothers. Jesus took no offense at any of this, and in accepting the presupposition by the answer that he rendered, he also accepted the validity of all seven marriages. The realization that the flesh is the essence of the joining explains all. When death dissolves the flesh, it also dissolves the marriage. Until death dissolves the flesh, nothing can by any other means dissolve the marriage.

Do we then have any part whatsoever in the formation of a marriage? Yes. God has given to us, consistent with the essential freedom of the will, the choice of a spouse or of the single life. We choose both the time and the person. We are not married until we choose to marry, and God does not select our mates.

The Father never coerces the will of man. Still, once the man and the woman have chosen and have realized the joining, heaven seals the marriage while the flesh endures. This choice of a mate is, because of its absolute permanence, one of our most important decisions. It is not surprising, therefore, that many cultures have assigned to the parents the duty of making this choice. They, unlike the children, are not motivated by passion and should make a wiser decision. Anyhow the choice is a human choice and, once the joining has occurred, permanent marriage results.

What consummates the joining? Sexual intercourse. The legal precepts have generally viewed this correctly. Marriage is not consummated until the male and the female are joined, because it is in its essence the joining of the two. Correspondingly, whenever two virgins (or unmarried persons) thus join, they marry. This may not have been their intention; they may have made no conscious commitment to one another. But they did choose to have intercourse; therefore they chose to marry because only the Father defines the joining that we call marriage. It does not depend on any condition subject to human adjustment. While both parties live in this world, heaven knows any sexual relationship they may choose to have with anyone else by one name only —adultery. It is adultery because it is an adulteration of their marriage, in which God has joined them, and therefore it is also sin against God. Any man and woman who consent to share the sex act *are married, unless either or both of them were married already, in which case they are adulterers.*

The absolute temporal permanence of marriage means that it also includes a very specific commitment that is distinguished from all others in that it is a "once in a lifetime" rendering of one person to another to begin and continue to the end a commitment of their persons. Once consummated, it is permanent and irrevocable.

"Trial marriage" is thus a contradiction. It does not and can never exist. The same is true for a "temporary marriage," which would exist if divorce were valid, for the marriage was temporary if one can divorce a spouse. Marriage, like birth and death, is a "once in a lifetime" experience except for the case of one who remarries after the death of a spouse. After a marriage has been consummated, further sexual intimacy, cohabitation, legal ties, and procreation play very important roles, but the marriage exists with or without them all.

The wedding ceremony is not essential to the marriage, but if it is included its proper place is at the beginning, unless that were impossible. Some couples join quietly and without fanfare; others spend a fortune on the fanfare of a public wedding. This alters nothing, for when two virgins come together in sexual union, they marry. They might dwell remotely, on a desolate frontier without benefit of either witnesses or ceremony, yet they are married still. Of course, they do have a witness even there — the Father in heaven who notes and records their union for all time.

There is today great confusion about marriage in many cultures. Young people join and decide to cohabit and they say to unsettled parents, "We intend to marry, but not until we have enough money," or, "We will get married before we have children." They are thinking of a ceremony and a legal document recognizing their union as something that constitutes the marriage, but this is incorrect. They are married already, whether they realize it or not, for they are joined to one another and have become one flesh. Heaven decrees this to be a marriage; call it "common law" if you will, but it is no less a marriage. Death is the only release from it. Just as it is the sexual union that consummates the marriage, only marriage gives legitimacy before heaven to the sex act. Outside of marriage all sexual intercourse is, at worst, rape, which in the Scriptures merits capital punishment (Deuteronomy 22:23, 24). At best it is adultery, which in the scriptures merits eternal condemnation (Deuteronomy 22:22; Leviticus 20:10; 1 Corinthians 6:9). More than this, when a man and a woman come together as pure virgins to experience the rapturous delight of sexual passion, their action seals their union. Each has become totally vulnerable to the other in the knowledge that each has of the other, that he or she has maintained purity for this union, and so remains pure forever, provided each remains faithful. Such a couple is to be envied by all who have squandered their virginity in a premarital sexual liaison, for their purity and their fathomless faith in each other. The husband by his faithfulness is saying to the wife, "You are the one person to whom I give my virginity, and I trust you to be the mother of my children and to be the prime influence in their young lives as we rear them, you and I together." The wife responds, "You also are the one person I trust to be the caretaker of my life, to be the parent of my children, and to provide for us for so long as we live. I also give to you my virginity, and I trust you to maintain its purity for so long as we both shall live."

Well, that is a fine beginning, you may be saying, but suppose he turns out to be a scoundrel. Or suppose she is faithless and sells her body on the streets. Or suppose one or the other becomes insane and requires confinement until death. What then? Are you saying that there is no release from marriage in cases like this? Suppose that one turns homicidal and attempts repeatedly to murder the other? Do you say that even in such extreme cases there is no divorce?

Yes. Exactly, except that I did not say it. It is the Word of God! There is no condition that justifies divorce because, in heaven, divorce is nonexistent. It is the creation of perfidious man. The Father does not acknowledge it, never has and never will for he does not change. Surely Jesus has made that clear in setting these words before us:

What God has joined together, let not man put asunder.

If a man or a woman could, by conduct, justify the other in ending a marriage relationship, would not man be putting them asunder?

This is a sharp contradiction of the Law of Moses, which served as the basis for Hebrew society and for the practices and teaching of the Pharisees. This law made ready provision for the dissolving of a marriage. If one wished to divorce one's wife, one need only write her a notice of divorcement and send her away. This "certificate" was her proof that she was free to marry whomever she would, and of course he was free to do the same. The Pharisees therefore considered the practice as approved of God, and for this and other reasons unnecessary to mention they held divorce in high regard. Knowing that Jesus disapproved, they sought to convict him of sin, that is, of disapproving what God had approved. So they approached him publicly with the question: "Is it lawful for a man to divorce his wife?" It was a crafty question intended to embarrass him publicly as they proceeded to prove from the Scriptures that he was in error. But Jesus, who could out-crafty the craftiest when the occasion demanded, responded: "What did Moses command you?"

By this question he drew out of them what was to have been their "big gun" without committing himself. They answered as expected, "Moses allowed a man to write a certificate of divorce, and to put her away."

Then Jesus replied:

For your hardness of heart he wrote you this commandment. But from the beginning of creation, God made them male and female. For this reason a man shall leave his father and mother and be joined to his wife, and the two shall become one. So, they are no longer two, but one flesh. What therefore God has joined together, let not man put asunder (Matthew 19:3-8; Mark 10: 5-9).

After this there was nothing for the Pharisees to say, and they quickly retreated from their public humiliation.

His disciples also heard his words and they were dumbfounded. No divorce? They had never before considered the idea, and they rushed to ask him about it. He responded:

Whoever divorces his wife and marries another, commits adultery against her; and if she divorces her husband and marries another, she commits adultery (Matthew 19:9; Mark 10: 11-12).

This account comes from Mark's version of the incident where his teaching corresponds exactly with Luke 16:18:

"Every one who divorces his wife and marries another commits adultery, and he who marries a woman divorced from her husband commits adultery."

There is absolutely no exception provided by these utterances, and those disciples who heard him immediately understood that this was his doctrine. Yet many churchmen take a position akin to the Pharisees in that they approve of divorce under certain conditions. They feel that they have scriptural authority to sustain them, quoting words of Jesus himself. For example, they are apt to quote the following from the Sermon on the Mount:

> *It was also said, whoever divorces his wife, let him give her a certificate of divorce. But I say to you that everyone who divorces his wife, except on the ground of unchastity, makes her an adulteress; and whoever marries a divorced woman commits adultery* (Matthew 5:31-32).

At first reading, it might be that one could misunderstand this language to provide grounds for divorce, for it does provide an exception of some sort. To hear Jesus granting a justification for divorce would be the normal thing for one whose mind was already disposed to accept such. Yet this utterance simply does not justify divorce under any condition, and an open-minded reading would not understand it to do so. It does the very opposite, showing clearly that even under the extreme grounds of adultery there is no justification for divorce. What, then, is the meaning of the exception so clearly expressed, if not to justify a divorce? Here, again, is the utterance in question:

> *... every one who divorces his wife, except on the ground of unchastity, makes her an adulteress; ...*

I have extracted only the essential language for the sake of simplicity. Now, solely for the sake of still further simplification, let me temporarily remove also the reference to an exception, and we have:

> *... everyone who divorces his wife ... makes her an adulteress.*

But is this a reasonable statement? Look at it carefully. Something is wrong. As it stands, without the exception, it is not according to good reason in at least one circumstance. If a man sets out to divorce his wife because she has committed adultery, there is no way that his action can contribute to making her an adulteress. She has already done that!

So, what Jesus said, plain and simple, is that whoever sets out to divorce his wife makes her an adulteress, excepting only when she has already made herself such. This exception then says absolutely nothing about justifying the divorce, for in every case, he continues:

> ... *whoever marries a divorced woman commits adultery* (Matthew 5:32).

Far from providing an exceptional justification of divorce, Jesus, by this exception, excludes any justification whatever because always, without exception, whoever marries a divorced woman commits adultery. This can only be because, in the eyes of the Father, she remains bound to her husband. This utterance is then perfectly consistent with Luke's and Mark's versions. The latter two disciples included no other teaching on the subject, and so wrote their entire accounts of the life and utterances of Jesus without any need to specify exceptional grounds for divorce. They surely would have done so if it were possible, seeing that this was a most objectionable doctrine that hindered the acceptance of the Gospel everywhere, and which they first viewed with great disdain. Instead, they recorded the words of Jesus that admit of no exceptions. If he had elsewhere provided an exception, he would have been contradicting himself.

Jesus was careful to avoid ambiguity. Had he intended to provide a justification for divorce, he would have done so plainly and simply. He might have said, for example: "Whoever divorces his wife, except on the grounds of unchastity, and marries another commits adultery with her." But, in Truth, this is not what he said. What he did say provided an exception of a different sort, to avoid any seeming ambiguity. Had he not inserted this particular exception, he might have been understood to say that whoever divorces his wife, thus moving her to seek another husband, was making her to become an adulteress even if she seemed such already. But if he makes her to become such only after the divorce and remarriage, then her pre-divorce infidelity was not adultery! Opening the door to such conclusions could lead to misconceptions and so he both slammed and locked it by the exception given.

There is one other record of Jesus' teaching on this subject, parallel with the utterance in Mark. Not surprisingly, we find it in Matthew (chapter 19:9):

Whoever divorces his wife, except for unchastity, and marries another, commits adultery.

Now perhaps you will say to me, "There! That is exactly the language of the statement that you said he might have uttered in Matthew 5, but didn't."

I concede that you have a strong point. If he did use this language, there can be no doubt that he justified divorce on the grounds of "unchastity." He also would be contradicting himself in every other utterance on the subject. He would have been thoroughly inconsistent. The fact is that the translators of the *Revised Standard Version* chose to select one manuscript rendition of many for inclusion here. Other manuscripts present the exception exactly as rendered in Matthew 5:

Whoever divorces his wife, except on the ground of unchastity, makes her commit adultery.

Therefore, since the RSV rendition presents Jesus as contradicting himself, it must be an erroneous account of this utterance. It is probable that scribes somewhere in the dark past, with access to Matthew's Gospel, altered the language of Matthew 19 to conform to their incorrect interpretation of Matthew 5. They did this to satisfy those in the church who insisted that God must do what he has never done: provide a justification for divorce. Scribes of a more recent dark past similarly selected an erroneous version of Jesus' teaching for inclusion in Matthew 19, a version that contradicts not one but every other utterance of Jesus on this subject.

Suppose that you were such a scribe — a modern churchman-scholar assigned the task of selecting, from contradictory versions in different but generally equally reliable manuscripts, the one version that truly represents the Word as uttered by Jesus. Suppose further that as a cleric you also have officiated at the weddings of divorced persons, thus giving these "marriages" the sanction of both your person and of the church. Would you, under this condition, choose the version that perfectly matches every other utterance of Jesus but contradicts your practice and that of your church? Or would you opt for the version that accords with your practice but contradicts every other relevant utterance of Jesus? Well, we know now what the RSV scholars did, and that they then sought to salve their consciences with footnotes!

The record is astonishingly lucid and uncomplicated. Jesus as God's spokesman made absolutely no provision for divorce, but instead denied any such provision saying:

> ... *whoever marries a divorced woman commits adultery* (Matthew 5:32),

and:

> ... *what therefore God has joined together, let not man put asunder* (Matthew 19:6).

Jesus presented every near relative as an object of forsaking when he uttered the Hundredfold Promise of Mark 10:29,30. He then told us that one would receive a hundredfold of every relative forsaken, except that he omitted two — the spouse and the father. All the others — mother, brother, sister, and children — he included.

Why did he omit the spouse and the father? If one is promised a hundred mothers now, in this present age, why not a hundred husbands, wives, or fathers? He had good reasons, but the reasons for the two exclusions are different and so I will address them independently. His reasons for excluding the spouse have been the basis for the present chapter, and the reasons for excluding the father will become clear in the next chapter.

So, why did he not promise a multitude of husbands or wives? This is a simple question, and it has a simple answer that can be framed in its essence by only two words: marital fidelity.

Since the requirements of discipleship may include the forsaking of every near family relative, one might infer that Jesus has a careless view of marriage and the family. This is not so. Such an inference is the grossest of errors, for in the Word of Jesus there is no human institution more sacred than marriage. There, marital fidelity is on the same level as fidelity to God. We begin to realize this when we acknowledge that he provided absolutely no grounds for divorce. Since God had provided for but one spouse and no divorce, Jesus, as God's spokesman, would hardly promise a hundred of them to everyone who forsakes a spouse for the sake of the Kingdom of God!

The carnal marriage relationship is a metaphor of the spiritual bond that exists between God and his people, whom he has called out from the world. The apostles and prophets used this metaphor, and so did Jesus. The Old Testament spoke of God's people, who had deserted him, as "whoring after other gods" (Exodus 34:15-16; Deuteronomy 31:16; Judges 2:17; 1 Chronicles 5:25). In the New Testament, Jesus presents himself as the bridegroom at his marriage feast (Matthew 9:15; 25:1-10; Mark 2:19-20; Luke 5:34-35). It is a suitable metaphor only if there is no divorce provision, according to which the bridegroom might divorce his "bride". Then we could not rely upon him to save and keep us. He might not keep his commitment to us. He might divorce us.

Marriage is also a test of individual integrity. If anyone does not keep the marriage vow for any reason, how is one to keep vows made to God? The spouse you can see and interact with immediately, but God you see only through the eyes of faith, and interactions with him seem often long delayed. Jesus foretold that God's children will suffer adversity in this world *because* they are God's children. Therefore, if a person is such that he or she does not keep vows to the spouse whom one can see immediately, just because some adversity arises, neither will that person faithfully keep vows to the invisible God in the day of adversity.

Jesus understood the power of the sex drive and the resulting purely human difficulty with this Truth. When his disciples first heard it they objected, saying "If such is the case of a man with his wife, it is not expedient to marry" (Matthew 19:10).

He replied:

> *Not all men can receive this precept, but only those to whom it is given; for there are eunuchs who have been so from birth, and there are eunuchs who have been made eunuchs by men, and there are eunuchs who have made themselves eunuchs for the sake of the Kingdom of Heaven. He who is able to receive this, let him receive it* (Matthew 19:11-12).

Marriage is not a human creation. Far from that, it is the most sacred ordinance of God, which he provided from the beginning. Divorce is the profane ordinance of perfidious man and lacks acknowledgement in the sight of our creator. Heaven makes all genuine marriages. Men on earth make all divorces. The Father does not acknowledge them. Therefore it is true as Jesus said:

> ... *whoever marries a divorced woman commits adultery with her* (Matthew 19:9; Luke 16:18).

From this we see that such a second marriage is no marriage. Well, then, you may say, let us take a different tack. Suppose a man gets a divorce to remarry someone who recently has struck his fancy. Years go by. Is the first wife still not free? There was no fault in her. Is she to live out her life without a mate because of his faithlessness?

Yes. She remains married to him. His divorce changes nothing because divorce does not exist in heaven where marriages are made. God is his judge, and he does and will bear the penalty of his faithlessness. She, if she is faithful, will be rewarded.

Why go on seeking exceptions when there absolutely are none? Marriage is the Father's sacred ordinance. He is the one who has joined us, and only he can separate us. He does this when one marriage partner dies, and only then is the surviving partner justified in seeking a new marriage. Still, there is no divorce; there is death instead. Divorce is invalid in absolutely all circumstances. It does not exist except in the fanciful imaginations of men and women. Always remember:

> *What God has joined together, let not man put asunder* (Matthew 19:6; Mark 10:9).

"If such be the case", you may be thinking, "then God is unjust." To this I respond by saying that I have introduced nothing new to your experience of God by the assertion that divorce lacks reality in his sight, whatever the circumstances. You have seen or heard of traffic accidents when innocent persons were permanently maimed. They are living out their lives on earth in an afflicted condition — perhaps burned or blinded, while the person responsible for the accident survived unscathed. You have seen or read of tornadoes that killed or maimed all in their paths, from the tiniest baby to the eldest reprobate, without distinction. You have seen or read of the airliner crash that killed all on board, from the vilest sinner to the purest saint. There are the proliferating numbers of innocent infants born to drug abusers and AIDS carriers who are themselves hopelessly addicted or infected due to evils of their parents. You have heard of the famines that ravish some pitiful places, and you have seen the pictures of the hopeless faces and distended bellies of the starving children. You have heard of the plagues and pestilences that moved across whole continents with suffering and death, sorrow and pain, again without distinction between the innocent and the wicked.

So you see why I said that I have introduced nothing new to the supposed problem of the suffering that afflicts us without regard to guilt or innocence. The Father does not annul the law of gravity to restore the falling babe to the balcony, uninjured. He does not annul a bad or painful marriage to restore a man or woman to a new marriage, uninjured. Neither does he annul a birth to grant a new one into more favorable circumstances!

The natural law operates without exception and men and women have learned to live with it, but not happily. They are always attempting to overcome it with serum, parachute, ladder, and CARE packages. Sometimes it appears that they have had some success in their efforts to abrogate the natural law of God. They take encouragement from the eradication of various pestilences and the introduction of safety measures on the highways and in the airways, yet they have not touched the laws of God. They have only altered their circumstances, thus minimizing the probability of immediate injury. So it is with marriage and divorce. Men and women have not changed the moral law of the Father, which is even more inflexible than the natural law. They have only altered the circumstances, thus again minimizing the probability of immediate injury. Then, they deceive themselves with the thought that they have ended one marriage and begun a new one!

We are dealing here with the so-called "problem of suffering," in which people strive to understand how God, who is just, can abide a system of being wherein the innocent suffer. You accept the natural law of gravity. You must, because there is nothing you can do about it. You accept the finality of your birth. You must, for there is no way you can rebirth yourself into more favorable circumstances. So, accept also the moral law of marriage, for there is nothing you can do about it. This acceptance also will move you a giant step forward in the direction of understanding it. By accepting both, one can constantly apply this acceptance to the task of altering the circumstances of any situation to minimize or eliminate injury, both here and hereafter.

You are, for example, alone, never married, and seeking a spouse. You understand and acknowledge the moral law — if you marry, you irrevocably commit yourself for life to the person to whom you are joined. Thus, the acceptance of this view of marriage, including its irrevocability, results in a lifelong irrevocable commitment to whomever you choose. You will therefore exercise extreme care in the selection of a marriage partner, knowing that there is no way to undo a mistake. Then, when you have found a partner and have made a commitment, you will do so in perfect faith and trust in your partner's love for you. This commitment will do much to sustain a marriage relationship for all time. Your marriage partner will, of course, make the same commitment with the same understanding of irrevocability, for you will have exercised careful judgment to select such a partner. Then the two commitments, working together, will create such a bond as can never be broken by any force on earth. How is that? Simply because both understand and accept the irrevocable nature of the ties that bind them.

What is the option? It is to marry with the mistaken idea that, if it should fail to work out, one can get a divorce and try again. Where, then, is the trust? Where is the commitment? Where is the basis for an enduring relationship? You have risked nothing, you think, for you can always try again if this is a mistake. By this means every day becomes, not a day of trust, but a day of trial ... whether the relationship is good enough to last one day more. No matter how otherwise well motivated you are to make a marriage last, you have lost it at the outset if you enter it believing in divorce.

Now it is very important to point out something that Jesus does not say about marriage. Never did he say or imply that marriage partners must never separate. The violation of the moral law of God begins only when there is an attempt at remarriage. It is at that point that one commits adultery. Separations may justifiably result for many reasons, including personal and religious incompatibility. Jesus set forth one specific reason that results, not in penalties, but in great rewards:

> *There is no man who has left house or wife ... for the sake*

of the Kingdom of God, who will not receive manifold more in this time, and in the age to come, eternal life (Luke 18:29-30).

Yet the marriage, as a commitment and divinely ordained union, remains intact while both parties live in this world. Any pretension to the accouterments of a new marriage, such as cohabitation, ceremony, sexual liaison, or whatever, constitutes adultery.

Now when we consider the significance of adultery, we should first ask, "What is being adulterated?" If, for example, someone has added an impurity to the drinking water so that it becomes undrinkable, the water has been adulterated. If someone takes the author's manuscript and on the way to the printer pauses to make an insertion, then the manuscript has been adulterated. If someone steals into the gallery and alters the artist's masterpiece, the painting has been adulterated. Also, when a married person takes to bosom a person other than a genuine spouse, for sexual intercourse, it is the marriage that is adulterated, because this act is reserved by the Father for the marriage relationship. It belongs exclusively to the marriage, just as the author's words belong to the manuscript, and just as the artist's paint belongs to the portrait. As the foreign substance, one that does not belong, defiles and corrupts the water, just so, the marriage is corrupted and defiled and therefore adulterated whenever anything is added to it or taken away from it by anyone other than its author, the eternal artist, the Father in heaven!

Like the water, the book, and the portrait, the marriage has its pure form and substance, which its creator has imparted to it. The elements of its form and substance include monogamous sex, cohabitation, economic sharing, birthing and parenting children. These things are pure when, and only when, we experience them as elements of marriage. Whenever we enact them apart from the first and only legitimate marriage, they are impure.

Whenever we willingly experience sex before marriage it then constitutes a marriage, though that was not our intent. How is that? Again, it is simple. When pure hydrogen and oxygen come together and interact, they become water without reference to the intentions of the hydrogen and the oxygen. It is God's natural law. In precisely the same pattern, when pure man and woman come together and sexually interact, they *are* marriage, without reference to the intentions of the man and the woman. It is God's moral law. Of course, all aspects of the two situations are not precisely the same. The hydrogen and the oxygen have no choice in the matter: when put together and catalyzed with the addition of a spark, they cannot help becoming water. The unmarried man and the woman cannot thus be forced into marriage, but if they mutually consent to have sexual intercourse, they marry. Look again at Jesus' words:

> *But from the beginning of creation God made them male and female. For this reason a man shall leave his father and mother and be joined to his wife, and the two shall become one flesh. What therefore God has joined together, let not man put asunder* (Matthew 19:4-6; Mark 10:6-9).

The sexual distinction is therefore the sole basis of a marriage. The marriage exists only because of the sexual distinction of male and female, and because of the necessity of the two coming together for the procreation of children. A "unisex marriage" is a contradiction. No such marriage is possible. As contrived by humans, it constitutes but another adulteration of marriage. Therefore, unisex "marriages" are but another form of adultery.

Perhaps in no other area of life is the will of God and the free will of humanity more clearly illustrated than in marriage. There God reveals his will as the permanent, irrevocable joining of male and female that only he can break. Contrary human divorce codes and marriage practices reveal the operation of our free will. The Father does nothing to enforce his will. He has only informed us through the Word of Christ. We remain perfectly free to respond or not to respond. There are no sure punitive temporal consequences should we choose to ignore his will by divorcing and entering a new, pseudo-marriage relationship.

No discussion of marriage and divorce can be complete apart from a definition of the motive that underlies them. What motivates people to seek divorce and remarriage? This question has a simple answer. They are motivated by the love of life, which cannot be understood without first considering other utterances of the Lord about the hatred of life. This consideration is the subject of Chapter 7.

Finally, everyone who seeks to become a disciple of Jesus and take his words seriously (the only way to take them!) must inevitably investigate their significance for every situation. What about the present subject? Let us first define the spectrum of possible situations. They are: (1) unmarried virgin, (2) married as a virgin, (3) unmarried non-virgin, (4) married as a non-virgin, (5) divorced, (6) divorced and remarried, (7) widowed, and (8) widowed and remarried. This categorization represents a human point of view, since that is the way you, the reader, are most likely to view them. The alternative is the point of view of Christ, who sees these things differently.

The first situation, or circumstance, is easy to analyze. Without contradiction, such a person, an unmarried virgin, is perfectly free to seek, as a marriage partner, anyone of the other sex who is also an unmarried virgin. One can go even further and say that such a person is also free to seek as a spouse anyone who is in Truth unmarried, though perhaps not a virgin. This would be a person whose prior sexual experience was, in Truth, adulterous, or a widow or widower. Also, of course, the unmarried virgin is perfectly free, in Truth, to remain an unmarried virgin. Keep in mind that any two unmarried virgins, male and female, who join in sex, are, in Truth, married.

The second circumstance is that of the person who married as a virgin. For this case it is only necessary to ask whether the marriage partner was, in Truth, unmarried. If so, the marriage is legitimate. That the spouse may have been an adulterer or adulteress does not invalidate the marriage. It is only necessary that they be, in Truth, unmarried.

The third circumstance involves an unmarried person with sexual experience. The question to ask is, "Am I, in Truth, unmarried?" If the prior sexual experience included anyone who was at the time, in Truth, unmarried, they are not truly unmarried. They are married to the first such person with whom they joined. All other experience was adulterous. If such is your case, you are married to that person as long as he or she lives, and thus you are not free to marry anyone else.

The fourth circumstance prevails when you were not a virgin when you married. Here, to determine your status, in Truth, you must ask two questions: (1) What was my status, in Truth?, and (2) what was the status of my spouse, in Truth? If all your prior sexual experience was adulterous, or was with a spouse now deceased, then you were, in Truth, unmarried and free to marry. As regards the second question, if your partner was either a virgin, or one whose sexual experience was, like yours, all, in Truth, adulterous, or with a spouse now deceased, both were unmarried and therefore free to marry, and your marriage is, in Truth, valid. Any other circumstance results in an adulterous relationship, and no marriage.

The fifth circumstance is divorce. Here, to define your status in Truth, you must ask, Was I ever really married? You need only answer the same questions specified above with regard to yourself and your former spouse. If you find that you were, in Truth, married, then you are married yet. If you find that you were, in Truth, unmarried, then you are unmarried yet. The divorce is irrelevant in either case.

If you are divorced and remarried as specified in circumstance No. 6, the same questions again apply, keeping in mind that the divorce is irrelevant. If any prior "marriage" was, in Truth, a marriage, and if that partner yet survives, your current marriage is adulterous. You are already married.

Circumstance number 7 is that of the widow or the widower. You must again ask the question, Was ours a true marriage? If so, then you are, in Truth, a widow or widower, and you are as unmarried as if you had never married. You are free, in Truth, to remarry. But if not, the death of your apparent spouse was irrelevant to your status. You may still be, in Truth, married to someone else with whom you had sexual experience, or you may never, in Truth, have been married.

The last circumstance on the list, No. 8, prevails if you are widowed and remarried. Your status, in Truth, is established by the answers to the same questions which prevail in all the other cases. You need only consider two basic premises:

(1) Marriage is consummated by the sexual "joining" of two unmarried persons, male and female; and (2) marriage is terminated only by the death of either person. Divorce is, in Truth, irrelevant.

You see, there are not many status options, in Truth, from which to choose, regardless of your circumstances. One is either a virgin, married, an adulterer, a widow or widower, or what is very likely, both married and an adulterer. In the latter case, the marriage may have preceded the adultery, or may have come subsequently. It may have issued from your current "marriage," or from a previous one. In no case, however, can one be a virgin and married, because the latter is consummated only by sexual intercourse.

God has had the first word. The extreme seriousness of adultery was manifest long ago when he made its prohibition one of the Ten Commandments. He will also have the last word, as stated by the Apostle Paul: "Do you not know that the unrighteous will not inherit the kingdom of God? Do not be deceived; neither the immoral, nor idolaters, nor adulterers, nor homosexuals, nor thieves, nor greedy, nor drunkards, nor revilers, nor robbers will inherit the kingdom of God" (1 Corinthians 6:9).

Call no man on earth your
father, for you have one
father, who is in heaven.

Jesus, Matthew 23:9

4
THE FATHER

The Fatherhood of God is the prime focus of the words of Jesus. This chapter describes how God, through those words, views fatherhood as an exclusive relationship that properly applies to him and to no one else. His *exclusive* fatherhood is the foundation of our eternal salvation. Therefore the following commandment takes precedence over all others introduced by Jesus:

> *Call no man on earth your father, for you have one father, who is in heaven* (Matthew 23:9).

This is the most important, because it is essentially the same as that which Jesus designated the first:

> *You shall love the Lord your God with all your heart and with all your mind and with all your strength, and with all your soul* (Deuteronomy 6:5; Matthew 22:37; Mark 12:30; Luke 10:27).

If you are uncertain about the sameness of these two commandments, then consider how they are related. First, both are commandments that God relayed through Jesus, although, of course, he first introduced the language of the first commandment through Moses. He commands total love, and he commands exclusive fatherhood; I conclude therefore that he would have us love him, and only him, as Father.

Yes, and as more than "Heavenly Father" as distinguished from the earthly father. We are to love him as Father *exclusively*, calling no man "father." You have not loved God according to the first commandment, with "all your heart and with all your mind and with all your strength, and with all your soul," until you have loved him exclusively as Father. It is simple. If you love someone else, some man on earth, as father, then you have divided your love, and you are not loving God with *all* of anything. Claiming both God and man as father is precisely the same, from the Father's viewpoint, as claiming two wives or husbands, from the viewpoint of the first wife or husband. Don't forget that Almighty God is eternally jealous! We are called upon to be monogamous in sexual relationships. We are similarly called upon to be monopatriarchial in personal relationships.

Consider Jesus' example. Joseph and Mary took him up to Jerusalem for the Passover Feast when he was about twelve. They were returning home when they missed him after the first day of the journey. Then they returned to the city seeking him. The story continues: "After three days they found him in the temple, sitting among the teachers, listening to them and asking questions; and all who heard him were amazed at his understanding and his answers. When they saw him they were astonished; and his mother said to him, 'Son, why have you treated us so: Behold, your father and I have been looking for you anxiously.' "

And he said to them:

> *How is it that you sought me? Did you not know that I must be in my Father's house?* (Luke 2:49).

Since they understood the temple to be God's house, we learn the following from this illuminating transaction: (1) Mary considered Joseph to be the father of Jesus, and called him such. She seems to have expected him to consider the home in Nazareth to be "my Father's house."

(2) Jesus hastened to deny this relationship by calling God "my Father." His words constituted a rebuke to Mary for not knowing exactly where to find him — in his Father's house — and for calling Joseph his father.

(3) After twelve years with him, Joseph and Mary did not consider Jesus to be of extraordinary parentage. If they had they would not have been astonished to find him sitting with the rabbis in the temple

— and they would have known exactly where to find him — in his Father's house.

(4) Jesus' self-knowledge arose from within himself at an early age, but this was probably the first time he had declared it to Mary. Otherwise, she would have learned from earlier experience not to call Joseph his father. Afterwards, Jesus returned to Nazareth with them and we read that Mary "kept all these things in her heart" (Luke 2:51). In like manner, following the birth of Jesus and the visit of the shepherds, we read that "Mary kept all these things, pondering them in her heart" (Luke 2:19). These comments are strong evidence that Mary did not tell Jesus the details of his miraculous conception. Instead, she pondered these things ... in her heart ... and there she kept them. Perhaps she almost forgot them as the years passed, because she *did* call Joseph his father. But Jesus knew. From an early age he knew, and he never attributed to Joseph the relationship of father. God, and God only, was his Father.

How did he know God as his only Father? Was it through a knowledge of his conception by the Spirit in a virgin that he knew? Not necessarily, and there are good reasons for saying this: (1) His utterances contain no mention of a virgin birth; therefore I conclude that this was not a factor in his self-knowledge. It was not important to his message to the world. The message is crucial; how it arrived is irrelevant. (2) He makes no distinction between himself and his followers regarding the attribution of Fatherhood, although they were not virgin-born. He calls no man Father, and he commands us to do the same. There is therefore no good reason to suppose that the virgin birth played any part in Jesus' understanding of the exclusive Fatherhood of God.

So, I am not writing of a relationship with God that is unique to Jesus due to the immaculate conception, but of a relationship that can become valid for anyone on earth who seeks it, following Jesus' precept and example. It is, however, an exclusive relationship that does not exist while we persist in also attributing it to some man. Fatherhood, if it is to involve God, must exclude man — otherwise why would Jesus have commanded us to call no man Father? We have either an earthly or a heavenly Father, but we cannot have both.

The purely human idea of fatherhood is necessary for reasons other than genetic. I am tempted to say that it is a "necessary evil," since that is the practical effect of the way things are. If things were different, such that the idea of fatherhood were unknown, we could not possibly choose God for our Father. Therefore the earthly father relationship is evil in that it is outside and contrary to God's will for us, yet it serves God's purpose by introducing us to an idea that makes our alternatives intelligible.

The father-idea is exceedingly strong among the Jews, and has always been so in that patriarchal nation. This helps to explain why the truth arose from within the Jewish nation. Where the father-child bond is strongest, our turning to God as Father is of the most profound significance. There is a paradoxical element in this, because the stronger our bond with the earthly parent, the less likely we are to break it to realize the bond to the Heavenly Father. The best candidate for divine childhood is therefore the most improbable one, and the New Testament Jews were the most improbable people on earth. The father-bond was so strong among them that it became, in their view, the one thing that qualified them to inherit the promises of God (Matthew 3:9; Luke 3:8). By holding the earthly fatherhood in the highest regard, and by carefully preserving genealogies, they could trace their descent from "Father Abraham," to whose offspring God had directed his promises (Genesis 17:7-9). They believed that, as inheritors of the promises of God, they were uniquely blessed among all peoples.

The relationship to the immediate father was supremely precious to each because it was the tie that linked each to "Father Abraham," and, ultimately, to God and his favor — or so they supposed. They were therefore exceedingly well prepared for the choice of the heavenly alternative that Jesus set before them. Yet, precisely because the bond to the earthly parent was so very strong, not many would break it to realize the heavenly bond. It is ironic that the very bond in which they trusted to secure the favor of God was the barrier standing between them and God. They were therefore not well disposed toward this man in their midst commanding them not to call Abraham, or any other man, "Father" (Matthew 23:9). Here was treason most heinous — the betrayal of the ethnic heritage by which they supposed God's favor and the national welfare were secured.

They did think of God as Father, but in a relationship resulting from intermediate linkages and not directly. Luke listed this genealogical chain, tracing the genealogy of Jesus all the way back to Adam, and thence to God (Luke 3:23-38). It was the intermediate linkages that distinguished men from the deity. Therefore, when Jesus expressed a direct bond to God as Father, they perceived him as a blasphemer by making himself thus equal to God (John 5:18). They applied the death sentence to such transgressors, fully persuaded that they were serving God in the process.

John the Baptist understood their folly in this matter because he attacked their reliance on the bond with "Father Abraham" in the most direct and powerful manner, as follows: "He said therefore to the multitudes that came out to be baptized by him, you brood of vipers! Who warned you to flee from the wrath to come? Bear fruit that befits repentance, and do not presume to say to yourselves, We have Abraham as our Father, for I tell you, God is able from these stones to raise up children to Abraham" (Matthew 3:9; Luke 3:8).

Jesus' acceptability to the Jews was further hindered by their reading of the prophets, who identified the Messiah as a son of David and of Abraham. As "Son of David," the Messiah was uniquely qualified to inherit the kingship that God promised to David's offspring (1 Kings 2:4). Therefore the Jews, in their passion for the restoration of the Kingship of David (which they took also to be the Kingdom of God), determined to accept as Messiah only a Son of David. It does appear from the genealogical record that Jesus was of the royal line of descent. He could have legitimately based his claim to Messiahship on this fact. Had he done so, his position before the people would have been much stronger, and his Messiahship much more acceptable to them. Some did honor him as Messiah, and when doing so were prone to address him as "Son of David" because of the promise of the kingship to David and his line.

Yet Jesus steadfastly refused to acknowledge sonship to David. Instead, at an appropriate time, he made a public issue of the matter. Here is Matthew's rendition of this event:

"Now when the Pharisees were gathered together, Jesus asked them a question, saying:

" 'What think you of the Christ? Whose son is he?'

"They said to him, 'The Son of David.'

"He said to them, 'How is it then that David, inspired by the Spirit, calls him 'Lord,' saying:

> *The Lord said to my Lord, sit at my right hand, till I put thy enemies under thy feet?' If David thus calls him 'Lord,' how is he his son?* (Matthew 22:41-46).

Jesus dealt similarly with the idea of being a son of Abraham. The context is the eighth chapter of John's Gospel, where, at the conclusion of a long and very enlightening dissertation devoted to the father-son relationship in Judaism, he said:

> *Your Father Abraham rejoiced that he was to see my day. He saw it and was glad* (John 8:56).

The Jews then said to him, "You are not yet fifty years old, and have you seen Abraham?"

Jesus said to them,

> *Truly, truly, I say to you, before Abraham was, I am* (John 8:58).

So they took up stones to throw at him; but Jesus hid himself, and went out of the temple. They felt fully justified in stoning him. In their estimate, he had blasphemed by making himself precedent to Abraham and equal with God by claiming a direct relationship apart from the linkage with Abraham.

As a fellow Jew he might have said, with the rest of them, "*Our* father, Abraham." This he did not do, but in a manner consistent with the Truth, he made it clear to all that he did not even call the man Abraham "father." Those who ended by killing him were the same ones who, a few minutes earlier and at the beginning of this incident, had believed in him. The controversy started when Jesus stated:

> *If you continue in my word, you are truly my disciples, and you will know the truth and the truth will make you free* (John 8:31-32).

These words greatly offended them. Jesus knew that they would be offended by the implication that they were bondslaves. He also knew that the root of the offense was the pride they took in being sons of Abraham. More specifically, they were the offspring of both

Abraham and Sarah, the "free woman," in contrast to Hagar, the "slave woman," who bore Ishmael to Abraham (Genesis 16:15). So they said to Jesus, "We are descendants of Abraham and have never been in bondage to anyone. How is it that you say, 'You will be made free?'" (Galatians 4:22-23). Jesus then led them into an interchange that issued in his identifying them as sons of the devil, and in their attempt to stone him to death. Why did he do this? He took a group of fellow Jews who were benevolently disposed and who "believed in him" (John 8:32) and with a few words turned them into mortal enemies. Why challenge them because of their dependency upon lineage? Why not accept them as they were? What could possibly be wrong with their claiming to be sons of Abraham? They were, weren't they? So was Jesus! What was to be gained by deliberately offending them over a seemingly innocuous tradition? What could justify inciting so violent a response?

Such action can only be justified if their reliance on Abrahamic sonship was a radical contradiction of the Truth the Father sent him to announce. Then, he could do nothing other than to confront them with the Truth, inflammatory though it be. If the very basis of their culture opposed the Truth, how could he have done otherwise? He did it because he knew that they founded their faith in him on a total misconception of whom he was, where he came from, and what he came to do. He knew they could never endure his words — that in their hearts they were disposed to kill the man he was, and would attempt to do so when they came to know him correctly. He knew that they must break the link with Abraham, in their hearts, if they were ever to forge a link with the Father in heaven. It is understandable that they were not receptive, since it was the link with Abraham that they trusted to join them to God. It condenses to this: they were trusting in their condemnation for their salvation! Jesus did not avoid the issue, for their sakes. It was for our sakes, as well, that this event has been preserved in the Word for two millennia. He could do nothing else, for only by pushing his blade to the hilt could he bear an enduring testimony to the Truth of the Father.

We see on close analysis that he proceeded in the following stepwise fashion: (1) Knowing that they would not endure his words, he made this a condition of discipleship in the words already quoted. They would have shouted "Amen," had he only omitted the phrase, "shall make you free." He said this knowing what would be their response, and it was for that reason that he had to say it. They responded exactly as expected, saying, "We are descendants of Abraham and have never been in bondage to anyone. How is it that you say, 'You will be made free?'" (John 8: 32-33). (2) Now to redefine freedom and slavery, and thus to clarify their true parentage. Jesus had set a trap for them in the first step, and they tripped it by asking their question, as he knew they would. So he answered:

> *Truly, truly, I say to you, everyone who commits sin is a slave to sin. The slave does not continue in the house forever; the son continues forever, so if the Son makes you free, you will be free indeed!* (John 8:34-36).

Now recall that the linkage to Abraham, through Isaac, is the root of the controversy. Abraham cast Ishmael, the son of the slave woman, out of his house, but Isaac, the son of the free woman, remained (Genesis 21:10). This is the pattern upon which Jesus is building his case; the pattern only, not the reality, as is clear from his statement, "The son continues forever" (John 8:35). He founded his position upon the realities of eternity, not those of human, temporal genealogy. (3) Next he drew them further into his trap by leading them on to make a direct assertion of their relationship to Abraham. They had used the term "descendants" (seed), and Jesus agreed with them as he continued:

> *I know that you are seed of Abraham; yet you seek to kill me, because my word finds no place in you* (John 8:37).

Then he opened the trap yet wider as he continued:

> *I speak of what I have seen with my father, and you do what you have heard from your father* (John 8:38).

They took the bait and said, "Abraham is our father!" (4) Having gained this assertion, Jesus denied it and then explained the reason, accusing them again of seeking to kill him. Yet again they grasped the bait and said, "We were not born of fornication. We have one father, even God!" (John 8:41). By this assertion they had accepted the challenge of projecting the question of their parentage into the eternal realm. Jesus proceeded to the next and final step, which was to define their true parentage from the perspective of eternity. (5) So he said to them:

> *If God were your father, you would love me, for I proceeded and came forth from God. I came not of my own accord, but he sent me. Why do you not understand what I say? It is because you cannot bear to hear my word. You are of your father the devil, and your will is to do your father's desires. He was a murderer from the beginning, and has nothing to do with the truth, because there is no truth in him* (John 8:42-44).

So, they are the children of the devil, the murderer, because they want to kill Jesus. They are also the children of the devil, the liar, because the words of Jesus, the words of Truth, offend them and in their rage they cannot deny it. Now comes the final blow:

> *He who is of God hears the words of God. The reason why you do not hear them is that you are not of God* (John 8:47).

The reality is that only the Son, Jesus, continues in God's house forever, and only he and his brethren (those who hear his words) are free. The Jews, even "those who had believed in him," are the children of the slave, Satan, who was cast out of the Father's house and who, with all his children, is in bondage to sin.

It was at this point that the Jews yielded themselves to violent rage, and took up stones to stone him to death. Jesus, who had not yet finished his work, chose to hide himself from them. He had revealed the true colors of those Jews who thought that they believed in him. He also redefined the father/child relationship as a divine, eternal bond having no validity on the human, temporal level, except as the relation of man to God, or to Satan (John 8:44), as the individual case might be. The fatherhood of Abraham is nothing. In the words of John the Baptist, "God is able of these stones to raise up children unto Abraham!" (Matthew 3:9; Luke 3:8). And if that is void, so is the fatherhood of every other man. Only the fatherhood of God has validity, or is genuine, and the only alternative is to be fathered by ... Satan!

Jesus had also put forth a two-fold test that establishes the parentage of everyone, as it did for "those Jews who had believed in him." First, the child hears the words of the father (John 8:47). The child of God hears the words of God, as uttered by Jesus. Whoever cannot bear the Word of God is the child of father Satan, and hears, believes, and repeats the words of his father, which are lies (John 8:44). As Jesus said, the child does the works of the Father:

> *I speak of what I have seen with my Father, and you do what you have heard from your father* (John 8:38).

And also:

> *If you were Abraham's children, you would do what Abraham did* (John 8:39).

Satan was a murderer from the beginning; therefore those who seek to kill Jesus are the children of Satan. This second "test" grows out of the like characters of father and child. The child does the deeds of the father because the child is like the father, which reminds us of the common saying, "Like father, like son." It follows that to become a child of the Father in heaven, one must become like him in essential ways. Jesus observed that the life-giving warmth of the sun, and the refreshing rain, come both to the righteous and the wicked, without discrimination. Since the Father is thus merciful to all, both the wicked and the righteous, we can become his children by acting similarly. By praying for those who persecute us (Matthew 5:44), by loving our enemies (Matthew 5:44; Luke 6:27), by doing good to those who do us evil (Matthew 5:44; Luke 6:27), and by lending to those who will not repay (Luke 6:34-35), we become the children of God (Luke 6:35).

> *Love your enemies, he said, and do good, and lend, expecting nothing in return; and your reward will be great, and you will be the sons of the most high; for he is kind to the ungrateful and the selfish. Be merciful, even as your Father is merciful.* (Luke 6:35, 36).

Those who act otherwise in that they love only those who love them, lend only to receive as much again, and do good only to those who do good to them, Jesus calls "sinners."

Jesus told two parables to illustrate this divine quality of mercy and to describe the consequences of either having or not having it. One, the Parable of the Unmerciful Servant (Matthew 18: 23-35), describes the penalty for failing to be merciful after having received the Father's mercy. The other focuses our attention upon the positive example of The Good Samaritan (Luke 10:29-37), who showed mercy to the man fallen among thieves, whereas the religious personages passed him by. It is extremely important to recognize that Jesus commands us to do these things for one reason: "So that you may be the sons of your Father who is in heaven (Matthew 5:45). This is the sole motive. He makes no comment on any other anticipated result. We are prone to think of other reasons for responding to Jesus' ethical imperatives: to turn an enemy into a friend, to make a better world, even to "witness" for Jesus. Such thinking is far from the word of Jesus and, for that matter, also far from the final consequence of his acts of mercy, which was his crucifixion before a mob of people for whom he had done nothing but good. The children of God cannot realistically expect that their acts of mercy will have a different result from those of their Lord, who put the matter concisely when he said:

> *If they have called the master of the house Beelzebub, how much more will they malign those of his household?* (Matthew 10: 25)

and,

> *If they persecuted me, they will persecute you;...* (John 15:20)

There is, then, only one acceptable motive for obeying Jesus — to become a child of God. This is the good and perfect will of God (Romans 12:2), and it leads us back to the first test of the father/child relationship: The child hears the words of the father.

I do not mean to imply that there are no good consequences to follow the merciful act. On the contrary, Jesus said, "Your reward shall be great" (Luke 6:35). By this he spoke of a reward in heaven, not on earth. He said elsewhere:

> *If you then, who are evil, know how to give good gifts to your children, how much more will your Father who is in heaven give good things to those who ask him!* (Matthew 7:11; Luke 11:13).

I have already stated that the Jews misunderstood who Jesus was, where he came from, and what he came to do. A careful reading of John's Gospel reveals that this misunderstanding is prominent there. Those who knew him as a young man in Nazareth knew him to be the son of Mary, of the city of Nazareth, a carpenter (Mark 6:3). Others, in particular those who held only ill will for him from the beginning, knew him to be a Galilean from Nazareth, from which no good comes (John 1:46). Or they knew him to be a Samaritan, demon possessed, who comes for no good (John 8:48). All the Jews understood that the Messiah was the Son of David, and of Abraham, who would come from Bethlehem to restore the rule of David in Jerusalem. Those who understood that Jesus was Messiah continued to believe these things, in some confusion, but still mounted a movement to take him to Jerusalem and force the scepter upon him. Jesus would have none of this. When the Jews sought to make him king, he hid himself from them, for neither Nazareth nor Bethlehem played any part in his self-identification or self-knowledge (John 6:15). He knew himself to be the messiah who has only God for his Father and who came neither from Nazareth nor Bethlehem, but down from heaven to do the will of God, not the will of the Jews.

Jesus was and is the Son of God ... directly. His sonship thus bypasses all the genealogical intermediaries. It was an idea heinous to the Jews, who thought it blasphemy. Jesus persistently forced the idea upon them and they responded by attempting to stone him to death according to the dictates of their law (John 8:59). His Jewish disciples were from the same tradition and they also found it difficult to accept the idea of direct sonship. It was the barrier that, having finally been breached, became for the early disciples the key to salvation. For example, John testified: "Whoever confesses that Jesus is the Son of God — God abides in him and he in God" (I John 4:15). This was the "good confession" first made by Peter at Caesarea Philippi, where Jesus asked the gathered disciples:

"Whom do men say that the Son of man is?"

They responded, "Some say John the Baptist, and others say Elijah, and others Jeremiah or one of the prophets."

He said to them:

"But who do you say that I am?"

Peter replied, "You are the Christ, the Son of the living God."
Then Jesus responded:

> *Blessed are you, Simon bar (son of) Jonah, for flesh and blood have not revealed this to you, but my Father who is in heaven* (Matthew 16:17).

Of course it was not flesh and blood that had revealed it — for all the flesh and blood in Peter's experience called it blasphemy. Yet here he was, courageously confessing the truth that lies at the core of the Gospel! This was surely a major insight toward the development of Peter's comprehension of the truth, yet he was still far from a full realization of it, as Jesus knew. Jesus acknowledged this when he addressed the disciple as "son of Jonah" (Matthew 16:17), the earthly parent, implying that he was not yet a son of God. Jesus continued to identify him with Satan, as we learn by reading a little further. Yes, Jesus called him "blessed," and promised him the keys of the kingdom — but then immediately confronted him with a test that he failed miserably (Matthew 16:21-22).

He began by showing Peter and all the disciples how he must go to Jerusalem and suffer and be killed and raised on the third day. In Jesus' mind this announcement would have come as wonderful news to any true friend who fully perceived the significance of his being the Son of God. He was, through death, to go to his Father in heaven — to share with him the glories of eternity. But Peter still loved his life on earth and wanted Jesus to remain in the earthly life, that is, in the flesh. This talk of suffering and being killed offended him so that he took hold of Jesus and cried out, "God forbid, Lord! This shall never happen to you!" Then Jesus turned and spoke these terrible words:

> *Get behind me, Satan! You are a hindrance to me; for you are not on the side of God, but of men* (Matthew 16:23; Mark 8:33).

Then followed one of the hard sayings:

> *Whoever would save his life will lose it, and whoever loses his life for my sake will find it* (Matthew 16:25).

Peter was far from realizing that to love heaven is to hate earth;

that to identify with God in heaven is to cut the bond with earth; that to make God his Father is to set himself apart from the earthly parent — yes, to *hate* the earthly, to use a word selected by Jesus (Luke 14:26).

Peter still did not understand on the day of crucifixion. He revealed his love of temporal life when, in fear for it, he even denied that he knew Jesus (Matthew 26: 69-75). But after the resurrection — surely he understood then? No, not even then. John's Gospel relates the account of an appearance of the resurrected Lord to the disciples by the Sea of Tiberias. Some disciples had been together the day before the appearance and Peter said, "I am going fishing" (John 21:3). Now it is important to recall at this point that Peter was beforehand a fisherman, and he was plying this trade when Jesus called him to leave it and follow him. Jesus is now dead, and Peter wants to return to fishing. Well, the others followed Peter's lead and went with him. They fished all night and caught nothing. Then at daybreak they saw (but did not recognize) Jesus standing on the beach. He called to them to cast the net on the other side. They did this and caught so many fish they could not haul them into the boat. One of the disciples said to Peter, "It is the Lord." Then we read how Peter, always the impetuous one, put on his clothes and swam ashore while the others rowed, dragging the net full of fish.

They found that the Lord already had a fire with a breakfast of fish and bread laid out for them. He commanded them also to bring some of the fish they had just caught. Then he invited them to breakfast, giving them to eat of the bread and fish he had already prepared. After eating he turned his attention to Peter and said:

"Simon, son of Jonah, do you love me more than these?"

What did he mean by "these?" The fish, of course. And why did he say "son of Jonah?" Because, in the mind of the Lord that is exactly what Peter yet remained. He had not yet become a son of God because he continued to love this life and its fish!

Finally, why did he say "more than these?" Because Peter had gone back to the fish although his Lord had long before called him away from them to become a fisher of men. Twice more he asked him, "Do you love me?" as though to counter, one by one, Peter's three denials at the foot of the cross. Each time he commanded Peter saying, "Feed my sheep!" and then told him what manner of death he would die as an old man — a death by which he would glorify God. Finally, he commanded, "Follow me" (John 21:19-22).

Perhaps Peter recalled that day when Jesus first called him and commanded, "Follow me." It was a day much like this one, in which Jesus passed along the seashore and saw Simon and his brother Andrew casting their net into the sea. On that day Jesus said to them:

Follow me, and I will make you to become fishers of men (Matthew 4:18-20).

They had followed immediately.

Another disciple, on being commanded by Jesus to follow him, sought first to bargain and responded, "Lord, let me first go and bury my father." To this Jesus replied:

Follow me and leave the dead to bury their own dead (Matthew 8:22).

Surely Peter needed this message also!

This utterance has often been erroneously interpreted to focus on the man's mistaken priorities, in which case the word "first" becomes the key to his meaning. But now, considering Jesus' utterances on the subject of fatherhood, we see clearly that what was unacceptable to Jesus was his referring to his male progenitor as "father." Jesus did not mention priorities, but instead implied that his identification with the dead was to cease.

Leave the dead to bury their own dead (Matthew 8:22).

While this disciple wanted to postpone following Jesus until his "father" was dead, Jesus considered him to be dead already, together with all those who had the task of burying him. It follows that anyone who establishes his or her identity through a man whom one calls "father" is in God's sight dead already, and only those who call *only* God "Father" are alive to God. To establish one's identity by recourse to human forebears is to identify with the dead, and that is death indeed.

This incident also provides a basis for an evaluation of Jesus' attitude toward the law of Moses. The commandment, "Honor your father and mother, that your days may be long on the earth, which the lord your God gives you" (Exodus 20:12; Deuteronomy 5:16) means that one should care for his parents in their old age, and then bury them at their deaths. The children would then do the same so that one's life would be prolonged, and thus one's "days would be long on the earth." Jesus considered this to be a commandment to the "dead," since the dead are the ones who wish to extend their lives on the earth, and this disciple was only asking to be permitted to obey this commandment. But when God, and only God, is Father, we fulfill this commandment by honoring God and the result is eternal life, not length of days on the earth. Therefore, Jesus would not permit this disciple to obey the commandment, because it would identify him with the dead. It was not because of priorities, for if it was to be done at all it must be done first.

Jesus elsewhere stressed the breaking of this earthly father-son bond in the most unmistakable language, when he said:

> *Do not think that I have come to bring peace on earth; I have not come to bring peace, but a sword. For I have come to set a man against his father ... and a man's foes will be those of his own household* (Matthew 10: 34-36).

Yet again he said:

> *If any one comes to me and does not hate his own father ... he cannot be my disciple* (Luke 14:26).

So with Jesus it is always either/or and never both/and as the religionists of this age would have us believe. Either God is your only Father, and you acknowledge him as such, or else Satan is your father (John 8:41-44). The exclusivity of divine Fatherhood is the key to this principle, and that is why Jesus commands us to call no man on earth "Father" (Matthew 23:9). If in Truth we are disciples of his Son, Jesus, and if we can receive his words, then we have only one Father, even God.

Why must the relationship as children of God be exclusive? Does God have to explain his reasons to us? Of course not! Yet it is not difficult to conceive of good reasons for this principle. What if God's sole motive for creation is to produce sons and daughters for himself alone? And what if this requires that those who exist because of the creation first desire from the heart to become his daughters and sons and to call only God "Father?" And what if we fail to respond? Do we not therefore abort the cardinal purpose of the creation, and render all the Father's efforts vain endeavors, including not only the creation itself, but also the sufferings of the Christ? Could any sin be greater than this?

The Father's sole motive for the creation of the heavens and the earth and all things therein is that we might become his sons and daughters in Glory. He therefore is an eternally jealous God who wills to be our only Father. Jesus exemplified the ultimate expression of the Father's will by refusing to call any man "Father," by motivating all his disciples to do all things "so that we might be the children of our Father in heaven," and by attacking and condemning the propensity of the Jews to identify with the dead through their devotion to the patriarchs. Then he commanded all who follow him to "call no man on earth 'Father.' " Therefore, our propensity to identify with human parentage and to call our male progenitors "father," with all the trappings of patriarchal devotion, constitutes the ultimate violation of the will of God. As disobedience to the first commandment, this must be the cardinal sin! He made our positive response to this teaching a prime qualification for discipleship when he said:

If any one comes to me and hate not his father ... he cannot be my disciple (Luke 14:26).

Therefore I tell you, the
Kingdom of God will be
taken away from you and
given to a nation producing
the fruits of it.

Jesus, Matthew 21:43

5
THE NATION

Was Jesus a nationalist? Was he a patriot? How did he view the nation and the state authority, and how did he respond to their demands? How should his disciples respond? These are among the questions addressed in this chapter.

The utterance on the previous page suggests that the Kingdom of God was a major determinant of Jesus' attitude toward the nation. The Kingdom was a primary theme of the Logos (or Word), and as such deserves much attention in any analysis of his message. I will therefore give it detailed consideration in a later chapter; here it is only necessary to discuss it in a limited way as it relates to Jesus' view of the nation.

One should first realize that when Jesus spoke of the Kingdom of God, he was not introducing a new term. On the contrary, it was among the most common ideas and was fundamental to Jewish nationalism. The Old Testament prophets often wrote of it, and the Jews drew their views from the prophetic texts. The general view was that God would send his Messiah to restore the Davidic monarchy. He would, of course, deal appropriately with their Roman conquerors. The national agenda of the Jews therefore looked to the restoration of the monarchy of David in all its glory and world power. First, the Messiah; then the consolidation of the people in his cause, then they would proclaim him king. He would command the scene, ejecting the Romans and proceeding to extend the sway of the Jews over the world. Thus did their zealots envision the Kingdom of God in its coming on earth. Jewish nationalism, therefore, focused on the hope of the Kingdom. Jews often spoke among themselves of the coming of the Kingdom, for which they fervently prayed. Certain people devoted themselves to praying for the Kingdom and seeking the Messiah to join his fight against the Roman rulers. Such persons were said to be "seeking the Kingdom" (Mark 15:43; Luke 23:51). Jesus was only one of many Messianic figures. Therefore, those who were seeking the Kingdom compared the many claimants to Messiahship to establish which was the Christ.

Jesus also spoke often of the coming of the Kingdom, and he urged his disciples to pray for this wonderful event (Matthew 6:10). He urged on them the task of seeking the Kingdom, much as the others were doing. He therefore shared with the Jews this intense interest in the Messiah, the coming of the Kingdom, and the devotion to seeking it. It appeared that Jesus was exactly what the nation sought — a Messiah who would bring the Kingdom. Many felt they had good reason to think he would respond favorably to their expectations of him (Acts 1:6), but this he did not do. Why? Because the Jewish nation, although rightful heir to the Kingdom, had utterly failed to qualify for it. Therefore, as Jesus said, the Kingdom was to be taken away from them and given to another nation that would produce the fruits of it.

What is this other nation? (Matthew 21:43). Luke presents a discourse of Jesus on the care for earthly things that includes the following utterance:

> *And do not seek what you are to eat and what you are to drink, nor be of anxious mind. For all the nations of the world seek these things; and your Father knows that you need them. Instead, seek his Kingdom, and these things shall be yours as well. Fear not, little flock, for it is your Father's good pleasure to give you the Kingdom* (Luke 12: 29-32).

This "little flock" of disciples, to whom God only is Father, constitutes the other nation to which the Kingdom is to be given. It will differ from every other in that its citizens seek first the Kingdom instead of the necessities of life on earth. The citizens of this "little flock" are few, and they follow Jesus as sheep follow the Good Shepherd (John 10:11, 14, 27).

There will come a day when he will gather all nations before the Christ for final judgment. This will include not only all the nations of the world, but also the little flock. There, he will separate them the one from the other as the shepherd separates the sheep from the goats — an individual, person-by-person selection. Then he will say to those at his right hand, the sheep:

Come, O blessed of my Father, inherit the kingdom prepared for you from the foundation of the world (Matthew 25:34).

This is if the disciples devote themselves to seeking first the Kingdom instead of food and clothing, in contrast to "all the nations of the world." It appears that they had not convinced Jesus that they qualified, for in the same context he issues a stinging rebuke, calling them "O men of little faith."

There are therefore now two categories of nations: "All the nations of the world" and "the little flock." Historically, God called the Jews out from all other nations and gave them the promise of the Kingdom of God if they should bear the fruit of the Kingdom. They failed, therefore he took the Kingdom from them and gave it to the "little flock." The Jewish nation then became but another of the large category. Jesus excluded them from the Kingdom on two grounds. First, they sought the things of this life like all the others, and second, they did not bear the fruit of the Kingdom. He instructed the little flock to seek the Kingdom, in contrast to the large category, and he promised that they would receive it.

Is this "new nation" composed then of only a few from the larger Jewish nation? (At this point most and possibly all his disciples were of Jewish origin.) No. Jesus expects this new little flock of a nation to be enlarged by the addition of other sheep that are not of the Jewish fold. Consider this utterance from John's Gospel:

Other sheep have I which are not of this fold. Them too I must bring, so there will be one flock, and one shepherd (John 10:16).

All the nations of the world are distinguished individually by ethnic considerations. The new nation cannot be so distinguished since its individuals have their origins in one or the other of the other nations. Its distinction therefore requires a new ethnicity that will simultaneously free its citizens from the old one. Jesus created this new ethnicity by the command:

Call no man on earth 'Father', for you have one Father, who is in heaven (Matthew 23:9).

Then he pounded the nail home with the command to hate "father, mother, brother, sister, wife, and children" (Luke 14:26). I have already explained how he set the example for us; how he replaced the old relatives a hundredfold by a new set of relatives characterized as those "who do the will of my Father" (Matthew 12:50). Thus, a new *spiritual* ethnicity, rooted in the direct bond to God as Father, dissolves and replaces the carnal human ethnic heritage. Jesus is the mediator of this new ethnic bond. All who share in it belong to the "little flock" that is the nucleus of a new nation. The Spirit, not the flesh, therefore bonds the citizens of this little flock of a nation and they assert their identities accordingly.

People who respond to the call to belong to the little flock come, like Jesus, out of a nativity associated with nations of the world. They are no more participants in the nations of the world, nor do they wish to be. Their separation is effected both by a change in their personal loyalty and by the response of the world: hatred. Jesus experienced the intense hatred of the nation. In this he served as an example for his disciples. He had taught that they were to be hated by all nations. Therefore there is no nation that does not hate his disciples (Matthew 24:9). He always chose his words with care to convey his meaning. Whenever he said, "all nations," he meant exactly that. Also, of this we may be sure: whoever is not hated by all the nations of the world has no part in the little flock. Jesus said expressly that such would be hated by all nations. This, then, becomes a criterion by which we evaluate our hope of sharing in the inheritance of the Kingdom. Remember his word:

You shall be hated by all nations (Matthew 24:9).

We change our personal loyalty because we no longer have much in common with the nations. We share neither father, nor family, nor treasure, nor quest, nor life, nor friend, nor enemy. He cancels the loyalty of the first nativity and replaces it with a new one arising from a second nativity or rebirth. Thus patriotism, as usually centered in one's earthly nation, becomes a focus of evil. We are no more patriots in the national sense, for patriotism means "fatherism," and we have supplanted the old fatherism, which focused on "the fathers of the nation" and the progenitor fathers, with a new one centered in the Father in heaven.

This second nativity is nothing less than the new birth that Jesus made essential to seeing the Kingdom of God. It was to Nicodemus that he said:

> *Truly, truly, I say to you, unless one is born anew, he cannot see the kingdom of God* (John 3:3).

This new birth acts in precisely the same way as the old one, in that it provides one with a new parentage, a new family, and a new nation and citizenship. Every relationship arising from the first birth is replaced by the new relationships arising from the second, or new birth. There is only one close family relationship that does not arise from the new birth, which is the spousal relationship. It is no surprise, then, that this is the one relationship not replaced by the new ethnicity provided by Jesus. Within the new ethnicity, God is the new and only Father; those who do his will are the new mother, brother, sister, son, and daughter. The new nation is the little flock, and the new citizenship is that in the little flock, or more fundamentally, citizenship in the Kingdom of God, since it is to the little flock that the Kingdom is to be given.

Now, this new birth is to be distinguished from the old, or first birth, by being "of the Spirit" rather than of the flesh. Jesus proceeded to answer Nicodemus' question, "How can a man be born when he is old? Can he enter a second time into his mother's womb and be born?" by saying:

> *Truly, truly, I say to you, unless one is born of water and the Spirit, he cannot enter the kingdom of God. That which is born of the flesh is flesh, and that which is born of the Spirit is spirit. The wind blows where it wills, and you hear the sound of it, but you do not know whence it comes, or whither it goes; so it is with everyone who is born of the Spirit* (John 3:5-8).

Still not comprehending, Nicodemus responded, "How can this be?"

Jesus rebuked him saying, "Are you a teacher of Israel, and yet you do not understand this?"

This rebuke implys that Jesus expected Nicodemus to understand. And if he could, we can also. Nevertheless, this "born again" experience is widely misunderstood and misinterpreted throughout Christendom. How are we to understand it?

First, there is no birth without a sperm, or seed. What then is this seed that produces a birth of the Spirit? The seeds are the words of Jesus, for in his parables Jesus identified the seed as the word that, like seed, is broadcast in the world. Furthermore, he equated his Word with the Spirit. He said:

It is the Spirit that gives life, the flesh is of no avail; the words that I have spoken to you are spirit and life (John 6:63).

From this it is clear that to be born of the Spirit is to be born of his Word — and this occurs when we receive his Word. It is precisely as he said to those "Jews who had believed in him,"

He who is of God hears the words of God; the reason you do not hear them is that you are not of God (John 8:47).

It is also clear that the words he refers to as "the words of God" are those specific words issuing from the mouth of Jesus.

Therefore, the key to the new birth is the reception of his words into our hearts. Those words are the sperm (Greek, seed) that, if received, impregnate our hearts and produce the birth of the children of God. This is mysterious, of course, yet we can easily understand it because it follows precisely the same pattern as the birth according to the flesh.

One of the great errors of Christendom, and especially of the fundamentalist sects, is the practice of encouraging new believers to seek an "experience" as testimony of the fact of rebirth. This event, they think, needs to be manifested in some way. One needs to be overcome by emotion, to be possessed by a euphoric mood, to speak in tongues, to feel the peace of God in the soul. Yet Jesus said nothing about the necessity of such "experiences." Can you remember when you were first born? Neither must you remember exactly when you were born of the Spirit, since it is not necessary that it be marked by emotional manifestations. We must be born again, but he said nothing about feeling it. The mark of the new birth, in the message of

Jesus, is one thing, and one thing only: "He who is of God hears the words of God."

What assurance does anyone have of the new birth? If you can receive the words of Jesus, if you continue in them, you have been born of God, you are "of God." There is no other valid test of the new birth. The outward manifestation of this must primarily be one of attitude and conduct, as you turn from following the ways of the world to live by those principles enunciated by Jesus. Will you feel different? I would hope so, for surely one must feel better when, for example, bitterness and hatred have been replaced by love and compassion.

Jesus said, "My sheep hear my voice." That is the key to the Kingdom, and the door of admission to the "little flock," that new nation with a spiritual ethnic heritage that produces new relationships and new citizenship. This radical transformation, which is nothing less than a rebirth, must also effect a new attitude and disposition toward those relationships of the world, including the national ones. What was Jesus' attitude toward the nations, the non-Jewish ones and that of the Jews?

His attitude toward non-Jewish nations was non-Jewish, which greatly contributed to the animosity he experienced from his countrymen. Consider, for example, the early discourse delivered to the inhabitants of his native village, Nazareth (Luke 4:16-30). He began this message in a well-received manner so that there was immediate acclaim. Then, in the space of a few moments, he converted them into a bloodthirsty mob intent on destroying him. He did this by reference to incidents in the experience of Elijah and Elisha in which God's prophets preferentially ministered to non-Jews (Luke 4:25-27). To Jesus, the Jews became but one nation among many, distinguished primarily by their gross hypocrisy. That he could sustain his position by reference to their prophetic Scriptures only infuriated them.

As another example, consider the temple-cleansing incident. He rebuked the Jews he found there, saying,

> It is written, my house shall be called a house of prayer for all nations, but you have made it a den of thieves (Mark 11:17).

In Jesus' view, God had from the beginning given special status and attention to the Jews. He considered them his "vineyard" and placed them under his care and protection, but they had not produced the desired fruit. In the Parable of the Barren Fig Tree (Luke 13:6-9), Jesus presents himself as their advocate and last hope. The Father had given them up as barren but he had interceded, and his presence among them, digging and fertilizing, was a last effort at redemption. But very early he concluded that they were hopeless. He foresaw the impending destruction of Jerusalem and the Jewish nation. They were to be cut down, and this implies that they are never to be resurrected as a nation of God. Paul utterly misinterpreted their status when, in writing to the Romans, he expressed the hope that the Jewish nation might again be grafted into the "olive tree" (Romans 11:17-21). Their rejection as a nation was complete and final, and was because, as Jesus also said, "you did not know the time of your visitation" (Luke 19:44). Once Jesus had reached this conclusion, the Jewish nation became for him but one among many nations of the world — perhaps worse than others due to hypocrisy and to their failure to produce fruit. Henceforth, if the Jews were to again be related to the Father, they must seek it as individuals in the same way as individuals from every other nation — by admission to the "little flock." After that, he focused on the task of redeeming a remnant from the national failure, whose members would be the charter members of this little flock. He conceived that its numbers would always be few (Matthew 7:14; Luke 13: 23-30), but would expand to include individuals from all the nations of the earth (Matthew 8:11; Luke 13:29). It would be different from them, though, in that it would bear the fruit of the Kingdom for God. It would seek first the Kingdom instead of the necessities of physical survival. The latter were the focus of the efforts of all nations, including the Jews. This new nation, composed of a people whom the Father included according to his judgment of each individual, would be hated by the others (Matthew 24:9).

If the Kingdom agenda of Jesus had resembled that of the Jews, the Davidic Monarchy definitely would have been restored. However, it was not God, but Satan, who had promised him all the kingdoms of the world. Thus this was a temptation that Jesus had already overcome so as no more to consider it. John tells us how, when the people were persuaded by his wondrous signs and were intent on taking him by force to make him king, "Jesus withdrew again to the hills by himself" (John 6:15).

Soon his early popularity began to sour, as the result of this and similar action, and he became the object of growing animosity that he did nothing to counter. On the contrary he continued to utter strong words of rebuke that only fueled the fires of their passions. Finally the day came when all, yes, all, forsook him and fled, leaving him to the Jewish rulers to fulfill his prophecy of them, that they would kill him.

He refused to involve himself in national affairs and took no position on the public issues of his time and nation. I hasten to say that this does not imply a lack of concern. He was concerned to the point of tears when he envisioned the fate of rebellious Jerusalem (Luke 19:41). Yet he did not involve himself with words and deeds designed to rescue the nation from Roman dominion.

Jesus made himself the prime example, for the sheep of the little flock, of how to relate to the nation. First, he accepted all national entities, neither saying nor doing anything designed to alter, overthrow, or otherwise change the realities of the national status-quo. The prominent Jewish leaders, who maintained their positions by collaboration with the Romans and who had much to lose from radical changes in the world, misinterpreted his motives and thought he meant to attempt a revolution. These are the ones who feared that his activity would cause "the Romans to come and take away our Holy Place and our nation" (John 11:48). They brought the charge of sedition against him before the governor, but no proof was forthcoming and Pilate resolved to release him (Luke 23:16). That they were unable to back their charge with convincing evidence strongly suggests that Jesus never engaged in seditious activity. It was the multitudes of the Jews who were fired up with sedition — the Jews whom Jesus avoided by retreating into the wilderness when they aspired to force the scepter upon him.

So Jesus inflamed the Jews, seeming deliberately to court their hostility. Then he went on to condemn all the nations of the world because of their quest for earthly things (Matthew 6:32; Luke 12:30).

To his disciples, the new nation, he issued a command designed to redirect their aspirations from that of other nations, saying:

> *"Do not lay up treasure on the earth," and "Do not be like all the nations in seeking what you shall eat and what you shall drink and what you shall put on"* (Matthew 6:19, 31, 32).

We see then how it was that Jesus lived within his native nation as a stranger and an alien. His goals, values, and national agenda as Messiah were so radically different from theirs that death-dealing hostility was inevitable. They looked for a Kingdom of God on the earth as it was in the days of David and Solomon, but he taught his followers to pray for the coming of God's kingdom on the earth as it is in heaven (Matthew 6:10).

Jesus accepted the national distinctions that exist everywhere. He affirmed the legitimacy of the existing authorities, both Jewish and Roman, while knowing that these same authorities would conspire to put him to death. Of the Jewish rulers he said:

> *The scribes and Pharisees sit on Moses' seat; so practice and observe whatever they tell you but not what they do ...* (Matthew 23:2-3).

Then he moved on to say to those same scribes and Pharisees,

> *But woe to you scribes and Pharisees, hypocrites! because you shut the kingdom of heaven against men; for you neither enter yourselves, nor allow those who would enter to go in* (Matthew 23:13).

To the Roman governor, Pilate, he said:

> *You would have no power over me unless it had been given you from above ...* (John 19:11).

He said this knowing that Pilate was about to authorize the Jews to crucify him. He also accepted the authority of the Romans to collect tribute, in the confrontation with the Pharisees on this subject (Matthew 22:21; Mark 12:17; Luke 20:25).

He concluded this latter incident with one of his most definitive utterances about the proper response of his followers to the worldly authority. The Pharisees and Herodians were seeking to lure Jesus into a seditious public statement. They guilefully asked him if it was lawful (from the Jewish perspective) to pay tribute to Caesar. Of course, the collection of tribute is the prerogative of conquerors, but its payment is always onerous to the conquered, and especially to the Jews. Posing this question, publicly, was a shrewd effort at entrapment, for it appeared that any answer he might give would be damaging. If he responded positively, he would lose support from Jewish followers. If he answered negatively, he might be charged by the Roman officials with sedition. If he responded evasively with some neutral comment, both results might well follow. Then Jesus deftly turned the thing against them.

> *"Show me," he said, "the money for the tax"* (Matthew 22:19; Luke 20:24).

They presented a coin and he asked them,

> *Whose likeness and inscription is this?* (Matthew 22:20; Luke 20:24).

They fell into his trap and answered, "Caesar's." He responded:

> *Render to Caesar the things that are Caesar's, and to God the things that are God's* (Matthew 22:21; Luke 20:25).

He dumbfounded his enemies by dramatically focusing on this principle. The Jews, following the Genesis account of creation (Genesis 1:26), ardently professed that man bears the likeness of God, having been created in his image. They may not have drawn from this the logical conclusion that man is the exclusive possession of God because he has the stamp of God's image upon him. So Jesus thrust the truth upon them in a way that was intellectually undeniable, using the coin as an example. For as the coin belongs to Caesar, it is right to render it to Caesar; and as the man belongs to God, it is right that man renders himself to God. The common element in each case is that both bear the likeness of their respective creator-owner. It follows immediately that, since man thus belongs to God, he does not belong to Caesar. It is as wrong for him to render himself to Caesar as not to render to Caesar his tribute in coin of the realm. Had the Roman representatives of Caesar been quick-witted, they would not have liked these words, for Caesar definitely laid claim to lordship over men. This was his primary claim! Instead, they focused on the subject, tribute, and so missed the clear implication. Jesus surely denied Caesar, or any national government, any legitimate claim on the persons of humanity. The same extends to his successors into the Twentieth Century and beyond, even to the end of the world.

He gave another commandment appropriate to the Roman tribute collection:

Give to him who asketh thee ... (Matthew 5:42; Luke 6:30).

Caesar was asking. What could Jesus say but "Give?"

Jesus always maintained his perfect consistency by never making any claims on mammon (money, material wealth), and by giving all their dues. Here, the same principle applies as for fathers, for with them it is also a case of an absolute either/or concerning earth, Caesar's locale, and heaven, God's locale. He spoke of "all the nations of the world" (Luke 12:30) as one category. He singled out the two closest to his immediate experience (the Romans and the Jews) for special affirmation of their authority to rule and collect tribute. He commanded submission to the rulings of the scribes and Pharisees because they "sit on Moses' seat." He affirmed the emperor's appointed governor, Pilate, as one whose power was from above. Yet Jesus did not approve of the actions of any of the governing powers. His order to other Jews regarding Jewish rulers was to do as they say, but not as they do. Then he entered the most terrible, harsh judgment against them: hypocrisy (Matthew 23:2, 13). He urged on his disciples a conduct and quest far different from that of "all the nations of the world," whose peoples spent themselves in the quest of food and drink.

The Roman presence was the major public issue in the Jewish nation. Suppose, by way of analogy, that Germany had won World War II and that today, after forty years, all Europe and America were hosts to German troops and forced to pay tribute to Berlin. That is the condition that existed, but Jesus would do nothing to change it, though he could have done so. Some may respond: "Jesus did not act to establish Jewish independence because he is the Messiah, and as such was bound to follow heaven's agenda. The church, however, lives in the real world of the Twentieth Century and our calling is to preserve the freedom that he won for us." The facts are correct, but the conclusions faulty, because I have never read where he taught his disciples to do anything other than to follow him. Of course, this results in their following him while he follows heaven's agenda, which has not changed so as now to embrace revolutionary activity. The Roman taxation was a hot public issue that he refused either to support or oppose. When they publicly challenged him to take a position, his only response was one of acceptance coupled with a deeper insight into underlying principles (Matthew 22:15-21; Mark 12:13-17; Luke 20: 19-25). For Jesus it was not an issue, and there is strong reason to think he never broached this or any similar subject. You see, public issues such as this all center on earthly values, interests, and goals, whereas the focus of Jesus' interest is heaven, and he instructed his disciples, saying:

> *Do not lay up treasure on the earth, where moth and rust corrupt, and thieves break in and steal. Instead, lay up treasure in heaven, where moth and rust do not corrupt, and thieves do not break in and steal. For where your treasure is, there will your heart be also* (Matthew 6:19-21).

If Jesus' heart were not in heaven, he would have been a poor one to teach others!

In summary, Jesus came into the Jewish nation expecting to bring them into the coming Kingdom, but they rejected him and his words and therefore failed to qualify. He then extracted a faithful remnant, defined as a new nation, the little flock, distinguished by the fact that they receive his words. The citizens of this nation seek, with Jesus, to follow Heaven's agenda as opposed to those who follow the agenda of the nations of the earth, and to them the Kingdom is to be given. In consequence, the new nation is to be hated by all nations of the world. He accepted the legitimacy of all the earthly authorities, but condemned their actions. He was among them all, including the Jewish nation, as an alien and a stranger because of the radical differentiation of his goals from theirs, and he announced the final judgment as a separation of the little flock from other nations of the world. He presented the most fundamental principle of how to relate to the state in the discussion of payment of tribute to Caesar. He established a new ethnicity for the new nation, for those born again through receiving his words, by calling on them to commit to the exclusive Fatherhood of God, to render themselves exclusively to God, and to seek spiritual, heavenly goals instead of earthly treasures.

How should we relate to the nation? Are things different in America today because we live in a representative democracy?

No, nothing has changed, because the principles of Jesus are founded on the eternal realities of the Kingdom of God and are absolute and unchanging, and because the world and its nations always remain fundamentally the same. We who would be his disciples are in this world, whatever the nation, aliens and exiles (Hebrews 11:13). This is not bad, for if we have truly received his word we are born again into a new nationality and our citizenship is in heaven (Philippians 3:20).

Jesus accepted all national entities and did nothing to overthrow any of them. This must mean that they are ordained of God for this world. We must also accept all nations and do nothing to overthrow any of them. The disciples of Jesus are submissive to authorities. We pay taxes and abide by all laws that are not contrary to the law of Christ, which consists of the commandments expressed in his words. But we do not have Caesar's image upon us, and therefore we do not belong to Caesar, or to the state, whatever that state or nation may be. We do have God's image upon us, and therefore we belong to God and his Kingdom. As Jesus said, we are not of this world, and therefore we cannot be citizens of any nation of this world. It follows that we have none of the benefits which are peculiar to citizenship, and none of the rights that accrue exclusively to citizens. The disciples of Jesus are most emphatically aliens in this world, all the more so because, unlike most aliens, they can never become citizens. Our nation is the little flock, our loyalty is to the Kingdom of God, and our citizenship is in heaven.

… They are not of the world,
Even as I am not of the world.

Jesus, John 17:14

6
THE WORLD

Jesus addresses this topic as one who has a perfect grasp of the subject. He speaks, authoritatively and without equivocation, of the world's beginning and end. He knows what was before it and what is to follow it, and, although within it, he speaks as one who sees the whole from the perspective of eternity. He is accurate when speaking of both the future and the past. This is not at all surprising if we recall that his words are the words of the eternal Father and not the words of Jesus, the man. This he also said (John 12:49).

Consider the biblical word for "world." In the New Testament Greek, it is *cosmos*. This word may have either of two general definitions. One is the total creation, the orderly arrangement of "stuff" that comprises the physical universe. It appears in the parables as a field, or container, of events (Matthew 13:38). It also may connote the world of men, the container of human events, as when he speaks of "all the nations of the world" (Luke 12:30). This is the primary and most frequent application of the word.

Jesus never dwells, like a scientist, on the mechanics of the world. He speaks instead as one who came into it to be a Savior and Redeemer of its content, which is men. As the world of men, it has not known God, and therefore is in darkness. Jesus has come as light into this darkness (John 8:12), and he commissioned his disciples to continue this function after him (Matthew 5:14). They are to do this by declaring the good news of the Kingdom of God to men. The darkened body of men, which is the world, is ignorant of God and thus is prone to sin. For this cause Jesus pronounces woe upon it. See how he pronounced woe upon the city of Jerusalem because it also was ignorant of God and thus "knew not the time of its visitation" (Luke 19:44).

Jesus manifested unsurpassed care, love, and concern for the world of men, which is not only dark, but also dead. He desires only to bring life to it, and to this end he says:

> *The bread which I give for the life of the world is my flesh* (John 6:51).

By this he does not at all mean the yielding up of his body on the cross, as he proceeded to explain:

> *It is the Spirit that gives life; the flesh is of no avail. The words that I have spoken to you are spirit and life* (John 6:63).

Here, he metaphorically identified the flesh with the words that the flesh uttered, or for which the flesh was but a vessel (of words). It is the words that give life to the world when they are cast, seedlike, into the field that is the world. Wherever men hear and believe, they receive the word and spring to life, and when they have root, they endure. It is thus that he gives his flesh for the life of the world.

The world always responds to him with hostility. It has an adverse relationship to Jesus and his followers that will never change. Jesus is "not of the world" (John 8:23). His disciples also are "not of the world" just as he is "not of the world" (John 17:14, 16). The world hates Jesus, his word, and his disciples (Mark 13:13). He identified Satan and his subserviency — that is, Caesar and his predecessors and successors — as "the prince of this world" but the kingship of Jesus "is not of this world (John 18:36). Whenever he speaks of the world as hating both him and his followers (John 7:7; 15:19), he always means the world of men. The same is true whenever he speaks of "all the nations of the world" (Luke 12:30).

The single word "men" in the utterances of Jesus defines a category that includes all people of the world. The following utterances are examples of this usage of "men" in the word:

> *Beware of men ...* (Matthew 10:17).

> *But he turned and said to Peter, Get behind me, Satan! You are a hindrance to me; for you are not on the side of God, but of men* (Matthew 16:23; Mark 8:33).

The Son of man is to be delivered into the hands of men, and they will kill him, and he will be raised on the third day (Mark 9:31).

Blessed are you when men hate you, and when they exclude you and revile you, and cast out your name as evil, on account of the Son of man (Luke 6:22).

(To the Pharisees) *You are those who justify yourselves before men, but God knows your hearts; for what is exalted among men is an abomination in the sight of God* (Luke 16:15).

I do not receive glory from men (John 5:41).

His disciples are those who have heard and received his Word, and who are distinguished from others by being "not of the world." This distinction arises from an inner reckoning of the disciples, according to which they resolve to abide in his words. The disciples are to beware of men because God is on one side and men are on the other. Men oppose God. Whoever is justified before men does not receive glory from God. Whoever is justified before God does not receive glory from men, but is subject to being delivered into their hands to be killed by them. The disciples must therefore beware of men, but should consider themselves blessed when men hate them. This means that they have God's approval.

The enmity of men toward God is so basic and strong, the hatred of men for the Word so inevitable and bitter, that there can be no neutrals, so that:

He that is not against us is for us. For truly, I say to you, whoever gives you a cup of water to drink because you bear the name of Christ, will by no means lose his reward (Mark 9:41).

He was, for emphasis, prone to express this teaching from the opposite perspective, saying elsewhere:

He who is not with me is against me and he who does not gather with me scatters (Matthew 12:30; Luke 11:23).

Therefore, anyone who aids, abets or ministers to a disciple must have crossed the line of hostility from the side of men of the world to the side of Christ. Such a one is the same as a disciple, for he will surely be hated by the world as such. He will be received as such by Jesus. There will be some happy surprises at the last judgment when they say to the Lord: "Lord, when did we see you hungry and feed you, or thirsty and give you drink? And when did we see you a stranger and welcome you, or naked and clothe you? And when did we see you sick or in prison and visit you?" Then the king will answer them:

> *Truly I say to you, as you did it to one of the least of these my brothers, you did it to me* (Matthew 25:40).

Those who "did it not" will have an unhappy surprise:

> *Truly I say to you, as you did it not to one of the least of these, you did it not to me* (Matthew 25:45).

These latter ones will go away into eternal punishment, but the righteous into eternal life. Jesus is not speaking here of general works of charity but of works directed specifically to those whom the world persecutes because of their identification with him. Those who minister to the disciples should expect to share in the persecution of the disciples because they will be identified with them by the persecutors.

To illustrate, a prison ministry to persons imprisoned for their crimes of larceny or violence is not included here. It is to the shame of Christendom that one can hardly find in the world today an example of what *is* included. This reminds us of yet another utterance of the Lord:

> *Yet shall the Son of Man find faith on the earth when he comes?* (Luke 18:8).

The line is so sharply drawn, the hostility so intense, the hatred so unwavering, that anyone who goes to the aid of a disciple who genuinely bears the name of Christ identifies with that disciple and receives both the persecutions and the rewards of a disciple. Such a person has crossed over and, like the disciples, is no longer of the world and can expect to share with the disciples in the hostility of the world. As one who thus identifies with the disciples, such a one counts as a disciple.

How do you dispose yourself toward men? This is a crucial question in this day when the line between Christians and the world is so faintly drawn that it seems not to exist. In reality the line is always bold and unmistakable, and one's disposition toward men boldly defines it because of the intrinsic hostility. Jesus said on this point:

> *You are those who justify yourselves before men, but God knows your hearts; for what is exalted among men is an abomination in the sight of God* (Luke 16:15).

From Luke's Gospel, this utterance is in the same context as the one on the two masters that focuses on money. In Matthew the context is different. One might conclude that Luke's sources did not agree with Matthew; therefore the two Gospels do not agree on the time of this utterance. One also might conclude that the abomination utterance represents a fundamental truth that Jesus applied repeatedly to different situations. This is my conclusion because, although the saying is definitely applicable to men's love of money, it also applies to many other things. A different application is specified — that is, the desire to be exalted among men. Besides, the plain application is to anything whatsoever that is exalted among men. Whoever receives praise and glory from men surely fits the application, and this applies to the Pharisees to whom he immediately addressed the utterance. These persons are an abomination in the sight of God; and if the thing exalted is an abomination, how great an abomination is that thing in men that motivates them to seek exaltation among their fellows! So, elsewhere addressing his disciples, he instructed them saying:

> *Beware of practicing your piety before men in order to be seen by them; for then you will have no reward from your Father who is in heaven* (Matthew 6:1).

Jesus himself was among his contemporaries as one who serves and, therefore, was not exalted. Fulfilling prophecy, he was despised and rejected of men (Isaiah 53:3). Wherefore, as Paul testifies, "God has highly exalted him and has given him a name which is above every name, that at the name of Jesus every knee should bow and every tongue confess that Christ is Lord" (Philippians 2: 9-11).

Jesus addressed this theme repeatedly. In Luke's version of the Beatitudes, he presented it "coming and going," as follows:

Blessed are you when men hate you, and when they exclude you and revile you, and cast out your name as evil, on account of the Son of man! Rejoice in that day, and leap for joy, for behold, your reward is great in heaven; for so their fathers did to the prophets. (Luke 6:22-26).

I conclude from this that God, through Jesus, assigned an absolutely inverse relationship to the estimate of either a thing or a person. If the estimation of men (in general) is high, God's estimation is low; if the estimation of God is high, that of men will be low. There is no provision at all for the remotest possibility that God's estimate will agree with man's when the estimate of man is high. Still, there is a provision for agreement when the estimate is low, for it is only when the estimate of men is low "on account of the Son of man" that God's estimate is inevitably high.

Although Jesus does not address the point, he leaves open the possibility that the two estimates agree when they do not involve the Son of man, and when they are low. Consider these examples: criminals, murderers, and tyrants may at once be abominations to both God and men. But I must repeat, for emphasis, that if the estimate of men is high, God's is low. Since it is God's word that Jesus announced, the nature of things must be such that God despises anything or anyone exalted among men.

Is this arbitrary? No, although it might as well be so since the result is the same. It is because of the fundamental nature of things. Anyone or anything that men exalt also will be, without regard to the estimate of men, an abomination to God. For example, any person who is of a character such that he or she seeks the exaltation of men, is also of a character that is abominable to God. Also, the character of Jesus and the nature of men are such that he is always and inevitably despised and rejected by men. Everyone who follows him in Truth is always approved and exalted by God.

Finally, consider how we are again dealing with the same absolute either/or. Men are on earth, while God is in heaven, and in consequence heaven clearly disapproves of whatever earth approves, and earth inevitably disapproves of Christ. The earth despises the one heaven approves, and heaven holds as abominable the one earth approves.

John's Gospel presents this same dichotomy, except that the term "world" replaces "men" or "earth." He said:

If the world hates you, you know that it has hated me before it hated you (John 15:18),

and

The world has hated them because they are not of the world, even as I am not of the world (John 17:14).

What is the appropriate response of disciples when they face the hostility of the world? Like everything else in the Word, Jesus presents this response in a simple, concise manner.

Do not resist one who is evil (Matthew 5:39).

Can any word be clearer than that? Only by the addition of specific examples, which Jesus proceeded immediately to provide: when one strikes you on the cheek, when one sues you, and when one forces your service. This is all compatible with love for your enemies, which Jesus also specifically enjoined. There is a great mystery here, but the result of this response is that whoever practices it has overcome the world, just as Jesus declared that he himself had done:

Be of good cheer. I have overcome the world (John 16:33).

THE PURPOSE OF THE WORLD

The Father called the world into being by his Word (John 1:1-3). By the same word we see that the world has only a hostile, antagonistic relationship to the Father, to his Son, and to the disciples. Now it is hardly reasonable to suppose that the Father did not know before hand that he was creating an adversary, so I conclude that this feature of the world is essential to his purpose.

The Word also reveals this: he wants but one thing from the world — a harvest. This he defined in the Parable of the Weeds:

The kingdom of heaven may be compared to a man who sowed good seed in his field; but while men were sleeping, his enemy came and sowed weeds among the wheat, and went away. So, when the plants came up and bore grain, then the weeds appeared also. And the servants of the householder came and said to him, 'Sir, did you not sow good seed in your field? How then has it weeds?' He said to them, 'An enemy has done this.' The servants said to him, 'Then do you want us to go and gather them?' But he said, 'No; lest in gathering the weeds, you root up the wheat along with them. Let both grow together until the harvest; and at harvest time I will tell the reapers, Gather the weeds first and bind them in bundles to be burned, but gather the wheat into my barn (Matthew 13:24-30).

Later, seated in the house with his disciples, they asked him to explain and he responded,

He who sows the good seed is the Son of man; the field is the world, and the good seed means the sons of the kingdom; the weeds are the sons of the evil one, and the enemy who sowed them is the devil; the harvest is the close of the age, and the reapers are angels. Just as the weeds are gathered and burned with fire, so will it be at the close of the age. The Son of man will send his angels, and they will gather out of his kingdom all causes of sin and all evildoers, and throw them into the furnace of fire; there men will weep and gnash their teeth. Then the righteous will shine like the sun in the kingdom of their Father. He who has ears, let him hear (Matthew 13:37-43).

So! The field is the world! Also, the single and precise purpose of the world is to serve as a field for the production of a harvest. Like the farmer in the midst of his struggles against the vicissitudes of weather and soil and pests, there is but one object: the day of harvest! To this day the Father similarly looks expectantly for the gathering of the sons of the Kingdom into his glory. But an enemy has been at work sowing weeds that are springing up everywhere in great numbers and making the field inhospitable to the few who are sons of the Kingdom. Now, in the normal vocation of farming, the farmer would send out his servants with hoes and plows to root out the weeds; but here the analogy breaks down. In this field, the world, the roots of the weeds and the wheat are so mingled that the sons of the evil one cannot be rooted out without also rooting out the sons of the Kingdom, and so both continue to grow together to this day. While the good seed means the sons of the Kingdom, the latter are those that the good seed produces. Like wheat, they produce more good seed from generation to generation. So there is an intimate identification and interdependence of the seed and the plant, which produces more seed. Yet there also is a distinction, because the seed obviously precedes the fruit-bearing plants. Furthermore, it is the Son of man, Jesus, who first sows the seed in the field, which is the world. The seed itself he defined as the word of the Kingdom, which he announced in the world. This one learns from the Parable of the Sower, the other of the two parables which Jesus expressly interpreted for the disciples (Matthew 13: 1-9, 18-23).

In this latter parable, the evil one (Satan or the devil) snatches away the Word, or seed, which was sown in the heart of the hearer. This is like seed sown on the path. Some seed falls on rocky ground, and springs up only to die when tribulation arises because it lacks depth. Other seed, sown among thorns, also springs up but the thorns choke it, and it is unfruitful. Only seed that falls on good soil is fruitful, and multiplies thirty, sixty, and a hundredfold. In this latter parable, the field is not the material world itself; it is the hearts of the people in the world. The sowing of the seed in the field, which is the world, is the broadcasting of the seed, which is the Word, into the hearts of men through the medium of hearing. It is the response of individuals to the Word of Jesus that reveals the nature of the soil (or hearts) of men. The Pharisees specifically exemplify poor soil:

> *Why do you not understand what I say? It is because you cannot bear to hear my word. You are of your father, the devil, and your will is to do your father's desires ... He who is of God hears the words of God; the reason that you do not hear them is that you are not of God* (John 8:43-47).

Finally, we see how everything contributes to a single end, which is the harvest. So also with the Parable of the Seed Growing Secretly. The sower sows the seed, then retires. The seeds sprout and grow up and the earth produces of itself, first the blade, then the ear, then the full grain in the ear. Then when the grain is ripe, the sower rises and puts in the sickle, for the harvest has come. Here again, the sole objective is the harvest.

So also with the Parable of the Net (Matthew 13:47-50), in which the world is the sea and the harvest is the harvest of the sea with its two differing kinds of produce, the good and the bad. The angels gather both and separate them for judgment, precisely as Jesus described in his portrayal of the final judgment in Matthew (Matthew 25: 31-33).

So also with the Parable of the Wicked Tenants that Jesus told against the chief priests and Pharisees. The point is that "When the season of fruit drew near, he sent his servants to the tenants to get his fruit" (Mark 12:2; Luke 20:10).

So also with the Parable of the Vine, in which the Lord says:

> *I am the true vine, and my father is the vine-dresser. Every branch of mine that bears no fruit, he takes away, and every branch that does bear fruit he prunes, that it may bear more fruit* (John 15: 1, 2).

In these parables, whether a field, the sea, a vineyard, or a vine, there is but one purpose manifest for the world and that is the harvest. This is the only purpose for the existence of the world; if we search the word for another, we search in vain. So, the world is not an end within itself and is therefore expendable. It does not justify itself, but finds its sole justification in a purpose beyond itself.

At an early point in his earthly sojourn Jesus expected a rich harvest from the Jewish nation. It was this expectation that prompted the following words:

> *Do you not say, there are yet four months, then comes the harvest? I tell you, lift up your eyes, and see how the fields are already white for harvest. He who reaps receives wages and gathers fruit for eternal life, so that sower and reaper may rejoice together. For here the saying holds true: one sows and another reaps. I sent you to reap that for which you did not labor; others have labored, and you have entered into their labor* (John 4: 35-38).

The patriarchs, kings, and prophets had labored, and the vineyard was let out to tenants. These were the chief priests, scribes, Pharisees, and the Jews. Those whom he had sent out into the nation to reap became with him the sowers of the seed in the wider field of the world, and the harvest of that field is to come at the end of the world, as he described it in Matthew's Gospel.

First, though, it is necessary that:

> *This gospel of the Kingdom will be preached throughout the whole world, as a testimony to all nations, and then the end will come* (Matthew 24:14).

Therefore absolutely everything looks to the harvest; but that is also the final judgment and the end of the world. Since the world does not remain after the harvest, it will have fulfilled its only purpose — that of producing the fruit that the Father desires.

In the Parable of the Seed Growing Secretly (Mark 4:27), the man who has sown the seed then retires and sleeps and rises "night and day" while the seeds sprout and grow without any further attention. "The earth produces of itself," first the blade, then the ear, then the full grain in the ear — all with absolutely no further activity, or even presence, of the sower. Only after the grain has ripened, at the harvest, does he again visit the field.

It is the same in the Parable of the Weeds of the Field, in which the field is the world. After the sowing, we find that the men have retired and are sleeping while the enemy is at work sowing the weeds. Now when all come up and the weeds appear, the servants want to return to the field and gather them. The farmer would not permit this and instead issued this instruction:

> *No, lest in gathering the weeds, you root up the wheat along with them. Let both grow together until the harvest* (Matthew 13:29, 30).

Obviously, the earth is producing of itself as the weeds and the wheat grow together without any attention from the sower or any other attendant. It is the same in the world. Jesus came and sowed the Word of the Kingdom, then he left. He will not return until the harvest is ripe. In the interval, today, both are growing together and the earth is producing of itself, with absolutely no interference from the Christ.

What is he then doing in the interval? Why, I do believe he said that he would be preparing a place for his harvest.

Make no mistake. He has gone, and he flatly stated:

The world will see me no more (John 14:19).

But to the disciples he said:

I will not leave you desolate ... but you will see me. Because I live, you will live also (John 14:19).

Then the disciple Judas (not Iscariot) asked, "Lord, how is it that you will manifest yourself to us and not to the world?"

That is, perhaps, your question also. Let us then allow Jesus himself to answer:

If a man loves me, he will keep my word, and my Father will love him, and we will come to him and make our home with him. He who does not love me does not keep my words; and the word which you hear is not mine but the Father's who sent me (John 14:23-24).

Then he added:

The counselor, the Holy Spirit, whom the Father will send in my name, he will teach you all things and bring to your remembrance all that I have said to you (John 14:26).

Thus he sets before us yet again the extreme importance of the words that the Father gave him to deliver in the world. He and the Father, as the Holy Spirit, come only to those who keep his Word, for that is the test of their spiritual genealogy. Others who do not keep his Word are not like him but are like the Pharisees of whom he said:

Why do you not understand what I say? It is because you cannot bear to hear my word. You are of your father the devil, and your will is to do your father's desires ... he who is of God hears the words of God; the reason why you do not hear them is that you are not of God (John 8:43-47).

It is thus that the men of the world go on their way neither knowing nor seeing him, and hating him and his words. His sheep, however, listen to his voice and have his words abiding in their hearts, and so he lives in them, and they in him (John 10:3-4, 16, 27; 15:1-7).

Everything, yes, absolutely everything, depends on our hearing and keeping his Word — the words uttered by Jesus himself. It is impossible to overemphasize this point. If I hear his words but do not take them seriously, I do not receive them into my heart. If I do not receive his words into my heart, neither do I receive him or the Father into my heart.

THE DESIRE TO CHANGE THE WORLD

Finally, in Christendom one hears on every hand the thought that one has a Christian responsibility to change the world — to make it a better place. To most people it will seem ungodly of me to raise the question whether this is a proper goal of Christian living. Yet I must do it, for the open mind is essential to the perception of truth. The multitudes accept this as a given axiom — a truth so obvious that it needs no proof. This, however, is an attitude symptomatic of the darkness that is in the world. I am reminded here of the apostles' admonition to "prove all things." The problem is that we have a strong aversion to the questioning of entrenched ideas that are also dear and long nurtured, for to do so seems somehow disloyal, even traitorous. Besides, "My pastor said all God's people should work to bring the Kingdom of God on earth, and he should know." But is it true?

We will not know until we have examined the idea with great care, with open minds, and in the light of Truth — that is, of the utterances of Jesus. What is his position on the matter?

First it is necessary to define the subject more specifically. I am not speaking here of superficial changes. I am speaking of bedrock transformations that endure. We all know that the world is changing rapidly because of the knowledge explosion of the past five hundred years. These changes are continuing daily and we all contribute to them just by working and paying taxes, if not in other ways. These may seem to you to be very fundamental changes, but no — I consider them highly superficial. They seem so significant precisely because they are superficial and therefore highly visible. A little rouge and lipstick can work wonders with a person's face — yet the inner character remains untouched. The whole world of humanity is like this. We are continually applying cosmetics and cosmetic surgery to the face of civilization, which feeds the beloved delusion that we are changing the world, but we are not. If you will hear me out, I hope you will agree.

Now to be very basic and specific, what is it that we are all seeking from life? Happiness! Whatever you may think it takes to make you happy — that is not the point. The point is happiness itself, and on that, at least, we should agree, just as the framers of the American Constitution recognized our common devotion to its pursuit. Now, do you really think that people are happier today than they were five hundred years ago? Or fifty? Or five? You may at first say "Yes," for you will think of the demise of once fearful superstitions, the defeat of once deadly maladies, and the overthrow of once oppressive monarchies. But, quickly call to mind also the despair in today's urban ghettos and the failure of marriage and family. Think next of the disillusioned youth committing suicide with drugs. Then go on to consider the recent "iron curtain," the threat of doomsday war and nuclear accidents, and the new malady called AIDS. I could go on, but surely you get the point. No one can make a sure judgment on this question because happiness meters were not available five hundred years ago and they still are not available. Apart from firm data, any opinion must be a guess. There is plenty of evidence both pro and con, but ... that we cannot give a reliable answer either way is significant, for it suggests very strongly that there has been no real change in the happiness quotient of the world. If there has been a significant change, there ought to be strong evidence to confirm it.

Because we can point to major sources of massive unhappiness in today's world, many of recent origin, without having any ready solutions, we must conclude that if things have changed at all, they cannot have changed much for the better. Therefore I maintain that my view, which is that the world hasn't changed in a significant degree in its ability to produce happiness, is well supported by the available evidence. Why is this so important? Because happiness is the one universal goal of all people, and its pursuit is the most worthy of occupations. A "better world," therefore, is by definition a happier world. I see, therefore, that the world cannot have been made better and that the many efforts to that end have been futile. They probably have been counterproductive. Yet happiness continues to be our goal.

It is a worthy goal, one that Jesus assumed without question, as he does in the Beatitudes (Matthew 5:1-11). Each of these begins with the Greek word, *makarios*, which defines a state of extreme happiness. Let us examine these verses briefly to see what, in Jesus' view, is the key to true happiness:

"Happy are the poor in spirit ... "

"Happy are they that mourn ... "

"Happy are they that hunger and thirst after righteousness ... "

"Happy are the merciful ... "

"Happy are the pure in heart ... "

"Happy are the peacemakers ... "

"Happy are they which are persecuted for righteousness' sake ... "

"Happy are you when men revile you ... "

You are thinking that something must be wrong here? Peace, mercy, and purity of heart make sense — but how on earth are we to find happiness through mourning and weeping? Or through poverty, hunger, persecution, and false accusation? Ah! There, exactly, is the rub ... we do not find this happiness on Earth.

The content is perfectly clear about this. These things render those who experience them happy because they result in great rewards "in heaven." The poverty is now; likewise, all the other things that result in happiness: the persecution, the mourning, the meekness ... all are in the present tense. Yet Jesus tells us to rejoice and leap for joy — not because of what we experience now, but because of the promise of eternal rewards in heaven.

Now examine the other side of this coin, which is the woe (Luke 6: 24-26):

"Woe to you that are rich ..."

"Woe to you that are full now ..."

"Woe to you that laugh now ..."

"Woe to you when all men speak well of you ..."

Now do you see it? In truth ... that is, in the words of Jesus, which are the words of the Father, there is an inverse relationship between happiness here and happiness hereafter. Those who experience happy things here and now will experience woeful things hereafter. Therefore, their happiness is not true happiness because it is very tenuous and temporary, and ends in eternal woe. On the other hand, all who are subject to temporal woe (for righteousness' sake) are eternally happy. Therefore, according to their faith, their happiness begins here, in the midst of the woes, such that they should "rejoice" and "leap for joy." Clearly, Jesus here assumes that any testimony to truth and righteousness will inevitably result in persecution, vilification, poverty, false accusation, and the like, for that is the nature of things. Therefore he has told us:

I have chosen you out of the world, therefore the world hates you (John 15:19).

We may draw the following conclusions from all this:

(1) Happiness is a valid goal. The Father wants his children to be happy, and it is OK to want and to seek this happiness.

(2) No one finds true happiness in terms of temporal circumstances; the world itself makes no one happy, for thus has the Father made both it and us.

(3) We have eternity in our hearts, and only eternity can produce happiness, but it can do that even now, in the midst of worldly woes. He did not say, "Happy will you be," but "Happy are you!" Therefore, within the context of a genuine commitment to eternity, the world lacks power to make us unhappy. He said therefore:

Be of good cheer; I have overcome the world (John 16:33).

(4) The world itself is a given entity, unchanging in its inner character, and unchangeable!

(5) Efforts to change the world are therefore futile; and the desire

to change the world, made unchangeable by the Father, is therefore evil.

Now focus on the kinds of changes in the world that people think they require to make them happy. Consider the following list:

(1) The elimination of poverty and unemployment, so that everyone has adequate resources for every need; no lack of food, shelter, clothing, and medical care anywhere in the world.

(2) The elimination of war, so that all nations have peace that is secure and lasting. There will be no armed forces or military weapons anywhere in the world.

(3) The elimination of broken homes and marriages, so that everyone has loving support from spouse, parents, and children.

(4) The elimination of oppression, so that justice and political, economic, and religious freedom prevail everywhere.

(5) The elimination of major disasters, including the so-called acts of God, so that there will be no more earthquakes, volcanic eruptions, deluges, droughts or famines.

I stop the list here to leave room for some imperfections. Many more "eliminations" could be added: Ignorance, crime, fraud, accidents, deadly diseases, bankruptcies, addictions — so, when we have realized the first five changes, something will be left for our descendants to work on. Of course, there is always death and aging; wouldn't their elimination make a marvelous contribution to our happiness?

A brief scrutiny of the items listed suggests that none of them, except the last, can be realized without first changing the character of man. Surely our hearts must undergo a transformation. Can poverty go while greed remains? Can peace prevail while violence, pride, arrogance, suspicion, fear, and the will to power survive? Can divorce go while infidelity and brutality abide? Can oppression go while prejudice and fear linger?

Looking at it in this way, whenever we set out to change the world, what we are really attempting to do, what we must do to realize success, is to change people! But here we collide with the immovable object, for the people we are trying to change is them, and the people they are trying to change is ... us, and the consequence of this is ... war, domestic strife, personal conflict, oppression, and poverty.

Consequently, all efforts to change the world are self-defeating. This desire in man to change his world is one of the primary maladies of the world. Perhaps it is the most fundamental, for it vigorously fuels the others.

The problem of the world can be distilled to one in which everyone seeks to change the world, but the various factions militantly disagree on what changes to make. It also follows that I, who believe that all attempts to change the world spring from evil, do not make any effort to stop others in their drives to that end, lest I come to excel them in guilt. To be consistent regarding this evil, I must and do accept the world exactly as it is, including the drive of its constituents to change it — that is, to change one another. More specifically, I must accept you just as you are, and this, dear neighbor, lies at the root of obedience to our Lord's second commandment:

"You shall love your neighbor as yourself."

Is it possible to effect changes within oneself? Whenever one understands the essence of the world, one sees that these things that I have listed as objectives of the world-changers, including the desire to change the world, lie within the scope of the world-essence. If one were to succeed in thus changing the world, the world would be the world no longer, but something else entirely. So, correspondingly, I cannot even effect such changes within myself and continue as a constituent of the world. Yet I can do it because Jesus has shown the way, and he said:

You are not of the world, even as I am not of the world (John 15:19; 17:14).

It is therefore possible for me to accept the world just as it is, and to accept you just as you are, because I do not accept myself as a part of it. Jesus has set me free from it as he promised:

If you continue in my word, you are truly my disciples, and you will know the truth, and the truth will make you free (John 8: 31-32).

What I have not said here is also very important: I have not said that I do not want you to change, or that I do not care. On the contrary, if I were to come to know you as a person of the world, I would very much want you to change. Yet I can make no effort to change you, but must accept you just as you are. The change that I want in you is a change only you can make. Yet you cannot make it until after you learn to want it, just as I want it for you. Now hear again what I have not said. In saying that I may want to see a change in you, I have not said that I want to change the world, for that I do not want. And how is that? Because the change I want to see in you is that of changing from "of the world" to "not of the world" while the world itself remains unchanged. I do not want to change the world, because it is precisely as my Father made it. The same principle that Jesus applied to marriage also applies here:

> *What God has joined together, let not man put asunder* (Matthew 19:6; Mark 10:9).

Applied to the present subject, the principle reads: "What God has put together (that is, the world), let not man change."

Now, recalling that Jesus uttered words of God, absolute Truth, let us examine them to see if he said either that the world will change, or that he had come to change the world. Look again at the items previously listed:

1. Poverty:

> *The poor you have always with you* (Matthew 26:11; Mark 14:7; John 12:8).

2. War:

> *Do not think that I have come to bring peace on earth; I have not come to bring peace, but a sword* (Matthew 10:34).

Also:

> *You will hear of wars and rumors of wars; see that you are not alarmed; for this must take place, but the end is not yet. For nation will rise against nation and kingdom against kingdom ...* (Matthew 24:6-7; Mark 13:7-8).

3. Broken homes:

> *For I have come to set a man against his father, and a daughter against her mother, and a daughter-in-law against*

her mother-in-law; and a man's foes will be those of his own household (Matthew 10:35-36).

Also:

Brother will deliver up brother to death, and the father his child, and children will rise up against parents and have them put to death ... (Matthew 10:21; Mark 13:12).

4. Oppression:

Then they will deliver you up to tribulation, and put you to death; and you will be hated by all nations for my name's sake ... (Matthew 24:7-9).

5. Major disasters:

Nation will rise against nation, and kingdom against kingdom; there will be great earthquakes, and in various places famines and pestilences, and there will be terrors and great signs from heaven (Luke 21:10-11).

Add to these utterances others such as the parable in which Jesus makes it known that both the weeds and the good seed are to grow together until the harvest, and we see that there is no expectation of change for the world. Instead, there is only the bittersweet mix of good and evil that is to continue until the end.

What is clearer still is that Jesus knows that the injection of the Gospel into the world is not going to change the world one whit for the better. It will only cause more war, more oppression, and more broken homes. The world is as it is because man is as he is, and man is as God made him. The world does not change because man does not change, except cosmetically. At heart he remains the same forever. Only individuals are changed by the Lord, by the word that makes them clean. This is repentance, which is central to the call of the Gospel. It does not change the world, it only delivers individuals from the world while the world itself goes on unchanged. They become "not of the world," wherefore their change of status in no way changes the world. It can be expected to retain its intrinsic character and to show this by turning on them with hatred and violence.

This is not all. There is yet something else amiss with

Christendom's perpetual busying of itself with changing the world. Consider these words of the Father as uttered by Jesus:

Do not lay up for yourselves treasures on earth, where moth and rust consume and thieves break in and steal. But lay up for yourselves treasures in heaven, where neither moth nor rust consumes, and where thieves do not break in and steal. For where your treasure is, there will your heart be also (Matthew 6:19-21).

If a young man invests most of his time and money in fixing, polishing, and proudly driving his old clunker about among his peers, then he definitely values, or treasures, it. Also a householder, who spends all his time and resources repairing, remodeling, enlarging, and otherwise changing it for the better, treasures his house. Such persons "treasure" the objects of their devotion. They testify to this by all the attention they heap upon them and by all the resources they invest in them. As we often say more truly than we realize, "He has put his heart and soul into it."

In his words on treasure quoted above, the Father has by the word "treasure" given the broadest possible definition. It may be on earth or in heaven; it may be tangible or intangible. It is definitely out of our reach when it is in heaven, and therefore intangible. It also may be an intangible treasure on the earth. It can be and is absolutely anything that has a claim on our hearts, for that precisely is our treasure. The Father thus makes it plain that the only characteristic of our treasure that interests him is its location, whether it is in heaven, or on the earth. He wants our hearts, and he has them only when they are attached to treasure in heaven.

So, therefore, the setting of one's heart on heaven is one way of expressing the only righteousness. All else is evil, and this alone is righteous. Seeing that the earthly treasure is not acceptable — he says first, "Do not lay up treasure on the earth." So, in a manner consistent with this, Jesus also uttered these words of the Father:

Blessed are the pure in heart, for they shall see God (Matthew 5:8).

Just as one's living body cannot simultaneously be in both Washington and Moscow, so also one's living heart and soul cannot simultaneously be on earth and in heaven. God has spoken, through Jesus, and that establishes the facts of the reality with which we have to deal.

Have you agreed with me that the youngster improving his car, and the man improving his house, have both treasured the objects of their respective devotion? Then you also should agree that their hearts are on the earth, since that is the location of their treasure. Good; now you also must agree with me in this: whoever dedicates himself or herself to the task of changing the world through efforts to improve it — that is, this world of humanity that is on the earth — also must treasure what is upon the earth because "his heart is in it." You also must agree with me in this: to the extent that such a person also caters to heaven, that catering is rejected because the heart is divided, and therefore impure. There is only one purgative for this impurity, and this also the Father uttered from heaven through the lips of Jesus:

You are made clean by the word which I have spoken to you (John 15:3).

Not only does the world never change, according to Jesus' utterances, but also the Word never inspires the disciples to attempt to change the world. In the present interval between the sowing and the harvest, both kinds of produce are growing together and will continue to do so until the end. Don't change it. "Let both grow together" (Matthew 13:30).

Think again for a moment of that precious, intangible treasure, peace. The word of God never brings outward peace; Jesus was very specific in instructing us not even to think that he came to do that. It brings division instead, and results in the disciples bearing the full force of the hostility of the world. The people of the world cannot bear to hear the Word of Truth. Instead, the spirit of evil that is in the world compels them to react to it violently.

Were you expecting the operation of the Gospel in the world to purge it of evil? Did you think it would result in the establishment of a worldwide reign of righteousness on the earth? No; the very opposite is happening, and will continue to do so until the end. The world is even more sinful than it ever was before the appearance in it of the Christ, and this is perfectly consistent with his utterances. Consider this:

If I had not come and spoken to them, they would not have sin; but now they have no excuse for their sin. He who hates me hates my Father also. If I had not done among them the works which no one else did, they would not have sin; but now they have seen and hated both me and my Father (John 15:24).

PURITY OF HEART

Soren Kierkegaard rightly said, "Purity of heart is to will one thing."* This is what we are really speaking of, for if one's heart is divided between heaven and earth, it wills two contrary things and is thus impure. So Jesus announced:

Blessed are the pure in heart, for they shall see God (Matthew 5:8).

He expressed this principle in many ways, but all arise ultimately from the world/heaven either/or. In one case he said:

No one can serve two masters; for either he will hate the one and love the other, or he will be devoted to the one and despise the other (Matthew 6:24; Luke 16:13).

Keep in mind that these are words that Jesus has heard from the Father; so therefore they are the words of God. It is God himself then who says, "you cannot serve God and mammon." The reason is clear: God will not accept the service of one who also seeks to serve another master — Mammon. The utterance comprehends all, for "No one can serve two masters," and therefore no one is accepted who offers divided service.

The principle is universal. It makes no difference what the identification of the masters may be. That is, it applies to all masters without exception. Yet the example given to illustrate the point suggests that the Word is only concerned with two masters in particular — God and Mammon. We see that, just as with fathers and

----

* S. Kierkegaard, "Purity of Heart Is To Will One Thing" (tr. Douglas V. Steere; Harper & Row, 1948).

treasures, so also with masters — we are dealing with the mutual exclusiveness and absolute antipathy of the world and heaven. God is in heaven, and the world of men is on this earth, as is Mammon. God is the only master to be considered in heaven, because his will prevails there. In contrast, many wills are active on earth, for every person has a will and exercises it freely. Jesus might just as accurately have said, "You cannot serve God and country," or, "You cannot serve God and family." He chose the term "Mammon" because the service of money and material wealth is comprehensive in that earthly wills all push in that direction. This utterance gives another reason one cannot lay up treasure at once on earth and in heaven: from heaven's point of view that would be the service of two masters having contrary wills. So heaven says, "No."

The world has as many wills as there are persons in it, but some are dominant and have more than an individual influence. Besides the will to wealth, there is the will to power, and all serve a common interest. The will of the state expresses itself through corporate bodies and elected or militarily imposed officials. The will of a great corporation expresses itself through its directors. One person may at once serve two or more of these masters because their common goals result in the conformity and cooperation of their wills. The will to secure domestic tranquility motivates the officials of the state, but this also motivates the corporate board, being a necessary condition for profitable operation. The will to profit motivates the corporate board. It also motivates the officials of the state because it results in job security, in the wealth essential to domestic tranquility, and in taxes that become salaries of the officials. So, though the people involved in the two differing entities on earth may at times seem to will different things, they really do not. The differing things are so compatible that they are one in essence. In these particular examples, money is a point of mutual concern. So Jesus, knowing that this holds for most earth-bound wills, chose mammon as the common denominator of earthly servitude.

He who loves his life loses it,
and he who hates his life in
this world will keep it for life
eternal.

Jesus, John 12:25

7
THE LIFE

The words of Jesus reveal that in his mind, and so in the mind of God, there is an absolute either/or relationship between heaven and earth. It is applicable to fathers, masters, treasures, and to the renderings we make of ourselves and of our possessions. These happen to be major constituents of the life of every person. From "fathers" we derive our identities, our national status, and our lineage — thus establishing who we are in the world. Whom we serve establishes the major dedication of life. What we treasure establishes our lifelong value systems and dictates life's major decisions. To whom we render our very selves establishes the object of our love and devotion. Of what, more than these, can life consist? So, Jesus encompasses everything in a single all-embracing either/or: life itself.

Can there be any mistaking the meaning of this utterance?

> *He who loves his life loses it, and he who hates his life in this world will keep it for life eternal* (John 12:25).

Absolutely everything hinges on our attitude to life! He stated it concisely and simply. This is the definitive statement, to man, of the key to eternal life — in the words of the only eternal God. The precept is universal, including everyone on earth. It allows for absolutely no exceptions, beginning as it does with the words, "He who." There are none of the complications that would arise had he said instead "Some who" or "Most of those who" or "All except." No one can misunderstand it.

Now, since it is all-inclusive, it must include Jesus. Indeed, it is coincident with events leading to the end of his life on earth that he

107

uttered these words. First he stated the truth, then he immediately applied it to everyone. Next, he proceeded to exemplify its correct application by applying it to himself. It is helpful here to repeat the utterance with its context:

> *And Jesus answered them, The hour has come for the Son of man to be glorified. Truly, truly, I say to you, unless a grain of wheat falls into the earth and dies, it remains alone; but if it dies, it bears much fruit. He who loves his life loses it, and he who hates his life in this world will keep it for eternal life. If anyone serves me, he must follow me; and where I am, there shall my servant be also; if any one serves me, the Father will honor him* (John 12:23-26).

So, the hour has come. Jesus, like a grain of wheat, is about to fall into the earth and die so that he does not remain alone. This saying presupposes the resurrection to glory, which is the focus of his attention. We know this because of the way he identified the hour. He did not say, "The hour has come for me to die," although, from a human point of view, it had. In his mind, it was the hour to be glorified, and that he said.

Then he uttered another absolutely all-inclusive statement:

> *If any one serves me, he must follow me* (John 12:26).

This saying parallels the Synoptic utterance,

> *If any one would come after me, let him deny himself and take up his cross and follow me* (Matthew 16:24; Mark 8:34; 10:21; Luke 9:23).

How severe! How hard it is for us, who are prone to avoiding crosses, to accept this as applying to ourselves. But look at the wonderful promise:

> *If any one serves me, the Father will honor him* (John 12:26).

There are only two options: love and hate. There is therefore no provision for a neutral attitude to life in this world. It is the nature of things. If we love our lives, we will lose them. Only by hating them can we save them. Someone will say, "Suppose I love my life only a little, so long as it is not more than I love God?" There can be only one reply to this. Look at the Word:

He who loves his life, loses it.

Or did it read, "He who loves his life only a little will keep it for eternal life?"

A truly marvelous thing about the Logos is that it is so concise that it is not possible to misunderstand it. (*Logos* is Greek for "word," and here is a generic term including all words uttered by Jesus.) Oh, sure, there are many to whom it means something else. They think he surely didn't mean that we must hate our lives to acquire eternal life, but that is precisely what he said. Such persons are only believing what they want to believe. As for the Word, they haven't heard it.

Jesus was not content to say only, "He who loves his life loses it," although that is sufficiently clear. But he presented the truth from its other side also, leaving no grounds at all for erroneous implications:

He who hates his life in this world will keep it for eternal life (John 12:25).

Then, to avoid any misconceptions of what he meant by the word "life," he concisely defined it as "life in this world" as distinguished from "eternal life." Then, at the end, to forestall any confusion over what he meant by loving and hating life, he made himself an example of the hatred of life by laying his life down at the cross. Finally, to rule out any thought that they crucified him against his will, he said also:

No man takes my life away from me; I lay it down of myself (John 10:17-18).

There can be no doubts about this. His death on the cross was his doing, an event that he controlled from beginning to end. It served a two-fold purpose. First, it was essential to his glorification that he hate his life in this world. Since there are no exceptions, the principle applied to him the same as to others. Second, by displaying his hatred of life so dramatically, and so publicly, he insured that his testimony to the hatred of life would stand forever.

He did it for himself, but not for himself only. He also did it so that we might see and understand and follow suit. It was so that he might not remain alone as the produce of the world, but that he might be the first born from the dead.

If he had loved his life, he would have saved it, for it was within his power to do so. But then he would have lost the life eternal. By losing his life through delivering it up upon the cross, he saved it, and established for his followers the supreme example of the hatred of life. A Synoptic version of this teaching is precisely in this save/lose terminology:

> For whoever would save his life will lose it, and whoever loses his life for my sake, he will save it (Luke 9:24).

His life in the world ended, and was temporal. Therefore, the life that one is to hate is life in time, or temporal life as distinguished from eternal life in glory. On the one hand there is then temporal life in this world, and on the other hand there is the option of eternal life in glory. Since it is the former that must be hated to acquire the latter, it was necessary that Jesus come to the earth to show life-hatred to us who are in the life of this world. So, he has confronted us again with the same heaven/earth dichotomy as in the previously considered utterances. Now, the location becomes the critical consideration. Life in this world is life on earth and, if we love it, we will lose it. We keep it only by hating it — but then it becomes life eternal, life in the heavenly glory with the Father and in his house. As life on earth, there is no means by which we can save it. We are again confronting the same absolute either/or: heaven or earth! "Life" is the comprehensive term, and one displays the utmost hatred of it by laying it down for the sake of life eternal.

However, the other utterances also exemplify life-hatred in its application to selected aspects of life. Refusing to call any man "Father" is to hate that relationship and to deny the man the place he cherishes. It is the proper and acceptable response to another utterance of Jesus that is even more specific:

> If anyone comes to me and does not hate his own father and mother and wife and children and brothers and sisters, yes, and even his own life, he cannot be my disciple. Whoever does not bear his own cross and come after me, cannot be my disciple (Luke 14:26-27).

To deny servitude to any earthly master is to deny him (or it) the normally expected domination, and that, too, is the hatred of life. This is most obvious when the earthly master is the state. Then, the denial of servitude is the denial of that allegiance that the state anticipates from all born within its domain. However, one who serves God does not render to the state what bears God's image and inscription — that is, one's very self! Despising earthly values, or treasures, is also surely an act of hatred for life in this world, which depends for its day-to-day sustenance upon such things.

What of exaltation among men? What wrong can there be in seeking good reputation among one's fellows? Precisely this: the striving for exaltation among men is the practice of those who devote themselves to this life. This is the utmost love of life.

All who seek the glory of this world, and thus spurn the glory of God, are captive to it. We all have this thirst for glory and it is legitimate. We are not to be blamed for it, seeing that we are born with eternity in our hearts. We do ourselves a terrible wrong, however, when we shortchange this thirst with a quaff of the ale of the glory of this age. We are again considering the inevitable either/or: If we seek the glory of men — we will forfeit the eternal glory. If we so love this life that we endeavor to garnish it with more and more glory, of the fading variety, we will lose it all. Jesus set the proper example for us in his earthly sojourn, affirming it with the words:

I receive not glory [honor] from men (John 5:41).

Jesus delivered these utterances to men on earth, having come from heaven for this sole purpose. They are keys to the understanding of his whole message, and in them we have two mutually exclusive and inimical alternatives. We cannot avoid the choice, because between them they are all comprehensive.

To the left stands life in this world with all its appurtenances, including parentage, possessions, nation, status, service, commitment, and the glory of this age. To the right eternal life beckons, with its Father in heaven, its eternal glory, rewards, status, and treasures. This decision confronts us while we are in the midst of the temporal experience. It comes when we have been here for so long during the growing-up process that we have thoroughly conformed. We have attached all our hopes and dreams to temporal aspirations. Therefore, the failure to choose eternity results in the choice, by default, of time. Even if we are never aware that there is an alternative to the life on earth, we have by default chosen it because that is all we know. In our darkness, it is all that we have. So, in one way or another, the choice is inevitable.

The terminology of the utterances defines the two alternatives with great clarity. There is the human father, the human ruler, the earthly treasure, the temporal life, and the human status. That is all one option. The other option comes to us as a Heavenly Father, a heavenly treasure, heavenly allegiance, eternal rewards, and life eternal, of which all transcend the temporal experience.

The inimical nature of the alternatives forbids any dual commitment. If we choose the Heavenly Father, we call no man on earth "Father." If we choose the heavenly treasure, we seek no earthly one. If we serve him who has the heavenly authority, whose image we bear, we serve not the state. If we seek heaven's esteem we will neither seek nor receive human honors. If we dedicate ourselves to eternal life, life in time will be hated. If we are not of this world, the world will hate us; but if we are of this world, the world will love its own.

There is no clearer statement of the qualifications for eternal salvation than this utterance regarding life. There is no valid hope of eternal glory for those who choose to continue to love life in this world. They are to lose it. They will keep it for life eternal only if they hate it.

It cannot be rationally denied that, according to Jesus, life in this world and life eternal are mutually inimical alternatives. We will inevitably love one, and hate the other, or hate one and love the other. We are reluctant to believe this. In Christendom, it is the calculated strategy of the world to oppose Jesus by affirming the compatibility of the two, in direct opposition to the Word of God. A prime illustration of this strategy is the commitment to "God and country," to which most citizens subscribe due to life-long indoctrination. This exposure begins in the cradle and becomes so much a part of us that we cannot entertain the thought that it is a contradiction — that a commitment to one's country is treason to God! The beauty of the Anthem is ringing in our ears! The Scout pledges are deeply ingrained! Also, we understand aright that God created the world.

How then can it be in total enmity with him? He seems a poor creator who only creates an enemy!

Organized religion is a barrier to the perception of this Truth. Catholicism long ago concocted a marriage of convenience with the state and the world. It has since consistently engaged in a cover-up of the significance of the utterances of Jesus. The reformers (Luther, for example) opened the word to everyone but shepherded our attention toward Paul and away from Jesus, with the same result. The utterances of Jesus have baffled the theologians, who devote their intellectual resources to the task of explaining how Jesus could not have meant what he said.

THE PROTECTION OF LIFE

Jesus hated his life on earth and his words and deeds bore a consistent testimony to this fact. But we must understand that he came into the world for the specific purpose of bearing witness to the Truth. Therefore, he could not relinquish his hold on life until the witness was complete. He was aware that his "hour" for glorification was before him and that he must preserve his life until that moment. Otherwise, he would abort his mission.

When the devil tempted him to cast himself down from the pinnacle of the temple, it was a subtle temptation to commit suicide. But this was not the focus of the temptation. Satan was appealing to the desire for temporal glory as he reinforced the temptation with the words, " ... it is written, 'He will give his angels charge of you,' and 'On their hands they will bear you up, lest you strike your foot against a stone' " (Psalm 91:12). To be caught in mid-air by the angels! What a powerful public proof of his messiahship! What glory it would bring to his life! Had he cast himself down, and had no angels appeared (suicide), Satan would have triumphed in that the world would never have heard his words. Ah, but if the angels had appeared, what a glorious moment in the history of man that would have been! Yet Satan would have triumphed again because Jesus would have been yielding to the love of life by seeking to enhance it.

In either case Jesus would have been testing the promises of God and transgressing the commandment, "Thou shalt not tempt the Lord thy God" (Matthew 4:7; Luke 4:12). As one who was disobedient to the commandment, he would have been a sinner like all the rest of us, and so would have brought himself under condemnation. It was therefore necessary that he turn a deaf ear to this temptation and that he remain in this life until he had deposited the Logos in the earth. Thus Satan hoped not only to destroy the man, but also to captivate the soul. The world would interpret the event as the suicide of a desperate or deranged man.

Jesus not only overcame this temptation, but he continued to protect his life from other threats until he had fulfilled his purpose. When the enraged citizens of his home town sought to cast him off a cliff, he escaped their hands (Luke 4:28-30). When his siblings sought to persuade him to go to Jerusalem, where they knew the Jews were seeking him to kill him, he responded, "My hour has not yet come" (John 7:6). Later he did go, but privately to protect his life until he had finished his work. As the months of testimony passed and his earthly mission was approaching its conclusion, the Pharisees took counsel how to put him to death (Matthew 27:1; John 11:53). Again Jesus protected himself in that "he no longer went about openly among the Jews" (John 11:54). Yet, in all this he displayed his hatred of life by the speed with which he finished his testimony. What might have required thirty-six years, he did in thirty-six months or less as he sought a quick end to the business. He desired only to return to the Father in heaven. So the time came quickly when he addressed himself to the Father in prayer, saying:

> *Father, the hour has come; glorify your Son that the Son may glorify you, since you have given him power over all flesh, to give eternal life to all whom you have given him. And this is eternal life, that they know you, the only true God, and Jesus Christ whom you have sent. I glorified you on earth, having accomplished the work which you gave me to do; and now, Father, glorify me in your own presence with the glory which I had with you before the world was made* (John 17:1-5).

Such was the grand destiny to which he aspired! Truly it was, as Paul said, "for the joy set before him that he endured the cross, despising the shame."

This is not all! Wonderful news of the Gospel! For, according to Jesus, this same destiny lies in wait for all who follow him in the way:

> *If anyone would come after me, let him deny himself and take up his cross and follow me, that where I am, there may my servant be also* (Matthew 16:24; Mark 8:34; Luke 9:23).

So, Jesus preserved his life until he had finished his work on earth, but he also displayed his hatred for it. He refused to become concerned about tomorrow, and never invested any energy in the task of laying up a supply to meet tomorrow's need. He knew that the Father was perfectly capable of providing for him from day to day. Nothing and no one threatened him, and he never for a moment considered any retaliatory measures against his enemies to make his life secure. He never said or did anything to advance his reputation among men and thereby taste the glory of this world. He explained this by saying,

> *I receive not glory from men* (John 5:41).

Although his wonderful works elicited adulation from the poor and the lame, he did them only out of compassion. Never for an instant did he seek the glory of men. He denied any semblance of identity with the people of the world among whom he had his earthly origins. This began at home where he refused to acknowledge Mary as mother, Joseph as father, or his siblings as brothers and sisters. This practice extended to the national level, where, as we have already seen, he refused the sonship of either David or Abraham (Luke 20:41-44; John 8:58). He offered no allegiance or service to his state and refused to make any commitment to Caesar. His only master was his Father, and to him alone did he offer service. With his hope steadfastly set upon the glory of the Father, he absolutely refused to accumulate earthly treasure. Finally, when he had finished his work, he laid down his life on the cross. This was the ultimate demonstration of life-hatred. It was also necessary to his repossession of the life of eternal glory. Throughout all, he counseled those who would be his followers to hold to the same course by following him in the Way. In finally evaluating the Father's love for him, Jesus gave a single reason for it, saying:

> *For this reason the Father loves me, because I lay down my life in order that I may take it up again* (John 10:17).

The Father's love depended upon his laying down his life that he might raise it up as life eternal. Had he sought to save his life, after the completion of his mission, he would have been lost as surely as any other person!

We find Jesus' heavy emphasis on the hatred of life in all four Gospels, where he stated it several ways. Here is a listing of the primary utterances:

From Matthew:

> *He who finds his life will lose it, and he who loses his life for my sake will find it* (10:39).

> *For whoever would save his life will lose it, and whoever loses his life for my sake will find it* (16:25).

From Mark:

> *For whoever would save his life will lose it; and whoever loses his life for my sake and the gospel's will save it* (8:35).

From Luke:

> *For whoever would save his life will lose it; and whoever loses his life for my sake, he will save it* (9:24).

> *If anyone comes to me and does not hate ... even his own life, he cannot be my disciple* (14:26).

> *Whoever seeks to gain his life will lose it, but whoever loses his life will preserve it* (17:33).

And finally, again, from John:

> *He who loves his life loses it, and he who hates his life in this world will keep it for eternal life* (John 12:25).

These are all very similar statements. Although some are plainly duplicate accounts of the same utterance, evidently Jesus voiced this theme repeatedly. Matthew recorded it twice, while Luke recorded it no less than three times as utterances from different occasions, and all the Gospel writers were careful to include it.

The meaning of these utterances is simple. Whoever is to participate in the blessed estate of eternal life must view his life in this world of time as totally expendable. Anyone who wishes to attain to eternal life must hate temporal life. Everything depends on one's attitude to life. It is unrealistic to anticipate the best of both worlds. The prospect of temporal woe must be accepted by anyone who would qualify for the eternal blessing. Whoever receives blessings from this life and responds by loving it has received his reward; there is nothing good to follow. As though in a tug of war, time and eternity strain at each of us, pulling in opposite directions and holding us in tension until we make the choice. Yes, the choice is ours to make, and we will go whichever way we ourselves decide. What must be emphasized repeatedly is the exclusiveness of the two appeals. There is a categorical decision to be made — a choice of eternal consequences. It is a decision against this life, while yet in it, to lay hold of that one before entering it. In their appeals to us, it is earth against heaven, time against eternity, stuff against spirit. Heaven never bestows her favors on earth's darlings, so the choice is both mandatory and inevitable. Like two suitors competing for the hand of the same maiden, these court us each in its own way. Heaven presents the grand promise of an unseen eternity through Christ, while earth points to the immediacy of its favors.

The gist of the maiden's decision is this: whether to accept the offer of immediate tangible benefits that will grow stale and pass away, or to join in matrimony with a promise of surpassing, but unseen, treasure that will never pass away. Earth entices: "My beloved, a bird in the hand is worth two in the bush." "No," says heaven; "Two in the bush which never die are worth far more than an in-hand bird doomed to perish." The earth pushes its case: "You have never seen the bush with two birds nor has anyone else. If you spurn me you will have given up this stately bird of mine for nothing!" "But of this you may be sure," responds heaven, "No one can deny that the bird in the hand will shortly perish. What will you have then?" Recall that Jesus said:

> *Thou fool, this night shall your soul be required of you.*
> *Whose then will these things be?* (Luke 12:20).

These utterances have been called paradoxical, and superficially they have such an appearance. It is not so. Each one is a simple statement of a profound truth, without any element of paradox! Jesus said:

He who finds his life will lose it (Matthew 10:39).

It is fact, not paradox.

Jesus said also:

Whoever would save his life will lose it ... (Matthew 16:25).

It is fact, not paradox.

Again Jesus said:

Anyone who comes to me and does not hate his own life cannot be my disciple (Luke 14:26).

It is fact, not paradox.

Jesus said yet again:

Whoever seeks to gain his life will lose it ... (Luke 17:33).

It is fact, not paradox.

Finally, Jesus also said:

He who loves his life, loses it ... (John 12:25).

It is fact, not paradox!

The word "paradox," so often heard in seminary classrooms and from pulpits and Sunday School lecterns, is nothing more than a smoke screen that the preachers throw out to discourage quests for the truth of the matter. Many will object to this, saying "Everyone knows what a good thing it is to love life!" Not according to Jesus of Nazareth. To him, this is the root of condemnation. Away, then, with the evil idea of paradox applied to these sayings.

Two different kinds of life are under consideration: temporal life and eternal life, and to love one is to hate the other! *This is the fundamental principle of the doctrine of Christ.* He never ceased to communicate it to the world, even to his last moments on the cross. There, he gave the supreme demonstration of it by displaying hatred for his earthly life. He also found yet another way to illustrate it, using the dispositions of the two others who were crucified with him. Both were cardinal sinners guilty of weighty crimes and both justly condemned before the law of man. There was absolutely nothing in their experience to justify any distinction between them. Yet Jesus, speaking to them for eternity, accepted one and ignored the other (Luke

23:32-43). Why? Was it because one was penitent and the other only fearful? No, not at all; both had a measure of fear and repentance and both sought help and consolation. If one were more penitent than the other, as the record suggests, it was because he realized the hatred of life in the hour of his death. Simply put, one sought to save his life, crying out to Jesus: "If you are the Christ, save yourself and us!" Jesus evaluated this plea according to his earlier utterance:

Whoever would save his life will lose it (John 12:25).

The result was that Jesus ignored him, because the saving of his life was his concern. This man definitely knew how to love his life as he sought a way to preserve it.

The other man was not similarly concerned. Hating his life in the moment of its greatest danger, he laid it down readily. I do not mean that he was unconcerned, but that he directed his concern to a different object when he cried out to his companion. He acknowledged personal sin and guilt and then addressed Jesus: "Lord, remember me when you come into your kingly power." This was a plea to which Jesus could respond gladly, and he did so in the light of his other utterance:

He who hates his life in this world will keep it for life eternal (John 12:25).

Jesus replied:

Truly I say to you, today you will be with me in Paradise (Luke 23:43).

The essential difference between these two men was their attitudes to life during the short time preceding and continuing to their deaths. One sought to save his life, and he lost it. The other, hating his life in the world and desiring to be rid of it, concerned himself only with the life that is to come. He hated his life for the sake of the life eternal.

The dying sinner who repented of his love of life was far more righteous than Peter. The latter had lived with the Truth for years and had made a firm commitment to the hatred of life. He had said to Jesus, "Lord, I am ready to go with you to prison and to death" (Luke 22:33). But he marched to a different drummer when the threat of sharing in the crucifixion of Jesus hovered near. When identified as a disciple, he cried out, "I do not know the man!" (Matthew 26:72). There is a lesson in Peter's example for all who have heard the Truth and have made a commitment: we are wise not to become cocksure about our attitude to life. While one may consciously make a decision to hate life in the world, the contrary attitude may yet be the master of the heart and, "As a man thinketh in his heart, so is he" (Proverbs 23:7). When Christ returns to receive his followers unto himself and to put an end to earth and history, it will be as when ". . . the flood came and destroyed them all" (Luke 17:27). On that day, the attitude to life of each will settle his or her eternal destiny. Wherever you are, if you rush to save your life or your treasure, you will lose everything. But all who commit themselves to eternity will reach out eagerly to grasp eternal glory!

Jesus has forewarned us about that day, saying:

> On that day, let him who is on the housetop, with his goods in the house, not come down to take them away; and likewise let him who is in the field not turn back. Remember Lot's wife. Whoever seeks to gain his life will lose it, but whoever loses his life will preserve it. I tell you, in that night there will be two men in one bed; one will be taken and the other left. There will be two women grinding together; one will be taken and the other left (Luke 17:31-36).

Do not confuse this with the utterance about the "desolating sacrilege" (Matthew 24:15; Mark 13:14). The latter does not refer to the Day of the Coming of the Son of Man, but to the impending destruction of Jerusalem, "when you see Jerusalem surrounded by armies" (Luke 21:20). This latter utterance instructs the disciples to flee to the mountains. This flight will be necessary for the few witnesses then alive because, like Jesus, they must preserve their lives until they have completed their testimony. This utterance undoubtedly refers to the destruction of Jerusalem by the Romans about 70 A.D., and it would be no benefit to the cause of Christ for his followers to perish with the Jews at the hands of the Romans. Ah, but when the earth begins to shake and the fire begins to fall, those who rush into the house to snatch up their treasures and run with them to the caves and rocks of the earth will lose their lives because, and only because, they attempted to save them. All these will remain for destruction and judgment, but whoever opens arms and heart to the earnest expectation of the everlasting glory "will be taken."

DEATH AND LIFE

Truly, truly, I say to you, he who hears my words and believes him who sent me, has eternal life; he does not come into judgment, but has passed from death to life (John 5:24).

Ordinary understanding presupposes that death follows life; one is born, lives, and then comes death. Not so with Jesus, who brings unique insight to bear on an old idea. In his mind, and therefore also in the mind of the Father, life does not precede death — it follows it! The above utterance illustrates this sequence. It is typical of Jesus thus not only to broach new ideas, but also to turn things in reverse to what we ordinarily think. Therefore, with Jesus, one passes not from life to death, but from death to life. Furthermore, since the life of which he speaks is everlasting, that is the end of the matter. Jesus has revealed that each has a destiny. We are moving forward to a new experience out of an old experience that we will never repeat. We are not on a cyclic journey through various orders of being and back — but we move on, progressively, never to return. The thing that the children of God are moving toward is life with the Father in glory. This is the "eternal life" of Jesus. It follows that, in the mind of Jesus, death is ever upon us.

What men have here, which they call life, is, in reality, death. It is a cruel deception that foists upon us the universal delusion that we are alive. In Truth, we experience death constantly, every day. So, when Jesus observed people engaged in their daily activities, following the course of this world, he surveyed death, not life, and he labeled it as such.

Two examples of specific incidents come to mind. In the first he confronted the Pharisees with this scathing rebuke:

You are like whitewashed tombs, which outwardly appear

beautiful, but within are full of dead men's bones and all uncleanness (Matthew 23:27).

He saw their physical bodies and interpreted them as tombs! Nothing more than the vessels of death! They thought of themselves as very much alive, but to him, their bones were dead men's bones.

The second example was when a would-be disciple approached him wishing to follow, but who wanted to go first and bury his "father." Jesus replied:

Leave the dead to bury their own dead (Matthew 8:22).

He made no fundamental distinction between those in need of burial and those accustomed to minister to that need! All belong to the category of the dead. Continuing from the words already quoted, He said:

Truly, truly, I say to you, the hour is coming, and now is, when the dead will hear the voice of the Son of God, and those who hear will live (John 5:25).

By the words, "and now is," he revealed that he was speaking to the dead whenever he addressed the multitudes in that long ago time. The "hour" began then, and it yet continues, when his words go forth across the earth to the dead. The fact is fearsome but the promise is glorious: "those who hear will live" (John 5:25).

Clearly, Jesus' conceptions of death and life differ radically from the generally accepted ideas. We think that we are alive; he states that we are dead. We think that our lives will end with death; he proclaims that our deaths may end with life — if we hear his words.

What does he mean by "the dead?" We have heard of the parent who has been offended by the conduct of a son or daughter and who cries out in anger, "Go from here and never darken my door again! To me you are henceforth dead." This, to Jesus, is exactly the significance of death. "The dead" are those who so offend the Father in heaven that he declares them to be dead. There is a difference, though, for the proclamation fails to settle the destiny of the child when the parent is human. But when God is the Father, and we are the children, our fates are sealed. When the Father is the Creator whose purpose in creating is aborted by the creature, then a mysterious and hidden change occurs in the status of the creatures. They were to have been his children but instead are forever separated from the Father. That separation is death. So, death does not imply a termination of being, but a dreadful and eternally permanent separation from the giver of life.

That being so, "life" in the utterances of Jesus must mean the initiation of an everlasting union with the Father, which is "eternal life." We who are in this world are dead, but he permits us to continue our being in hope that we will hear the Word of Christ and repent.

Those who hear will live (John 5:25).

This is the only escape from death and it must be seized while we are yet in this world. Otherwise, death is an absolutely permanent state.

Two more words must be introduced here to provide a firm basis for understanding this truth. One is "sin." The other is "love." First, consider sin. The Scriptures elsewhere tell us that "the wages of sin is death" (Romans 6:23), and that "sin is the transgression of the law" (1 John 3:4). With this in mind, continue to the following utterance of Jesus: "And behold, a lawyer stood up to put him to the test saying, Teacher, what shall I do to inherit eternal life?" (Luke 10:25).

He said to him,

What is written in the law? How do you read? (Luke 10:26).

And he answered, "You shall love the Lord your God with all your heart, and with all your soul, and with all your strength, and with all your mind; and your neighbor as yourself."

And he said to him,

You have answered right; do this, and you will live (Luke 10:27).

Sin, in its essence, is then the transgression of the law — of this law that, according to Jesus, is the essence of the law. It is failure to love God with all our being — with everything that we are and have. But love, the second word with which we need to deal, is a unifying and joining force; when it is genuine, nothing can overcome it. When it is the love of God, we want to be joined with him in his presence and glory forever; but then we do not want to remain trapped in time.

This implies that we hate our "lives" in this world! That, of course, is exactly what Jesus has told us. If I love God or anyone or anything else, I reach out in my heart to him, her, or it. I yearn to be with Him, her, or it ... in the very presence and not separated by anything. But we are here, and God is in his glory. If we want to remain here, what does that mean? It means that we love life on earth because we do not wish to leave it. It also means that we do not love God, regardless of what we may say. We would want to go to him if we did. Failing thus to love the Father, we abide in death, not having heard or received the Word of Christ. We are transgressors of the First and Great Commandment! We have transgressed the law of the love of God, which is the essence of divine law. This is the sin that issues in death wages, for we cannot enter into life with God when we do not love him with our whole being. This is not the result of an arbitrary judicial decree. It is simply because we do not want to, and he will not drag us, screaming and kicking, into his glory. So we remain in death until that love consumes us — because death is our choice!

We stand apart from God, and therefore dead, until we put on that love that "binds all things together" (Colossians 3:14). Therefore, love is the force that issues in life. When our love truly binds us to God the Father, we are in Truth joined with him in life everlasting.

Sin, seen in this light of Jesus, is simply the temporal orientation of love. A person who loves his or her life in the world is both dead and sinful because of the orientation of love. Alternatively, a person who loves God the Father with his or her whole being abides in life. This is the righteousness of Christ. This person desires only to be with the Father. It follows that this person hates, or wishes to separate from, his or her life in this world. It is very simple, isn't it? Consider also how marvelously, yes, how perfectly consistent Jesus is in all his utterances!

One may very well be a good person from every human point of view — altruistic, humanitarian, charitable, considerate, honest, industrious. Yet if one also retains the love of life, all is in vain. All the deeds are good, but the whole life is a sin because it is rooted in the love of life in this world. Such a person is lost to God, and in need of redemption, because the reason to exist is null and void.

Jesus calls that thing "death" that we call "life." Then what we call "death" also must be viewed differently by him. When his friend, Lazarus, "died," he did not announce it by saying "Lazarus is dead." Instead, he said to the disciples:

Our friend, Lazarus, has fallen asleep (John 11:11).

Then the disciples, uncomprehending, replied, "Lord, if he is sleeping, he is getting well" (John 11:12). He responded to their blindness by descending to their level of comprehension, and said,

Lazarus is dead! (John 11:14).

Yet Lazarus was indeed "getting well." To Jesus, the experience that men call "death" is, for the children of God, only a welcome rest between temporal and eternal experience. It is sleep. It is not death in any sense because even in this sleep one remains in union with the Father, much as the sleeping baby on its mother's bosom is in union with the mother.

A ruler once came to Jesus with the plea: "My daughter has just died; but come and lay your hand on her, and she will live" (Matthew 9:18). Jesus rose and followed him, with his disciples. When he came to the ruler's house and saw the flute players, and the crowd making a tumult, he said:

Depart; for the girl is not dead but sleeping (Matthew 9:24).

They laughed at him. Then they put the crowd outside and he went in and took her by the hand, and the girl arose.

Reading the Gospels from a purely human point of view, one could easily conclude that Jesus had a morbid obsession with death. He looked to the hour, he strained forward to when he would say, "And now, Father, I am coming to you." But no. This was an obsession with life, not death! He displayed this "obsession" in many other sayings, such as the following:

I am the bread of life (John 6:35, 48).

I came that you may have life, and have it more abundantly (John 10:10).

Because I live, you shall live also (John 14:19).

Failing to comprehend Jesus' conception of life, men usually take this to mean a promise of adding to the luster of the earthly experience. But Jesus was thinking of the union with God the Father in Glory, which we must "die" to realize. That is the only abundant life, and he came to show, and to be, the way to its realization.

In reality, his promise of abundant life is a detriment to life in this world, and he recognized this in many utterances, as follows:

> *The way that leads to life is hard, and few there be that find it* (Matthew 7:14).

> *Marvel not if the world hate you, for you know that it hated me before it hated you* (John 15:18).

> *Men will hate you and cast out your name as evil on account of the Son of Man* (Luke 6:22).

Nothing can be more heinous to the mind of Christ and of God than preaching in his name that godliness is worldly gain. It is a priceless gain, but it costs one everything. Jesus said it:

> *Whosoever does not renounce all that he has cannot be my disciple* (Luke 14:33).

That which seemed a death wish as Jesus and his disciples marched to the cross and to martyrdom was not such at all. It only seems so to those of us who have refused the enlightenment that Jesus introduced into the world by his Word and Way. They all were motivated by the very opposite of a death wish — that is, a life wish. They were persuaded that only by following Jesus was it possible for anyone to receive the life that is life indeed. They went to martyrdom because they turned against the tide of the pseudo-life that has overwhelmed the world, a tide that is contrary both to good common sense and to the doctrine that we have in the utterances of Jesus.

Deep in our hearts, every one of us knows better than we speak or practice. The eternal God created us, so that in our hearts we are eternal beings. Yes, we have eternity in our hearts! There are no exceptions. Therefore we are always forlorn and despairing when we seriously think about life from the merely human point of view. We know that it must end, and we cannot adapt ourselves to the idea of the cessation of being. So, powered by the drive for eternal experience, we foolishly strive to postpone the dread encounter. We strive to extend our longevity on the earth while knowing, deep within, the futility of it all. It is because we refuse to comprehend that our commitment to life is in Truth a commitment unto death. The thing that the world has taught us to fear and to hate more than anything else is, in Truth, the only access to the life our inmost being craves.

The life-wish of every person is an eternal life-wish. It can never be satisfied by temporal experience. Yet we persistently, stubbornly, blindly, go on striving vainly to satisfy it by the earthly experience of death that is death indeed. I mean, by our temporal separation from the God who is the source of true life. What a deadly self-deception!

EVOLUTIONARY IMPLICATIONS

It can be argued that the doctrine of Christ is incompatible with the evolutionary development of man and the universe. How far would the process have gone, had the species been endowed with this "hatred of life," instead of the innate commitment to temporal self-preservation that now prevails? Not far, to be sure. Therefore, we have evolved and persevered because the drive for self-preservation motivates our species. When presented with a threat to life, we don't have to think about it for a moment. We react immediately with whatever evasive, defensive, or protective action is possible. We are therefore the products of a creation-old process of natural selection that results in the survival of the fittest, and we are the survivors.

It was necessary to the purpose of God that we have our being after this manner, but it does not follow that we are doomed to an infinite succession of generations of frustrated life-preservers. It is not unreasonable to think that this cycle of evolutionary self-preservation has an end. We generally agree that it had a beginning, and as our generation is the first to learn, it also must have an end when the sun burns up its nuclear fuel. That is, if another disaster does not overtake the earth long before that distant event. All the cycles of nature end after making their contributions to ultimate destiny. The earth will cease its cycles about the sun. Long before that, the life-sustaining water will cease its cycle of "ocean-sky-rainfall-river-

ocean." Before that, many other life cycles will cease, having fulfilled
the purposes of the Creator. It is as though the cycles were, like
wheels, rolling on toward the fulfillment of the purposes of God and
bearing upon their axles the vehicles of the children of God, convey-
ing them all into his ultimate presence.

Look at illustrations closer to our immediate experience. Consider
the infant. Daily it rises, totters, and falls. Again and again, day after
day and week after week, it rises, totters, and falls — until one day
the cycle ends when it rises and walks, taking its first steps into the
world. We knew all along that it would happen in its time. We
understand that all the rising, tottering, and falling was to this end,
that the whole series of cycles might culminate in the ability to walk.

The athlete attempts repeatedly to vault over the highest pole. He
backs off, he runs, he vaults, he dislodges the pole, he falls. Back off,
run, vault, hit pole, fall; back off, run, vault, hit pole, fall; back off,
run, vault, hit pole, fall; thus the cycle repeats until, at last, over the
pole he gracefully sails! The cycle is broken when he achieves his
purpose. Likewise, the evolutionary cycle of the generations of life-
preservers is broken when they vault over the "pole" and sail gracefully into the glorious liberty of the children of God! At that point
the whole purpose of the evolutionary process is fulfilled. And when
the purpose is fulfilled, the process is ended. Thus all temporal cycles
will be broken when the full number of the children of God has
entered his kingdom.

Jesus once told a parable in which these cycles are implicit:

> The kingdom of God is as if a man should scatter seed upon
> the ground, and should sleep and rise night and day, and the
> seed should sprout and grow, he knows not how. The earth
> produces of itself, first the blade, then the ear, then the full
> grain in the ear. But when the grain is ripe, at once he puts
> in the sickle, because the harvest has come (Mark 4:26-29).

He sleeps and rises, night and day, as the cycle repeats itself.
Likewise the growing seedlings experience the continuing cycles of
night and day. But something else is also happening —slowly, almost
imperceptibly, there is growth — he knows not how. Eventually the
desired end is attained — the seedlings grow up and the harvest
comes. Likewise the evolutionary cycles will end when the harvest

has come! This harvest is the sole goal and purpose of creation —
that it might produce the children of God for his glory (Isaiah 43: 5-7;
Hebrews 2:10).

For I am come down from heaven, not to do my will, but the will of him who sent me...

Jesus, John 6:38

8
THE WILL

Here is Jesus' definitive expression of the Father's will:

All that the Father gives me will come to me; and him who comes to me I will not cast out. For I have come down from heaven, not to do my own will, but the will of him who sent me; and this is the will of him who sent me, that I should lose nothing of all that he has given me, but raise it up at the last day. For this is the will of my Father, that everyone who sees the Son and believes in him should have eternal life; and I will raise him up at the last day (John 6:37-40).

Since this is Jesus' definitive expression of the Father's will, it therefore defines the concept in all his references. It follows that, if we examine other utterances in the light of this one, we will realize this significance in them. We also will draw new insights from them as their Truth comes to light.

First, though, I am going to state a conclusion drawn from a careful study of all the utterances and you will see, as you proceed, how well it corresponds to the Truth. This conclusion is: The will of God consists of but one primary objective; all other things that contribute to the realization of that objective are secondary expressions of his will. This single objective is the destiny that the Father desires for everyone, which is the goal of being, the Resurrection at the last day. If we seek to incorporate other ideas, objectives, or conditions into our views of the will of the Father, we will depart from the Truth unless those things also contribute to the realization of the one objective. Even then we also must acknowledge them as secondary expressions, or we will continue to err. Now, referring again to the utterance quoted above, what is this one single objective? Obviously, it is eternal life with the Father, which we acquire only by: (1) believing in Christ, and (2) participating in the resurrection at the last day.

It is necessary to define "believing in Christ" because of the erroneous interpretations that Christendom has applied to this idea. For example, the preachers have often told us it means "to believe that Jesus died for my sins," or that "Christ is the Son of God." Both ideas are correct as far as they go, but they are inadequate expressions of the crux of the faith. They have misplaced their focus, and those who build their faith on such confessions are like those who build, without foundations, houses doomed to fall. Their error is precisely identical with that of the one who "hears these words of mine and does not do them."

By believing in him, Jesus had in mind that we should believe his words. This is the crux of true faith. He intimately identified himself with his words, so much so that there is no way to know him except through the knowledge of his utterances. The only effective faith in him is faith in his Word. This alone is the faith that issues in salvation. The only genuine response to him is a response to his Word. It is the utterances that are the personification of the man. He came down from heaven specifically to utter them, and so to believe in him is to believe the words.

You will understand this better by reference to another of his utterances:

> *Whosoever loves his life loses it; but he who hates his life in this world will keep it for life eternal* (John 12:25).

He also said that the will of God is that everyone who sees and believes in him should have eternal life. When he said that we obtain eternal life only through the hatred of life in this world, we see how he intends us to understand belief in him. For unless one believes what he said, i.e., that only he who hates his life in this world receives eternal life, one will not receive eternal life, whatever else one may have believed about Jesus.

Let us look at typical Brother A. as an example. Brother A. believes in Jesus with all his heart, or so he supposes, because he believes in the Jesus that his teachers at church have defined for him. Brother A. also loves his life in this world, which means, in essence, that he does not want to part with it. He believes that this love of life is a good thing. He even says "Amen" when the pastor, speaking from the pulpit, eulogizes a "hero of the faith" as one who was a lover of life. So, does Brother A. really believe in Jesus? Absolutely not! If he does not believe his words, he does not believe in him, and he does not believe his words because he loves his life contrary to the Word. Therefore he cannot receive eternal life because he does not believe in Jesus. That is, he does not believe the words of Jesus. On the other hand, if he were to hate his life in the world in a manner consistent with the words of Jesus, he would receive eternal life. He may never have heard of Jesus, yet he would believe in Jesus because he would believe in the Truth expressed in the Word.

The will of God is then that all arrive at that particular destiny that Jesus defined as "the Resurrection at the last day." Now, since the will of God more generally includes all things that contribute to transporting us to that particular destiny, and since only by the hatred of life can one receive eternal life, it follows that the hatred of life is also the will of the Father. It transports us to the point where it is God's will that we be, namely, the Resurrection at the last day.

Jesus also stated that "he who loves his life loses it."

Then it follows that such a person fails to receive eternal life. He fails to arise to eternal life at the Resurrection at the last day, which is the Father's will. It follows also that the "love of life" is not the will of God. Also, since it is the love of life that absolutely precludes one's arrival at the Resurrection at the last day, which is the Father's will, one can say that the love of life opposes the will of God. It obstructs the Father's will when anyone is guilty of the love of life. Let us go a step farther. It is reasonable to say that sin is whatever opposes the will of God. Therefore the love of life is the essence of sin, and to "repent" of one's sin is to repent of the love of life. This is the essence of repentance, apart from which there is no repentance.

Now consider the second means to the single objective, which is the Resurrection at the last day. The will of the Father cannot be realized apart from the Resurrection. This informs us that the single objective that constitutes the will of the Father refers not to this world or to time because we realize it only through the Resurrection at the last day. The will of the Father is life eternal as distinguished from life temporal. Therefore, in this world nothing has any significance as the will of God except only those secondary things that contribute directly to the realization of that will, which is eternal life at the Resurrection. One of those things is the hatred of life in this world!

This hatred also must be a primary element in the Father's will. Jesus expressly stated it as a prerequisite to the realization of the Father's will, which is eternal life through the Resurrection at the last day. This idea radically contradicts the views of most churchmen. It is not my purpose here to expand into a discussion of the failings of the churches, but it is important to acknowledge that they are among the most influential institutions in Christendom, and their influence is pervasive throughout the world. The result is that Jesus' sharply defined idea of the will of God is inundated by falsehoods that render the Truth generally inconceivable. He has, again, been betrayed by a kiss!

The churches tend to teach their adherents to think of the will of God in either of two ways: corporately, as the realization of some general earthly condition such as "world peace" or "political freedom," and individually, as the decision which "God would have us make" when seeking a spouse, selecting an occupation, and resolving personal problems or perplexing questions of conduct. Again, consider our beloved Brother A., who has come into a considerable inheritance and needs to know how to invest it wisely. Should he enter the stock market, and if so, what stocks should he purchase? Should he buy a business and quit his job? Should he pay off his home mortgage? Should he give to a worthy charity?

According to Jesus, absolutely none of this has any relevance to the will of God unless it contributes to the goal of eternal life at the last day. Giving the money away conceivably falls into this category. Nothing else of those things mentioned does because all contribute to the enhancement of life in this world and fall under the category of the love of life. If we restrict the options to those of investing it in an earthly, temporal way — the Father has no interest. So I repeat for the sake of clarity: the will of God is the fulfillment of a single goal, which is the Resurrection at the last day. That is all we need consider, because that is the Father's sole concern. Absolutely nothing else has any positive significance in his sight. He has no interest in the outcome of our wars or of our national and world peace. This is purely a temporal affair that lacks relevance to eternal life. He does not concern himself with the eradication of poverty or of disease, since these things only contribute to the quality of temporal life that we are to hate. He does not care whom you marry, or whether you marry, since this is purely a temporal condition. Jesus stated that, in heaven, there is neither marrying nor giving in marriage. He cares not a whit about your occupation, nor the extent of your education. He gives no attention to the degrees of your success in this world.

How can I make it any more plain? Jesus has spoken — not his words as the words of a man, but the very words of the Father in heaven. One might wish that it were otherwise, but it is not and we must reckon with this, either here or hereafter.

Doubtless the will of God embraces much, much more than this one single objective. I do not mean to say in an absolute sense that God concerns himself with nothing else. What is clear is that He has no other desires concerning us. Therefore we can know nothing else about his will than this, which he has revealed through his Son, Jesus. We have no need to know anything else. Perhaps in eternity we shall know much more — but now we can know nothing else for this is all he has chosen to reveal.

How dark, oh how very dark is this world! See how people commit themselves to the pursuit of the will of God conceived in temporal terms, and look at the result: "holy war." Christians war with Christians, Jews, Muslims, anyone who threatens them in the conviction that they are doing the will of God. Jews war against Arabs, Muslims against Jews, Christians, and themselves all in the conviction that the war is holy, that it is God's will that they fight and win. All would be resolved and peace would prevail if all men realized the one simple fact that Jesus set forth long ago: the will of God is eternal life, this and nothing more! In saying this I do not mean to imply that such a peaceful world is a goal of divine will. To the contrary, the world functions precisely as divine will has ordained from the beginning. It has no prospect of any radical change for the better, according to Jesus' prophetic utterances about the future of man on earth.

When one believes, as I do, that God created the world, this interpretation of the Father's will leads directly to another conclusion: the purpose, the sole purpose of the creation, was and is our realization of eternal life at the Resurrection. I am stating this here because of its immediate relevance, but an extended discussion will be presented later.

DOING THE WILL

The preceding presents the Father's will as goal — as the destiny that he would have us attain. How does this relate to "doing" the will of God? Jesus was very interested in this aspect of the Father's will. His intense interest stands out in the following utterances:

(1) In the prayer instruction to the disciples:

> *Pray then like this: Our Father who art in heaven, Hallowed be thy name. Thy kingdom come, Thy will be done, On earth as it is in heaven* (Matthew 6:9-10; Luke 11:2).

(2) At the conclusion of the Sermon on the Mount:

> *Not every one who says to me, 'Lord, Lord,' shall enter the kingdom of heaven, but he who does the will of my Father who is in heaven* (Matthew 7:21).

(3) And in Gethsemane:

> *My Father, if it be possible, let this cup pass from me; nevertheless, not as I will, but as thou wilt* (Matthew 26:39, 42; Mark 14:36; Luke 22:42).

And he came to the disciples and found them sleeping; and he said to Peter,

> *So you could not watch with me one hour? Watch and pray that you may not enter into temptation; the spirit indeed is willing, but the flesh is weak* (Matthew 26:40-41).

Again, for the second time, he went away and prayed,

My Father, if this cannot pass unless I drink it, thy will be done (Matthew 26:42).

Jesus provides the key to understanding his emphasis on "doing" the will in the utterance in John's Gospel that appears at the beginning of this chapter. There he said,

... for I have come down from heaven, not to do my own will, but the will of him who sent me (John 6:38).

Taking his every word very seriously, as he intended, we immediately derive from this that in his mind, "doing the will of God" was his unique task. He was of course also interested in the doing of the will of God by others, as when he said,

... whoever does the will of my Father, the same is my mother, and brother, and sister (Matthew 12:50; Mark 3:35).

He was unique in that his was the task of doing it first. He was to show and teach the way for others to follow. Before his coming, the Father's will was not being done on the earth by anyone. The whole world was in darkness and he came, as he said, to be the light of the world. He sought to enlighten everyone about the will of the Father and how to do it. This meant that he must first do it himself for if he, who understood it, did not do it, then no one would. Thus it was that he came down from heaven to be the first to do the will of the Father. Jesus was the original pioneer of the Father's will.

The apostles rightly acknowledged him to be subject to the temptations characteristic of all, and he experienced all the human frailties. Even Jesus was unsure of his ability to fulfill his calling as he sought the prayerful support of his friends when he counseled them to pray:

... thy will be done, on earth as it is in heaven (Matthew 6:10; Luke 11:2).

This was nothing less than a petition for their prayers in his behalf — that he might be equal to the task of doing the Father's will on the earth, as he well understood that it was and is done in heaven. He had been mightily tempted in the wilderness, and he knew that the devil had only left him for a more convenient season. That convenient season arrived in Gethsemane (Matthew 26:36-45; Mark 14:32-41).

There, struggling against the "weak" flesh and valiantly clinging to his spiritual resources, he won the conclusive battle with Satan.

We note his extreme disappointment in his friends, who were oblivious to the cosmic struggle occurring within him — so much so that they chose to take a restful nap. Listen to his plaintive words:

So you could not watch with me one hour? Watch and pray that you may not enter into temptation; the spirit indeed is willing, but the flesh is weak (Matthew 26: 40-41; Mark 14: 37-38).

His victory, however, was secured by his strong resolve as expressed in the following words.

My Father, if this cannot pass unless I drink it, Thy will be done (Matthew 26:42; Mark 14:36).

He had come down to do the will of his Father; the time for doing was at hand. He had battled victoriously with the opposing human forces within and the demonic forces without. These sought to divert him from his resolve — from his whole purpose in coming to the earth. Thus far he had prevailed. He had not failed and was continuing his resolute march to the cross and to the event that would be the first doing of the will of the Father on the earth, as it is done in heaven.

When he said,

Not everyone who says to me, "Lord, Lord" shall enter the Kingdom of Heaven, but whoever does the will of my Father who is in heaven (Matthew 7:21),

he was thinking first of himself — how he, as a man, would enter the Kingdom if, and only if, he was faithful to the task of doing the will of the Father. He hoped for and expected that others would follow him in a similar doing of the Father's will, for only on that basis does anyone enter the Kingdom. Here we see his strong distinction between those professing to believe in him and acknowledging him as Lord but failing to hear him and follow in doing the will of the Father, and those who listen to him, take him seriously and follow him in doing the Father's will. It is only the latter who truly believe in him, for they not only believe "in" him, they actually believe *him*. They believe what he said!

He did the will of his Father when he yielded up his spirit on the cross, when he uttered his last gasp and died. All parties present conspired in some way to deflect him from this resolve. Yet he, who might have come down from the cross, who might have called out to the Father to send angels to destroy all his enemies, did no such thing. Instead, he held true to his calling to do the Father's will. It is in his suffering and death that he showed what he meant when he spoke of doing the Father's will on earth as it is in heaven. It was there that he held true to the love of the Father and of life eternal by hating his life on earth. It was to go to his Father and share again in the Glory of Eternity (John 17:5, 13; Hebrews 12:2). Thus also he left us an example that time can never erase, which all must follow who would enter the Kingdom.

God's will is done in heaven by everyone who is blessed to achieve that wondrous estate. And his will, which they are doing, is simply that they love being there. None of them would wish to be anywhere else, and it is not the Father's will that they should be removed from him. He loves them all and would hold them to himself eternally. For this cause Jesus emphasized that he did not come down from heaven because he wanted to, but the Father sent him to do his will on earth as it is done in heaven. It is obvious, then, that the Father's will is not being done by anyone, anywhere, who does not want to be with him in his glory but who desires to reside somewhere else. This is of course the perfect description of anyone who seeks to prolong his life on the earth, for while we cling to this life, loving and embracing it, do we want to be with the Father? I tell you, no! Therefore only by hating life in this world can anyone do the will of the Father, which is that we hate this life so as to experience the life eternal in his presence in glory.

This is also the significance of the commandment of God that Jesus designated as "first" — "Thou shalt love the Lord thy God with all your heart and with all your mind and with all your soul and with all your strength" (Deuteronomy 6:5; Matthew 22:37; Mark 12:30). Loving God the Father in this way can mean only one thing. It means that we reach out to him with our whole being. It means that we desire above all other things to join him in his Glory as a son or a daughter for eternity. And if this is the case with any person, that person does not want to remain in the life temporal and therefore can be said to hate it. Conversely, it follows that anyone who loves his life in time clings to it and by that signifies that he does not love God.

The will is the hinge pin upon which the whole universe swings. It is a key to the comprehension of all that Jesus conceived when he spoke of "Truth." Apart from an accurate understanding of the will, one can never realize the light of Christ, but must forever wander in the darkness of the world, without light and without hope. To be more specific, nothing is more important to us than an accurate understanding of what "the will of God" signifies in the utterances of the Lord.

I have shown what was in his mind when he said,

> *I have come down from heaven, not to do my own will, but the will of him who sent me* (John 6:38).

Other ideas have been advanced, such as the ones listed here:

(1) He conceived that, day by day, he was to live an exemplary life on the earth as a pattern of conduct for all men to follow. Thus he would be doing the will of God on earth that he said he came to do.

(2) God's will for mankind is the perfection of society issuing in a utopian world of righteousness, peace, and joy. Jesus came to show us how to realize this goal and to inspire us to strive for it with all our might. He did both and thus he did the will of him who sent him.

(3) Jesus came to give his life a sacrifice for sin so that men and women might be forgiven. This he did and thus he did the will of his Father.

Doubtless many other options might be set out for our consideration, but these are more than sufficient for this discussion. About the first option, the presentation of himself as an example of righteousness for all men to follow ... it is correct to say that he did present himself as an example to be followed; however, he did not expect many people to respond:

> *The way is broad that leads to destruction, and many there be that go in thereby; but the way is hard that leads to life, and few there be that find it* (Matthew 7: 13, 14).

> *For judgment I am come into the world, that those who do*

not see may see, and that those who see may become blind (John 9: 39).

The following utterance is also encumbered with similar difficulties:

I came not to call the righteous, but sinners to repentance (Matthew 9:13; Mark 2:17; Luke 5:32).

These utterances are characteristic of the general tenor of his message, in which mankind consists of two major categories. One will hate and persecute him and his followers; the other will love and follow him. The latter category is very small in the expectation of Jesus, while the former, which includes his persecutors, will include almost the whole of mankind. In view of these difficulties, it is not reasonable to suppose that the first option constituted the will of God in the mind of Jesus.

Now consider the second option. It can be eliminated handily by examining other statements given by Jesus as constituting in some way his purpose in coming down from heaven. He did say that he came down to do the will of the Father, that is, of him who sent him (John 6: 38). In another place he also said:

Do not think that I came to send peace on the earth; I came not to send peace but a sword (Matthew 10: 34).

Yet again he said:

I came to cast fire on the earth, and would that it were already kindled! (Luke 12:49).

He came to do God's will, but he did not come to send peace on the earth. He came to do God's will, but he also came to cast fire on the earth. Therefore, the doing of God's will on the earth by Jesus is in some way associated with the sending of the sword and the casting of fire. It follows that one can eliminate the utopianization of society from consideration, since a fiery earth at war is hardly consistent with the Utopia of which our species dreams.

Also, none of his visions of the future of the world has even a hint of optimism about its state. He said:

You shall hear of wars and rumors of wars, but the end is not yet (Matthew 24:6; Mark 13:7).

The poor you have always with you (Matthew 26:11; Mark 14:7; John 12:8).

These statements are typical of his expectations of this world. The intervening two millennia have fulfilled his predictions.

We also can eliminate the third option by similar means. This one conceives of the will of God as consisting of Jesus' offering up of himself as a sacrifice for sin; but this cannot be the case in view of the following utterance:

Those who are well have no need of a physician, but those who are sick. Go and learn what this means, 'I desire mercy, and not sacrifice.' For I came not to call the righteous, but sinners (Hosea 6:6; Matthew 9:13; 12:7).

The quotation from Hosea, "I desire mercy and not sacrifice," was mentioned repeatedly by Jesus, and suggests that he understood that God does not desire a sacrifice. Now, to speak of "God's desire" is, of course, to speak of God's will. Since this was his view of that matter, he could not have understood that God had sent him into the world to do what he does not desire — to render a sacrifice. I will discuss this idea more fully in a later chapter on the topic of salvation, in response to the heavy, but mistaken, emphasis on sacrifice throughout Christendom.

God's will, in its absolute essence, is to have children in his presence in glory. Everything which contributes to that end is, of course, also his will in a general sense. The will of God is then a family affair, in which a father begets children to share his life with him. God's means to this end is the creation of the world and the evolution of man, with the subsequent inspiration of man by the eternal spirit of the Father, but individually as each qualifies. The Father sent Jesus down to teach us how to qualify, and then to show us the way. So, when he was uttering the words of God, he was doing the will of God in that the words tell us to respond to the divine call to glory. Subsequently, when he laid down his life on the cross in demonstration of both the hatred of life in this world and the love of eternal glory, he was showing how each can and must qualify. So, in his death, he was doing the will of God by showing the way to God.

Finally, as a man among men, he fulfilled the Father's will in his person by desiring the Father's will above all earthly considerations. Thus he went joyfully to his Father to become his child in Glory — the firstborn of many sisters and brothers.

I submit to you that this is all we need know to realize fully the significance of the will of the Father in the mind of Jesus. Whatever other dimensions there are in the will of God remain unknown to us. Nor have we any need to know of them. The will of God finds expression in a single idea, and if we do not respond to that, we have no need to know of anything else. A positive response to the one essence is the sole qualification for entry into the will of the Father.

In spite of this, men and women never tire of interpreting the Father's will in terms of their particular desires. This only leads them astray from the divine will, not into its realization. This is the prevailing practice, not only in Christendom, but also in every other culture that acknowledges God. For example, we all want a peaceful earth devoid of war and its horrors and so that becomes "the will of God."

Jesus avoided making any intrusion into the definition of the Father's will. And let there be no mistake: he had a will that was distinct from that of the Father. He was careful to acknowledge this. Not only so, but his will, like ours, tended to be contrary to that of the Father. This stands out in the following prayerful utterance:

> ...*not my will, but yours be done* (Matthew 26: 39; Luke 22: 42).

In the mind of Jesus, then, the Father's will is children in heaven, together with everything that contributes to that end. From this perception of the will of God comes the answer to many questions that were previously unfathomable. For example, why must there be enmity between heaven and earth? As far as I know, Jesus did not explain this other than to point out the impossibility of serving two masters. He accepted it as a given state of things that is fundamental to Truth. The absence of an explanation raises questions. Either it is not important, which cannot be the case given Jesus' focus upon it, or others had already revealed it, which does not seem to be so, or it is so obvious that it needs no explanation. The latter, I believe, is the case. It became clear to me while I was considering the following tenets of faith:

(1) God in heaven created the world (Genesis 2:4; Isaiah 42:5; 45: 8, 12, 18; Ephesians 3:9).

(2) God then created man in the world, in his likeness (Genesis 1: 26-27; 9: 6; 1 Corinthians 11:7).

(3) Heaven is the glorious eternal state of being (Isaiah 63:15; Acts 7:55).

(4) God wills that we become his children in heaven (Isaiah 43: 6-7; Hebrews 2:10).

All these are in some form affirmed by the prophets, and Jesus affirmed the prophets (Not that he affirmed everything written by them). Jesus focused on the last one, giving it special emphasis, illustrating and illuminating it in every way. For example, he defined the Father's will as follows:

> *This is my Father's will: that I should lose nothing that he has given me but should raise it up at the last day* (John 6:39-40, 44, 54).

He amended and explained this utterance when he promised that the meek will inherit the land (Psalm 37:11; Matthew 5:5), that he has gone to prepare a place for the children (a place in the Father's house, see John 14: 2, 3) and that he will return, at the Parousia, to receive them unto himself that where he is, there they will be also (John 14:3).

I am not dependent upon the New Testament Epistles as source material, but it is useful to show that those whom Jesus taught directly also came to understand this as God's will and purpose for man. Witness these statements:

"For those whom he foreknew he also predestined to be con-formed to the image of his son, in order that he might be the firstborn among many brethren" (Romans 8:29).

"He destined us in love to be his sons through Jesus Christ, according to the purpose of his will" (Ephesians 1:5).

"For it was fitting that he, for whom and by whom all things exist, in bringing many sons to glory, should make the pioneer of their salvation perfect through suffering" (Hebrews 2:10).

So therefore, the Father's will and purpose for man is the resurrection. This is unmistakably the resurrection to his eternal glory, to be with him in his house, as his sons and daughters. It is important to acknowledge that this is the Father's only will and purpose for man — that we become his children in glory. Every legitimate expression of his will ultimately derives its significance from this. Now, understanding as we do that the eternal God changes not, I can only conclude that this has always been his purpose for man, even from before the creation of the world.

Keeping the above four tenets in mind, now let us explain the obvious — that is, the only method by which the creator can realize his purpose of adding children to his glory. God, had he been temporally minded, may have desired to realize the children immediately, but even he could not do this because of the nature of children: they are in the parent's likeness. Since his likeness includes a perfect freedom of the will, they too must possess this divine attribute. But if they enter glory with unrestrained free will, there will be disagreements. There will be rebellions, factions, and even war in heaven and glory will be glory no more. Better to do without such children! His purpose would be defeated. On the other hand, if he compels their wills to conform to his, they will have lost their freedom. They will no more be in the Father's likeness; his purpose will be defeated. But God is resourceful and proceeded to resolve this seeming dilemma by providing another place, planet earth, where the children can come into being and work out their rebellion. Those among them who freely come to will for themselves the same purpose that is the Father's will become like minded with the Father. They will therefore desire to become his children in glory.

This response to the Father's will has, however, no real significance unless the children have at least one other attractive option. This he provided by the creation of the world and the life that is in it. This option must have very desirable features. It must attract, woo, and entice the children. Above all, it must cause them to think that it alone offers the promise of fulfillment. If, in spite of the vigorous courting by this world someone spurns it, discovering and opting for another fulfillment in eternity, this world must punish him. It must vent its rage upon him, rendering this course so unattractive in its immediate results that others will be discouraged from following. It also must strive to realize within itself an alter-glory, and so to accomplish within itself that same unification of the will that is the Father's purpose for us. To this end the authorities arise to persuade, coerce, enlist, indoctrinate, enforce, and finally, destroy, so that there can be at least a degree of unity and peace in this world.

Women and men are therefore the prize for which heaven and earth contend, and within our free volition lies the battlefield upon which they wage their war. So it is inevitable that there be enmity between these two realms that contend for us in a contest that seals our eternal destinies.

It is against this background that Jesus said:

> *If you were of the world, the world would love its own. But because you are not of the world, but I chose you out of the world, therefore the world hates you* (John 15: 19).

The life that is of the world is then at enmity with the life that is not of the world. The latter is alien, threatening, suspicious, incomprehensible, and therefore hateful to the former. The world therefore hates all who are not of the world, precisely because they are not of the world. That is the only explanation necessary to understand the inimical relation between these two adversaries that contend for the soul of every person.

The Truth becomes astonishingly clear in the light of the words of Jesus if only one can get beyond that great and formidable obstacle: the love of life. Then we see that the whole creation owes its being to the desire of the Father to have children, children of free will like unto himself, to share his eternal glory. It was out of a consideration of the freedom of the will of these children that he created the universe of space-time and energy. It was so that they might have their origins under conditions that preserved the freedom of the will while offering options to his desire for them. We conceive of the whole universe as a fruit of the Father's will. He brought it into being by the exercise of divine will. He said simply, "Let it be" (Genesis 1:3, 6, 14), and it was so!

It was also fitting that the creation be subjected to decay, not of its own will but of the will of its creator, as Paul truly wrote (Romans 8:20, 24). Jesus also acknowledged this when he urged us to lay up our treasure in heaven where, in contrast to earth, thieves do not break through and steal, and rust and moth cannot corrupt (Matthew 6:19, 20). Otherwise, it might stand forever over against the Glory of the Father, hopelessly captivating, by its sham glory, all creatures exposed to it.

The creation is perfect, for the Father's purpose, just as it is. It gives us a taste of glory to whet the appetite and drives us to seek the utmost glory, but it also drives us to despair at the futility of this age. This moves those who are wise to seek that glory that is glory indeed.

Finally, at the right time, at the fullness of time (Galatians 4:4), the Father sent the Son to explain all. He was also careful to make known the option of eternal glory to those who are called out of the world to become his children in heaven. He did this, and more; for after his words came his victorious example as he showed us the way that we need only follow. I mean when he hated his life in this world and put it away from himself at the cross so that he might participate in the joy that was before him, and that is before us all if only we follow him. And what was it he said he came to do?

> *I came down from heaven, not to do my own will, but the will of him who sent me* (John 6:38).

Thy kingdom come,
Thy will be done,
On earth as it is in heaven.

Jesus, Matthew 6:10

9

THE KINGDOM

Jesus quickly focused on the Kingdom. The primary thrust of early sermons was a call to repentance based upon an urgency imposed by the nearness of the Kingdom. He said: "Repent! For the kingdom of God is at hand!"(Matthew 4:17; Mark 1:15). In this he was continuing the major theme of John the Baptizer, whose preaching had first aroused wide public interest. He was also gaining attention by appealing to the Jews' intense interest in this theme. But Jesus' call to repentance based on the nearness of the Kingdom was different from that of John. John's was a call to a higher state of morality, whereas Jesus was calling the people to change their whole attitude to life (Matthew 3:8-10; Luke 3:7-14). This was to be done by resetting their minds from earth to heaven and from time to eternity. He tied this call to the Kingdom, for it was because of the nearness of the Kingdom that he issued the call. Why repent? Because the Kingdom of God was at hand!

THE COMING

Both Jesus and John understood that the prophetic promise of a Kingdom of God, as conceived in the Messianic expectation, was not yet fulfilled. I mention this to establish a point of reference in time. The Kingdom was not yet come when Jesus and John were issuing their calls to repentance based on its nearness. The Kingdom promised by the prophets had not yet appeared. Now, beginning at this point, I propose to set forth the exact time of the coming, give or take a few seconds. As always, I will do this by focusing on the utterances of Jesus. Here is an initial clue: When Jesus gave prayer instruction to the disciples, he inextricably tied the coming of the Kingdom to the doing of the will of God on earth as it is done in heaven. The utterances quoted on the previous pages, and again here, strongly suggest this:

> *"But when you pray, say:*
> *Our Father who art in heaven,*
> *Hallowed be your name.*
> *Your Kingdom come,*
> *Your will be done,*
> *On earth as it is in heaven."* (Matthew 6:9-10; Luke 11:2).

Here, then, is the clue: The coming of the Kingdom is simultaneous with the act of doing the will of God on earth as it is done in heaven! Jesus' joining of these two ideas in one breath at the outset of this prayer strongly suggests that they are simultaneous in time, and may be identical. When one is praying for the Kingdom to come, one is also praying for God's will to be done on earth as it is in heaven. The two events may even be synonymous! This also implies that the will of the Father had not yet been done on the earth as it is in heaven, as of the day and hour when he uttered these words.

I am aware of the widely accepted interpretation of this prayer for the doing of the will of the Father. This is that it is a petition of a general nature and that it only asks for earthly conditions to improve. It conceives that men will rise to a higher state of righteousness, then the Kingdom will come. I, too, once understood it in that light, but do so no longer. Now I know that Jesus was only asking the disciples to pray for him, that he alone might persevere to perform certain actions defined in his mind as "the will of God," as explained in the prior chapter. Then the Kingdom of God could and would come! The following discussion clarifies this view.

Many generations of subjugation to foreign kings had intensified the yearning for the Kingdom, as they perceived it, throughout the Jewish nation. There flourished in the hearts of Jewish patriots, then as now, the grand dream of the restoration of the rule of David with all its earthly pomp and glory. God had promised, and Jesus and John were not the only preachers asserting its nearness. It was a topic of wide interest, and the people were sure to go out of their way to listen to anyone who spoke of it with authority. The following quotations illustrate how Jesus responded to this interest in the Kingdom, and in particular to its coming.

> *Being asked by the Pharisees when the Kingdom of God was coming, he answered them, the Kingdom of God is not coming with signs to be observed* (Luke 17:20).

> *So when they [the disciples] had come together, they asked him, 'Lord, will you at this time restore the kingdom to Israel?'* (Acts 1:6).

> *Now there was a man named Joseph from the Jewish town of Arimathaea. He was a member of the council, a good and righteous man, who had not consented to their purpose and deed, and he was looking for the Kingdom of God* (Mark 15:43).

You see then how it was that the Pharisees, the disciples, and good men, such as Joseph, were asking questions about the Kingdom. They were intensely interested in its coming, and they were earnestly seeking it. The most common and fervent question was, "When?" It was into this arena of intense interest and expectation, discussion and speculation, that Jesus stepped with his bold and authoritative proclamations. It is not surprising that he quickly gained their attention; he would have done so even without the dramatic miracles, especially since he emphasized the nearness of the event.

Two things need to be clarified before we proceed. First, the New Testament expressions, "Kingdom of God" and "Kingdom of Heaven" are synonymous. Jesus probably used the terms interchangeably. It is not possible to tell which of the two occurred in any particular saying because the New Testament accounts are not uniform. Matthew typically quotes Jesus as saying "Kingdom of Heaven," whereas the other Gospel writers render "Kingdom of God" on the same occasions. Matthew preferred "Kingdom of Heaven" and used it almost exclusively. The others used "Kingdom of God" exclusively, and thus, "Kingdom of Heaven" not at all. So you see that for us there can be no significant distinction. Failure to realize this has led many to err in their quests of the Kingdom.

Second, when Jesus said that the Kingdom "is at hand," he used the New Testament Greek word that means "has drawn near" or "has come close." It implied that the Kingdom had drawn so close that its arrival was imminent. He applied the word similarly in other passages, reproduced here, that lead us to believe in the immediacy of it.

Behold, the hour is at hand and the Son of Man is delivered up into the hands of sinners (Matthew 26:45; Mark 14:41).

Behold, he is at hand that betrays me (Mark 14:42).

And having drawn near, he asked him, What do you desire that I shall do to you? (Luke 18:40-41).

In the first instance, Jesus had hardly finished speaking when soldiers appeared to take him into custody. In the second instance, Judas, the betrayer, was already close. In the third instance, the two are already about as near as they could be.

It was with this immediacy, then, that Jesus proclaimed the nearness of the Kingdom to his contemporaries.

I think of it as when I was a lonely farm lad. If we expected guests, I would be found on the front porch swing (or, in winter, with my face glued to a window). My eyes were eagerly scanning across the fields for a glimpse of their car turning off the gravel road onto the rutted dirt road a mile away. Is that it? No ... but there it is! I would jump excitedly from the swing and rush into the house, loudly announcing to all inside, "They're here! They're here!"

That was exactly the kind of nearness Jesus expressed when he announced the coming of the Kingdom. Perhaps also it was with a similar attitude: eagerly! happily! The glad time has come! Close enough to see, close enough to hear, close enough that there is no mistake. It is at the very door! It is not necessary that the actual arrival be within a day, a week, a month, or even a year, considering that they had been expecting it for centuries. But it is necessary to suppose that the coming was to be a part of the experience of those who heard him. Otherwise, the "at hand" could have no relevance to them. Suppose that we had been among those multitudes, hearing that proclamation of the Lord. We would have understood his message to have relevance to us, and would have expected to experience it in our lifetimes, and very soon. If Jesus had only meant that the coming would be a hundred years or more from the time of the proclamation, he would have deceived us. More than this, he would have known that his teaching was deceptive. In other words, he would have been lying. That, of course, is a possibility which any earnest truth seeker must consider. I have even entertained the thought that Jesus did not know what he was talking about, but long ago, as the evidence mounted, I laid aside all doubts. Jesus is the Truth — of that I am convinced. His word is perfectly reliable.

The coming of the Kingdom continued to be a frequent theme of the Lord. He returned to it often during the two to three years usually allotted to this phase of his life on earth. He seems to have wanted its coming intensely, as suggested by his teaching the disciples to pray for its consummation. "Thy Kingdom come ... " is the very first petition of his prayer instruction, which suggests that this was a thing uppermost in his mind. Had something else been more weighty, he probably would have asked for it first. The coming, the doing of the will of the Father, the provision of daily bread, the forgiveness of debts, and deliverance from evil, are of great significance. But the emphasis was on the coming.

Seeking other clues to the time of the coming, let us focus our attention on the following utterance:

> *Truly, I say to you, there are some standing here who will not taste death before they see the Kingdom of God come with power* (Matthew 16:28; Mark 9:1; Luke 9:27).

This passage confirms what I have already affirmed: that Jesus' prophecy had relevance for that generation. People who were hearing the teaching were to see its fulfillment. The writer of the Epistle to the Hebrews clarifies the significance of the expression "taste of death" when he wrote that Jesus should "taste death for every one" (Hebrews 2:9). So, the coming of the Kingdom "with power" occurred before some of those hearing him could qualify for their graves. But when? The saying suggests also that at least one person standing there must taste of death prior to the coming. The author of the Hebrews points to Jesus as that man.

Jesus understood the Kingdom perfectly, and knew all the prior conditions essential to its coming. The prime condition was that the will of God must be done on earth as it is done in heaven. Jesus further understood that he alone must be the one to do God's will on earth so as to initiate the Kingdom. He also knew what action and attitudes this entailed, but he was not certain that he was equal to the task. He had as much free will and personal liberty as any other man, and he was tempted in all points common to others (Hebrews 4:15). Therefore he did not know with certainty that it would come according to plan.

He also did not know the exact moment of the coming in that he could not pin a date to it. He based his teaching of its soon appearing, then, on the presumption of his faithfulness to the end. It was properly stated because, apart from his faithfulness in this matter, his earthly sojourn would be without purpose. When he instructed the disciples how to pray, and told them to say, "Thy Kingdom come, thy will be done on earth as it is in heaven," he was soliciting their prayers for himself to the end that he might be faithful in doing the Father's will on earth so that the Kingdom might come. He also understood that the Father's will would be done by himself through the performance of a specific action. It was action of which the prophets had spoken that would be manifest to the people and to the disciples. He also knew that the people who witnessed the action would be unaware that it coincided with the Kingdom's coming. Not even the disciples would know! It would not be such an event as they were expecting and would continue to expect for some time afterward. So, if they understood that the Kingdom was to come as they witnessed him performing this action, they would not believe and would be offended. Yet he wanted both them and us to understand. So he chose to introduce an enigmatic clue, one that they would little note until the teaching ministry of the Holy Spirit acted upon their minds. This clue he provided at the last supper when he said:

> I shall not again drink of the fruit of the vine until the Kingdom of God comes (Luke 22:18).

With these words in mind, we need only search the Scriptures to find when he next drank of the fruit of the vine. If we can establish this (and if Jesus spoke accurately), we will know the exact moment of the coming of the Kingdom of God. Then we can consider only three possible conclusions: Jesus never said this or he said it and was mistaken, or the Kingdom came exactly as he said.

The search need not be a long one. Follow the story in the Gospels and you will shortly read the account of his crucifixion. While hanging from the cross, he cried out as follows:

> *After this, Jesus, knowing that all was now finished, in order that he might fulfill the scripture, said, "I Thirst." A bowl full of vinegar stood there, so they put a sponge full of vinegar on hyssop and held it to his mouth. When therefore he had received the vinegar, Jesus said, "It is finished!" And he bowed his head and gave up his spirit* (John 19:28-30).

What was this vinegar? It was wine — a sour wine, but nonetheless a fruit of the vine. Jesus' executioners had earlier offered him a drink of wine but he had refused it. Now you know the answer to a great mystery: Why Jesus, who fasted forty days in the wilderness, seemed to yield to the lust of the flesh with his last few breaths, though he knew that "all was now finished." He had been on the cross many hours, with his mouth parched with thirst and his body in agony, but had refused drink until he knew it was all over (Matthew 27:34). He also knew that it was too late for the drink to give any relief. At that point he reversed his earlier refusal and asked for the drink — and "received it" as the fruit of the vine. Now you know why he earlier refused the drink — it was not the moment of the coming of the Kingdom. You also know why he drank at the last moment: the Kingdom was come!

Throughout the agonizing crucifixion, he was subject to a continuing uncertainty about whether he would be faithful to the end. If he were not ... if he should yield to temptation and come down from the cross (as was in his power), he would not have done the Father's will on earth, and the Kingdom would not come. So he waited to signal the coming, by drinking the fruit of the vine, until he knew that "all was now finished." He had been faithful! He had done the Father's will! The Kingdom was come! His last words and action informed us of this wonderful event.

Now, when he announced the clue in the Upper Room, he was probably not drinking vinegar but rather the more desirable form of the fruit of the vine (Mark 14:25; Luke 22:18). Therefore he did not say "From now on I shall not drink vinegar ... " because that was not what he was then drinking. No, but to establish a connection he used a term applicable to both the wine and the vinegar, that is, "fruit of the vine." Jesus wants us to know the exact moment of the coming. Otherwise he might better have drunk of the fruit of the vine when they first offered it. But he did not. When he had tasted of it, the scripture clearly states that in the first instance he "would not drink" (Matthew 27:34). Perhaps he thought it might have been water. So he tasted it. Determining that it was a fruit of the vine, he immediately refused it to preserve the validity of his clue.

Is it really so simple? How is it that the learned theologians, both Protestant and Catholic, have not realized this truth? Their ponderous tomes contain many convincing arguments pointing to this or that time; how is it that they have overlooked this?

I suggest first that the reliability of their conclusions is questionable because they often disagree with one another. Their methods of derivation of biblical truth are similar, if not identical. Therefore their diverse conclusions cast a heavy shadow of doubt over the methods. My method, in contrast, is of the utmost simplicity and consists in listening to Jesus — to his very utterances as recorded in the four Gospels — *and in believing him.* The theologians, on the other hand, have fallen into confusion through considering the sayings of Jesus as only one source of truth among many. They examine his words alongside the law, the prophets, and the apostles. On this basis they tend to find in the Bible almost anything they seek. I do not mean to imply that the other sources are without value. I mean only that apart from a prior and separate consideration of the utterances of Jesus, the others cannot be understood. Jesus alone is the Truth (John 14:6).

So, their method is one reason for their failure, but this is not the main reason. The main reason is this: they are prone to have a conception of the Kingdom that does not admit of the truth that it has already come. Conditions on earth do not accord with their views of what must follow the coming of the Kingdom. Also, their views of the event of the coming tend to be characterized by apocalyptic co-events that they do not see at the death of Jesus. These views, firmly implanted in their minds, block the conception of the Truth. It is unthinkable. Examples of such views include (1) the initiation of the reign of perfect justice among men; (2) the dissolution of national distinctions; (3) the advent of secure, worldwide peace; the end of war; (4) the return of the Lord, visibly, to reign over the Earth from Jerusalem, and (5) The elimination of poverty and hunger. These things have not become reality, of course. Therefore the thought that the Kingdom is already fully come is to such men the utmost idiocy! They cannot think it, they cannot hear it, and therefore it is impossible for them to hear the truth as announced by the Lord. They have failed, utterly failed, to avail themselves of the Lord's promise:

> *If you abide in my word, you will know the Truth and the Truth will make you free* (John 8:31-32).

This tells us much about such men. If they were genuinely dedicated to Truth, they would first examine the utterances of Jesus, who is the Truth, and then formulate their views of the Kingdom. Instead, they proceed in the reverse order: they form their views of the Truth, then bend the words of Jesus accordingly. Or perhaps, as here, they ignore them entirely.

I should hasten to say that it is not really so simple as I have suggested, due to the variants in the texts of the three Synoptic Gospels. Each renders the key Upper Room saying, upon which our knowledge of the definite time of the coming depends, somewhat differently. They read as follows:

From Matthew:

> *I tell you I shall not drink again of this fruit of the vine until that day when I drink it new with you in my Father's Kingdom* (26:29).

From Mark:

> *Truly, I say to you, I shall not drink again of the fruit of the vine until that day when I drink it new in the Kingdom of God* (14:25).

And from Luke:

> *I tell you that from now on I shall not drink of the fruit of the vine until the Kingdom of God comes* (22:18).

The versions are all similar, but have differences as follows:

(1) Only Luke speaks of the Kingdom's coming; the others refer to activity in the Kingdom.

(2) Both Matthew and Mark include an idea not found in Luke: the word, "new." To what does it refer? To the fruit of the vine, to the act of drinking, or to something else?

(3) Matthew is unique in including the words "with you."

(4) Matthew speaks more specifically of "this" fruit of the vine. The others record "the" fruit of the vine.

(5) Both Matthew and Mark include the expression "that day," not found in Luke.

How are we to explain this diversity? Not by saying the different writers recorded three different sayings, for each is most explicit in asserting that these are the words uttered by Jesus when, in the Upper Room, he took up the cup. So, we have several options, some of which I list here:

(1) All the witnesses erred in recording his words.

(2) One was correct, the others erred.

(3) All are partly right, partly wrong.

(4) Each accurately recorded different portions of the statement.

(5) Errors of transmission have altered the sayings from an original uniformity.

(6) Some combination of the previous five.

I have come to favor (4) as the most likely explanation, with perhaps a little of (5). After all, none of the Gospel writers claimed to have recorded all Jesus' words, and here it is particularly evident that there are omissions. Luke, for example, completely omits any mention of the introductory words of both Matthew and Mark, "This is my blood of the covenant which is poured out for many," and Matthew follows with the phrase "for the forgiveness of sins," that Mark fails to mention. Let us therefore see if the accounts can be combined to provide a complete statement that is reasonable and in harmony with the facts. Could the full statement have been something like this?

"Take this and divide it among yourselves; for I tell you that from now on I shall not drink of the fruit of the vine until the Kingdom of God comes.

I shall not drink again of this fruit of the vine until that day when I drink it new with you in my Father's Kingdom."

The complete statement is thus the sum of the witnesses, in which Mark represents a fusion of the other two, and which preserved the key the/this contrast. Both beverages were "the fruit of the vine," which accounts for their relevance to Jesus as he presents the clue.

Jesus knew the Psalmist had prophesied that they would offer him "vinegar" to drink at his crucifixion. Therefore he needed to make the clue perfectly unambiguous. There must be no confusion to cause us to think that the coming was associated with the drinking of "this" new wine. He also may have known that he would drink again of the new wine after the coming, in the Kingdom, and with the disciples. If he thus foresaw two separate events, he introduced the second one into the statement only to resolve any ambiguity in the clue. Then the second event, the drinking of "new wine" with the disciples "in" the Kingdom, would follow as a confirmation that the Kingdom had already come.

This raises yet another question: Has Jesus yet partaken of the new wine with the disciples "in" the Kingdom? There is a very good reason to think that he has, based on this statement of Peter from the Acts: "but God ... made him manifest ... to us ... who ate and drank with Him after He rose from the dead" (Acts 10:40, 41).

Our knowledge of the times and dining practices of Jesus and the disciples inclines me to think that what they drank was the "new" wine, not the "vinegar." The implication of this is that, after his resurrection, they were with him in the Kingdom as they had not been before. This can be explained only by accepting that the Kingdom had come in the interval between the Last Supper and their supping with him after his resurrection. That would be consistent with its coming at the moment of his death. I therefore conclude that Mark's rendition is a mix of the two separate portions of the statement. It blends them into one and is thus not as accurate as the others. The objection, that this is unlikely because Mark wrote his account first, is not valid. It is more likely that later accounts would be more accurate because their authors may have sought to make up what was lacking in Mark's version. Are not the modern versions of the Scriptures considered more accurate than earlier ones because the later translators have corrected the texts to conform to more accurate manuscripts? It is certain that the Gospels do contain such inaccuracies as those suggested here. For example, when they asked Jesus, "Which is the great commandment of the Law?" Matthew omitted the words, "All your strength," which Mark included.

Or, more to the point of the present subject, consider the contrasts in the following parallel sayings about the coming and the Kingdom. From Matthew:

> *For the Son of man is to come with his angels in the glory of his Father, and then he will repay every man for what he has done. Truly, I say to you, there are some standing here who will not taste death before they see the Son of Man coming in his Kingdom* (Matthew 16:27, 28).

And from Mark:

> *For whoever is ashamed of me and of my words in this adulterous and sinful generation, of him will the Son of Man also be ashamed, when he comes in the glory of his Father with the holy angels. And he said to them, "Truly, I say to you, there are some standing here who will not taste death before they see the kingdom of God come with power"* (8:38; 9:1).

Here we encounter options similar to those we applied to the Upper Room sayings. From the uniformity of contexts there can be no doubt they are reporting the same utterance. The question arises: did he say they would see the Son of Man coming in his kingdom, or did he say they would see the Kingdom of God come with power, or perhaps both? These accounts cannot be both accurate and complete.

Luke's account of the Upper Room saying, while incomplete, is accurate in that there is no misstatement. This clearly explains why he refused to drink when the drink was first offered, then asked for drink when he was at the point of death. It answers many questions provided only that we can believe that the Kingdom came "with power" when Jesus received the fruit of the vine and "yielded up his spirit" (Matthew 27:50; Mark 15: 37; Luke 23: 46; John 19:30).

There are objections to this conclusion. Some will ask, "Why so enigmatic? Why not simply tell them, and us, that the Kingdom was to come at the moment of his death?" And why were they still asking him, following the resurrection, "Lord, will you at this time restore the Kingdom to Israel?" (Acts 1:6). If the Kingdom was fully come, why put them off with an evasive answer beginning with the words, "It is not for you to know the times or the seasons?" (Acts 1:7-8).

We can best answer these questions together. It will be seen that the facts on which they are based reinforce the belief that the Kingdom had already fully come, before the ascension, and that they were even then "in" the Kingdom. There were at least two reasons why Jesus both evaded their question about the times, and gave them a clue to the time in an enigmatic fashion. First, as I have already said, Jesus was not certain that he was equal to the task set before him. Therefore he did not know with certainty that the Kingdom would come at the point of his death on the cross. Had he evaded the cross, or had he come down from the cross, or otherwise acted to save his life, then he might have survived to die a death unrelated to the coming of the Kingdom. To have told them, then, that the coming of the Kingdom would be coincident with his death might have turned out to be inaccurate. He would have deceived them.

Second, he knew the disciples, and he understood that they had typical Jewish kingdom preconceptions. Society had already falsely answered their questions before they thought to ask them, as in our case, and so the questions, the key questions, were never asked. Not until after they had witnessed the crucifixion, the resurrection, and the ascension, and had received the Holy Spirit would they be inclined to accept any modification of that view. Therefore they remained unqualified to receive the Truth when Jesus ascended into heaven. Why tell them what they were not prepared to hear?

Consider what their response might have been — those yet geocentric men! Would they not all have responded as Thomas did when he was told of the resurrection: "I will not believe?" (John 20:25).

Later, after receiving the Holy Spirit, he would take these words of Jesus ("what is mine") and "declare" it to them (John 16:15). Thus the Truth would (and did) arise from within their hearts and they would not be offended but would receive it with joy.

Surely some of them would have related the Upper Room saying to the drinking of the fruit of the vine, the vinegar, and realized its import? No, the mystery was secure. Their minds were too firmly set on the hoped-for visible glorification of the realm of the world to entertain such notions. Similarly, most theologians of the Twentieth Century read the utterance just as I have done, yet without ever considering its obvious significance.

Jesus' other utterances regarding the Coming of the Kingdom also conform to this insight, but let us first examine the "taste of death" sayings in Matthew and Mark. Both passages refer to two separate comings that, as I shall show presently, are entirely different and widely separated in time. One of them, described as "the coming of the Son of Man in the glory of the Father and with the holy angels" (Matthew 16:27-28; Mark 8:38—9:1; Luke 9:26-27), is associated with divine retribution on sinners. Then it is that he will "repay every man for what he has done" (Matthew 16:27). Everyone will see and recognize this "Coming" since it is not possible for "every man" to be judged and "repaid" without being aware of the highlights of the event. Since therefore we have not yet seen this coming, it has not occurred.

He clearly speaks, in the same breath, of a coming that some of those standing there and hearing him would see before they would taste of death. This latter "coming" is that of the Kingdom, which all except Jesus saw before tasting of death. Of course they did not recognize it as such, or even observe the actual coming. Had they done so, Jesus would have been in error when he earlier said,

> *The Kingdom of God is not coming with signs to be observed*
> ... (Luke 17:20).

Matthew says that Jesus used the words, "the Son of Man coming in his Kingdom," whereas Mark relates that he used a different expression, "the Kingdom of God come with power." The two versions of the same utterance, being different, cannot be both accurate and complete. I consider that either Matthew was inaccurate, or else early scribes introduced an aberrant version, for he speaks of a "coming of the Son of Man," albeit "in his Kingdom," as distinguished from coming "in the glory of his Father." However, the "coming of the Son of Man" phrase carries a special significance for Jesus. He separated it from the "coming of the Kingdom." Therefore it is unlikely that he would describe the coming of the kingdom as in any sense a coming of the Son of Man.

There is no difficulty in Mark's rendition of this utterance, which speaks explicitly of the coming of the Kingdom "with power." This is exactly what transpired with the death of Jesus. It is possible to see in Matthew's rendition yet a third "coming," when they were to see Jesus coming into their midst "in the Kingdom," since the Kingdom had already come at the time of his death. In this view, Jesus' words in Matthew are tantamount to a prediction of his visible resurrection. It suggests that everything that happens on earth after his death is "in" the Kingdom. A more complete account of the utterance may then be as follows:

> *Truly I say to you, there are some standing here who will not taste death before they see the Kingdom of God come with power, and before they see the Son of Man coming in his Kingdom.*

Why did he condition their observations by the thought of tasting of death? The answer is simple. He knew that he, alone, must taste of death before the Kingdom's coming, since that was the sole condition of its coming. Therefore the tasting of death was, in his mind, constantly associated with the coming of the Kingdom. They were inseparable events. But this association applied only to him, since he alone had to die to effect the coming of the Kingdom. There were some standing there (everyone excepting only himself) who would not taste of death until they had either seen the Kingdom come in power or the Son of man coming in his kingdom, or perhaps both, since either is true.

His other statements about the coming of the Kingdom are consistent with this view. First, there is the opening petition of the Lord's Prayer, which begins, "Thy kingdom come ... " and continues, "Thy will be done on earth as it is in heaven" (Matthew 6:10; Luke 11:2). We now see, as I have already suggested, that this instructive prayer is a request for their prayers on his behalf, that he might be faithful to do the Father's will on earth as it is done in heaven. He knew full well how he must do the Father's will, but he did not know that he *could* do it. Temptation was intense. What was the nature of this temptation? It was to save his life — and so to lose it! Of course, we now know that the prayer was answered affirmatively. He was equal to the task; he did do the Father's will on earth as it is done in heaven. The Kingdom did come, exactly as he said. He refused to save his life, and therefore he kept it for himself and everyone else, as life eternal.

What of those sayings in which he spoke of the Kingdom as though it had already come in the days of his flesh? Two utterances are of special interest here:

> *But if it is by the Spirit of God that I cast out demons, then the Kingdom of God has come upon you* (Matthew 12:28; Luke 11:20).

The second, also addressed to the Pharisees, is from Luke:

> *Being asked by the Pharisees when the Kingdom of God was coming, he answered them, The kingdom of God is not coming with signs to be observed; nor will they say, Lo, here it is, or there, for behold, the Kingdom of God is in the midst of you* (Luke 17:20-21).

We rightly draw the conclusion from these utterances that in some sense the Kingdom was already present on earth before the death of Jesus. I take it to mean that in the presence of the Lord, or wherever demons were being exorcised by the power of the Spirit of God, the authority of the Kingdom was dominant. This, however, was not the "coming" to which Jesus looked. He constituted a beachhead of the Kingdom, which had invaded the world in his person and was in mortal combat with the forces of evil. Yet it had not won the decisive victory, the issue was yet in doubt, the beachhead was not secure. The authority of the Kingdom was not universal and it was not effective, outside the presence of the Lord, to do the will of God on the earth. God's sovereignty was active in the presence of Jesus, but not in the world at large. The latter was yet subject to a different monarch.

The Coming of the Kingdom was to be a total overthrow of the power of Satan over the world (Hebrews 2:14, 15). It would be the final establishment of a new rule of God following the crucial victory of Jesus. He would win a fierce battle of the spirit by the giving of his life.

Clearly, the Kingdom did not come with signs to be observed. It definitely did not come so that men could recognize it and point it out to others saying, "Lo, here it is!" or "Lo, there!" This should not surprise us, nor should we have expected such signs to accompany its arrival. Jesus has already informed us that it "comes not with observation" (Luke 17:20). His statement is final and authoritative. There was, of course, a sign — the drinking of the fruit of the vine. But no one recognized it to cry out, "Lo, here!" because the sign was not such as they sought. Only in retrospect, under the tutelage of the Holy Spirit, can anyone recognize the coming. They are those to whom "it is given" to know the secrets of the Kingdom of God (Matthew 13:11; Mark 4:11; Luke 8:10). Others cannot receive it, not even when it is stated clearly and simply. They may hear it, as sounds in the air; or they may see it, as ink on the page, but they cannot receive it because to them it has not been given.

The *King James Version* of Luke's rendition of these verses easily leads one to think that the coming of the Kingdom is "into" persons (Luke 17:20), and it is often so misunderstood. Surely it was not inside those blind Pharisees to whom Jesus addressed the statement? No, it was not. Understood correctly, Jesus was saying to them, "When it comes, you blind Pharisees will never see it. Why, it is right here in your midst already!" No. Jesus nowhere speaks of the Kingdom being inside anyone, for that would not be consistent with its real character.

I have already stated that the "coming of the Kingdom" is different from the "coming of the Son of Man," to which Jesus also refers repeatedly. It is necessary to emphasize this distinction because so many have erred in associating the two in time, as they continue to do. A common belief is that the Son of Man will some day come to judge the world. After that, his Kingdom will come as he "sets up his Kingdom on earth and begins his millennial reign." It is ironic that the error of equating the two comings results from Jesus' speaking of them together in the same sayings. The error could be easily avoided by careful consideration of what he said about each. The Lucan passage listed above is a case in point.

Concerning the coming of the Kingdom, they will not say, "Lo, here!" or "Lo, there!" (Luke 17:20-21) because it will not come with observable signs to incite such an outcry. On the other hand, neither will they say to us, "Lo, here!" or "Lo, there!" (Luke 17:22-24) at the coming of the Son of Man — but for a different reason. Absolutely everyone will see it for himself or herself and there will be no one in ignorance to whom to herald the event. Every eye will see him! (Luke 17:24; Revelation 1:7). So, in one case, there will be no heralds because no one will see it. In the other, everyone will see it so that there will be no need of heralds. If there are heralds of the coming of the Son of Man, Jesus tells us not to believe them because all will see him when he comes. So, in contrast to the coming of the Kingdom, which is not with observation, the coming of the Son of Man is with universal observation. No one can fail to see it. Thus, when it occurs, it will after all be like the coming of the Kingdom in that there will be no heralds shouting, "Lo, here!" and "Lo, there!" but for radically different reasons. Therefore Jesus mentions the two events together, not only here but in Mark 8:38-9:1 and parallel passages. It serves his purpose of helping us to understand both events by specifying similarities and distinctions made evident by the association with heralds.

The "Synoptic Apocalypse" (Matthew 24:4-44; Mark 13:5-37; Luke 17:22-38) confirms what I am saying here about the coming of the Son of man. There, Jesus describes this dramatic event in vivid detail. He compares it with lightning in that "the lightning comes from the East and shines as far as the West." This is truly an event of universal observation!

I do not mean that no one saw the coming of the Kingdom. I mean that those who saw did not recognize it because it did not match their preconceptions. Jesus had stated that some would "see the Kingdom come with power" (Mark 9:1). John's Gospel clarifies the puzzle when it quotes Jesus as saying, "Except you be begotten again, you cannot see the kingdom of God" (John 3:3). The apostles had not been begotten again at the time of the crucifixion and the coming of the kingdom; therefore, none of then recognized it in its coming. They saw the events, to be sure, but they did not perceive their significance. They could not, because the Spirit had not yet come to them. On the contrary, the victorious event that was the fulfillment of their earnest desires for the Kingdom seemed instead to be defeat. It inspired in them only disappointment and despair of the worst kind. They mumbled out of the depths of their despair to that stranger on the road to Emmaus, "We had thought that this was he who is to redeem Israel!"(Luke 24:21).

Jesus stated that the Kingdom would come when he next drank of the fruit of the vine (Luke 22:18). He expected this would be at the moment of his death by crucifixion, and so it came to pass when he cried out, "I thirst!" and then received the vinegar (John 19:28-30). It was his last act. The Kingdom did come. It came consummately, exactly as he predicted.

It is tragic when anyone cannot believe it. Sadly, almost no one can. Nearly always it is because their preconceptions, hopes, and expectations of the Kingdom are inspired by the love of life. Therefore their expectations cannot possibly match the realities of the Kingdom. If only they would dwell on the utterances of our King, they would quickly learn better. He repeatedly warned of the consequences of the love of life in the world, and made our salvation directly and solely dependent on learning to hate life.

The apostles must soon have come to realize this Truth, for there is no hint of a yet future coming of the Kingdom in their New Testament epistles. Instead, their comments on this subject are thoroughly consistent with the prior coming of the kingdom. Consider, for example, Paul's bold proclamation to the Colossians: "He has delivered us from the dominion of darkness and transferred us to the kingdom of his beloved Son, in whom we have redemption, the forgiveness of sins" (Colossians 1:13, 14). Or consider that there is no New Testament record of anyone repeating, or instructing anyone else to repeat, the "Lord's Prayer" with its opening petition, "Thy Kingdom come ... " (Matthew 6:10; Luke 11:2). Is this not a very strange omission, considering that his apostles were men who had been, before his death, eagerly seeking the Kingdom? No, not if they had already realized the Kingdom's coming as a finished event in history. They did not continue to utter this prayer after the death of Jesus because the prayer had been answered!

THE PROPHECIES

Jesus knew the Old Testament prophets well. He professed a positive relationship to them, saying:

I came not to abolish but to fulfill (Matthew 5:17).

and,

> *Not one jot or one tittle shall pass from the law until all is*
> *fulfilled* (Matthew 5:18).

Now, suppose you and I had been standing before him and hearing his words. We would have understood him to mean that it was his intention to fulfill the prophets in consequence of his coming, and that he would do so very shortly. Jesus was not unaware of how his hearers understood his words — it was to impart that exact idea that he had uttered them.

We who come hundreds of years later often fail to consider what his words conveyed to those to whom he was immediately speaking. This is often the first question we should ask: What did his immediate audience understand him to be saying? This is surely a major key to interpretation, and we are likely to err if we fail to consider it. The words may at first impart a very different idea to us who have come two thousand years later. Here, those among us who do not see the prophets fulfilled are apt to suppose that he came to set in motion a long chain of events that would eventually, many thousands of years later, produce the fulfillment of the law and the prophets. This is a mistake because that is not what he said.

Neither was it what his immediate hearers understood him to say. Thus, we are apt to conclude that he was mistaken and that the prophets remain unfulfilled. Otherwise, the only logical responses are to conclude that he lied to them or that he was mistaken. Either option does nothing for his reputation. However, if he spoke the truth, the perfect Truth that he intended to be understood by those who heard him immediately, we must acknowledge that the prophets have been long fulfilled. Those who say he spoke specifically for us who have the benefit of the centuries to aid our interpretation, and not for those who heard him immediately, do him a disservice. They put him in a position where it was not possible for him to speak the Truth directly to those who heard him and also to us who only hear him through the recollection of those immediate ones. Thus they render his words subject to the vicissitudes of time — meaningless because they can mean anything from the differing points of view of the centuries.

But no! Jesus' Truth is absolute and therefore unaffected by history or time. Anyone who understands him aright must hear him in the relationship of contemporaneousness.* Are we so foolish as to think Jesus did not know how easy it would be for us to understand him immediately simply by considering how those to whom he spoke in immediacy must have understood him? Hearing him thus, as contemporary with him, all can understand, the centuries notwithstanding. Jesus was not foolishly caught in the contradictory position of having to lie to them to get the Truth to us!

So, from this we see that, according to his words, his reason and purpose in coming was to fulfill the Law and Prophets, while here. If he did not fulfill them in that long-ago time, we must consider that he was subject to err just as we are. But then he is not the personification of Truth as he claimed when he said, "I am the Truth … " and we should consider him an impostor.

Additional support for this view comes from another utterance in which he said:

> *The law and the prophets were until John; since then the good news of the Kingdom of God is preached, and everyone enters it violently* (Luke 16:16).

Here Jesus considered that the Law and the Prophets had already, beginning with John, encountered their terminus. He was then living in the age of their consummate fulfillment, and was himself the personification of that fulfillment. These words make it rationally impossible to understand Jesus' view of the prophets as one that projected their tenure through the centuries to come. This terminus, or fulfillment, is implied in the Sermon on the Mount each time he entered the phrase, "You have heard that it was said … but I say to you…" (Matthew 5:22, 28, 32, 34, 39, 44). His word stands in relation to the Law and the Prophets in these cases as a supplanting contrast — a word vastly different from the one it supplants. It is so different that it represents an absolute discontinuity having no relationship to its predecessor save this, that it is its fulfillment! The discontinuity is not to be represented by a gap, as though there were a great leap

----

*see Kierkegaard, "Training in Christianity," *A Kierkegaard Anthology*, 375, 408 (New York: Random House, 1946).

between them. No, but they were separated by a distinct boundary, or interface, which is ... the Kingdom of God.

Therefore he said, in the words already quoted,

The Law and the Prophets were until John (Matthew 11:13; Luke 16:16).

What since then?

The good news of the Kingdom of God is proclaimed! (Luke 16:16).

Thus it is the coming of the Kingdom that constitutes the terminus of the Law and the Prophets. They were prophets of the Kingdom who could only look forward to it. They did not know how to look backward to it. Therefore, they are no more.

Again, what did Jesus say? He said that they were until John. So, therefore, they are no more. Ah! The good news of the Kingdom! Not "new prophecies of the Kingdom." Not "new light on the old prophecies of the Kingdom." Not "good news about the under-standing of the prophecies of the Kingdom." No! None of those. What, then, is it? Wonderful good news!

Now good news pertains to something "good" that has already happened or that is to happen immediately. Otherwise, it is only a "good prophecy" of something yet to happen. If it is "good news of the Kingdom," it can only mean that the coming of the Kingdom has either already happened, or that it is about to happen very quickly. It must happen so quickly that the news of its nearness is joyful "good news" to the hearers — that is, to those who hear it immediately. By no stretch of logic or imagination can a Kingdom which still has not come on earth, in this year of our Lord, have been "good news" to Peter, James, and John. Yet this is exactly the word imparted to them by both Jesus and John the Baptizer.

The good news of the Kingdom, preached to and by the first disciples, was no lie. Therefore that good news, which was that the Kingdom of God was at hand, is good news no longer. It is not "news" of any kind, any more so than last year's, or last century's, newspaper. Therefore, any "good news of the Kingdom" that we now proclaim must be different. It must be this to those who hear it for the first time in any century: The Kingdom of God has come!

This is never good news to most theologians, who cannot admit the thought that the Kingdom has already come on the earth. Their views of the consummate kingdom are in sharp contrast to today's realities and to the realities of the history of the last two millennia. They cannot "see" the Kingdom, and in their blindness they plunge on into the abyss of theological speculations. These speculations generally picture Jesus as mistaken in his expectations of the coming of the Kingdom. They present his words as words that cannot have relevance to the real world of our times. Perhaps Jesus himself, in anticipation of these late naysayers, diagnosed their condition when he stated:

> *Except you be born again, you cannot see the Kingdom of God* (John 3:3).

THE SIGNIFICANCE

The spokesmen of Christendom have generally insisted that the Kingdom of God and of Christ must conform to the pattern of the kingdoms of this world, though Jesus has expressly stated otherwise. As usual, they ignore Jesus to cling to their dreams for the future of the world. Listen to what Jesus had to say:

> *My kingship is not of this world; if my kingship were of this world, my servants would fight that I might not be handed over to the Jews; but my kingship is not from this world* (John 18:36).

In saying, "My kingship is not from this world," and in illustrating how this results in a radical effect on the conduct of himself and of his disciples, he shows that the characteristics of his Kingdom are "wholly other" from those of the worldly kingdoms and authorities. Some characteristics of the kingdoms of this world are: They are inspired by the human lust for power. They are established by military action, and thus secured. They are governed by a king and his agents who rule from a palace in the capital city. Their endurance is dependent on the loyalty of many subjects, and so on. Now, the Kingdom of God is not like this. If it were, then the hope of Christendom would be realized by a visible return of Christ at the head of heavenly armies, to vanquish the kings of earth at Mount Megiddo. We would see him victoriously leading his forces across the Kidron Valley, past the tombs of the prophets, and up the steep slope of Moriah. Then he would pause while construction workers labor to pave a way across ancient Arab cemeteries and to reopen the Golden Gate for his entrance into the Holy City. Finally the last obstructing stone would be removed, and such a shout would go up as could be heard on the Mount of Olives, all the way across the Kidron Valley. The procession would then move through the gate to occupy the holy Mount Moriah with its Mosques of Omar and El Aksa. There, in Jerusalem, the King would establish the seat of world power, sending out his agents and armies to secure a thousand years of peace on this earth! The Kingdom of God would be come!

But no! His Kingdom is not like this. If it were, the disciples (his servants), would have fought so that he might not be delivered to the Jews. Something else has happened instead. Where men looked for a mighty ruler marching in triumphal procession, a young man, executed and disgraced, is taken down "dead" from a cross. Where men looked for a benevolent monarch to reign in peace from Jerusalem, we see instead a Jerusalem divided and forsaken, cast from one ruler to another as a pawn of political and religious power, the object and prize of war. Where men looked for a worldwide reign of one government unifying the nations in justice, peace, and prosperity, we see instead the persistent blooming of divisive racism, nationalism, cultism, and ideology, until today the whole world labors fearfully under the threats of nuclear, chemical, and military genocide.

I see all these things, and yet I know and am persuaded that God's Kingdom has come on the earth. The weight of the biblical revelation is too powerful and convincing to deny. We must, in faith, believe it, contrary to the testimony of the natural senses. Also we must conclude that the Kingdom of God has a reality and significance radically at variance with the traditions of Christendom. The purpose of the following pages is therefore to investigate the real character and significance of the Kingdom.

A kingdom that was consummated at Calvary cannot mean the realization of a just society on earth — either by a slow process of spiritually inspired social revolution, or by the sudden, apocalyptic overthrow of the forces of evil by God's universal rule of righteousness. The Kingdom has fully come, and yet poverty and suffering abound worldwide. We read of famines, earthquakes, floods, tornadoes, and pestilences (Matthew 24:7; Luke 21:10). Crime and immorality thrive. Warfare grows ever more fierce and destructive. The unification of the race remains an elusive dream in this epoch when new, bellicose ideologies and nations are rising around the globe. Even old ones, long thought dormant, are rising anew to press their militant claims. Of what use is a Kingdom that seems to have no corrective influence in the world? Why bother with seeking it? Most people turn away from the Truth at this point, as almost everyone raises these questions. They are few who go beyond them to the eventual realization that such evidence as I have just cited is confirmation of the operation of the Kingdom in the world today.

Here, briefly, is an example of what I mean. Both Daniel and David prophesied that the Messiah would shatter the nations, dashing them in pieces like a potter's vessel (Psalm 2:9; Daniel 2:40-41). Now, isn't that exactly what is happening, such that today we look out upon a potsherd world? It is the rule of God in his Kingdom that first destroyed the Pax Romana and that now continues to frustrate all human aspirations toward "one world." Most recently, the fragmentation of the Soviet Union manifests the operation of the rule of God in his kingdom.

The human, churchly expectation is in diametric opposition to the reality of God's rule. Failing to understand the will and purpose of God, men have embraced a geocentric "attitude to life," and the result is utter blindness to the Truth. Tragically, pathetically, Christendom continues to insist that God's Kingdom must order the world according to a human point of view. Men forget that in its very essence, the coming of God's Kingdom must mean that God's will is done, as distinct from man's. It is as though they expect God to rule the world according to their dictates! Why, then God would only be man's vassal King!

The coming of God's Kingdom means that God in Christ has defeated all contenders for ultimate power and has taken up his great power and begun to reign. This is precisely what Jesus arose from the tomb to announce to us and to the world:

All authority, in heaven and on earth, has been given to me
(Matthew 28:18).

This is also the cosmic event that the angels of Revelation heralded
when they sang out:

We give you thanks, Lord God Almighty, that you have
taken your great power and begun to reign! (Revelation
11:17).

The apostles likewise focused on the cross as the crucial victory
that brought the kingdom and crowned a king. Paul, writing to the
Colossians, said:

"And you, who were dead in trespasses and the uncircumcision of
your flesh, God made alive together with him, having forgiven us all
our trespasses, having canceled the bond which stood against us with
its legal demands; this he set aside, nailing it to the cross. He disarmed
the principalities and powers and made public example of them,
triumphing over them in him" (Colossians 2:13-15).

In consequence of this, he also said:

"For in him the whole fullness of deity dwells bodily, and you have
come to fullness of life in him, who is the head of all rule and
authority" (Colossians 2:9-10).

If at the cross he triumphed over the principalities and powers, if
he was invested with all authority both in heaven and on earth, and
if he is in consequence the head of all rule and authority, in heaven
and on earth ... what else can be required for God's Kingdom to come
on earth as it is in heaven?

The Kingdom of God came on earth, as it is in heaven, at the hour
of Jesus' death on the cross. In view of the direct and consistent
biblical testimony to this fact, not only from Jesus but also from the
apostles, what can be the end of those who search the Scriptures and
yet do not believe?

Jesus became King of Kings and Lord of Lords. He is, as Paul
declared to the Colossians, the head over all things, and all things
have been put under his feet. Therefore, Christ has ruled the world
since that day, and he will continue to rule it until the end. If, as the
writer of the Epistle to the Hebrews stated, "We do not yet see
everything in subjection to him" (Hebrews 2:8), that is our blindness,

not his limitation, but it is true nevertheless. The reluctance of men everywhere to accept the Truth grows out of this simple fact: Jesus as King of Kings is not administering his kingdom on the earth in a way that pleases the will of men. In their affection for life on earth and for the world that nourishes that life, men are prone to insist that the world itself must become a paradise. Therein lies their great error. Contrary to human speculation, the world is exactly as God wills it to be. It is wholly consistent with the active exercise of the power of Him who has taken up his great power and begun to reign.

Jesus stated that the heavens and the earth will pass away (Matthew 24:35; Mark 13:31; Luke 21:33). That is his statement of what Paul called its bondage to futility. Being very specific, Paul said: "the whole creation was subjected to futility, not of its own will, but of the will of the creator" (Romans 8:20). The King is actively ruling to maintain this bondage to futility that is expressly attributed to the Father's will. Therefore, there can be no enduring peace on earth. There can be no end of poverty. There can be no end of pestilence, corrosion, and thievery. There can be no end of that which men call death.

What, then, is different in consequence of the coming of the Kingdom? Just this: The Usurper had appropriated the rule of the world of men, and the Christ has wrested the authority away from him. He has triumphed over him by refusing to love his life or to fear death. As a direct result of this cosmic victory of the Christ at Calvary, he compelled the earth to resume its only legitimate function. It has begun to yield, to the Glory of the Father, those who respond to his call to become his sons and daughters.

Everything must be understood through the comprehension of the freedom of the will of every man. The Christ maintains the world in its bondage to futility lest men find their glory here. This drives us to despair for the world and to seek our consummation in the Heavenly Glory. When that becomes our will, our only will, then we are qualified to enter it — for that is the sole purpose of our being here. That is the only purpose of our existence.

That the words of Jesus have been preserved is dynamic evidence of the rule of the Kingdom of God in the world. This is exactly as he prophesied, saying:

Heaven and earth will pass away, but my word will not pass away (Matthew 24:35; Mark 13:31; Luke 21:33)

Men strive for one world brotherhood, but Christ in his Kingdom effectively frustrates all their efforts to produce it. He will never permit it to be realized. The breakup of old empires and the persistent fragmentation of the nations of the earth is evidence of the rule of God in his Kingdom. Thus has he fulfilled the prophecy of the Psalmist: "You will dash them in pieces like a potter's vessel" (Psalm 2:9).

Because of all this, somewhere, every day, someone is deciding, of his or her free will, to hate life in this world so as to inherit eternal life in the Glory of God. Remember that the whole creation has absolutely no purpose outside that of fulfilling its intended function of producing children for the Glory of the Father. When anyone, anywhere, hears that word of the King:

Whoever loves his life loses it, but he who hates his life in this world will keep it for life eternal (John 12:25).

And also that word that says:

Call no man on earth "Father," for you have one Father, which is in heaven (Matthew 23:9).

And when one not only hears, but responds from the heart by the yielding of his will to conform to the will of the Father, and desires with all his heart to leave this world and to enter the Father's Glory in eternal union with the Father as his child, then the Father's will is done again on earth as it is in heaven. The Father's will is being done exactly as it was when Jesus died on the cross to bring the Kingdom to the earth. Whenever anyone thus yields his or her will to God, that also is the living proof that His Kingdom has been consummated on the earth.

All kings in all kingdoms rule to the single end that the will of the king is done throughout the realm. The Kingdom of God is the same, in that God in Christ rules to the single end that the world yield up the children of the Father to his glory.

"We give you thanks, Lord God Almighty, that you have taken up your great power and begun to reign!" (Revelation 11:17).

The earth was barren before the coming of the Kingdom. It had been created for the specific purpose of bearing the fruit of children of God for the glory of the Father, but none were forthcoming. Therefore all was lost, futile, and vain, and the whole world was under the power of darkness. (Luke 22:53; John 3:19; 8:12; 12:46; Ephesians 6:12). But, now that God in Christ is ruling, divine children are being born into the realm of the Father's Glory. The earth has become fruitful. It must be, for the Kingdom of God has come!

The coming is therefore not at all to be viewed as a progressive, continuing process such as some have taught, in the belief that it is somehow to be equated with the development of civilization. No kingdom comes partially or incompletely. Either its authority is complete and effective, or else it has not yet gained the power to rule. The Kingdom of God is no exception, and the New Testament presents its coming in the Greek punctiliar action. Such action is like this: first, it has not happened; then, instantly, it has already happened. Related events may lead up to the coming, but these are not the coming. When finally it comes, it has already happened. It is over and past and no one can rightly speak of it in the present tense as though one could see it happening progressively. No. One can only say "The Kingdom is at hand"; then suddenly he says, "The Kingdom has come!" This is the way it was when the Kingdom came on earth as it is in heaven.

It is also the same in its coming into the consciousness of every individual. With everyone who has received the Truth, there was a time when each spoke of the coming of the Kingdom as a future event saying, "O, Lord, let thy Kingdom come!" But then the heart was opened and the light burst forth with splendor and one could suddenly say only, "Praise the Father that his Kingdom came!" This moment of Truth, when suddenly the light has already burst forth into consciousness, is surely the most blessed and joyous moment in all this life until that hour when we shall see him in his glory. (Matthew 16:28; 25:31; Mark 8:38; 13:26; 14:62; Luke 9:26; 21:27; John 1:51; 2 Thessalonians 1:7-10; Revelation 1:7).

"The Kingdom of God was consummated on the earth when Jesus died on the Cross." On hearing this statement a seminary professor once retorted derisively, "Do you mean to say that the Kingdom of God has fully come while war, poverty, and injustice continue rife on the earth? No one can believe it!"

I mention this man because his geocentric view is typical of churchmen who insist that God cannot be actively ruling while these evils continue. They assert that the rule of God aims to produce a utopian society and thus they betray the earth-centeredness of their thinking. By this I mean that their primary values are earthly ones, also their primary threats. This prohibits their accepting a heavenly kingdom that does not bring an earthly peace. If we first allow for their refusing to take the teaching of Jesus seriously for all their professed devotion, then we should acknowledge that such objections are honest.

The maintenance of seemingly evil conditions under the rule of God certainly calls for an explanation. There is first the matter of appearances. Human rulers appear to abide the same as ever, in their full spectrum from the malevolent dictators to the benevolent monarchs. When Jesus wrested his victory from Satan, Caesar, and the Sanhedrin, there was no apparent end of Roman rule, nor any visible change in administration. The Romans continued to exercise their authority, except that they suddenly received it from a different source. This change in power at the highest level was invisible to men, so that the Romans themselves were unaware of any change in the sources of their power.

When Daniel prophesied of the four beasts, "Their dominion was taken away, but their lives were preserved for a season and a time" (Daniel 7:12), he was speaking of this very thing; for the Romans' dominion, as something of themselves, was taken away from them. Yet their lives were preserved in that we yet see their successors carrying out their functions as though nothing had happened. The writer of the Letter to the Hebrews must have been speaking of this when he wrote, "We do not yet see everything in subjection to him" (Hebrews 2:8). Since he wrote this after having specifically stated that nothing had been left outside his (Christ's) control, I understand this statement to have reference only to the limitations of our vision, and not in any sense to call in question the extent of Christ's rule.

There is no *real* contradiction between what is and what we see to be. To be sure, many see an apparent contradiction due solely to their misconceptions of the Kingdom. But if their apparent contradiction were to be resolved in favor of their ideas, there would then be a real contradiction in Truth, which is a thought unreasonable. For the biblical and reasonable testimony (as of two witnesses) agree consistently in that whatever is eternal is to us unseen, and the Kingdom is eternal. It follows, therefore, that the Kingdom itself must forever remain unseen as an object of objective human perception. To be sure, we see it vividly through the eye of faith, having been born of the Spirit in accord with Jesus' statement:

> *Except you be born again, you cannot see the Kingdom of God* (John 3:3).

There the matter rests, and the eye of faith would not have it otherwise.

Consider this saying of the Apostle Paul:

"We look not to the things that are seen but to the things that are unseen; for the things that are seen are transient, but the things that are unseen are eternal" (2 Corinthians 4:18).

It follows that anything, to be eternal as is the Kingdom, is and must ever remain unseen. If it can be seen, it is only a component of the temporal reality that passes away, in the same manner as that of the whole world. This is precisely as John also wrote:

"And the world passes away, and the lust of it" (1 John 2:17).

Therefore, whatever can be seen in this way is of the world. Yet Jesus has been careful to teach, in sharp contrast to this, that the Kingdom is not of this world (John 18:36). I must conclude, then, that any kingdom that we can see will pass away. It is subject to the temporal futility that binds the whole of creation and therefore it cannot be the Kingdom of God!

We must now finally consider the divine imperative, which is our legitimate choice and which I have already discussed at length. I ask this question: "If God's surpassing eternal Kingdom and Glory were evident to objective observation, where would be the grounds for our choice in the freedom of the will?" Would not everyone be compelled to select the glory of eternity rather than the relative puny and fading splendor of this age? So therefore the essential choice is and must ever remain an act of pure faith precisely because of the unseen character of the eternal verities, and so it continues to constitute a legitimate choice.

Do you ask, "How can one make a legitimate choice of an entity that cannot be seen?" Would not a "genuine choice" require an equal exposure to all the possibilities? Is it not understood, for example, that before a jury can make a decision concerning innocence or guilt, both defense and prosecution must be granted an equal hearing?

This seems a reasonable question. But a little reflection will show that the questioner has not grasped the least part of what I am saying; for it ought to be obvious that if anyone insists on having the same kind of visible evidence of the unseen as of the seen in order to make a choice between them, then for that person the unseen has never been seriously considered as an option. The perceptual distinction that differentiates between the seen and the unseen also must differentiate between their respective testimonies. The testimony to the objective reality of the world is essentially visible, whereas the testimony to the reality of the Kingdom of God is, like the Kingdom itself, essentially invisible so that the choice begins not with a consideration of the entities themselves, but with a consideration of their respective testimonies. If one chooses to heed visible witnesses to the world as credible above the invisible witnesses to the Kingdom, he has already made his choice in favor of the world without ever giving the Kingdom a hearing. So therefore the choice is clear and pure from the very beginning, not only with regard to the unseen entities, but also as regards their testimonies.

Those who have already chosen the world have acted as though the unseen testimony of the Kingdom were no testimony, whereas in fact it is the most powerful and credulous testimony of all. Just as it was written that "God has nowhere left himself without a witness," so in this age abundant witnesses give their evidence for him and his Kingdom. The rule of God is indeed effective in the seen world, but so as not to be recognizable as such to men. On the contrary, the visible consequences of the rule of God are often such as men, including churchmen, do not like to see. They are often frustrated because the changes they promote are contrary to the will of God — and God is ruling. It is for this reason that for all their efforts men have never been able to unite the world since the coming of the Kingdom. There is such a vast difference between the mind of man and the mind of Christ that the rule of God prohibits the very changes that men demand as evidence of the rule of God.

Nevertheless, when one has at last made the choice of the unseen Kingdom of God, it is discovered that even the visible testimony of the world bears witness to it, although indirectly. God in Christ exercises the regency of the Kingdom to the end that, above all things, the freedom of the will of man is protected and preserved, since only by the operation of the freedom of the will is it possible for children in the Father's image to be delivered into his glory. Apart from that, his whole purpose in creation would be thwarted and no one could be saved. That this also results in terrible inequities, transgressions, and sufferings due to the conflicts of the will of men means only that we are the sinners who bring it all upon ourselves. The Father stands always at the window, grieving, yearning, hoping for the prodigal's return.

Be of good cheer;
I have overcome the world.

Jesus, John 16:33

10
THE VICTORY

The world acted to destroy Jesus as soon as he was born. Satan, who was the prince of this world, immediately recognized Jesus as his eternal nemesis and quickly marshaled his forces for a war unto death. The combatants in this cosmic struggle are the focus of this chapter. It describes their strategies, defines the essence of their warfare, and explains the ultimate victory of our Lord.

John dramatically describes the hostility in his Apocalypse, where he shows us a woman "clothed with the sun, with the moon under her feet, and on her head a crown of twelve stars; she was with child, and she cried out in her pangs of birth, in anguish for delivery" (Revelation 12:1-2). Then another portent appears in the heavens: "Behold, a great red dragon with seven heads and ten horns, and seven diadems upon his heads. His tail swept down a third of the stars of heaven, and cast them to the earth" (Revelation 12: 3-4). Next, we see the dragon standing before the woman, that "he might devour her child as soon as she brought it forth . . ." (Revelation 12:4).

This is precisely the setting of the birth of Jesus. Satan's subregent, King Herod, resolved to destroy the infant, and when he learned the location of the birth, he dispatched a detachment of soldiers to destroy him. Not knowing the specific identity of the child, but only the place of birth, he resolved to kill every male infant in Bethlehem and its surrounding territory (Matthew 2:16). Jesus escaped this slaughter only because a dream forewarned Joseph to flee to Egypt, which was outside Herod's jurisdiction (Matthew 2:13). The Apocalypse skips over the details of the conflict to the victory itself, as it continues: "She brought forth a male child, one who is to rule all the nations with a rod of iron, but her child was caught up to God and to his throne" (Revelation 12:5).

This is victory language. The reference to a "rod of iron" reminds us of a prophetic passage that foretold this conflict. I refer to the Second Psalm, where we read: "Why do the nations conspire and the peoples plot in vain? The kings of the earth set themselves, and the rulers take counsel together, against the Lord and his anointed, saying, Let us burst their bonds asunder, and cast their cords from us" (Psalm 2:1-2).

We are reading here of the hostility and bitter enmity that characterized the conflict between two opposing sets of allies. The gentiles and the peoples of Israel, allied under the Kings of the earth and the rulers of Israel, are joined in combat with the Lord (God) and his anointed one (Jesus). As in the Apocalypse, the Lord is victorious and sets his Messiah on the holy hill of Zion with authority over all nations. There he makes the nations his heritage and the ends of the earth his possession. The prime consequence of this is that the Messiah is to "break them with a rod of iron, and dash them in pieces like a potter's vessel" (Psalm 2:6-9). Take note of the common element, in both the Psalm and the Apocalypse — the rod of iron.

Thus were the battle lines drawn from before his birth until the moment of his victorious death on the cross. Jesus lived within the world as an alien invader in a hostile land. He committed himself fully to the tasks of overthrowing its government and inaugurating a new administration that was wholly and radically contrary to the desires of all people. He viewed the rulers of Israel and of the whole world as the enemy — wicked, hostile and vicious — which had set itself to destroy him. It was not only the rulers whom he identified as the enemy. Taking his cue from the Second Psalm, which portrays the "gentiles" and "peoples" as plotting against him, he broadened the scope of his identification of the enemy to include *all men.* He appropriated the word, "men" as his generic term for the enemy. Listen:

> *Get behind me Satan, for you are not on the side of God, but of men* (Matthew 16:23; Mark 8:33).

These words, spoken as a rebuke to Peter at a crucial point in the war, show how Jesus defined the two opponents. On the one side we have Jesus and his Father, God. On the other is Satan, men, and, at that moment, Peter, all corresponding perfectly with characters in the Second Psalm. Jesus obviously saw himself allied with his Father in a conflict with Satan and men. Thus when Jesus refers to "men," he generally is defining a category of hostile opponents in alliance with Satan, as in the following examples:

To his disciples:

> *Behold, I send you out as sheep in the midst of wolves; so be wise as serpents and innocent as doves. Beware of men; for they will deliver you up to councils, and flog you in their synagogues, and you will be dragged before governors and kings for my sake, to bear testimony before them and the gentiles* (Matthew 10:16-18).

> *Blessed are you when men revile you and persecute you and utter all kinds of evil against you falsely on my account. Rejoice and be glad, for so men persecuted the prophets who were before you. You are the salt of the earth; but if the salt has lost its taste, how shall its saltiness be restored? It is no longer good for anything except to be thrown out and trodden under foot by men* (Matthew 5:11; Luke 6:22).

Jesus always characterizes men as utterly hostile, not only to himself, but also to the disciples who come from their ranks.

In what sense does he describe the disciples as the "salt of the earth?" The disciples are the salt that, to men, has lost its savor. The result is that men cast them out and trod them underfoot. The disciples, therefore, are deviant turncoats from the mainstream of the human race. They are traitors to the human cause. Men deal with them as abhorrent radicals. They are scandals to the masses of mankind. They are good for nothing and therefore worthy only to be cast out and trodden down. So it was that Jesus, in fulfillment of Isaiah's prophecy, "was despised and rejected of men" (Isaiah 53:3).

But Jesus categorized those few from among the ranks of men who desert to his cause as "the blessed." He said to them:

> *Blessed are you when men hate you and when they exclude you and revile you, and cast out your name as evil, on account of the Son of Man* (Luke 6:22).

He also said,

> *Woe to you when all men speak well of you, for so their*
> *fathers did to the false prophets* (Luke 6:26).

Jesus held the approval of men in utter disdain, saying of himself:

> *I receive not glory from men* (John 5:41).

Then he condemned the Pharisees because:

> *... you appear outwardly righteous to men* (Matthew 23:28).

It was in this attitude toward men that he instructed the disciples in the Sermon on the Mount:

> *Beware of practicing your piety before men in order to be seen*
> *by them; for then you will have no reward from your Father*
> *who is in heaven* (Matthew 6:1).

> *Thus, when you give alms, sound no trumpet before you, as*
> *the hypocrites do in the synagogues and in the streets, that*
> *they may be praised by men. Truly, I say to you, they have*
> *their reward. But when you give alms, do not let your left*
> *hand know what your right hand is doing, so that your alms*
> *may be in secret; and your Father who sees in secret will*
> *reward you* (Matthew 6:2-4)

> *And when you pray, you must not be like the hypocrites; for*
> *they love to stand and pray in the synagogues and at the street*
> *corners, that they may be seen by men. Truly, I say to you,*
> *they have their reward. But when you pray, go into your room*
> *and shut the door and pray to your Father who is in secret;*
> *and your Father who sees in secret will reward you* (Matthew
> 6:5-6).

So also, when he foretold the final outpouring of the wrath of God on the wicked, it is men who are the recipients. He closed such prophecies with the phrase,

> *There men will weep and gnash their teeth* (Matthew 8:12;
> 13:42; 13:50; 22:13; 24:51; 25:30; Luke 13:28).

In the mind of Jesus, and therefore in Truth, "men" are the enemy. Among them his disciples are as sheep in the midst of wolves who can expect only the worst treatment. He eschews any positive relationship with men for either himself or his followers, though the latter come to him from the ranks of men. He goes to the very taproot of human identity to sever all identification of the disciples with men by this commandment:

> *Call no man your father on earth, for you have one Father, who is in heaven* (Matthew 23:9).

All the testimony points to the attitude of Jesus, toward men, as toward those who are utterly hostile to God. He viewed Satan as the father of men. He identified the Pharisees in particular, and men in general, as being:

> *... of your father, the devil* (John 8:44).

Jesus engaged in mortal combat with Satan during the wilderness temptations. There he acknowledged that Satan was the possessor of "all the kingdoms of the world" (Matthew 4: 8-10; Luke 4:5-8). Had the case been otherwise, he would surely have responded differently when Satan offered them in return for his service. Jesus readily exercised power over demons, who characteristically fled his presence. His enemies explained his power over the demons by saying that he was their captain. They insisted that it was by Beelzebub, the Prince of Demons, that he cast out demons (Matthew 9:34; 12:24; Mark 3:22). Jesus responded by saying:

> *Every kingdom divided against itself is laid waste, and no city or house divided against itself will stand; and if Satan casts out Satan, he is divided against himself; how then will his kingdom stand?* (Matthew 12:25-26; Luke 11:18).

> *And if I cast out demons by Beelzebub, by whom do your sons cast them out? Therefore they shall be your judges. But if it is by the Spirit of God that I cast out demons, then the kingdom of God has come upon you* (Luke 11:19-20).

> *Or how can one enter a strong man's house and plunder his goods, unless he first binds the strong man? Then indeed he may plunder his house* (Matthew 12:29; Mark 3:27).

Jesus understood that this world was Satan's house. He pictured himself as the thief who has entered the "strong man's house" with intent to plunder his goods. What are the "goods" that he came to plunder? It is all those from among men whom he could steal away to the cause of the Father. It is all those whom he designated "blessed."

Jesus sees himself as the spearhead of God's invasion of the kingdom of Satan. More than that, he is the plunderer who sets himself to loot the house (or land) of its treasures and transport them to his Father's house. In this he would follow the pattern of King David who had invaded the lands of the Ammonites, Amalakites, and Philistines and took much plunder back to the house of God (1 Chronicles 18:11; 26:27).

Now, the nature of the conflict required that Jesus become a man, engage Satan, and claim victory over him. To do so as a God would not serve the Father's purpose. Therefore it was necessary that Jesus enter fully into the human experience, beginning with the usual birth and ending with the usual "death." He was therefore exceedingly vulnerable, especially in infancy and youth. Without some special advantage, there was no means by which he could have survived because Satan was aware from the beginning that there was an intruder in his house. Now, the record reveals that the Father compensated for this vulnerability by the "binding" of Satan, as Jesus suggested in this brief parable. The dream that warned Joseph to escape to Egypt with Jesus and Mary exemplifies this binding. After that, Jesus was incognito among men until the time of his revealing. The demons recognized him, so there is reason to think that Satan was always aware of his location and identity. This suggests another aspect of the binding: that it prevented Satan's revealing the identity of Jesus to men, who would have destroyed him before he could complete his work. This is the same binding that is mentioned in the Apocalypse (Revelation 20: 1-3). Therefore, when Jesus was conducting his teaching campaigns and otherwise waging his war of Truth, it was so that he might succeed in plundering the house of Satan. God had already bound the latter so that he could not prevent it.

Jesus very early conceived and developed the strategy of his warfare and tenaciously held to his plan. He neither deviated from his planned course nor retreated in disorder. The strategy, which the parable of the strong man's house also suggests, consisted of dividing

Satan against himself. I will show how this developed, but first let us review the scene as follows:

Satan deceived all men (beginning with the first man, Adam) and bound them to him through fear of death. They were in darkness as to the only fulfilling eternal life and vainly sought fulfillment in the temporal, earthly experience. Although, as the Scriptures state, what can be known about God was plain to them, they chose to believe a lie (Romans 1:18-25). This is the lie that says they can find fulfillment in the temporal setting. Their minds were darkened, and so it continued from generation to generation. They refused to reckon with the choices that the Father set before them and, by default, gave themselves to whatever was close — to earth and to time. Among them there was no one who understood or responded to the will of the Father by setting the heart and mind on the Father's glory, for which he had created them. Thus they brought themselves under condemnation. All life came to take its purpose and value from the earth experience. But since they were in the image of the Father, they never ceased their struggle to realize on earth all the conditions of life to which their hearts by nature inclined, due to the eternity that is in them.

Since the eternal Father finds pleasure in certain types of relationships and conditions of life (all eternal), men in his likeness have struggled vainly to develop here, on earth and in time, the like things for which he fitted them. What do they do who have left old England behind and journeyed to a new and virgin land? They build a New England! So men ceaselessly labor to render the earth their new heaven, wholly contrary to the purposes of God. Here all are misfits, and by seeking to conform, all render themselves unfit for heaven. Their hunger is, at its root, the hunger for divine, eternal glory — nothing less. Therefore the richest temporal goodies, doomed to pass away and therefore hopelessly bound to futility as the Apostle Paul so aptly stated, can never be truly satisfying. But no one realized the significance of this unsatisfied hunger. Therefore, there was no admission that the cause of the continuing dissatisfaction lay within themselves. Few would even acknowledge that the intense dissatisfaction existed. To do so would have undermined their desperate confidence in the only hope they knew. They all disdained the heavenly glory and the Heavenly Father and relied instead on earthly fathers to supply all their needs. Consequently, the gates to True Glory became for them the Gates of Death, from which they recoiled in fear and dread. Thus the world ... this dark, futile world ... applies itself to the task of capturing each new generation and convincing it of the wisdom of the "fathers" in seeking an earthly fulfillment.

Our Heavenly Father nevertheless continued to reach out to our forebears in eternal patience and love. He persisted in his intention to redeem them to his purpose. To this end he never permitted our predecessors to forget him, but manifested himself in many ways, peoples, and places. By the threefold processes of choosing individuals, preserving a remnant, and founding a prototype kingdom in Israel, he prodded history along the ascending way toward its destined encounter with the Kingdom of Heaven. Finally, at the proper time, the Father dispatched his beloved son with the commission to be the light of the world. The world responded by fulfilling the Second Psalm. The nations conspired, the peoples of Israel hatched vain plots, and the kings and rulers took counsel together. They set themselves for battle to the end that they might throw off the last of the binding cords of heaven. All the forces of Satan and man combined and set themselves to fight against the Lord and his anointed one — Jesus! It is understandable, then, that Jesus, who knew his identity as the anointed one and understood these things, considered himself an utter alien in a hostile land whose citizens joined in common cause against him. He told a parable to illustrate his circumstances as follows:

> A man planted a vineyard and let it out to tenants, and went into another country for a long while. When the time came, he sent a servant to the tenants, that they should give him some of the fruit of the vineyard; but the tenants beat him and sent him away empty-handed. Again he sent other servants, more than the first; and they did the same to them. Afterward he sent his son to them, saying, 'They will respect my son.' But those tenants said to one another, 'This is the heir; come, let us kill him, and the inheritance will be ours.' And they took him and killed him, and cast him out of the vineyard. What will the owner of the vineyard do? He will come and destroy the tenants, and give the vineyard to others

who will give him the fruits in their seasons (Matthew 21:33-41; Luke 20:9-18).

Now, the language of the second Psalm suggests that there must be the massing of great armies preparing to join in such a battle as would leave the world a desolation strewn with the bodies of the slain. But whom are such great armies to oppose? The Psalm presents all the human authorities as bound together against the numerically small alliance of only two — the Lord and his Messiah. Also, grand armies do not gather to do battle with spirits or with gods. No, there must be other grand armies for them to fight. Since the rulers of all the human forces belong to the same alliance, there can be no such battlefield carnage in fulfillment of this prophecy. There must be a different sort of warfare here — one in which the grand alliance of human forces and authorities, represented by the satanically inspired peoples and rulers of both gentile and Jew, unites for the single purpose of destroying the Lord's anointed.

When the time of the great final battle drew near, Satan's strategy was exposed. Victory over the Lord's anointed one must be realized by tempting him to save his life in this world. None of the peoples or rulers understood this; if they had, they would not have crucified the Lord of Glory (1 Corinthians 2:8). Satan understood the warfare, yet Jesus deftly maneuvered him into the condition of being divided against himself, and by that he was defeated. The supreme spirit-powers joined in the climactic battle for control of the world. For Satan, victory was to be won by enticing the Son of God to save his life by delivering himself from the threat of imminent death. Only thus could he put out the light that Jesus had sparked in the world and retain his hold on the allegiance of all men. As Jesus revealed in the parable of The Wicked Tenants quoted above, the Father had planted this vineyard, the world (or, in Jesus' immediate purview, the nation of Israel) for the sole purpose of receiving the harvest of its fruit. He had never yet received his harvest, because Satan had kept it all. Satan knew he was about to lose all this unless Jesus could be tempted to save his life on earth like other men.

Remember, now, that this conflict is a matter of the individual human will. To become fruit for the Father, one must will, or want from the heart, to go to him. Alas, they did not, they do not, have this want. Instead, men seemed universally to will to save their lives on earth, thus aborting any harvest that the Father might have anticipated. The fear of death was their condemnation and the seal of their continuing bondage to the Prince of this World.

Contrarily, for the Father and for Jesus, victory must be secured by the initiation and continuation of the delivery of a harvest of souls. To this end, two primary things must occur: the seed must be planted in the world so as never to be uprooted, and the Son himself must burst forth from the vineyard as the firstfruits of the harvest. It was only thus that he could blaze a trail for others to follow.

Now the Word is the seed, as Jesus elsewhere declared in parables (Luke 8:11). So it was first necessary for him to plant the Word in the world such that it would never pass away. This objective he confidently defined by the following statement:

Heaven and earth will pass away, but my words shall not pass away (Matthew 24:35; Mark 13:31; Luke 21:33).

Having done that, he must win the final victory, as a man, by luring Satan to destruction through the offering up of Jesus' own life on earth. By this offering, he would receive the eternal glory that, through him, the Father extended to all who follow. Only thus could he break the bonds of Satan that the fear of death imposed. By no other means could he deliver his harvest to the Father in its season.

The moment of this victory also would be the moment of the consummate coming of the Kingdom of God to the earth, for then Satan's enslavement of men would be broken forever. Thereafter the earth would continue under the rule of God. It would respond to the will of God that is ... this one thing ... that it deliver up its continuing harvest of souls to the Father's glory.

If we look at the scene from Satan's perspective, we see that his purposes would best be served by avoiding the final confrontation. His first effort to this end was to destroy the infant Jesus before he could come to maturity. He sought to do this through his servant, Herod, but could not because God had bound him. After that, no one except Mary, Joseph, and of course in time, Jesus himself, knew the lad's identity. Satan must use human agents to destroy him. These agents also would become aware of Jesus' identity. They might, in this knowledge, turn to worship Jesus instead of destroying him. There was no one as vicious as Herod on whom Satan could fully rely, and so he trusted no one. He dared not reveal to them the identity of the person he sought to destroy. He was therefore bound again — to keep his terrible secret. So he watched, helplessly, as Jesus grew to maturity and to the knowledge of his identity.

Of course, if the young Jesus would only commit some offense worthy of capital punishment, Satan would have his way with him. This Jesus was not about to do. Instead, his behavior was admirable and praiseworthy. Satan was so securely bound that he could not even advance a credible lie to convict Jesus by false accusation. So Jesus had a kind of protection in the world due to his incognito, and thus he grew up to manhood. Then Satan's strategy necessarily changed. Knowing the nature of this strange conflict and that Jesus was set to overcome him and to take away his kingdom, Satan assayed to salvage whatever he could by bargaining. He offered it all to Jesus if only he would enter the service of Satan as a subregent. This is the significance of the temptation in the wilderness in which Satan offered Jesus "all the kingdoms of the world and the glory of them" (Matthew 4:8). It also explains why Jesus absolutely refused to accept glory from men. Satan's failure thus to buy Jesus is well known to all readers of the New Testament. Thereafter he temporarily retreated from the field of battle, but he did not surrender. He could not; he had no choice. The circumstances compelled him to continue to do battle in every way, no matter how desperate his plight. Jesus would accept no conditional surrender.

Satan never withdrew the offer of the Kingdom. He continued to press it upon him in other ways, even working through the people of Israel to force Jesus to accept a position as his subregent. To this end he inspired the many admirers of Jesus to mount a movement to force the scepter upon him. We read of this in the Gospels also, and of Jesus' response (John 6:15). He removed himself from the people who were seeking to enthrone him, and went out into a solitary place to restore his exclusive commitment to the eternal treasures and glory.

Know you not that I must be in my Father's house? (Luke 2:49).

With these words the twelve-year-old Jesus revealed that his was a singleness of devotion to the glory of God, his only Father. He made the choice that is also God's will for us all, and he maintained this devotion with great tenacity. Earth and Satan try, and try again, but cannot claim him. His spirit is always free to make its departure from this world to the Father. He needed only to complete his work, and to that end he looked and labored with eager anticipation.

As the Epistle to the Hebrews has informed us, Satan had always used the fear of death to secure his power over man (Hebrews 2:15). How can one set the heart on God's glory, or have any genuine love for God, when one recoils in fear from the one experience that leads to God? Jesus was no exception in that the strait gate of death also stood between him and his restoration to the Glory of the Father. Therefore he was free of satanic dominion only while he did not fear death. If only Satan could cause him to fear death, he would fall into evil's grasp like the rest of mankind. It appears that, until his en-counter with Jesus, Satan's success rate in imposing this fear on men was one hundred percent. With this solid experience on which to build, Satan now resolved to deal with Jesus as with any other man — by imposing this fear upon him. In consequence, Jesus would not want to go to his Father because of the fear of death, and would find himself in Satan's power. He would act to save his life, and thus lose it!

Jesus' perspective was no less clear. First he must speak the word in such fashion that it would take root and grow among men. It would be of no use if, after his departure to the Father, the Truth did not remain securely implanted on planet earth. (The continuing opera-tion and maintenance of the Word on earth is therefore all the evidence we need of the operation on earth of the rule of God.) Second, he must become the personified expression of the Truth by conquering the fear of death, in the face of death. By thus maintaining his commitment to the Father's Glory under the most difficult cir-cumstances, he would be eternally victorious. Finally, he must engage Satan (and man) in battle and defeat him and his human servants. This defeat would end Satan's reign and initiate the reign of God on earth as it is in heaven. It is obvious that one cannot establish a new government without dealing with the already established authorities!

When his hour came, he claimed victory through refusing to yield to all temptations to love and to save his life, and by dividing Satan against himself. The result was sure. Satan's kingdom fell. Only one thing had ever been in doubt — would Jesus fear death in its hour? When he did not yield to fear, he resolved all issues and sealed Satan's doom. He broke, forever, the chains of the fear of death. He did it for himself, and for all who follow him. He delivered us from bondage into the freedom of the Kingdom of God.

No one should suppose that the way to the Father was easier for him than for others. Some do, when they speak of his advantage as the pre-existent Christ through whom the world was made. They reason that he came from the Father's Glory and thus knew by prior experience of the reality of eternal life, but we do not. We can know it only by faith, having never seen or experienced it. But recall that we all are the seed of Adam, who, like Jesus, also came from God, an eternal spirit breathed into the clay. We therefore have the same primeval heritage.

Whatever advantage Jesus might have had due to his pre-existent state was more than offset by his disadvantage. He knew that he must confront Satan as a man among men. He also knew that no man before him had ever succeeded in breaking the bond of evil that is the fear of death. He must therefore also have known how slim were his chances. Statistically speaking, he had absolutely no chance of victory. I can well imagine my despair, had I been in his place. I would have concluded that the assignment was impossible. Doubtless I would have found it most convenient to accept the Devil's offer of all the kingdoms of the world.

The mere humanity of Jesus lacked nothing. He entered the world as a babe like the rest of us. Everything he knew, he had to have learned. He had clearer consciousness of his eternal, glorious origin than do we, but it must only have been because he, as a man, never failed to maintain his commitment to the Father's glory. This was in spite of the formidable array of demonic/human forces mustered against him. How alone he was!

Looking at him in this light one is impressed, not by his advantage, but by his great disadvantage. No man has ever had to face and defeat such a concentration of evil power as converged upon this one man. Yet, as a man, he persistently maintained his devotion to the Father and the resulting fellowship transcended the limitations of ordinary sensibility. Still, if any one of us were to maintain a similar, sinless devotion, our assurance of Glory and our consciousness of the Eternal would be no less intense than his. Jesus won the battle with Satan and man as a man. It was as a man that he died, crying out, "My God, my God, why hast thou forsaken me?" (Matthew 27:46; Mark 15:34).

His choices were human choices, and his resources are no less available to us than they were to him. He spoke from experience when he said, "The gate is narrow" (Matthew 7:14).

To die fearlessly or to live fearfully was the issue in the cosmic spiritual struggle between Jesus and Satan. I have shown how, at first, it served the purpose of evil to seek the death of the infant. Even as late as the riot at Nazareth, the simple death of Jesus would have served its purpose of aborting this divine incursion into the realm of men and demons. But after Jesus had succeeded in consolidating his ground by implanting the Word of Truth on the earth, his simple death no longer served evil's purpose. It was essential to Satan to discredit the implanted Word, and he could only do this by discrediting the planter. The Word declared that "He who loves his life loses it, but he who hates his life in this world will keep it for life eternal" (John 12:25). Now, if only Jesus could be caused to manifest a love of life, his soul would be captivated by evil, and his words discredited. What a victory that would be!

So therefore it became essential to the purposes of evil to keep Jesus alive under the threat of death, by causing him, in the face of death, to fear death and to avoid it. This required for its accomplishment that Jesus face the genuine threat of impending death. But actually to kill him? No.

If Jesus accepted death without fear, then he would have credited the Word, so that this would become Satan's defeat. The latter would lose his kingdom beyond all retrieval. Jesus understood, then, that his victory could be won only by suffering a fearless death at the hands of men in a human struggle with the Prince of Demons. Such men have, as their motivating forces, the love of life and the fear of death. He knew that all human rule and authority were rooted in this fear and its corollary, the love of life. Therefore, men everywhere bond together and submit to rulers only to protect their earthly treasure and preserve their corporeal lives. The human establishment throughout the world exists to this sole end. Therefore, the struggle of Jesus was also with the establishment. It was in bondage to Satan through the same fear of death by which the demons would have bound Jesus to themselves. So, the time of the final and climactic battle, the New Testament "fullness of time" (Galatians 4:4), came when the primary establishment authority was centered in one ruler — the Roman emperor. God had permitted the Empire to assemble for this very purpose.

Jesus understood how the men of the world, in the bondage of their universal fear of death, are easily threatened by anyone who advocates ideas contrary to their geocentric value-set. Such a person always arouses hostility when he speaks against material wealth and advocates alien values such as "treasure in heaven," as Jesus did. Men saw him as a threat to their establishment and to their earthly lives and treasures. "See," they said, "how the whole world has gone after him" (John 12:19).

They suspected his motives and feared his influence in the expectation that he intended to take over political and military power. The idea that Jesus was no threat to their establishment was far beyond their fear-bound powers of comprehension. Neither could they conceive that their only valid fear was fear itself —the fear of death.

Jesus did not want their positions, their wealth, their earthly security, or the glory of men — but they could not but think that he sought them. When he refused to cooperate with the establishment but spoke in the harshest terms against the rulers, and that publicly, they could only assume, in that revolutionary country packed with zealots, that Jesus was plotting Messianic revolution. Their conclusion, and their fear, was that "The Romans will come and destroy both our Holy Place and our nation" (John 11:48).

This expectation of Roman intervention was realistic. The threat was always present and the Romans were acutely aware of the rebellious spirit of the Jews and took every appearance of seditious activity very seriously. Being themselves also bound by the fear of death and its corollary, the love of life, they also responded to the dictates of their particular geocentric interests.

Jesus deliberately proceeded to use these circumstances to his advantage, to the end that he might present the demonstration of a fearless death while engaged in a struggle with men motivated by that same fear. He was in complete control of events from beginning to end. As the climactic battle approached he carefully chose both his enemies and his friends, and pronounced a blessing on all who were not offended in him (Matthew 11:6; Luke 7:23). He skillfully arranged details to comply with prophecy, and when his hour came, it was Jesus who commanded the action when he said to Judas,

> *What thou doest, do quickly!* (John 13:27).

After that, he was punctual to the minute for his appointment across Kidron, in Gethsemane. There he remained in command most peculiarly, even giving orders to his captors, which they obeyed. When he said, "Let these men go" (John 18: 8-9), they could only let those men go. To one disciple he issued the command, "Put your sword into its sheath!" and he did so. He exposed the essence of the drama by saying to Pilate the Procurator,

> *You would have no power over me unless it had been given you from above* (John 19:11).

He was never for a moment in their power. They were in his power, to do with them as he would. He could at any moment have delivered himself, and he said so:

> *Do you not know that I could call upon my Father, and he would send twelve legions of angels?* (Matthew 26:53).

This was precisely the temptation that would have destroyed him had he yielded to it, for then he would have saved his life, and so, lost it forever. That is the essence of evil and the only barrier on the way to God.

His disciples were utterly bewildered by the events preceding the crucifixion — this even though Jesus had repeatedly impressed upon them that this death was to occur as they saw it, and that it was the will of the Father that it be so. We have, after all, seen a like thing in our time — the adherents of "Christianity" who betray him with a kiss, uncomprehending of his Truth. This they do though they have read the Words of Truth repeatedly during their study of the Gospels. It was in the first disciples to quarrel which of them was the greatest

(Mark 9:34; Luke 9:46; 22:24). They also were "pyramid climbers" as they shuffled for the key positions at his right hand and his left (Matthew 20:20-24; Mark 10: 35-44). They had not the ears to hear Jesus' frequent assertion that he was to be delivered into the hands of men, to be crucified (Matthew 16:21; 17:22; Mark 9:31; Luke 9:44). They objected to this prospect, as Peter did when he said, "No, Lord, this shall never happen to you" (Matthew 16:22; Mark 8:32). Jesus immediately recognized this as a barb from Satan and responded to Peter accordingly.

They were all convinced of Jesus' Messianic identity, much as are the vast majority of modern disciples. Now, as then, we hear the refrain, "Thou art the Christ, the Son of the living God!" Then, as now, they saw the Messianic office as created according to their geocentric imagery. This vision inspired their patriotic fervor and moved them to battle heroically for the realization of their earth-bound dreams for themselves, their children, and their nation. This was the fervor that inspired Peter to declare, "Lord, I am ready to go with you to prison and to death" (Luke 22:33). Yes, and he was ready. He would have done it, but for the wrong reason. He was in bondage to an earthly hero complex that paradoxically inspires life-loving, death-fearing men to die for an earthly cause. They do so knowing that they will yet live on in the hearts of their countrymen as heroes and martyrs, and that their deaths may enrich the temporal lives of their survivors.

Such heroism is no victory over death. It is defeat instead, because they lose ... both this life and the next. Their commitment to die is not for the sake of anything beyond death, and such soldiers are therefore seldom trained in the art of dying. Instead, they are skilled at killing. Their aim is to put the enemy to death and save this life for themselves.

Peter revealed his true ilk a short time later when, in fear of both prison and death, he denied the Lord three times, saying, "I do not know the man" (Matthew 26:70-75; Mark 14:66-72). Can this be the same person who had shortly before made so fearless a confession of loyalty? Yes, the very same, and there is no contradiction. When he made the confession, he could not conceive that the Messiah should suffer thus. He must have considered the occasion to be a test designed to elicit just such a response. Nor was he being insincere;

had events proceeded according to his idea of victory, he would willingly have become a martyr and a hero through death. But when he saw Jesus, seemingly hopeless to combat the enemy, he retreated to his basic life-saving stance. He was not about to lay down his life for a man who appeared to have deceived him.

When Jesus rebuked him for using the sword in his defense (he had brought it according to Jesus' command), and when Jesus even healed the enemy's wound, Peter must have felt that Jesus had denied him the privilege of becoming a hero. No wonder he felt confused and betrayed; there was ironic truth in the words of his denial, "Woman, I do not know the man." He had spent years as a disciple of Jesus, but still he did not know him. He did not even know himself!

Peter and all the apostles were both blind and deaf in that hour. When one sees how they responded to the crucifixion, one thinks at first that Jesus must have utterly misjudged them in saying:

> *Blessed are your eyes, for they see, and your ears, for they hear* (Matthew 13:16).

Jesus' knowledge of them must therefore have extended beyond the crucifixion. He saw that the resurrection would open their eyes so that they would both see the Kingdom and hear the Word. And so it came to pass. First, however, they had to endure trauma such as would render them receptive to the light. Then, the light did dawn within them and they understood why they were not permitted to fight in defense of their Lord. They also realized what he meant when he addressed the following words to Pilate:

> *My kingship is not of this world; if my kingship were of this world, my servants would fight that I might not be handed over to the Jews; but my kingship is not from the world* (John 18:36).

In the dawn of his understanding, in radical repentance and overwhelmed by tears, a different kind of Peter was about to emerge from the fleshly cocoon. The new Peter would confess his love and rise to take up his cross in response to a new commandment, not "to slay my foes" but "to feed my sheep" (John 21:16-17). This way of the cross would seal his earlier commitment, for it would lead him both to prison and to death — and, finally, to Glory.

The New Testament disciples were forgiven their lack of comprehension and slowness to believe before becoming witnesses to the resurrection. After all, the Word presented a new and unique wisdom to them and to the world, and they had absolutely no precedent for the ideas of Jesus. Not so the men and women of modern Christendom. We are without excuse who serve Christ for earthly gain or who entice others into the fold by the promise of temporal rewards. We have always before us the resurrection testimony made sure by the convincing power of the Holy Spirit who teaches and counsels us. We gain absolutely no earthly advantage through service to Christ and his Kingdom and all are without excuse who seek or promise such. We have instead been called to experience sufferings and hardships in this life precisely because we follow the Lord. We have the testimony of the Apostles as follows:

"To this you have been called, because Christ also suffered for you leaving you an example, that you should follow in his steps" (1 Peter 2:21).

The intensity of Jesus' suffering during the last hours remains far beyond our comprehension. We focus attention on the objective ordeal of extreme physical pain and underrate or little consider the subjective ordeal that raged within his heart. He not only had to endure an agonizing death at the hands of evil men, but he also had to endure the disappointed entreaties of his closest friends. Finally, he had to endure their abandonment as "they all forsook him and fled."

How wonderful and how mysterious the hour when the suffering Messiah, in lonely agony, forsaken and outcast, was yet the only one who understood the cosmic significance of the event and controlled it from the beginning to the end. No one else suspected the real significance of that high drama. He truly pleaded the ignorance of all parties to the crucifixion in his petition for their forgiveness:

Father, forgive them, for they know not what they do (Luke 23:34).

We can understand how Jesus divided Satan against himself only by first acknowledging that it was not Satan's intention to put Jesus to death. His sole purpose was to force the fear of death upon him, for only by this could he ensnare the man Jesus in the bonds that held all other men captive. Satan's victory required only one result — that Jesus default before God by saving his life. By this he would discredit the word of God that Jesus had planted in the world. Simultaneously, he would destroy the Son of God by bonding him to himself through the fear of death. To this end he must orchestrate the most fearful threat of death imaginable to maximize the temptation of Jesus to save his life. It was the demons of Satan who inspired the people to cry out for the sentence of death. It was the minions of Satan who inspired men to testify against Jesus before every judge. Yet Satan was mustering all his forces only to orchestrate his own destruction. Thus Jesus divided Satan against himself, and beguiled him into managing the events that were to issue in his eternal defeat.

Satan had good reasons to feel secure. He could lose only if Jesus offered no resistance to death. All other men had resisted without exception, and Jesus also would surely fall. Satan was further divided against himself in that he was compelled to tempt Jesus to save himself by coming down from the cross. This was counter to the desires of those who also served Satan by putting Jesus on that cross. Satan knew that Jesus could come down if he would.

He made the temptation most extreme by inspiring the spiteful taunts and derision of the spectators to the crucifixion. They mocked Jesus, spat upon him, and braided a crown of thorns and pressed it upon his head (Matthew 27:29; Mark 15:17; John 19:2). They then committed the supreme mockery by bowing to him in mock obeisance and saying, "Hail, king of the Jews!" (Matthew 27:29; Mark 15:18) and "He saved others; he cannot save himself!" Yet others said, "If you are the king of the Jews, come down from the cross!" (Mark 15:32).

What person among all who have ever lived on earth could have endured such taunts? He could have come down. He could have saved himself. He could have exalted himself in the sight of his foes ... he could have destroyed every one of them with a word, and Satan knew it! That is precisely what Satan was risking everything to cause Jesus to do, and thus he was putting forth his forces as sacrificial pawns. He knew that his own power and person could be saved only by the destruction of those persons loyal to him — and so in this also he was divided against himself.

Yet there on the cross Jesus remained — tortured, agonizing, alone, and forsaken. Yes, he was absolutely forsaken, not only by his friends, but also by his God and Father. This also Jesus acknowledged by crying out in the words of a familiar Psalm,

> *My God, my God, why have you forsaken me?* (Matthew 27:46; Mark 15:34).

Satan not only counted on succeeding in tempting Jesus the man to save himself and come down from the cross. He also hoped to move the Father himself, in his infinite love for his dear Son, to intervene and to deliver him from the hands of evil men. But Satan did not reckon on the force of the Father's love for *all* men. If the Father had intervened, he would have aborted the redemption of the world and left all men in bondage to Satan forever, without freedom and without hope.

Jesus faced the ordeal as a solitary human individual. He must fight the battle as a man if he was to win the battle for men. Therefore, the Father did not help him. He could not, without forever condemning all others. The crucial struggle was confined to the will of the man, so that at last a man might do the will of God on earth. The Father could not intervene in any way, not even to console and comfort, without compromising the freedom of the will of Jesus the man. Now we can better understand the significance of the words:

> *For God so loved the world, that he gave his only begotten son that whosoever believes in him should not perish, but might have eternal life* (John 3:16).

There was only one thing that would move the Father to intervene — the outcry of the dying Son. If Jesus had called upon the Father to deliver him, he would have done so. The battle would already have been lost.

Jesus knew that he must die a solitary man. He understood that the Father could not intervene to save him. Still, he was human and so cried out as though he did not understand,

> *My God, my God, why have you forsaken me?* (Matthew 27:46; Mark 15:34).

Yet he did not cry out, "Save me!" and so we can be saved.

Who else could have endured such taunts? I must shamefully admit that I would have come down from the cross. I would have cried out for the twelve legions of angels. I would have exalted myself in the sight of my foes. I would have done all these things — but not Jesus. He confronted the combined forces of the greatest concentration of evil the world has ever known, yet he remained true to the end. Thus he perpetuated the Word that his enemy sought to discredit and destroy:

> *Whoever would save his life will lose it; but he who hates his life in this world will keep it for life eternal* (John 12:25).

His great strength grew out of his devotion to Truth and his constant awareness of its realities. Therefore, the inspired Apostle wrote of him:

"It was for the joy set before him that he endured the cross, despising the shame, and is set down at the right hand of God there to await until his enemies should be made a stool for his feet" (Psalm 110:1; Acts 2:34; Ephesians 1:20-22; Colossians 3:1; Hebrews 1:3, 13; 10:12, 13; 12:2).

And also:

"Therefore God has highly exalted him and bestowed on him the name which is above every name, that at the name of Jesus every knee should bow ... " (Philippians 2:9, 10).

So Satan's division against himself consisted of his being put in the untenable position of trying to kill Jesus on the one hand, while trying to move him to save himself on the other. When he realized that he was losing the battle — that it was Jesus who had lured him into the battle under that particular set of conditions and that Jesus was not going to yield and save his life in this world, he then sought to call off the whole thing until "a more convenient season." He did this when Pilate said, "I find no fault in the man; I will chastise him and release him!" (Luke 23:4, 16). His control over Pilate had been his "ace in the hole" as Satan contemplated beforehand the possibilities of the conflict. One can well imagine him pondering, and concluding, "If he should refuse to save his life, I will inspire Pilate to call off the dogs."

We now know this did not work. Satan did not anticipate the insubordination of those human forces that he himself had set in motion, and thus did not imagine that he would lose control. As it turned out, nothing could check the rage of the Jewish rulers and people. Pilate could not control the outcome and therefore Satan could not control it. In this also, he was divided against himself! As for the people, "they knew not what they did."

Who was really in control? Obviously, Jesus. The victim was the victor, and the erstwhile ruler of the house saw it divided and tumbling about him in ruins. One is almost moved to pity Satan. Jesus adroitly maneuvered him into a battle in which Satan used his power to destroy himself and his authority over the kingdoms of this world. John understood what had happened there, and he expressed it in these words:

"The kingdom of the world has become the kingdom of our Lord and his Christ, and he shall reign forever and ever" (Revelation 11:15).

It is to this very day and hour and moment of the death of Jesus on the cross that the Scriptures consistently bear witness as the time of victory. Note the following examples:

"Since therefore the children share in flesh and blood, he himself likewise partook of the same nature, that through death he might destroy him who has the power of death, that is, the devil, and deliver all those who through fear of death were subject to lifelong bondage" (Hebrews 2:14-15).

Jesus said, after his resurrection:

All authority in heaven and on earth has been given to me (Matthew 28:18).

The crucifixion seems paradoxical, like so much in the experience of our Lord. The natural eye saw a miserable preacher executed for crimes according to due process of law, disgraced before his countrymen and discredited among his followers. In Truth, however, he was winning the critical battle of the spirits for the salvation of mankind. The very moment of his death was the point at which the men who crucified him considered him to be utterly vanquished. It was, in Truth, the moment of his eternal victory!

I do not suppose that we can ever fully realize the significance of Jesus' suffering and death. The more I dwell upon it, the more I am amazed by the eternal consequences of that stupendous event, clothed as it was in the garb of a public execution. The Lord was under attack by a vast alliance of foes, both from within and without. He struggled inwardly with the tempter, whose forces were immeasurable because of the paradoxical nature of the struggle. For him to die was ... to live. For him to live was ... to die! To suffer a human defeat was eternal victory for himself and all who follow him. To win a human victory was to suffer an eternal defeat, for himself and for all mankind.

Outwardly, the assemblage of foes included the nations (gentiles), the peoples (of Israel), the rulers (of Israel), and the kings of the earth (Herod, Pilate, and Caesar), all as listed in the Second Psalm. Thus all men, both Jew and gentile, both small and great, stand over against Jesus in the battle in which the prize of the victor is the authority to govern the earth. It was necessary that Jesus overcome the power of kings and rulers to take the rule unto himself. Also, those kings and rulers must be the representatives of supreme human authority so that Jesus might secure to himself the supreme authority over the world.

Satan offered to give it all to Jesus on the sole condition that Jesus would use it in the service of Satan, as other rulers had done (Matthew 4: 8-9). What Satan offered on that condition, Jesus by force of Spirit took without condition. He stripped the vanquished devil of authority and placed him, and the whole world, in subjugation to himself.

The Scriptures bear consistent witness that our Lord is now ruling all things, both in heaven and on earth. Consider his post-resurrection testimony, that all authority, not only on earth but also in heaven, has been given to him (Matthew 28:18). Consider also the mass of apostolic testimony such as this statement by Paul: "You have come to fullness of life in him, who is the head of all rule and authority" (Colossians 2:10; 1 Peter 3:22). And this from the Letter to the Hebrews: "In putting everything in subjection to himself, he left nothing outside his control" (Hebrews 2:8). Seeing, therefore, that absolutely everything is now under his control and that he is the sole head of all authority, he can be nothing less than the absolute monarch of the universe.

His strategy called for and produced total victory for himself and for his brothers and sisters, and total defeat for the adversary. The immediate consequence was the consummation of the Kingdom of God upon earth, as it is in heaven. This was the answer to the "Lord's Prayer" (Matthew 6:9-13) that Jesus had instructed his disciples to offer on his behalf. The Kingdom has fully and finally come, and all who refuse to acknowledge it stand on the side of the adversary. Only through maintaining men in ignorance of the Kingdom's coming and power can he retain any influence over the destiny of men.

The preachers stand on the side of the defeated Satan whenever they lead their congregations in the recitation of the "Lord's Prayer." How is this so? Because to pray for the Kingdom's yet coming is to teach by implication that it has not yet come.

It also follows that whenever anyone maintains the realization of the Kingdom in consciousness, that person is delivered from the power of Satan through perception of the truth that he has no power. That is why the Gospel of the Kingdom is such wonderful good news to all men. Thanks be unto God that Satan no longer has any power on earth or over any one of us, except only the power that we give him through ignorance of the Truth.

For whoever would save his
life will lose it; and whoever
loses his life for my sake,
he will save it.

Jesus, Luke 9:24

11

THE SALVATION

Salvation depends on the attitude to life. This is the foundation of all Jesus' teachings. Read it again:

Whoever would save his life will lose it (Mark 8:35).

This does not seem to make sense. But it does, for Jesus is only stating the contrast and mutual exclusiveness of the interests of temporal life in this world and eternal life in the Father's glory. Simply put, the meaning is that whoever seeks to save his life, in time, will lose it forever. Then he immediately continues,

… and whoever loses his life for my sake, he will save it (Mark 8:35; Luke 9:24).

This is the other side of Truth. When one willingly loses the temporal life for Jesus' sake, one will save it for life eternal. Salvation therefore applies to life so that when Jesus speaks of salvation, he means the salvation of your life.

The preachers have obscured the real meaning and deep significance of salvation as it applies to life by diverting the emphasis to the soul. It is typical of them to speak of the need of forgiveness of sin and the salvation of one's soul without mentioning the fundamental attitude to life upon which that salvation is wholly dependent. When we hear that the topic is the salvation of the soul, we understand immediately that a purely religious subject is under consideration, and there is no impetus to apply it to life. When one begins to think or to speak of the saving of life, rather than the saving of the soul, different ideas come into play. One is likely to respond by questioning how or in what manner one's life is in jeopardy, since there is no apparent threat or danger. It would then be appropriate to enlighten such an individual about the crucial significance of the attitude to life. I mean that if one is of a mind to save this life, it is utterly lost and in great need of salvation. The perception of safety can be very deceptive. So, when Jesus speaks of salvation, the emphasis is on the salvation of life that is solely dependent on the attitude to life. When Jesus looked out over the world, he saw a great loss — not of souls, but of life! Consider this utterance from John's Gospel:

> *I am the door; if anyone enters by me, he will be saved, and will go in and out and find pasture. The thief comes only to steal and kill and destroy; I came that they may have life, and have it abundantly* (John 10: 9-10).

Jesus is the door. To enter through him is to be saved. But what is saved? Life, for he immediately states that as the motive of his coming to earth. So also in this passage from Luke, he frames his motive for coming in terms of the salvation of life:

> *... for the Son of man came not to destroy men's lives but to save them* (Luke 9:56).

Jesus came into the world, then, to save men's lives. That is the focus of his salvation.

He also spoke of his motive in coming as the saving of the world:

> *If any one hears my sayings and does not keep them, I do not judge him; for I did not come to judge the world, but to save the world* (John 12:47).

> *For God sent the Son into the world, not to condemn the world, but that the world might be saved through him* (John 3:17).

He presents the purpose of his coming in an even more general sense in yet another utterance,

> *The Son of man is come to seek and save that which was lost* (Matthew 18:11; Luke 19:10).

I conclude from these utterances that the world was lost because the women and men of the world were lost. They were lost because their lives were lost, and Jesus had come to seek and to save the lost lives of the women and men of the world.

Now, how is the lostness of the world related to that of the lives of people? Viewing this question in the light of the preceding chapters and the utterances discussed therein, the answer becomes clear. The Father desires children with whom to share his eternal life in glory (Isaiah 43: 6-7; Colossians 3:4; Hebrews 2:10). As children, they will be like him in every way, being complete (perfect), as he is perfect (Matthew 5:48). They will therefore also be possessors of the freedom of the will. It follows that they will not inhabit Glory until they wish to do so. Otherwise, they would not retain the freedom of the will. What, then, are they to inhabit, and how are they to derive and maintain their being until they want to inhabit Glory? The solution to this problem was the creation of the world. The Father called it into existence for the sole purpose of providing an alternative to Glory, until the children freely choose the Glory of the Father. The lives of his children were lost to his Glory, and that is what Jesus came to save. By convincing men and women to hate their lives in the world so as to enter the Father's Glory, he would redeem the world to the fulfillment of its only justifying purpose. That is all that is necessary to fulfill his purpose. He would save the women and men who were lost through the misdirected will to live in the world. This is the sole significance of the salvation of men and women, and of the salvation of the world. The persons who are to become children of God through Christ are now being saved for his Glory through the redirection of the will-to-live. The world is being saved, or redeemed, because it has begun to fulfill the sole purpose of its creation. The lives of the children are being saved for eternity, and the world is responding positively to the rule of God by yielding a harvest. Therefore we know that, precisely as Jesus taught, the Kingdom of God has come on earth. His will is being done on earth, even as it is done in heaven.

From the perspective of eternity — that is, of God and of Christ, the creation enterprise was failing because people were seeking their glory on earth. They were in love with life, so that both the world and the people in it were utterly in vain. There was no one who truly desired from the heart to die so as to go to heaven, and therefore the lives of all were lost. The salvation initiative of Jesus was to save the lives of the lost, and so to save the world itself. He saved it by restoring it to the fulfillment of its sole purpose.

Now from our individual points of view, when once enlightened, we see that we have lost our lives ... lost to the glory of the Father ... and it is our lives that are in need of saving. The world was not producing the desired children before the victory of Jesus at Calvary. No one wanted to leave it to enter the Father's Glory, and so no one qualified for that transition. There was no one who even suspected that was the sole criterion for eternal salvation. Since this was the sole purpose in the creation of the world, the result is that everything and everyone were utterly lost, and were thus the objects of God's salvation. The Father created us for eternal life. We are lost while we spurn that life for the sake of life in this world, but when we receive eternal life, we are "saved."

One enters life eternal, just as into temporal life, through being born into it (John 3:3-7; 1 Peter 1:23). So, one who has been born into life in this world, has been born of water. Then, when such a person has been born anew, of the Spirit, that person enters, or receives, the gift of eternal life, or has been born into eternal life. Here is the relevant utterance:

> *Truly, truly, I say to you, unless one is born of water and the Spirit, he cannot enter the kingdom of God. That which is born of the flesh is flesh, and that which is born of the Spirit is spirit. Do not marvel that I said to you, 'You must be born anew.' The wind blows where it wills, and you hear the sound of it, but you do not know whence it comes or whither it goes; so it is with everyone who is born of the Spirit* (John 3:5-8).

Again I must emphasize that everything — the being saved, the being born again, the entering eternal life — everything depends upon and is coincident with the redirection of the will-to-life of the individual as expressed in this utterance:

> *He who loves his life loses it, and he who hates his life in this world will keep it for eternal life* (John 12:25).

The point when one enters salvation is the same as when one is born again and when one receives eternal life. It is the point of conversion when one decides to believe in Jesus through the redirection of the will in imitation of Christ. It is the moment at which one begins to will to hate temporal life for the sake of eternal life.

Our willful commitment to temporal life is all that separates us from the Father's Glory, for which he created us. This willful commitment is therefore all that separates us from God. It is therefore the essence of sin, and from it all "sins" derive their existence. To repent of our sins is therefore synonymous with the reversal of that commitment, in which one makes a considered, willful decision to hate life in this world for the sake of eternal life in the Glory of the Father. This is nothing less than "conversion." I understand, therefore, that repentance and conversion are synonymous each with the other, and both with being saved, being born again, and receiving eternal life. This is precisely the same point at which we become children of the Father, who had afore been children of the devil, or children of this world. These are but different ways of speaking of precisely the same event, depending upon the focus of one's interest when speaking.

Are you debating your circumstances? Consider this: The Father has done his part. He has done everything he can do to effect your salvation. Jesus the Christ has done his part. He has done everything he came to do to effect your salvation. Throughout all ages, his witnesses have done all they can do; the Word is near you, even before your very eyes and knocking on the door to your heart. Now it is up to you what your fate will be for eternity. You can love your life, and lose it, or you can hate your life, in repentance and in the imitation of Jesus, and save it for life eternal. You, and only you, will decide, and you must do so as a solitary individual. All he requires of you is an act of your volition, that you remove the only thing that prevents your entering Glory as a child of the Father — your desire to remain in this world through love of life. The freedom of the will brings with it a terrible responsibility!

The Father loves you but he will not force you. He cannot, for that would be the coercion of your will and the end of your freedom. You, and you alone, decide. If you do not decide for glory and Eternal Life with the Father, it is because you do not believe the words of Jesus our Lord. It is because you do not believe in Jesus; but if you decide for him, then you believe in him, for you believe his words. You also claim his promise, that whoever believes in him should not perish, but should have eternal life. So it is that your life may be saved, when you enter the salvation of our God and Father, and of our Lord Jesus Christ.

It is all so simple! I do not say it is easy; to the contrary, it is very hard, as Jesus was careful to state. The simplicity is part of the hardness. It would surely be easier to deal with if it were vague or complicated. Then we might justify trusting our destiny to those experts, the clerics, who claim to watch out for our souls. As it is, we have no need of them. If they would testify to the Truth, they could help us and minister to our need of guidance; but, sadly, they only confuse our perceptions of the reality with which we have to deal.

Salvation is an individual matter. One acquires it through an act of the will. It has no relevance to corporate associations. Jesus said nothing about joining a church to be saved. What he did say makes that irrelevant. Sacraments and ordinances of the churches are distractions that deceive us by providing a false sense of security. Fellowship is of great value, but it is fellowship in the hard way that is a help to us, not that fellowship in the easy way that leads us to destruction (Matthew 7:13). Where is that community of believers that is founded in the hatred of life? It is "wherever," for Jesus said,

Wherever two or three are gathered together, in my name, there am I in the midst of them (Matthew 18:20).

Baptism in water does not save one. "Last rites" do not save one. Prayers and offerings for the dead have no value when those dead ones died in the embrace of the love of life. These things benefit only the clergy, for it is their living. There is no salvation by association with earthly institutions. The essential nature of salvation dictates that it associate only with heavenly institutions!

Salvation lacks essential emotional manifestations. True, our emotions are important expressions of our happiness and other states of mind. Therefore we are likely to experience some emotion in association with salvation, but not necessarily. It is not essential that one have "feelings" of any kind to mark the experience. The tendency to expect or demand emotional manifestations is a great error in Christendom. Often, the expression of some emotion leads to the conclusion that one is "saved." When this is not so, it only seals one's condemnation, since one goes on erroneously believing he or she has been saved. If only we would listen to Jesus we would avoid these errors and, coincidentally, find salvation. Listen:

If anyone keeps my word, he will never see death (John 8:51).

He who hears my word and believes him who sent me, has eternal life (John 5:24).

In its essence, trusting Jesus for salvation simply means to trust his Word. He said that anyone who hears, believes, and keeps his Word will be saved ... will receive eternal life. So we believe and accept it because of this simple fact: he said it. After that, our assurance of salvation rests on the same simple fact: he said it! One listens, one is convicted of the truth of the utterances, and one chooses to believe. One makes the decision, a decision to believe Jesus and therefore to believe in Jesus, because the force of his utterances is so powerful and convincing. Then one continues to abide in that decision for the same reason: the force of his words in Truth is so powerful. His words reinforce the decision each time we hear them.

If you abide in my words, you will know the Truth, and the Truth will make you free (John 8:31-32).

There are two powerful deceptions at work in the world, and many remain under condemnation because of the false security that they provide. One is the trust in the corporate body of believers with its professional ministry and mutual affirmations. People believe because of the profound conviction with which the preachers proclaim it. Then they continue in the faith because of the affirmations they receive from the brothers and sisters who occupy the other pews. How can they question their salvation — how can they *not* be saved, when the corporate body of the historic church affirms them in every way? How can anyone doubt, when the highly respected pastor or priest expounds the message so powerfully? Here is a "person of God," deeply committed and often highly trained. One can do nothing but listen with deep assurance to one who speaks with so much enthusiasm.

The second deception springs up where the corporate body is not so historic and where the tradition is not so strong ... where it is only in the beginnings of its formative stages. Then one needs an additional boost to assuage the deep inner doubts. True, the force of the minister continues to be critical, for apart from his persuasiveness, one is not even involved. Still, one needs something more — and this one finds by appeal to the emotions. The Spirit seems surely to be in it because one feels it. One dances "in the Spirit," perhaps, or shouts for joy, or speaks in tongues, or weeps openly and shamelessly, or simply senses a deep feeling of peace and assurance. This experience is surely real, so one goes on with the profound assurance that what the preacher says has happened, has happened: one has been saved! One is even moved to proclaim, "I am certain of it!" "Saved and certain!" becomes the battle cry and the ground of assurance of the faithful. When anyone else cannot subscribe to this cry, that person cannot be saved. If he were "saved," would he not also be "certain?"

I was once a young pastor unhappily involved with just such a denominational experience as this. I think it was in consideration of this position, this "saved and certain" doctrine, that I first began to realize the Truth as Jesus has written it in my heart. It came to me, so forcefully and sensibly that I could find no reason to deny it, that this position is a fundamental contradiction. On the one hand, the church was proclaiming, and truly so, that salvation is by faith alone. On the other hand, the brothers and sisters found it necessary to attest to the "certainty" of it, without ever considering that when "certainty" enters the door, "faith" goes out, for it loses its very ground of being. Faith can exist only when there is no certainty. When you truly have faith in a thing, it is because there is no certainty, no surety, no "knowing," yet you believe and accept anyway, on faith (Hebrews 11:1-40). The biblical focus on faith as the grounds of salvation utterly eliminates any appeal to "certainty" or to "knowing." Therefore, anyone who appeals to certainty is denying faith, and therefore, also denying that salvation that rests upon faith as its ground of being. The young pastor was surprised to find that on acceding to this conviction ... the conviction that there is no certainty of salvation ... the ground of his faith became strong. His assurance became firm and his faith confident, whereas before he was prone to doubt. Deep in his heart he knew that nothing is certain, so that this appeal to certainty caused powerful doubts that undermined his faith.

Abandonment of certainty strengthened his inner assurance, which is the one that counts. The outer assurance was another thing, and that suddenly grew very weak. The brethren called me before them to give an accounting of my beliefs. As I was attempting to do so, a beloved elder brother spoke in my behalf: "Brethren, don't be too strong in your condemnation of Brother Ed. Stop and think. If we are honest with ourselves, we all have to admit that there have been times when we doubted our salvation!"

How I loved him! It took courage to say that. He did it because he loved me, and because he knew in his heart that they were doing wrong. Yet my heart ached for him because he completely misunderstood me. To him, the attestation of certainty was the remedy for doubt, so my refusal to subscribe to "certainty" must mean that doubts plagued my heart. The very opposite was the case. I did not doubt, where once I had, and the reason for the change was my turning away from certainty to the simple prescription of faith in the Word. I believed then, thirty-six years ago, as I still do, that the only valid ground of assurance of faith is faith itself. I fear that dear brother was using his attestations of certainty in vain attempts to smother the raging fires of doubt in his heart ... attempts that were only fueling the flames!

Faith is its own assurance. This faith is not "blind faith." It is rational, sensible, deliberate, and makes its appeal both to the heart and to the mind. How can one's faith be blind, when one perceives oneself walking in the light, as he is in the light? I believe Jesus. I have faith in him. I do this because I have listened to him carefully and considered the significance of his words, so that I am persuaded that he is Truth. He makes sense. His Word alone makes sense of the experience of my life in the world. It answers my questions and gives me a reason to exist and to go on. I am persuaded, like Paul, that he is able to keep secure what I have committed to him, and to deliver it into the Glory of the Father at the last day. The longer I live in his words, listening, questioning, accepting, the more I am persuaded.

Even the indirect references to certainty are convincing. When Jesus gave his prophetic description of the Last Judgment, he sorted all into two groups. He placed one, the sheep, on his right hand, and the other, the goats, on his left hand. Then he addressed those on his right hand:

Come, O blessed of my Father, inherit the kingdom prepared

*for you from the foundation of the world; for I was hungry
and you gave me food, I was thirsty and you gave me drink,
I was a stranger and you welcomed me, I was naked and you
clothed me, I was sick and you visited me, I was in prison
and you came to me* (Matthew 25:34-36).

This wonderful good news surprised the "sheep." They responded:

*Lord, when did we see you hungry and feed you, or thirsty
and give you drink? And when did we see you a stranger and
welcome you, or naked and clothe you? And when did we
see you sick or in prison and visit you?* (Matthew 25:37-39).

The Lord's answer, packed with implications, is as follows:

*Truly, I say to you, as you did it to one of the least of these
my brethren, you did it to me* (Matthew 25:40).

On his other hand are the "goats," whom he next addresses:

*Depart from me, you cursed, into the eternal fire prepared
for the devil and his angels; for I was hungry and you gave
me no food, I was thirsty and you gave me no drink, I was a
stranger and you did not welcome me, naked and you did
not clothe me, sick and in prison and you did not visit me*
(Matthew 25:41-43).

We receive the strong impression that these "goats" are just as
surprised as are the "sheep." They were not expecting this. They
responded with a question that strongly suggests that they had approached this event in the strong conviction, perhaps even the "certain knowledge," that they had done everything necessary to
salvation:

*Lord, when did we see you hungry or thirsty or a stranger or
naked or sick or in prison, and did not minister to you?*
(Matthew 25:44).

I can imagine their terrified, plaintive voices echoing through the
corridors of Eternity, and I hear a strong emphasis as they bear down
on the word "not." They are even more surprised than the sheep. It
is too late ... too late to do anything once one has heard those terrible

words. One can only listen in terror and fear, and then obey the last commandment of the Lord:

Depart from me, you cursed, into the eternal fire prepared for the devil and his angels ... (Matthew 25:41).

This "last commandment" is, of course, in contrast to the "First Commandment,"

You shall love the Lord your God with all your heart and with all your mind and with all your soul and with all your strength (Luke 10: 27).

The First Commandment is not mandatory; we have a choice whether we will obey it. The last, in contrast, will certainly be obeyed by all who receive it ... that is, by all those who do not obey the First. We have then this simple choice: whether to obey the First Commandment, or the last. Those who do not obey the first, will obey the last. Then, he will have taken the freedom of the will away from us. Now, the choice is ours. Then, it will be his. We see the basis of salvation in this portrayal of the Last Judgment.

The difference, the only difference, between the "sheep" and the "goats" is that the sheep ministered to the needs of "one of the least of these my brethren," whereas the "goats" did not. When Jesus said, "one of the least of these my brethren," he implied that this defined the same category that was listening to him then. The "sheep" were his brethren, and they had ministered to one another under the circumstances described, without realizing that they were also ministering to the Lord himself!

Why did they minister to him, and why did the "goats" not minister to him? The sheep are those the world hates, just as Jesus had also prophesied,

If the world hate you, you know that it hated me before it hated you (John 15:18).

Now, the world hates the sheep because they are those who hate their lives in the world. Since the world hates them, it also hates all who minister to them, and identifies them as one. Those who love their lives in the world will not do this. They are afraid, within the context of the love of life, to do anything that might place that life in jeopardy. They will do nothing that will identify them with those whom the world hates. Therefore, only those who hate their lives in the world will minister to those who are poor, hungry, thirsty, sick, or in prison, and whom the world also hates as it hates Jesus. This common attitude to life identifies them both with those whom the world hates, and with the Lord, whom the world likewise hates, because he also hated his life in the world. The "goats" do not identify with the "sheep" due to fear of the world that results from their love of life in the world. One of them might sympathize with the persecuted sheep … yet if one does nothing to minister to them for fear of being identified with them, the sympathy alone does not lead to salvation. They stand condemned because of their love of life that inspires the fear that, in turn, prevents acts of mercy.

Many have appealed to this portrayal of the Last Judgment to assert the belief that good deeds, as such, are the basis of eternal salvation. So they go about giving clothing and food to the poor of the world, and visiting those who are sick at home or in hospitals, and ministering to the convicts in prison. They do these things in the belief that this activity will secure their acceptance on that day … for they will surely be among the sheep!

Not so. While such activity is commendable in that it is the manifestation of mercy and of loving one's neighbor as oneself (The Second Commandment of Jesus), it does not obtain salvation because it is not motivated by the hatred of life. Instead, many do such things out of the love of life. They seek the glory of men, and find that the good reputation they secure enhances life in this world. Therefore they differ from Jesus, who "receives not glory from men." Jesus was therefore careful to counsel his followers, that when doing such acts of charity, they should not let the left hand know what the right hand is doing. Then their alms will be secret, and the Father, who sees them secretly, will reward them openly. Therefore, such acts of charity as Jesus listed in his portrayal of the last judgment are effective for salvation only when coupled with the hatred of life … that is, when they are directed to those whom Jesus called "these my brethren." These are those whose poverty, hunger, illness, or imprisonment results from their testimony to Jesus and to … the hatred of life. These are acts of charity that one does not do in secret. One does in secret only those acts of charity that would, if published, receive the approbation of the world.

The basis of salvation is the simple desire, as that of a child, to go to the Father in glory. This is the love of God. This is the fulfillment of the First and Great Commandment (Matthew 22: 35-38; Mark 12: 28-39). It is the desire to go to him ... now! Therein is the hardness. It is the love of God manifested by the child, Jesus, when he said to Joseph and Mary,

> *Know you not that I must be in my Father's house?* (Luke 2:49).

Jesus also expressed this in his "Parable of the Prodigal Son." There was nothing to prevent the son's acceptance by the Father, nothing to prevent his returning to the Father's house, except the lack of desire to go back. When at last he came to himself, when he finally resolved to return to the Father — now — the Father immediately accepted him. Why, the Father was rushing out to meet him even before he arrived!

This Parable, commonly called that of the "Prodigal Son," (Luke 15: 11-32) is associated with two others, "The Parable of the Lost Coin" (Luke 15: 8-10) and "The Parable of the Lost Sheep" (Luke 15: 3-7). Thus it might more fittingly be called "The Parable of the Lost Son," so that all are parables of the lost. The last lines of the parable are those of the Father, " ... for this your brother ... was lost, and is found" (Luke 15:32).

So we have three "Parables of the Lost," — "The Lost Sheep," "The Lost Coin," and "The Lost Son." Jesus was responding, in all three parables, to the self-righteous charge of the Pharisees and scribes that he "receives sinners and eats with them!" (Luke 15:2). They had noted how the tax collectors and other "sinners" were coming to Jesus (Matthew 9:10; Mark 2: 15-17), and so they judged him by the proverb, "birds of a feather flock together."

The first two, the Parable of the Lost Sheep and the Parable of the Lost Coin, share common elements. Jesus put the Pharisees and scribes in their place by showing that their attitude toward sinners was unreasonable. They would have nothing to do with "sinners," not even to seek to save them from the error of their ways. This attitude was without concern or interest in helping those whom they condemned. The "Lost Sheep" and the "Lost Coin" are saying that the sinners are of equal value with everyone else. They are only lost and therefore in need of finding. If any man of them had a sheep to wander from the fold, he would not only drop everything and rush to find it, but would be so overjoyed when he found and returned it to the fold that he would celebrate. So also with the woman who lost one of many coins. Here the emphasis of Jesus is on value, or worth. That the coin was lost did not in the least detract from its worth, but caused the woman to drop everything else to look for it. She was full of anxiety at the thought of her great loss should it remain lost. She, too, is overjoyed when she finds it and rushes to tell all her friends, saying, "Rejoice with me, for I have found my coin which I have lost!" (Luke 15:9).

It is precisely the same when we consider the lost lives of those whom God intended to become the children of his glory. Jesus, who came, as he said, ". . . to seek and to save that which was lost." is here, in the world, like the man who lost his sheep, or the woman who lost her coin. Like them, he is here seeking the salvation of lost sinners, and rejoicing greatly when he finds even one of them. It is the only reasonable response of love for the lost. Jesus could not turn a cold shoulder to sinners, as did the Pharisees (Matthew 9:11; Mark 2:16; Luke 5:30, 15:2). It was for their salvation that he had come.

The Parable of the Lost Son contains the same concern for the lost and the same rejoicing for the found as do the other parables. There are also differences that must be understood to perceive its full significance. First, the Lost Son is about the relation of a son to his father. It is about a human being, not about coins and sheep, and therefore we realize immediately that it is of a different order. In the parables of the sheep and the coin, the initiative for seeking and finding belongs totally to the man and the woman. The sheep and the coin can do nothing to find themselves. Not so with the lost son! Here the Father has evidently done everything he can do; now all depends on the son. The Father can do nothing but wait, grieving, loving, hoping that the son will yet return to his place in the Father's house. Everything, absolutely everything, now depends on the son because of his possession of free will. Considering the prime significance of the father/son relationship in the Word and the mind of Jesus, we can be certain that whenever he calls attention to it, he is referring to the Father, his only Father, and ours if we will have it so. This is no exception. Here he means to show how the Father in heaven (In the metaphor of the adult Jesus, the Father's house is heaven) is looking down upon all the sinners of earth, the Pharisees and scribes included. The Father grieves for them in their lostness ... lost to the Father, lost to his glory — lost, lost, lost! There is nothing the Father can do that he has not already done. Everything depends wholly upon the resolve of the lost ones. All that he requires of them, absolutely all, is that, like the lost son of the parable, they "come to themselves" and resolve to go to the Father's house with a plea for mercy.

The Word also reveals that the Father is so very merciful! This was another of Jesus' favorite themes ... that the Father is merciful (Luke 6:36). So, in the parable, he not only rushes to give mercy to the sinner, but also kills the fatted calf and calls for a great celebration, for "This my son was lost, and is found."

> *"Blessed are the merciful, for they shall obtain mercy"* (Matthew 5:7).

> *"But love your enemies, and do good, and lend, expecting nothing in return; and your reward will be great, and you will be sons of the Most High; for he is kind to the ungrateful and the selfish. Be merciful, even as your Father is merciful"* (Luke 6:35, 36).

So it is nothing less than the mercy of God that is the ground of our salvation, and those who would go to him must likewise show themselves merciful. Lack of mercy was the great sin and failure of the Pharisees as they looked down on those whom they deemed "sinners." It was Jesus' purpose in these parables to reveal their lack to them in the most forceful way by showing that it was without reason. The Parable of the Lost Son does not stop there. It goes on to glorify the mercy of the Father who now can do nothing but wait in patient sorrow until the child comes home. This is the kernel of the whole matter: the will of the child! In deference to the precious freedom of his will, he cannot be forced. If he is to be saved from his sinful condition, there is but one remedy: he must resolve, out of his free will, to go to the Father. But that also means leaving this world — therefore the hatred of life becomes the key to salvation. The

Prodigal Son received his salvation only after learning to hate his life in the pigsty. That was all that had ever stood in the way.

A second thing that distinguishes the Lost Son from the Lost Sheep and the Lost Coin is that a new actor comes onto the stage — the elder brother (Luke 15:25). Who is this elder brother? We might suppose, from the similarity of his attitude toward his younger brother to that of the Pharisees and scribes toward sinners, that this elder brother represents the Pharisees and scribes. Not so! Although this elder brother seemed to manifest an absence of mercy, he still is the loyal son who has ever pleased his father. "Son, thou art ever with me." Is this spoken by Jesus of the Pharisees? He spoke of them elsewhere, saying:

> *Woe to you, scribes and Pharisees, hypocrites! for you traverse sea and land to make a single proselyte, and when he becomes a proselyte, you make him twice as much a child of hell as yourselves* (Matthew 23:15).

> *You know neither me nor my Father* (John 8:19).

No, the elder brother cannot possibly be the Pharisees and scribes. Who, then?

The elder brother is Jesus. Here he is admitting us to the inner sanctum of his heart. It is his admission to us, the sinners, that he is tempted to despise us, just as the elder brother at first was tempted to despise the prodigal. He has been ever loyal and obedient to the Father. So when the Father expresses such great joy at the return of the lost son, who has never been faithful ... and when he even kills the fatted calf in honor of the occasion, it is almost too much. Yet we know that Jesus responded appropriately to the Father's mild rebuke, for he was here in the world, sent by the Father, to seek and to save the lost. He accepted the Father's rebuke. Had it been consistent with his purpose to have carried the parable farther, we would have seen the elder brother joining the celebration and rejoicing with the Father. But Jesus was not here to magnify himself ... therefore the parable stopped at this point.

The Pharisees generally despised sinners, holding them in contempt, unworthy of association. Jesus is showing us that, while he harshly condemns this unjustifiable, unreasonable attitude, he yet understands it ... for he has been tempted to it.

The Parable of the Lost Son must be interpreted in the light of its context, as a response to the evil attitudes of the Pharisees and scribes. More than that, it reveals the crux of salvation. The context begins, not with Luke 15:1, where the Pharisees and scribes are introduced, but a few verses earlier, with Luke 14:25, where we read:

> *Now great multitudes accompanied him; and he turned and said to them, "If any one comes to me and does not hate his own father and mother and wife and children and brothers and sisters, yes, and even his own life, he cannot be my disciple."*

The context, which begins with the hatred of life, ends with a vivid description of how one man came to hate his life in the pigsty (the world), and how that hatred was the sole condition of his salvation.

In the Parable of the Lost Son, Jesus has set before us the essence of salvation with all its major components. Here we see the elder brother, Jesus. Here we see the Father in heaven, in his house, yearning for the return of that which was lost. Here we see the lost sinner, the prodigal, loving the world and giving himself to it fully, contrary to the will of his Father. Here we see the Father not standing in his way, because he cannot do so without destroying the freedom of the will, without which one cannot qualify for sonship. Here we see the son "coming to himself," suddenly hating his life in the world and longing to be again with the Father in heaven. Here we see the Father rushing to meet him, to embrace and receive him in complete forgiveness. Why? The repentant sinner has ... hated his life in the world so that he might have life eternal. Here we see the love and mercy of God. Here is eternal salvation based on the one essential condition that even the Father in all his love and mercy could not abrogate: the hatred of life in the world. So there is one thing, and one thing only, that stands between the sinner and the Father: the willful love of life in this world.

There is no place in the utterances of Jesus, and therefore no place in Truth, for the atonement theology of Christendom. Jesus was not a sacrificial lamb. This monstrous error has its roots in the Apostolic Era, for there is no doubt that it is a central theme of the Epistles.

The Apostles, in turn, were drawing on prophetic utterances in their largely successful effort to relate Jesus to the traditional religion of the Jews so as to make him theologically palatable. Yet, I do not write off the Apostles. The Epistles also bear witness to the central place that they accorded the hatred of life in their exposition of the faith, so that there can be no doubt about their personal qualifications for salvation. When Paul wrote, "I have a desire to depart and to be with God" and "to die is gain," we know his heart is in the right place, that he is not a lover of life in this world. And I consider that one of the most inspired texts ever recorded is this from the Letter to the Romans: "So then, brethren, we are debtors, not to the flesh, to live according to the flesh, for if you live according to the flesh you will die, but if by the Spirit you put to death the deeds of the body you will live. For all who are led by the Spirit of God are sons of God. For you did not receive the spirit of slavery to fall back into fear, but you have received the spirit of sonship. When we cry, 'Abba! Father!' it is the Spirit himself bearing witness with our spirit that we are children of God, and if children, then heirs, heirs of God and fellow heirs of Christ, provided we suffer with him in order that we may also be glorified with him" (Romans 8:17). Peter, who once denied Jesus three times in fear for his life and out of the love of life, later came eagerly to anticipate his departure from this world: "I think it right, as long as I am in this body, to arouse you by way of reminder, since I know that the putting off of my body will be soon, as our Lord Jesus Christ showed me" (2 Peter 1:13-14). These were men of profound faith and mightily used of God, because they hated their lives in the world for the sake of life eternal. No one has since recorded words of greater inspiration. But the time has come to acknowledge that they, too, were human. They, too, blundered when they taught that the death of Jesus was an atoning sacrifice.

Now, one would never discover their error by listening to them. Within the context of their epistles one finds that much of the text can be brought to bear in support of this doctrine. Apparently they lacked any comprehension of the blunder they were committing. Later, when a similarly blundering ecclesiastical institution elevated their epistles to the same level as that of the utterances of the Lord, their error was installed as a keystone of the faith. But the utterances of Jesus are still with us, and we can still realize the Truth by abiding in them, if only we will. Yet, how hard it is to demote the Apostles, due to the powerful influence of ecclesiastical traditions!

The Parable of the Prodigal Son was elicited by the controversy with the Pharisees and their penchant for looking down their noses at "sinners." It was in an almost identical context that Jesus uttered the final word about sacrifices:

> *And as he sat at table in the house, behold, many tax collectors and sinners came and sat down with Jesus and his disciples. And when the Pharisees saw this, they said to his disciples, "Why does your teacher eat with tax collectors and sinners?" But when he heard it, he said, "Those who are well have no need of a physician, but those who are sick. Go and learn what this means, 'I desire mercy, and not sacrifice.' For I came not to call the righteous, but sinners"* (Matthew 9:10-13; Mark 2:15-17).

When Jesus lifted the phrase, "I desire mercy, and not sacrifice." from the prophet Hosea (Hosea 6:6; Matthew 9:13; 12:7), he elevated it to a principle in Truth that represents the mind of the Father. He does not desire sacrifice. What he does desire is mercy. The first, the Pharisees were all too ready to produce. The second, they did not understand and did not manifest, especially when they were self-righteously condemning the "tax collectors and sinners."

Jesus understood the contradiction between "mercy" and "sacrifice". The sacrifice is totally incompatible with mercy, and so the Father, in his mercy, does not require a sacrifice. So, also, when he looks upon us he desires of us the one thing, mercy, and not sacrifice. The sacrificial atonement makes no sense within the mercy of the Father. The Father does not withhold forgiveness pending the offering of a sacrifice if he is truly merciful. If he desired a sacrifice, he would not have rushed out to meet the returning prodigal. He would have called out through the closed door, "Where is your sacrifice?"

But the Pharisees chose to trust in their sacrifices. It was a grave error, as even they could have readily discerned if only they had heeded the wider message of their prophets:

"For you have no delight in sacrifice; were I to give burnt offering, you would not be pleased. The sacrifice acceptable to God is a broken spirit; a broken and contrite heart, O God, thou wilt not despise" (Psalm 51:16-17).

Therefore the merciful Father could not fail to accept the Prodigal Son, nor can he fail to accept anyone who thus comes to him. Is God a vampire that he must be sated with blood, and that the blood of the innocent one? Where is the mercy in that — where is the justice? Is God a leach, or a tic, or a mosquito, that his is an appetite for blood?

Nevertheless it is profoundly true that "without the shedding of blood, there is no remission of sin" (Hebrews 9:22). This is not because God demands a blood-sacrifice as atonement for sin. It is because the love of life is the essence of sin, so that the shedding of life-blood symbolizes the hatred of life. Therefore it was necessary that Jesus shed his blood to bring the Truth to bear upon us. Had he recoiled from the cross it would have been because he yielded to the love of life in this world. Thus yielding, he would have lost his life — and ours also, who would have lost our guide, our Savior, our example, our pioneer. It was then both right and necessary for him to shed his blood at Calvary. It was the definitive demonstration of the hatred of life.

The cross was not a sacrifice for sin, because it was not a real sacrifice. Jesus "sacrificed" nothing when he gave up his life on earth to enter his glory. The apostle was precisely correct when he said, "It was for the joy set before him that he endured the cross, despising the shame ..." (Hebrews 12:2). He was trading the futility of this age for the Glory of the Father. That is no sacrifice.

Jesus knew that the Father does not desire sacrifice. He saw the result of the dependence of the Pharisees on a sacrificial system and he hated it, for he perceived it as a prime contributor to their self-righteous hypocrisy. He knew that the same result would come from the dependence of his followers on sacrifice (and indeed it has!). He did everything possible to guide us away from the sacrifice and into the True Way, which is the Way of Mercy, and not sacrifice. Would he, then, have offered himself to God as a sacrifice? Never! The Pharisees trusted, for their righteousness, in their sacrificial rituals, and they despised others who were without similar benefit as "sinners." So Jesus said that he came "not to call the righteous, but sinners."

Today, many churchmen trust similarly in a sacrificial system. According to this system, Jesus is the sacrificial lamb by which they secure righteousness. They presume that all who are without benefit of this sacrifice are condemned sinners. Some call it Mass, some Holy Communion, and some The Lord's Supper, but in each case the result is the same: a body of people trusting a sacrifice for their righteousness and referring to others as "sinners." Now, when Jesus returns to receive his disciples unto himself and deliver them to the Father, his purpose will remain unchanged from that of his first visit. He will come, not to call the righteous, but sinners.

Yet Jesus extended the mercy of the Father even to the Pharisees and scribes, once they ceased to trust in their sacrifices and offerings. It was a scribe who came to him and asked, "Which commandment is the first of all?" When Jesus had finished his answer, the scribe responded: "You are right, Teacher; you have truly said that he is one, and there is no other but he; and to love him with all the heart, and with all the understanding and with all the strength, and to love neighbor as oneself, is much more than all whole burnt offerings and sacrifices." Then Jesus replied:

You are not far from the Kingdom of God (Mark 12:34).

He did not tell him that he was in the Kingdom, mind you, for the man still did not acknowledge that his offerings and sacrifices were of absolutely no value. But he was not far, because he had relegated them to a place of lesser value.

If Jesus had been of a mind to offer a sacrifice, he must have offered something of value. Even the Pharisees demanded the best of the flock, a lamb without blemish, for their sacrificial offerings. They were not accustomed to offer the dregs. Only the precious first fruits would do. Yet the testimony of the Gospel is, always, that Jesus counted his life of no value to himself, and therefore of no value to the Father. Surely, if he had been of a mind to offer a sacrifice, he would have offered something of value — his life in Glory. He would not have offered the pittance of life in time. He could have done that very thing — given up his life in Glory — had he but come down from the cross. But then we would not have seen the supposed sacrifice, would we?

What did Jesus say about his crucifixion? This is the key question, since it is the word of the Lord that must finally settle every controversy. I have already appealed to his statement:

I desire mercy and not sacrifice (Matthew 9:13; 12:7).

This should be sufficient to settle the matter without further ado. Still, let us examine the Gospels more thoroughly for other relevant utterances. Having done this already, I have discovered that he never presented any extensive dissertation on the subject of his crucifixion as either atonement, expiation, or sacrifice. While he did make at least one statement (Matthew 26:28; Luke 22:20) that might be applied to bolster the sacrificial interpretation of his passion, it is not necessary to do so. We will refer to this statement presently, but first, consider what he did not say. If the "sacrificial atonement" is as the preachers would have us believe, Jesus would surely have spoken to the issue. First, consider the metaphorical descriptions of himself. If he were the sacrificial lamb, as identified by John the Baptist (John 1:29, 36), would he not have spoken of himself as such? Yet one searches in vain for any reference to himself as the lamb. He did use many other metaphors for himself, and I list some of them here that are from John's Gospel:

1. I am the bread of life (John 6:35).
2. I am the light of the world (John 8:12; 9:5).
3. I am the door (John 10: 7,9).
4. I am the good shepherd (John 10:11,14).
5. I am the resurrection and the life (John 11:25).
6. I am the way, the truth, and the life (John 14:6).
7. I am the true vine (John 15:1).

So ... never did he identify himself as "the lamb." Instead, when he used anything in the pastoral category as a metaphor for himself he selected, not the lamb, but the shepherd. More curious yet, he selected a shepherd who dies for the sheep! Since he definitely had his mind on his unique death at the time of this utterance, it would have been necessary for him to have said, "I am the Lamb of God who sacrifices his life for sinners" if that had been his perception of his death. Without dispute, in the sacrificial system it is the sheep that dies for the man, not the man who dies for the sheep! So, his metaphorical language is precisely the opposite of that demanded by the doctrine of the sacrificial atonement. His followers, not himself, are the sheep; and he, the shepherd, a man, dies for the sheep. Yes, he even dies for the sins of the sheep!

His death for the sins of the sheep was not an atoning sacrifice. It resulted from the simple facts: the sheep (the men) are in bondage to Satan (the wolf, or dragon) through fear of death (Hebrews 2:14-15), and in complete darkness about what to do about it (John 12: 35,46). Their sin is, in its essence, the acquiescence to this fear. There is no way of deliverance from that captivity to Satan and sin unless someone could show the Way and elicit followers. That is what Jesus did.

So all men are lost in sin, lost sheep wandering in the dark night (John 3:19). It is necessary to our salvation that Jesus come into the darkness of this world to lead us out of captivity. He also redeemed us from the bondage of Satan, the fear of death, and blazed a trail into the Glory of the Father that we can follow if only we will. If we lacked sin, we would know the way such that it would have been unnecessary for Jesus to suffer for us. It is true, then, that Jesus died for our sins. Except for our sins,he would not have needed to come and die, and the Father would not have needed to send him. So it was that he came as our Way and Way-shower, our Shepherd, our Pioneer. There is therefore no way by which his death can be correctly interpreted as an atoning sacrifice.

To call the crucifixion a demonstration does no damage to the true picture of the love of God and of Christ. That he suffered vicariously for us is beyond question. But to call it a sacrifice for sin greatly offends the growing capacity of men and women to comprehend the mercy of our loving, heavenly Father.

Jesus not only pictured himself as a shepherd, but as a shepherd who did not flee when he saw the wolf (Rome, Herod) coming (John 10: 11-18). He laid down his life instead, in defense of the sheep. In so doing, he both overcame the wolf, and then went on, by his resurrection, to prove his kingdom and authority over all things. This, of course, includes death, which no other king has conquered.

To recognize the essential nature of sin is to understand why a bloody sin offering can never be effective to wash away or secure the forgiveness of sin. Recall how the Father's sole will and purpose is that we become his glorified children. Recall also how the sole hindrance to this is our contrary quest for an earthly fulfillment. It is therefore our love of life on earth that is the essence of all sin. All transgressions spring from this one root as branches from the central trunk of the tree.

Recall also that repentance is the act of the will, by which we cease to love our lives in the world and begin to love God with all our being. The result is that we begin to hate our lives in this world, in imitation of Jesus. We fix all our hopes on that promised blessed communion with the Father in Glory. This repentance becomes a possibility only through Christ, for only he has brought us the light and shown us the way. Before him, none understood what the Father requires, and that his requirement is not an arbitrary one, but one made essential by the nature of the case. Jesus truly said, therefore,

No one comes to the Father but by me (John 14:6).

Because Jesus was of all men faithful to his earthly calling, the Father has greatly honored him and exalted him above all. It was, as the apostle expressed it, that he might be the first-born among many brothers.

The cross is both a symbol of God's love for us, and of our love for God. It also has a corollary significance — it symbolizes hate. First, it is symbolic of Jesus' hatred of his life in this world. Second, it symbolized our hatred of our earthly lives, provided we follow him by taking up our crosses in imitation of him. The cross of Christ will be of no benefit to us except it become an example that we follow in the Way. Jesus said:

If any man would come after me, let him deny himself, and take up his cross, and follow me; that where I am, there shall my servant be also (Matthew 16:24; Mark 8:34; Luke 9:23; John 12:26).

Another reason the teaching of the cross as sacrifice is heinous is that it leaves us with a false sense of freedom. We think we are free to pursue our lives in the world as usual, as most do, in the mistaken conviction that the blood offering covers all our sins. It also leaves us with a gross misconception of the nature of sin — that it is a multitude of miscellaneous transgressions of varying weights. I mean such acts as lying, cursing, stealing, adultery, murder, hypocrisy, and the like — even including also the consumption of alcoholic beverages (which Jesus did!). But these things are only the light froth resting on the visible surface of the boiling cauldron of sin, which is the love of life in this world.

The sinner is one who wants to go to heaven when he dies, whereas the righteous one truly wants to die, now, and go to heaven! No sacrifice offering can make the conversion from one of these states of mind to the other. But there is the dramatic demonstration of one who suffered for us that elicits — first our admiration, then our depths of appreciation, and finally, our imitation.

Another metaphor, by which Jesus likens himself to bread, is also highly significant for the present discussion. Found in the sixth chapter of John's Gospel, a careful reading is enlightening:

> *Truly, truly, I say to you, he who believes has eternal life. I am the bread of life. Your fathers ate the manna in the wilderness, and they died. This is the bread which comes down from heaven, that a man may eat of it and not die. I am the living bread which came down from heaven; if any one eats of this bread, he will live forever; and the bread which I shall give for the life of the world is my flesh* (John 6:47-51).

At this point, the Jews interrupted, disputing among themselves and saying, "How can this man give us his flesh to eat?" (John 6:52). How, indeed! An uninformed person could well conclude that the speaker had taken leave of his senses. Then Jesus continued:

> *Truly, truly, I say to you, unless you eat the flesh of the Son of Man and drink his blood, you have no life in you; he who eats my flesh and drinks my blood has eternal life, and I shall raise him up at the last day. For my flesh is food indeed, and my blood is drink indeed. He who eats my flesh and drinks*

*my blood abides in me, and I in him. As the living Father
sent me, and I live because of the Father, so he who eats me
will live because of me. This is the bread which came down
from heaven, not such as the fathers ate, and died; he who
eats this bread will live forever* (John 6:53-58).

The discourse becomes even more incredible. Surely the man is
speaking babble! Eternal life is dependent upon drinking his blood
and eating his flesh? How can anyone take him seriously?

He was speaking to a Jewish audience that included his disciples
but consisted predominantly of unfriendly Jews. Jesus was deliberately casting the Truth in such metaphors as would, although true, be
misunderstood. He must have known that this cannibalistic language
would be highly offensive. It also offended the disciples, so that it was
necessary for Jesus afterward to explain the metaphor to them.

*Do you take offense at this? Then what if you were to see the
Son of Man ascending where he was before? It is the spirit
that gives life, the flesh is of no avail. The words that I have
spoken to you are spirit and life* (John 6:61-63).

Here we have it! These are the words that should for all time put
to rest the heretical idea of the literal efficacy of the flesh and blood
of Jesus to cover sin as a sacrifice offering, or as a sacrament or
ordinance, or as anything at all!

"The flesh is of no avail." and, "The flesh profits nothing!" Why
are the priests and preachers deaf to these words? In this brief
statement is the simple truth that ends the giving of sacrifices for all
time. Even the flesh and blood of Jesus profit nothing, for that is
exactly the flesh and blood of which he was speaking. They are only
metaphors, nothing more. To probe this metaphor, which is multi-
layered, we need to enter it in stepwise fashion. First, there is the
bread. This corresponds to an ancient metaphor with which the Jews
were familiar — the manna in the wilderness. As the manna sustained
life, so this bread, the bread of life, also sustains life.

This bread also corresponds to the second metaphor of a series,
his flesh and blood, which he had just set forth in so offensive a
manner. Now the flesh and blood have particular significance, being
the medium through which the Father introduced his words into the

world. That is, it was through the medium of the flesh and blood of Jesus that the Father proclaimed the Word in the world. The flesh, then, corresponds to the logos, being the vehicle that conveyed the Word to the world. Therefore it is the words of Jesus that, manna-like, came down from heaven, and not the actual flesh, which was as earthy as yours or mine. Remember that Jesus always and in every way maintained that his words were solely the words of the Father:

He who sent me is true, and I declare to the world what I have heard from him (John 8:26)

Finally, we read that even the Word is but another metaphor, which corresponds to the life-giving Spirit. To be "filled with the Spirit" is to be full of his words! So, to partake of his flesh and blood, whether symbolically, as in the communion, or literally, as in the sacrament, or mentally, as in the doctrine of sacrificial atonement, will be of no use while our focus is upon the body of Jesus. It is his word:

The flesh profits nothing (John 6:63).

The Spirit, and only the Spirit, gives life eternal. Still, the Word mediates the Spirit, and the flesh and blood of Jesus mediate the Word. So to eat his flesh, to "eat me" as Jesus expressed it, is to eat or receive his words, which is to receive the Spirit, which is to receive life eternal! For his Word is Truth, and it is the Truth that liberates us from the power of sin:

If you continue in word, you are truly my disciples, and you will know the Truth, and the Truth will make you free (John 8:31-32).

The opening verses of John's Gospel present the significance of the metaphors of Jesus; it is the Word, not the flesh, that defines his being. Men know only to invest the flesh with being. Thus it was necessary that the person who is the Logos, or divine Word, become flesh to communicate with men and so it was written:

And the word became flesh and dwelt among us, full of grace and truth ... (John 1:14).

As in these days, when men measure the quality of food in terms of calories, so the Father measures the quality of the life-giving word

in terms of grace and truth. He who eats Christ feasts upon him —
that is, upon his words, and so is strengthened and built up in the
Spirit through grace and truth.

What does it profit if, in the ritual communion feast, one believes
that he participates in the body and blood of Christ, if he does not
heed the words that were mediated by that body and by that blood?
Truly the apostle declared, "such an one eats and drinks damnation
to his soul" (1 Corinthians 11:29).

Such a one brings condemnation upon himself due to hypocrisy,
for by participation in the ritual he makes a public show of participating in the Word (the body and blood) of Christ, which he does not
do. If, on the other hand, one truly eats Christ by ingesting his words,
his subsequent conduct will publish the fact. Where, then, is the need
of a ritual? There is none; and if one reads the Gospels carefully, one
sees that our Lord never authorized the so-called "Holy Communion." It is only another remnant of Christendom's Hebrew
heritage — a perpetuation of the Passover feast. The apostles erroneously propped up and preserved the ritual of sacrifice because
they could not bear to divest every vestige of their Jewishness.
Neither will the priests and preachers abandon it. It serves them too
well by holding the people in bondage to them, like sheep led to a
slaughter. When the child has been taught from infancy to hold the
priest in awe as a man of God in whom is vested the exclusive right
to administer sacraments or ordinances that assure him eternal
blessedness, he is not likely soon to see the priest or pastor in his true
colors. Instead, he continues all his lifetime to serve the minister as
a sort of bond servant. It becomes for them both, then, according to
the Word, that the blind leads the blind and both fall into the pit. The
church has by such practices become the perfect misrepresentation
of Christ to the world. Men continue to betray him — with a kiss!

Jesus deals with the same subject in yet another saying, found in
both Matthew and Mark:

> *The Son of Man came not to be served, but to serve, and to
> give his life a ransom for many* (Matthew 20:28; Mark
> 10:45).

This introduces "the ransom," a subject of lively theological debate
since the first century. If I wanted to avoid it, I could not, for the

passage is without doubt authentic. I have to acknowledge, therefore, that Jesus saw the giving of his life on earth as a ransom. It was a payment for the release of captives.

Now, if Jesus identified his death by crucifixion as a ransom, how can it possibly be a sacrifice? The offender offers a sacrifice, whereas the offended one offers a ransom. One offers a sacrifice to the offended one, whereas one offers a ransom to the offender. One offers a sacrifice for the release of the guilty one, whereas one offers a ransom to secure the release of the innocent one. Or, to put it all together, the evil one offers a sacrifice to the righteous one to deliver the guilty one, but the righteous one offers a ransom to the evil one to deliver the innocent one. So you must recognize that the two ideas are radically contradictory. Both include an offering, but there the similarity stops. Jesus could not have considered his crucifixion to be a sacrifice, because he did consider it to be a ransom, and to think of it as both is to be as irrational as to think of cold as hot, or of up as down. Sacrifice and ransom are veritable opposites!

How is it, then, that he considered it to be a ransom? Well, who was held captive, and by whom? And who extracted his life from him on the cross? The author of the Epistle to the Hebrews answered these questions: "Since therefore the children share in flesh and blood, he himself likewise partook of the same nature, that through death he might destroy him who has the power of death, and deliver all those who through fear of death were subject to lifelong bondage" (Hebrews 2:14-15). Satan, the captor, the arch-prince of this world, bound men and held them captive through fear of death. Jesus gave his life on earth up to Satan, through the agency of Satan's sub-regents, the Romans, who crucified him. Precisely as often happens when the captors go to collect their ransom — Jesus revealed and destroyed Satan by exposing him to the whole world. He stripped from him the capacity anymore to use the fear of death as the binding cord of those who are becoming the children of God.

Looking at the world as Jesus saw it, we see all men held in bondage to Satan, and to sin, through the fear of death. The sole release is for Jesus to enter among them and to deliver them from their shackles (the fear of death). He must do this by showing the impotence of the same through suffering the agonizing death that issued in the resurrection. Thus, through the giving up of his earthly life on the cross, he provided a way of deliverance for all mankind. Therefore the giving of his life followed the pattern of a ransom, and not that of a sacrifice.

Examine the death of Jesus, logically and rationally, and you will see that it matches the definition of a ransom in every respect. It was a payment, by Jesus the righteous one, to Satan the evil one, to redeem the innocent one — himself and all who take refuge in him.

Examine the death of Jesus, and you will see that it contradicts the definition of a sacrifice in every respect. In no sense was it an offering of an evil or guilty one, for if it were, then Jesus must be deemed evil or guilty. In no sense did he offer it to the righteous one, for it was Satan, through his subregents, Caesar, Herod, Pilate, and the Jewish rulers, who extracted his life from him. If it were an offering to the righteous one, then it must be that the righteous one is Satan, and the Father is the evil one! In no sense did it redeem the guilty — unless we call Jesus and those who follow him (in the hatred of life) the guilty ones. So it definitely was not a sacrifice. It was a ransom, and as such it could not have been a sacrifice.

The Apostle Peter understood that it was a ransom. He used the same (ransom) metaphor, but mistakenly combined it with the sacrifice metaphor in the following excerpt from his first letter: "You know that you were ransomed from the futile ways inherited from your fathers, not with perishable things such as silver or gold, but with the precious blood of Christ, like that of a lamb without blemish or spot" (1 Peter 1:18-19).

God, not desiring to punish us but seeking to receive us as dear children, sent his son, Jesus, incognito into the clan that captured us through the captivation of our wills. Jesus came into the world to liberate the captives. More specifically, his task was the liberation of the will. It would have been vain for him to have set us free in a forceful way without first persuading us to repent, or to effect the reversal of the will that had led us into captivity. His purpose was, and is, to persuade us, without any coercion of the will, to a reversal of the will to a righteous state, and to show the Way. He revealed the way to liberation and reconciliation to the Father by a martyrdom that the world can never forget. Thus it was that his life became a ransom for our release.

We should note that, in our day, the ransom often has a slightly different connotation than in biblical times. Now, we hear of a kidnapper who steals a child and holds it captive until the parents deliver a ransom. This follows the pattern of a biblical ransom, but the latter means more than this. Then, one nation overcame and captured another whole nation, as the Jews were held captive in Babylon and Egypt, and as they hold the Palestinians captive in Israel today. It was a kingly matter, in which one ruler captured the peoples of another, and demanded a ransom as the condition of their release. So it was that Jesus entered the world to pay ransom as required for the release of those held captive by the ruler of this world, Satan. When Satan moved to collect his ransom, the life of the Son of God, he was himself overcome and relieved of his kingly power.

Here is yet another set of sayings relevant to the present subject.

> *Now as he was eating, Jesus took bread, and blessed, and broke it, and gave it to the disciples, and said, 'Take, eat; this is my body.' And he took a cup, and when he had given thanks he gave it to them saying, 'Drink of it, all of you; for this is my blood of the covenant which is poured out for many for the forgiveness of sins. I tell you I shall not drink again of this fruit of the vine until that day when I drink it new with you in my Father's kingdom* (Matthew 26:26-29).

> *And as they were eating, he took bread, and blessed, and broke it, and gave it to them and said, 'Take this; this is my body.' And he took a cup, and when he had given thanks he gave it to them, and they all drank of it. And he said to them, 'This is my blood of the covenant, which is poured out for many. Truly I say to you, I shall not drink again of the fruit of the vine until that day when I drink it new in the kingdom of God'* (Mark 14: 22-25).

> *And he said to them, 'I have earnestly desired to eat this passover with you before I suffer; for I tell you I shall not eat it until it is fulfilled in the kingdom of God.' And he took a cup, and when he had given thanks he said, 'Take this, and divide it among yourselves; for I tell you that from now on I shall not drink of the fruit of the vine until the Kingdom of God comes'* (Luke 22: 15-18).

If these passages are familiar, perhaps it is because they are the same ones that I set before you earlier as keys to the mystery of the coming of the Kingdom. You know, then, that I consider these words authentic within the exegetical limitations outlined earlier, and it is obvious that they may relate to sacrifice. I refer in particular to Jesus' statement, "This is my blood of the covenant, which is poured out for many." Now, if one chooses to follow the apostolic interpretation of the crucifixion as sin sacrifice, this statement could be cited in support of that doctrine. It is thus unique among all the recorded utterances of Jesus. Paul, who was not present at the Passover feast, also recorded the statement as having been delivered to him by the Lord (1 Corinthians 11:23-25).

Let us examine these words again. Jesus did not mention a sacrifice, so that we must infer, if we choose to do so, that he had the sacrifice in mind. It is, then, only by inference that such a connection can be made. Now the question is, did Jesus intend such an inference?

Considering the various facets of the statement individually, it becomes immediately evident that the shedding of his blood definitely was for the forgiveness of the sins of all who trust him in Truth for eternal salvation. This is perfectly evident, and I give it wholehearted acceptance. But how is it that the blood of Christ effects the forgiveness of sins? As a sacrificial offering given to satisfy a bloodthirsty deity? No! The blood of Christ secures forgiveness in this manner: The whole world of men was under the condemnation of sin — the sin of loving their lives in this world. They were all in darkness, such that none of them knew any better and there was no repentance for lack of knowledge. Truly, they were an offense to God, who had designed them for his eternal Glory. The Father, in his mercy, was ready to forgive them whenever they would repent and turn from the world. But they did not even know how to repent, for they did not understand the nature of their sin. Thus their salvation required that someone enter the world to enlighten them, teaching them the way by word and example. This is precisely what Jesus did, and the teaching necessarily consisted of oral expression and visual aid, of precept and example. He distributed the words throughout the days of his ministry, but the final example came at the end, at the crucifixion. Without that, he could never have made the full impact of his words felt and known. By that example, he dramatically displayed the essence and the power of his words. Now we can know the full meaning of repentance and be moved to repent. We repent, then, by putting to death the earthly affections within us, and by resetting our affections on things above — on the Father, his Glory, and his eternal life. The Father's loving forgiveness follows quickly; but apart from the crucifixion we could not have understood the sinful significance of the love of life, could not have repented, and so he could not save us.

Even this is not the full story. The significance of the Kingdom is vital to our right understanding of the crucifixion. All that I have already written must be applied at this point, for the rule of the world was the central issue. Jesus could only gain this rule by laying down his life willingly, to enter the glory of the Father. It was by fear of death that Satan held men in bondage and ruled the world (Hebrews 2:14-15). Therefore, it was only by suffering a fearless death that Jesus could overcome him. Unless Jesus overcame Satan and the world of life lovers, he also would be a sinner and there would yet be no forgiveness. Thus it is that the death of Jesus secures the forgiveness of sins, and leads a host of captives (Ephesians 4:8). It is after this manner that his blood becomes effective for our salvation.

Consider now the other portion of Jesus' statement that makes reference to "the blood of the covenant." When Moses received the Law at Mt. Sinai, he wrote all the words of the Lord in a book, "The Book of the Covenant." Then he built an altar and there he read all the words to the people; he also offered sacrifices of oxen, and threw half the blood against the altar and half upon the people and said, "Behold, the blood of the covenant which the Lord has made with you in accordance with all these words." Thus, the first covenant was ratified by blood, and it is this pattern that Jesus had in mind when he spoke of his "blood of the covenant."

He was initiating a new covenant to replace the old; and it is fitting that, according to the pattern of the old, the new also should be ratified by blood. So it is true, precisely as the author of the Epistle to the Hebrews has explained, that without the shedding of blood there is no forgiveness of sins. It was true for the Old Covenant, it is true for the new covenant. Therefore most of the explanation found in the Epistle is correct. But, the new was of necessity different from the old, according to the prophet, and as quoted in the Hebrews: "The days will come, says the Lord, when I will establish a new covenant with the house of Israel and with the house of Judah; not like the covenant that I made with their fathers on the day when I took them by the hand to lead them out of the land of Egypt; for they did not continue in my covenant and so I paid no heed to them, says the Lord. This is the covenant that I will make with the house of Israel after those days, says the Lord:

> *I will put my laws into their minds, and write them on their hearts, and I will be their God, and they shall be my people. And they shall not teach every one his fellow or every one his brother, saying, "Know the Lord," for all shall know me, from the least of them to the greatest. For I will be merciful toward their iniquities, and I will remember their sins no more* (Jeremiah 31:31-34; Hebrews 10:16-17).

Therefore the New is far superior to the Old. According to the Old, ratification was by the blood of a dying sacrifice; but according to the New, ratification is by the blood of a victorious, living demonstration, and not by a sacrifice. Yes, the Old Covenant was ratified by the blood of a sacrifice. How different is the new one! It was ratified by the blood of one who taught that God does not desire a sacrifice.

It is easy to see how the apostles misunderstood the crucifixion. Superficially, it does resemble the blood-letting ritual of the ancients. The high priest was instrumental in the act, and the blood of a pure and innocent victim was poured out near, if not exactly upon, the altar of God. Yes, the suffering part of it might be so interpreted, but not so the actual death. That was no sacrifice by any standard! It diametrically opposed the definition of sacrifice. It was the very furthest thing imaginable from a sacrifice, for it was the means by which he took leave of this futile world (where he never wanted to be) and returned to the Glory of his Father. No reasonable person, aware of the facts, can consider that a sacrifice. I remind you of those apostolic words: "All the suffering of this present age is not worth comparing with the glory which is to be revealed" (Romans 8 :18).

There is nothing about the death of Jesus that truly can be called a sacrifice. The sacrificial animals lost their lives; but about the death of Jesus, everything is gain. Christ himself witnessed that he came into the world from the Father's glory, but he did not wish to come. He came only because the Father sent him (John 8:42). It was important to him that we understand that he did not want to come. Had it been his desire to come to us, from the Father's presence and Glory, he would have been guilty of the cardinal sin, the very sin that he had come to define as such for us — that is, the sin of loving the life in this world. He would have been following the folly of the Prodigal Son. He never loved it, though, and never wanted to enter it. He hated it before its beginning, and he hated it unto the end. Hating it, he refused to save it, and so saved it for life eternal. Because he did, you can too.

What of that other thing of which the preachers love to speak, the sin debt? How heinous an idea is this! That Jesus' suffering, bloodshed, and death were the payment of a sin-debt to God, without which the sin could not be forgiven. As for our being indebted to God, it is true. We owe everything to him. It is true also that our transgression of his will subjects us to a just penalty. It is true also that the debt is so great that none of us can pay it. Apart from this, the preachers have greatly confused Christendom, and Christendom has greatly confused the world, by teaching that the crucifixion was both a sacrifice and a debt payment, whereas anyone can readily see how it cannot be both. The two are a contradiction. A sacrifice was offered freely, a gift to God, so that if it was payment of a debt, it cannot be a sacrifice. Now I have already shown that it was not a sacrifice. Neither is it a payment of our debt to God, and this I trust you will understand also. All Jesus' teachings rest on the assumption that we can never pay our debt to God. It will be settled, either by condemnation or forgiveness, but never by payment. God's estate, unlike ours, is infinite. He never suffers loss through what he has entrusted to us, nor can we give to him anything that would add to him whose gain is infinite. There is one exception: the gift of our very selves as dear children to our God and Father. This, however, is not payment of a debt. If it were, each one could settle his account with God through the rendering of his person. No, for it is true, as the preachers usually proclaim, that the debt is so great that none can pay it.

Jesus mentioned a debt to God on at least three occasions. The first mention is in the parable of the Kingdom often called "The Parable of the Unmerciful Servant" (Matthew 18:23-35). Here, he likens God to a king who wished to settle accounts with his servants. One came before him who owed ten thousand talents — so great a sum that he could never pay. The king ordered him and his family to be sold into bondage toward payment. But the man's pleas were so pitiful that he was forgiven the debt outright, without any payment. Now, the servant did not share in the merciful spirit of the king. He went out and seized one of his fellow servants, who owed him a mere hundred denarii, and demanded immediate payment. Like himself, the fellow servant could not pay, and so fell down and pled for mercy, just as he had pled before the king. But he hardened his heart against his fellow servant and dealt with him unmercifully, casting him into debtor's prison. This enraged the king. He summoned the man and said to him, "You wicked servant! I forgave you all that debt because you besought me; and should not you have had mercy on your fellow servant, as I had mercy on you?" And in anger the king delivered him to the jailers. Then Jesus stated the lesson of the parable:

> *So also my heavenly Father will do to every one of you, if you do not forgive your brother from your heart* (Matthew 18:35).

Keeping this first teaching in mind, next consider the second one, from Luke's Gospel (Luke 7:37-48). Jesus had accepted an invitation to dine in the house of Simon the Pharisee. While there, a sinful woman entered bearing an alabaster flask of ointment. She then proceeded to stand behind him, at his feet, weeping. The tears fell upon his feet, wetting them, and the sobbing woman wiped them with her hair, kissed them, and anointed them with the ointment. Seeing that Simon was taking the typical Pharisaical attitude toward the woman, he said to him:

> *A certain creditor had two debtors; one owed five hundred denarii, and the other fifty. When they could not pay, he forgave them both. Now which of them will love him more?* (Luke 7:41, 42).

Simon answered, "The one, I suppose, to whom he forgave more."

Jesus replied, "You have judged correctly" (Luke 7:43).

Turning then to the woman, he continued speaking to Simon:

See this woman? I entered your house; you gave me no water for my feet, but she has wet them with tears and wiped them with her hair. You gave me no kiss, but she has not ceased to kiss my feet. You did not anoint my head with oil, but she has anointed my feet with ointment. Therefore I tell you, her sins, which are many, are forgiven, for she loved much; but he who is forgiven little, loves little (Luke 7:44-47).

Then he addressed the woman:

Your sins are forgiven. Your faith has saved you, go in peace (Luke 7:48, 50)

Third, once in teaching the disciples to pray, he said,

Pray then like this ... forgive us our debts, as we also have forgiven our debtors (Matthew 6:12).

There is a common element in all three of these teachings, which is that, before God, we can settle our debts amicably only by forgiveness. Neither we, nor anyone acting on our behalf, can settle them by payment. If Jesus had understood his crucifixion as in any sense a debt payment, it is in these passages that he would have incorporated such a doctrine. But no. Instead, the Word always presumes that one never settles such a debt by payment. Always it is settled by forgiveness, and only by forgiveness ... or by punishment. Furthermore, it is evident that the forgiveness is conditional on two things. The woman was forgiven because of her great love for God, and the forgiveness was contingent on that love. This was, and is, the primary factor — the love for God. There is no forgiveness apart from love for him. What is this love for God? It is the heart's desire to be united with the Father, in his presence, in Glory, unalloyed with any earthly affection. What can this mean ... but the hatred of one's life on earth? The woman was forgiven because she loved much; and because her sins were many, she was forgiven much. Because she was forgiven much, she loved all the more, so that these two things, love and forgiveness, work together for a mutual magnification of love that began when God the Father loved the woman, while she was yet a sinner, and sent Jesus to minister to her great need.

The second condition of God's forgiveness concerns our response to him after realizing that our own sins are forgiven. We must be imitators of his mercy if we are to receive mercy, for if we do not forgive others their debts, neither are our debts forgiven. Herein is the mercy of God manifest in the world — when his children forgive the debts of others, even as God has forgiven them. Therefore also Jesus commands us saying:

Lend, expecting nothing in return, and give to him that asks of you (Luke 6:30, 35).

In a similar way he pronounced a blessing on the merciful, those who forgive, saying:

Blessed are the merciful, for they shall obtain mercy (Matthew 5:7).

Why does anyone persist in exacting every cent from debtors?

Clearly, it is because of the love of life in this world, which results in the placing of great value on money for what it can do for us here and now. How can anyone forgive a large debt, but for the love of God and the hatred of life? All things then condense to one fundamental disposition of the individual will. You surely perceive by now why it is true, as Jesus said:

He who loves his life loses it, but he who hates his life in this world shall keep it for life eternal (John 12:25).

Perhaps now you also can appreciate the words of the Father first spoken through the prophet, Hosea:

I desire mercy, and not sacrifice (Hosea 6:6).

It is a crass and pagan conception of God that knows him as one who can be satisfied with the blood of the innocent one; or as one who must exact full payment of every debt, though it comes, unjustly, from one who has no debt (that is, from Jesus). It is a paltry grace that comes only to those whose debts are paid, by themselves or by someone else! Begone, you god of dark Christendom, you without mercy, who thirsts for blood, who demands full payment of every debt!

Enter by the narrow gate; for the gate is wide and the way is easy that leads to destruction, and those who enter by it are many. For the gate is narrow and the way is hard, that leads to life, and those who find it are few.

Jesus, Matthew 7:13-14

12
THE WAY

His Way is hard and narrow. No reasonable person seeks it as the goal of life. The other way, the way of the world, can be marvelously easy, and multitudes travel it in style. It is much, much more attractive, provided we refrain from considering its destination. But what sensible person chooses a way as an end? Only a tourist; but along the pathway of life we do not have the luxury of traveling for the sake of sightseeing, because there is no going back. Every day takes us another day's journey along the way, in one direction or another, and we cannot retrace a single step of it. A prudent person will therefore choose his or her way in life based on the destination, not the pleasantries of the journey. The destination, not the journey, should be our prime concern.

There are only two ways to go — the easy and the hard. Jesus has shown the significance of each. He, who was from the beginning invested with glorious eternal life, displayed his great love for us by condescending to experience the hard way. He jeopardized his status as Son of God to guide us to a proper destination. He is the living personification of the Way, and it is as such that he said:

I am the way (John 14:6).

Anyone who would follow Jesus to the Glory of the Father must traverse this world by the Way of Christ. His way is the hard way, but God is its destination. It is the only way to that destination. Remember his word:

No one comes to the Father but by me (John 14:6).

He was not optimistic about the numbers who would be influenced by him. He said that those who would follow are few, while many would traverse the broad and easy way. This is true, although the easy way leads to death and destruction, and the hard one to eternal life with the Father in heaven. Seeing it thusly puts the matter in a new perspective. Jesus does not urge us to make a *selfless* commitment to the service of God and others. Instead, he makes his appeal to our highest self-interest. A temporary inconvenience to the self is nothing when compared with the glorious destination. Christendom has misinterpreted self-interest. This error must be addressed before we can understand the True Way of life. I am about to make some statements that may be offensive to you because of the influence of this type of "Christendom thinking." Please do not turn away. If you continue, you should realize that we have all been mislead.

Jesus condensed all the commandments of the Mosaic code to only two: the first, the command to love God; and the second, to love neighbor. Now focus on the second and examine it in some detail. How are we to love our neighbor? Listen:

> ... *you shall love your neighbor as yourself* (Matthew 19:19; 22:39; Mark 12:31).

Do you see the clear implication? One must measure the love of neighbor against the love of self. If one does not begin by loving oneself, there is no basis, in this commandment, for loving one's neighbor. So, Jesus accepted self-love as a given entity, a base from which to reach out in love to others. He repeatedly displayed this acceptance by his assurances of a rewarding destiny for those who follow the hard Way. It is the Way that leads to eternal, abundant life for oneself, which is motive enough for following it. He knew that every person wishes for himself or herself the blessing of life and all good things that pertain to life. An inherent life-wish motivates us at the deepest level, and it is to that most fundamental of motivations that Jesus makes his appeal. Consider his instruction on treasure:

> *Do not lay up for yourselves treasures on earth, where moth and rust consume and where thieves break in and steal, but lay up for yourselves treasures in heaven, were neither moth nor rust consumes and where thieves do not break in and*

steal. For where your treasure is, there will your heart be also (Matthew 6:19-21).

He seems at first to be prohibiting the accumulation of treasure, but then we see that is not so. To the contrary, he urges upon us the accumulation, for ourselves, of the true treasure that cannot be consumed or stolen. It is the most secure and precious treasure imaginable, which is in heaven. So he is definitely not saying, "Do not lay up treasure for yourselves." Instead, he is instructing us to be discretionary in our choice of treasures. He would have us seek only the true treasure, rich above any earthly evaluation and absolutely secure! Go, then, for the gold!

He continued this theme through the Sermon on the Mount, where he instructs us not to be anxious about our lives — about what we shall eat or drink, nor about clothing — what we shall put on (Matthew 6:25, 31). Again, he did not base this prohibition on lack of concern for oneself. It is only that he would have us put first things first. He wants us also to inhabit Glory, and he wants this with the same fervor with which he wants it for himself. Thus he loved his neighbor as himself by coming to earth for us. Yet he never failed to maintain his self-interest. He never failed to want and to will one thing above all others for himself: that he might return to the Father. At the earliest possible moment, as soon as he had finished his work in the world by the sowing of the Word, he turned to the Father in prayer saying:

And now I am coming to you (John 17:13).

… now, Father, glorify me in your own presence with the glory which I had with you before the world was made (John 17:5).

The writer of the Hebrews expressed it well when he wrote

… it was for the joy set before him that he endured the cross (Hebrews 12:2).

Yes! Jesus was eager to return to the Father because it was in his highest and best self-interest. It was also necessary that he show the way for us to follow by manifestly hating his life in this world. So it is that he is the supreme example of loving one's neighbor as oneself.

Now consider once more the Parable of the Prodigal Son. Here Jesus presents a person who, in his willfulness, once thought it was in his interest that he claim his inheritance and go out into the world. This he did, only to lose everything. He finally "came to himself." Then, from the dregs of his miserable existence as a swineherd he resolved, "I will return to my Father's house and seek to become one of his hired servants, for they have bread enough and to spare, while here I perish with hunger." Thus it was by a resolve born of prudent self-interest that the young man found escape from his folly. Jesus recommends him to us as an example to follow if we are to escape the swineherd conditions of this life and enter the Father's house in glory.

He has not commanded us to love our neighbor instead of ourselves. He has not commanded us to love our neighbor more than ourselves. No, the command is plain and simple:

Love your neighbor as yourself (Matthew 19:19; 22:39; Mark 12:31).

He did not command these things, I suspect, for the simplest of reasons: they are impossible. That is, it is impossible to love your neighbor more than yourself, and it is impossible to love your neighbor instead of yourself. Therefore Jesus did not concern himself with these two impossible applications of love. He concerned himself only with what is possible — that we may love our neighbors less than we love ourselves, or that we may love them not at all while loving only ourselves, or that we may love them selectively. These are the possibilities that he abhors, the possibilities that exalt the self above others, including God the Father. He commands the one other possibility as the only acceptable characteristic of the Way that leads to the Father — that we love our neighbors exactly as we love ourselves, and that we love them thus indiscriminately.

I do not mean only that we are not to discriminate racially, culturally, or socially. Jesus intends us to go beyond all that. He selected as the object of love all who can be included in the word "neighbor." That means absolutely everyone within the sphere of our experience. To illustrate the radical extremity of this inclusiveness, he gave another much more specific commandment in the Sermon on the Mount:

Love your enemies (Matthew 5:44; Luke 6:27, 35).

How is this possible? Is not this a contradiction — to love oneself, and to love the hostile enemy who is intent on doing harm to that very self? Christendom has struggled vainly with this question because Christians have not correctly defined genuine self-interest. Lack of progress is evident in that the so-called Christian nations are as adept as any others at hating and destroying their enemies. They will never progress while they define self-interest in terms of temporal considerations, contradicting the Word of Christ, as they seem destined to do.

The highest self-interest, the only true and genuine self-interest, begins with the acceptance of an eternal set of values. When one has established such values, consistent with the doctrine of Christ, the command to love one's enemies and all similar injunctions become not only reasonable and practicable, but the essence of one's being.

To illustrate, let us yet again visit our familiar friend, the Prodigal Son, as described in the parable of Jesus:

> *"There was a man who had two sons; and the younger of them said to his father, 'Father, give me the share of property that falls to me.' And he divided his living between them. Not many days later, the younger son gathered all he had and took his journey into a far country, and there he squandered his property in loose living. And when he had spent everything, a great famine arose in that country, and he began to be in want. So he went and joined himself to one of the citizens of that country, who sent him into his fields to feed swine. And he would gladly have fed on the pods that the swine ate; and no one gave him anything. But when he came to himself he said, 'How many of my father's hired servants have bread enough and to spare, but I perish here with hunger! I will arise and go to my father, and I will say to him, 'Father, I have sinned against heaven and before you; I am no longer worthy to be called your son; treat me as one of your hired servants.' And he arose and came to his father. But while he was yet at a distance, his father saw him and had compassion, and ran and embraced him and kissed him. And the son said to him, 'Father, I have sinned against*

*heaven and before you; I am no longer worthy to be called
your son.' But the father said to his servants, 'Bring quickly
the best robe, and put it on him; and put a ring on his hand,
and shoes on his feet; and bring the fatted calf and kill it,
and let us eat and make merry; for this my son was dead,
and is alive again; he was lost, and is found* (Luke 15:11-32)

The Prodigal was impatient to get out into the world and to the
business of living. This impatience suggests that his values were of a
temporal nature. Now, the father in this Parable is the Father in
Heaven, where all the values are eternal ones. Yet he did not coerce
the will of the Prodigal, but granted all his wishes. He watched, sadly
no doubt, as the Prodigal strutted proudly out into the world. There
he proceeded to make a life for himself, but it was not such as he had
envisioned. He soon found himself forced to dwell in very unsatisfac-
tory circumstances. Then he became wise and looked back to his
father's house, to the eternal and eternally secure treasures he had
left behind, and realized simultaneously what a fool he had been. It
was also at this point that he learned to hate his life in the world.
Surveying his circumstances, he suddenly saw no hope, no future, and
nothing of value or in any way satisfying to his inner self. Suddenly,
life in his father's house appeared glorious. He yearned for it from
the depths of his heart. Yet he lacked any claim on it, having forsaken
it for the life of the world. Then, in the depths of his despair, a happy
thought struck him: *I will return and cast myself on Father's mercy.
Perhaps he will permit me to become a hired servant, for they have
everything they need.* Of course it happened — but see how it happened! The Father did not accept him until he had learned to hate
his life in the world, and until he realized what was truly in his best
interest.

Few are as wise as this Prodigal. He could have continued to plan
and scheme and try, again and again, to find satisfaction in the world.
This is exactly what most people are doing and have always done. He
hated it instead, and on that basis he returned to his Father, who
received him with great rejoicing. He radically revised his values,
which freed him to aspire to lasting treasures.

Now, let us augment the parable a little. Suppose that while
working as a swineherd, the Prodigal encountered an enemy intent

on displacing him from his job. Had the Prodigal maintained his earlier commitment to temporal values, he would have responded with hostility. After the radical reversal of his values, he would have found that such an enemy was no threat to him. So, he would have responded without resistance, free to love even this hostile opponent because he no longer valued what the enemy sought. Having deserted the pigsty and found acceptance in his father's house, he would have reached out with compassion to his enemy.

Now, consider the example of Jesus, how he could love his enemies. You will find that it was for the reason presented in the prior discussion of the Prodigal. He did not value what the enemy sought — not even his very life. Therefore those who would be his enemies were absolutely no threat. Since he loves all his neighbors as himself, including his enemies, he can, in the act of suffering death at their hands, plead with the Father for them:

Father, forgive them, for they know not what they do (Luke 23:34).

And what does he want for them — for them all? Nothing less than what he wants for himself — a place in the Father's house! It was to realize that very want that he came and suffered so much.

In summary, the foundation of the Way of Christ includes the acceptance of self and self-love, equal love for one's neighbors, and the eternal treasures as the exclusive value set. This all begins with becoming a child of the Father and learning to hate the life in this world, exactly as the Prodigal hated his life in the pigsty, and as Jesus hated his life in Israel. There can be no valid considerations of Christlike conduct by anyone who has not resolved these primary matters of self-acceptance and self-love. The same applies to anyone who has not resolved the contradictory temporal and eternal values by renouncing the former and adopting the latter.

This is not all. There is one other matter even more important than these that revolves around, not the second, but the First and Great Commandment:

You shall love the Lord your God with all your heart, and with all your soul, and with all your mind, and with all your strength (Mark 12:30).

This love is much more than you might imagine. Religious rituals can never satisfy it. To realize the depths of its meaning, look again at the Prodigal Son: he wanted one thing exclusively — deliverance from his miserable life in this world (the pigsty) through restoration to his Father's house. He wanted to be close to the Father, in fellowship with the Father, serving the Father. The moment he came to that radical resolve, that very moment, he renewed his love for the Father. For that is the significance of genuine love. It is the desire to reach out and unite with its object, as the small magnet attaches to the larger steel bar and clings to it tenaciously. When this yearning for God possesses the mind, the heart, the soul, and the body, expelling all contrary desires — then it is that one has obeyed the First and Great Commandment.

You see, then, how the love of God is contrary to the love of life in this world. One cannot simultaneously retain that life ... and go also, like the Prodigal Son, to be with the Father. You should now realize also how this love imposes a radical effect upon the conduct of the followers of Christ. Without it, there is no possibility of doing the will of God in any circumstance. There is nothing to be gained by attempting to do so, seeing that it is this love that *is* the will of God.

These, then, are the things that must be realized before there can be any profitable consideration of the Way of Christ:

(1) The love of the Father, with one's whole being;

(2) The love of oneself that reaches out to all;

(3) The radical rejection of the temporal treasures for the eternal ones, consistent with the very highest love of the self.

Now we can go on to the investigation of some particular commandments that Jesus gave to guide our conduct in the Way.

THE LAW

Pauline antinomianism is contrary to Jesus. Jesus' rendering of the First and Second commandments as the summation of the Law and the Prophets should set this matter to rest — yet he did not stop with that. He went on to address the matter more specifically in the following utterance:

> *Do not think that I have come to abolish the law and the prophets; I have come not to abolish them but to fulfill them. For truly, I say to you, till heaven and earth pass away, not an iota, not a dot, will pass from the law until all is accomplished. Whoever then relaxes one of the least of these commandments and teaches men so, shall be called least in the kingdom of heaven; but he who does them and teaches them shall be called great in the kingdom of heaven. For I tell you, unless your righteousness exceeds that of the scribes and Pharisees, you will never enter the kingdom of heaven* (Matthew 5:17-20).

Let us first acknowledge that he is addressing a condition that must prevail until "heaven and earth pass away." It is therefore a permanent condition. It continues to this day, totally untouched by later events, including the crucifixion and apostolic interpretations of Jesus and his work. Jesus must have stated this repeatedly to counter the later doctrines of the church about his person and work. Luke's rendition of such a saying is as follows:

> *But it is easier for heaven and earth to pass away, than for one dot of the law to become void* (Luke 16:17).

These statements leave absolutely no room for the end of the dispensation of law while the universe remains. Therefore the Law and the Prophets remain in force to this day.

Consider next how it is that, for Jesus, the Law is the basis of the righteousness of the Kingdom. Only by adherence to the law does one's righteousness come to exceed that of the Pharisees and scribes. Yes, it is very simple: one enters the kingdom, if one does so, solely by a righteousness that is the result of keeping the law. Jesus then proceeds, in the Sermon on the Mount (from now on called herein simply "The Sermon") to present six antithesis in which he modifies the law as delivered through the Old Testament. He first said that whoever relaxes one of the least of these commandments, and teaches men so, shall be called least in the Kingdom of Heaven (Matthew 5:19). Then he proceeded to take certain key legal

precepts of the Mosaic code and do the very opposite: to make them
much more stringent. He knew beforehand that there would be many
who would not only seek to relax the law, but even to do away with
it entirely. This is the tendency in Evangelical Christianity. Therefore
he did the opposite by giving six specific illustrations (antitheses) of
the nature of the modifications. In these, he deliberately rendered
the law more rigorous. His warning to those who would relax the law
applies especially to his modifications. The first antithesis is:

> *You have heard that it was said to the men of old, "You shall
> not kill; and whoever kills shall be liable to judgment." But
> I say to you that every one who is angry with his brother shall
> be liable to judgment; whoever insults his brother shall be
> liable to the council, and whoever says, "You fool!" shall be
> liable to the hell of fire* (Matthew 5:21-22).

The second antithesis is:

> *You have heard that it was said, "You shall not commit
> adultery." But I say to you that everyone who looks at a
> woman lustfully has already committed adultery with her in
> his heart. If your right eye causes you to sin, pluck it out and
> throw it away; it is better that you lose one of your members
> than that your whole body be thrown into hell* (Matthew
> 5:27-29).

The third antithesis is:

> *It was also said, "Whoever divorces his wife, let him give her
> a certificate of divorce." But I say to you that everyone who
> divorces his wife, except on the ground of unchastity, makes
> her an adulteress; and whoever marries a divorced woman
> commits adultery* (Matthew 5:31-32).

The fourth antithesis is:

> *Again you have heard that it was said to the men of old, "You
> shall not swear falsely, but shall perform to the Lord what
> you have sworn." But I say to you, Do not swear at all, either
> by heaven, for it is the throne of God, or by the earth, for it
> is his footstool, or by Jerusalem for it is the city of the great
> King. And do not swear by your head, for you cannot make*

one hair white or black. Let what you say be simply "Yes" or "No"; anything more than this comes from evil (Matthew 5:33-37).

The fifth antithesis is:

You have heard that it was said, "An eye for an eye and a tooth for a tooth." But I say to you, Do not resist one who is evil. But if any one strikes you on the right cheek, turn to him the other also; and if anyone would sue you and take your coat, let him have your cloak as well; and if any one forces you to go one mile, go with him two miles. Give to him who begs from you, and do not refuse him who would borrow from you (Matthew 5:38-42).

The sixth and last antithesis is:

You have heard that it was said, "You shall love your neighbor and hate your enemy." But I say to you, Love your enemies and pray for those who persecute you, so that you may be sons of your Father who is in heaven; for he makes his sun rise on the evil and the good, and sends rain on the just and on the unjust. For if you love those who love you, what reward have you? Do not even the tax collectors do the same? And if you salute only your brethren, what more are you doing than others? Do not even the gentiles do the same? You, therefore, must be perfect, as your heavenly Father is perfect (Matthew 5:43-48).

Jesus listed these six in detail so that you can see immediately how it is that he made the law much more demanding. It is so demanding that most people have despaired of ever keeping it. Churchmen have developed various theories to preserve a place for our lack of compliance with the law, while explaining why Jesus made it so rigid. There are a few exceptions (Tolstoy, for example), but nearly all have concluded that the law of Christ is totally impractical.* They view it as impossible to apply to life in this world. One writer advances the idea that Jesus gave us these commandments to drive us to despair.

---

* For a good summary, see Clarence Bowman, *The Sermon on the Mount—The Modern Quest for Its Meaning* (Atlanta: Mercer University Press, 1985).

Then we might forsake all efforts to become righteous and rely wholly on the grace of God. Another proposes an "Interim Ethic." This was valid only for the early disciples during the brief period that they suppose Jesus expected before the transformation of the world. Then, so it goes, the transformation did not occur, so the commandments can have no further validity. Yet others see them as defining the perfection that is our goal, while we continue to fail and rely on the grace of God for forgiveness. Then there are those who think Jesus' commandments are the law of the Kingdom that, so they go on to say, has not yet come. Therefore his commandments are not authoritative for this age.

Men designed all these ideas to relieve us of obedience to the law as expressed in the words of Jesus. It was precisely to counter these evasions that Jesus closed the Sermon with these words:

> *Every one then who hears these words of mine and does them will be like a wise man who built his house upon the rock; and the rain fell, and the floods came, and the winds blew and beat upon that house, but it did not fall, because it had been founded on the rock. And every one who hears these words of mine and does not do them will be like a foolish man who built his house upon the sand; and the rain fell, and the floods came, and the winds blew and beat against that house, and it fell; and great was the fall of it* (Matthew 7:24-27).

That serious and learned men can read such words yet continue to excuse themselves, and us, from taking them seriously has always amazed me. I realize now that their positions are logical developments of their mistaken ideas of the reality with which we have to deal. For one thing, the belief that Jesus concerns himself with the maintenance of the world has possessed them. From this they understand how his commandments do not make sense for the world at large. Why, if a whole nation responded to its enemies by loving them, they would quickly overcome it and evil would triumph!

They are right in this one thing: Jesus does not expect or intend that the world at large apply his commandments to the affairs of this life. He knows that the world is going to continue without any consideration of the application of his teaching to world affairs. But he does expect his followers, the relative few who are not of this world, to take him seriously and to apply his commandments now.

How is this possible? What distinguishes the follower from anyone else such that one can take Jesus seriously whereas the other cannot? The answer to this question is the very thing that I have all along been explaining: the hatred of life. When seen in the exercise of the hatred of life and its ancillary commitment to Eternity, the commandments of Jesus lose their problematical character and become the normal response to every circumstance. It is only in the application of this principle that they become sensible. Also, Jesus never expected anyone to take him seriously apart from the hatred of life. Those who do are the only persons who are acceptable children of God, and the only ones who have any hope of eternal life in glory. Let me remind you of his clear words again:

> *He who loves his life loses it; but he who hates his life in this world will keep it for life eternal* (John 12:25).

Now examine the above antitheses while keeping this utterance in mind, and you will see what I mean. In the first, he stiffens the command, "Thou shalt not kill," by the modification, "Thou shalt not be angry." It is easy to relate hatred of life to the original version. Suppose you are a policeman who answers a call to investigate someone seen carrying a pistol. You arrive, see the person with gun in hand, and do your duty. Drawing your weapon, you call out to the suspect to drop his. Instead of dropping it, he raises it in your direction. How are you to respond? If you do not shoot first, you may be killed — and you have only an instant for decision. You shoot. Why? Because you love your life. This compels you to protect it, which here means killing someone else. You have then transgressed the commandment that forbids killing, and the reason is plain — you love your life. Your response would surely be different if you hated your life. Then, your life or death is not a primary concern. Of course, if you truly commit yourself to the hatred of life, as taught and exemplified by Jesus, you would not likely be in this situation. But assuming you were, you can see how your attitude to life would dictate your actions.

Now what of the prohibition of anger? Jesus applied this to the attitude to a brother, for the Jews had always considered the prohibition of killing to apply only to a brother. They have never had compunctions about killing their enemies, any more so than any other tribe. Therefore, so as not to confuse the issue at this point in the Sermon, he applied the prohibition of anger specifically to a brother. To see the relevance of the hatred of life, we must first ask, what are the usual causes of anger?

We list a few: oral and physical abuse, lies, disrespect, theft and destruction of property— these are adequate for my immediate purpose. All are causes of anger only because we perceive them to threaten something of value to this life — for example, our bodies, our possessions, our reputations, and those we love. But, if these things have lost their value because we have replaced them with heavenly treasure, threats to them will no more stimulate anger!

In the second antithesis, Jesus stiffens the prohibition of the act of adultery by the prohibition of the very thought of adultery. This is consistent with the doctrine, "as a man thinks in his heart, so is he." So for a man to lust after a woman, or vice versa, is not, in the assessment of guilt, to be distinguished from the very act. Now, why does a person commit adultery? Is it not because he or she has a commitment to this life — to a kind of enjoyment that it affords, if only he or she will bend social conventions? A person who truly hates life in this world will therefore not yield to temptations to commit actions harmful to others for the sake of sexual pleasure. One who has truly settled the matter will not even entertain the thought.

In the third antithesis, Jesus took the Mosaic code regulating marital fidelity, which provided for divorce, and stiffened it by the elimination of this provision. Jesus does not acknowledge divorce under any condition. The people of the world pay him no attention, of course, but go on providing for divorce as always. In the churches, they assiduously seek interpretative schemes that continue to provide some basis for divorce.

Why? The explanation is precisely the same as for the first two antitheses. A person who loves life in this world easily reaches the conclusion that a spouse is no longer satisfactory. There are multifarious reasons, but the love of life fuels them all. Therefore, a spouse who seems not to be enriching this life as expected must be discarded for someone who will bring more enjoyment to the temporal experience. The enjoyment of this life takes precedence over any marriage commitment.

The response is entirely different whenever one who has learned to hate life in this world experiences marital difficulty. Such people always consider that their commitments take priority over temporary inconveniences. (And all temporal inconveniences are temporary.) They are not greatly upset when the marriage road becomes bumpy because they understand that there is no enduring fulfillment in this life in any case. Therefore, they can gracefully accept such trials and live with them indefinitely. More importantly, when a person values this life and its contents above other things, that person may feel justified in doing anything that offers the prospect of making life happier. If this means divorce, so be it! But when one values the eternal treasures and hates this life, one is free to accept whatever life brings. There is no compulsion to do things that may bring unhappiness to others or that would be a failure to keep commitments. Such a person is free to endure suffering in the expectation of an eternal reward that is more than compensatory. Then one can continue to be happy and to love a poor spouse since such a spouse poses no threat to one's true values. The result can be the cheerful endurance of a poor marriage in which one preserves self-respect and the hope of eternal glory. Everything depends, you see, upon acquiring and maintaining the hatred of life in this world taught and exemplified by Jesus.

The fourth antithesis is the one in which Jesus absolutely forbids the taking of oaths under all circumstances. "Let what you say be simply Yes or No," he said, and then added that anything more than this comes from evil. The practice of administering oaths, common in the world and especially in courts of law, is therefore evil.

Why do people continue to render such oaths? Because they do not question the practice, and because they are afraid of the consequences of refusal, for the authorities have not always taken such refusal lightly. The history of punitive action has produced a practice so intimately woven into the fabric of civilization that people accept it without question. But when a person hates life in this world, the punitive consequences of refusal are not a primary consideration. The hatred frees one from the conformity that the love of life would compel.

And why do the authorities compel the oath? Surely it is to establish the basis for the penalty of perjury should one lie, and so to increase the probability of hearing the truth. It is a very effective system for people who love their lives in the world, who would fear the consequences of lying on the quality of life. By the same reasoning, it would not be in the least effective with people who have learned to hate their lives. They would not fear the punitive consequence of perjury.

The key question is "Why do people lie?" They lie because they hope to gain by it, or because telling the truth would cost too much in terms of things dear to them. Now, if you examine these costs and gains, you will discover that people deem them such because of the love of life and the temporal value system. Such motivations do not exist for one who has learned to hate life in this world.

To use an extreme example, suppose you must testify against someone charged with serious crimes. The court will either convict or release this person because of your testimony, and the truth will convict. Suppose also that this person has a very mean and violent brother. The brother communicates to you this threat: "If you testify truthfully and they convict my brother, I will kill you!" You know he surely means it. What are you to do? Most people, committed to the love of life, will not long debate before lying to save their lives.

But Jesus said, "Whoever would save his life, will lose it." If, therefore, you have learned to hate your life in imitation of Jesus, you will not save it. You are free to tell the truth despite consequences. Then you require absolutely no oath to produce the truth, nor consequence of perjury to prevent your lying. You are free. The constraints that compel the people of the world to lie and deceive do not bind you. Since to save your life is to lose it, you know that you have nothing to gain by lying, and everything to lose. The motives for lying have left you, and you are free, utterly free, to tell the truth. How can you ever submit to the oath, which your Lord has forbidden, and has labeled "evil?" If you do submit, you are accepting the implication that, apart from the oath, you might be expected to lie. You are accepting the implication that you fear the penalty of perjury, and therefore that you love your life in this world. These implications utterly destroy any witness you might make about the life we have in Christ Jesus, who leaves us here for this very purpose! How, then, can you ever submit to the oath?

Anyone who has learned to hate life in this world has lost the motivation to lie — but such a person always has the motive to tell the truth. It is a matter of maintaining integrity — the integrity of one's person and the integrity of one's witness. Again, it is a matter of values, in which one values one's integrity above one's life. Such a person is absolutely free. No one can compel the free person to do anything contrary to his or her will. In the consideration of divorce, the integrity of one's commitment was the final determinant; so also with the oath. It is again the integrity of one's word that is the final determinant. Personal integrity is therefore at the heart of the Christ-commitment, because the person is the one entity that continues into eternity. It is therefore the one eternal treasure that we possess today, if we are careful to maintain it.

The person we permit ourselves to become, in this world, is the person who must face the judgment bar of the world to come, where no truth is hidden and no oath is required. The children of God will tell the truth, and nothing can move them from it. The children of God will not submit to the oath, and nothing can move them to it. They know the truth, they speak the truth, and the truth has made them free.

The fifth antithesis contains the commandment,

"Do not resist one who is evil."

This is a particular application of the sixth and last general antithesis:

"Love your enemies."

The application of the principle of the hatred of life to these two is obvious. About non-resistance, Jesus explains:

But if anyone strikes you on the right cheek, turn to him the other also; and if anyone would sue you and take your coat, let him have your cloak as well; and if anyone forces you to go one mile, go with him two miles. Give to him who begs from you, and do not refuse him who would borrow from you.

Each case illustrates a threat to life or to one of life's treasures. One can never deal with them as commanded by Jesus, on the grounds of non-resistance, unless one first deals with the attitude to life. While you love life and cherish its values, you are compelled to resist the threat. Forsake that love, and there is no threat from such attacks. The result is the possibility, nay, the inevitability, of non-resistance to the evil one. This is the key to the realization of love for that same enemy.

The one thing that is crucial, which alone enables us to take these commandments of Jesus seriously, is the "conversion" by which the love of life turns to hatred. Then arises a new value system centered in the eternal verities beyond the common disposables of time and of life in this world. The old treasures, doomed to pass away anyhow, consisting of material and bodily security, relationships and alliances, and ultimately life itself, no longer possess us. Threats to them no longer inspire us to resistance. Also, the enemy is helpless to threaten the new and eternal treasures, so he no longer poses a threat. He continues to value the temporal life and its securities. The only way he knows, or can know, to inflict harm is by attacking others at the same level. It is only when he attacks the followers of Jesus that he meets no resistance. He discovers instead that he has fallen into the arms of their redemptive love. Yes, not only is non-resistance possible, but one goes even further in response to the Second Commandment, and reaches out to the enemy in love — genuine, warm, and authentic love. This love goes beyond mere non-resistance to inspire a positive attitude to the enemy, which results in actions toward him that are such as you would have him do unto you. Jesus sums up this positive response to the enemy in the following words from Luke:

> *But I say to you that hear, Love your enemies, do good to those who hate you, bless those who curse you, pray for those who abuse you* (Luke 6:27-28).

Mere non-resistance might be motivated by any number of reasons: fear, weakness, cowardliness, or simple prudence as in the Gandhian model. The enemy will always assume that non-resistance comes from one of these reasons because these are the only ones he understands. He will respond to it with contempt and even more abuse ... unless it is accompanied by the positive, love-inspired service. This means that love does more than the enemy would compel one to do. Therefore Jesus illustrated the appropriate response of love with the commandment:

> *If anyone forces you to go one mile, go with him two miles* (Matthew 5:41).

One does such things because one loves the enemy, and one loves the enemy because he does not threaten, and he does not threaten because one's valuables are secure, and one's valuables are secure only when they are in heaven. You see, your response to such circumstances will be consistent with your self-interest. Only by placing self-interest in the eternal context can any rational person love one's enemy in this world. Then it becomes not only possible, but probable, as you extend your love for yourself to your neighbor consistent with the Second Commandment.

I must emphasize repeatedly that a proper perspective on the self is crucial to the response of Christ to the enemy. The unsolved problem of interpreters who have dealt with the Sermon has been the question, "How can one do justice to the self and also take Jesus seriously?" Now we have the answer to that question. Always, Jesus places the self in a key, central position as he seeks to motivate his followers in every place and age. This is nowhere more evident than his conclusion to these antitheses, where the reward motive continues to be accepted and presented as the basis of acting in this way:

> *For if you love those who love you, what reward have you?*
> *Do not even the tax collectors do the same?* (Matthew 5:46).

Luke's rendition is even more explicitly focused on self-interest:

> *If you love those who love you, what credit is that to you?*
> *For even sinners love those who love them. And if you do*
> *good to those who do good to you, what credit is that to you?*
> *For even sinners do the same. And if you lend to those from*
> *whom you hope to receive, what credit is that to you? Even*
> *sinners lend to sinners, to receive as much again. But love*
> *your enemies, and do good, and lend, expecting nothing in*
> *return; and your reward will be great, and you will be sons*
> *of the Most High; for he is kind to the ungrateful and the*
> *selfish* (Luke 6:32-35).

So you see how it is that Jesus always addresses us on the assumption of the reward motive ... of the desire for "credit."

Now, the ultimate reward is a place in the Father's house, as a child of the Father, but Jesus posits this childhood on conformity. That is, those who would be children of God must become like him in essential ways, especially in that quality of character called "mercy." Since, therefore, the Father deals with his enemies in a certain way, we must deal with them similarly. Then we become as he is.

> *You, therefore, must be perfect, as your heavenly Father is perfect* (Matthew 5:48).

Jesus illustrated this teaching with the following words:

> *... for he makes his sun rise on the evil and on the good, and sends rain on the just and on the unjust* (Matthew 5:45).

In the dispensation of his temporal blessings, the Father makes absolutely no distinctions between his children and his enemies. All receive the sun, all receive the rain. I can even go further to say that when any of these blessings are withheld, all suffer alike, both the just and the unjust. Even drought, earthquake, tornado, and volcano make no distinction between the evil and the good! Since the Father acts thus without discrimination, we, too, must

> *Be merciful, even as your Father in heaven is merciful* (Luke 6:36).

So, in the loving of your enemies, you are only acting according to the divine nature that is in you. You do it for a reward, the kind of reward that the Father values.

Those popular preachers who seek to motivate others by appealing to the desire for a reward in kind, such as, for example, promising material rewards to those who tithe, are speaking contrary to the Word and the Spirit of Christ. That they do it in his name renders theirs among the grossest of sins. They are only catering to the love of life — and to the temporal value system, which to Jesus is abhorrent.

Jesus continued the Sermon with instructions on piety; specifically, he issued guidelines for the giving of alms, prayer, and fasting. In all three cases his dominant concern has to do with motive. There are two common elements: his appeal to the reward motive that I have already discussed at length, and the command to secrecy. He concluded the instruction on almsgiving with these words:

> *... and your Father who sees in secret will reward you* (Matthew 6:4).

He concluded the instruction on prayer with these words:

> *... and your Father who sees in secret will reward you* (Matthew 6:6).

He concluded the instruction on fasting with the same:

> *... and your Father who sees in secret will reward you* (Matthew 6:18).

So you can see that always he makes his appeal to the need in each of us to receive rewards. Specifically, he urges on us the desire for and expectation of the rewards that only the Father can mete.

Now, in reviewing the context of these words in the Sermon, you doubtless have noticed that he does not accept the desire in us for a reward when we are looking to men as its donors, and when we are seeking it here in this life. He began this series of instructions with these words:

> *Beware of practicing your piety before men in order to be seen by them; for then you will have no reward from your Father who is in heaven* (Matthew 6:1).

Everything, you see, hinges on your motives. When you give alms or do other pious acts publicly to impress men favorably, something is happening that is terribly wrong in the sight of the Father. He will never reward you for such acts. Do you remember Jesus' response to Peter's objection to his first prediction of his sufferings?

> *You are not on the side of God, but of men* (Matthew 16:23; Mark 8:33).

Or do you recall what he said to the Pharisees?

> *You are those who justify yourselves before men, but God knows your hearts; for what is exalted among men is an abomination in the sight of God* (Luke 16:15).

The nature of things is such that the Father is on one side, men on the other. What men adore, the Father abhors! If this is true, as Jesus said, then what can be the Father's opinion of those who, like the ancient Pharisees or contemporary public servants, seek to justify themselves before men? To use Jesus' own words again, they are an abomination!

About himself, Jesus said,

> *I receive not glory from men* (John 5:41).

For his part, then, he solicited absolutely no plaudits from the category labeled "men." He also uttered harsh words against those who seek to elicit the praise of men, especially in the disposition of their religious duties. His typical comment on them is:

> *They have their reward* (Matthew 6:2, 5, 16).

This means, of course, that those who seek the praise of men for their reward can expect no reward from the Father, either here or hereafter. This basic enmity between men and God explains why Jesus expressed such strong concerns about the motives of our piety. Jesus instructed the disciples to keep their pious acts secret because the consequence of impure motives is so terrible, and the temptation to seek the approval of men is so strong. Listen:

> *But when you give alms, do not let your left hand know what your right hand is doing, so that your alms may be in secret; and your Father who sees in secret will reward you* (Matthew 6: 3-4).

> *But when you pray, go into your room and shut the door and pray to your Father who is in secret; and your Father who sees in secret will reward you* (Matthew 6:6).

> *But when you fast, anoint your head and wash your face, that your fasting may not be seen by men but by your Father who is in secret; and your Father who sees in secret will reward you* (Matthew 6:17-18).

Does this mean that the Father would have us never to do any of these things other than secretly? What about the offering of prayer during public worship? Surely that is not forbidden? Or what about the saying of "Grace" at the family table? If you will simply review his words, and take him seriously, I need say no more to answer your question. We can think of all the reasons in the world why Jesus could not have meant what he said. Yet there it is, in black and white (or in any other color your New Testament may contain). Always, the word is "secret." Secret, that is, to all but the Father, who sees "in secret," and therefore will reward you openly in his eternity.

Those who do such things are obviously transgressing the will of God as enunciated by Jesus. Does this, then, give us grounds for pronouncing condemnation on those who practice such things contrary to the instructions of the Lord? No, absolutely not. We cannot rightly judge what is in the hearts of other people, and they are under condemnation only when their motives are impure — that is, when they do it to impress their neighbors.

The Lord has made his will unmistakable, as usual: Do it, but do it secretly! Pray in your secret room. Give alms so your left hand does not know what your right hand is doing. Let your appearance when fasting be as though you do not fast. Then all will be in secret, and only you and your Lord will know of your devotion. These are his commandments, who also said,

If you love me, keep my commandments (John 14:15).

and,

He it is who loves me, who keeps my commandments (John 14:21).

Some pious acts are so patently designed to influence others that I have much difficulty in not expressing a very poor opinion about those who do them. This includes those who:

1. Say Grace at the table in public restaurants;

2. Claim a private communication line with God during ordinary conversation: "The Lord told me … ." or "I told the Lord;"

3. Post religious signs in their private businesses, on auto bumpers, or other public places, and

4. Publicly credit God for giving them special blessings as rewards for personal piety, which also gives them public credit for being so

pious. For example, a successful businessman may say, "The Lord has blessed me because I have always paid a tithe."

What of Jesus? Did he abide by his dictum? Did he do these things in secret? On giving alms: there is no record that he publicly shelled out of his pocket to help the poor. If he did it, he did it in secret. There were many poor persons in Israel who needed help. He did help them in a variety of ways, including feeding them miraculously and healing their diseases, but I know of no case where he paid out of his pocket to provide for their needs. He had plenty of resources, for when money was an object, he could readily supply it. Witness his instructions to one disciple to go catch a fish and remove the tax money from its mouth!

As for fasting, clearly he fasted during the wilderness experience of forty days, following which Satan tempted him (Matthew 4:1-2; Mark 1:13; Luke 4:1-2). He was there alone, in secret, and it was under these circumstances that he fasted in a manner perfectly consistent with his later teachings. We know of no other incident where he fasted, either publicly or not, so that any such practice must have been very secret. The record does say the disciples of Jesus were unique in that they did not practice fasting, although Jesus said they would do so after he left them (Matthew 9:15; Mark 2:20; Luke 5:35).

Jesus was a man of frequent prayer, and there are many places in the record where he addressed the Father. His practice was in good accord with his instructions to the disciples. Mark tells us, for example, that " ... in the morning, a great while before day, he rose and went out to a lonely place, and there he prayed." Matthew tells us of another, similar event: "And after he had dismissed the crowds, he went up into the hills by himself to pray" (Matthew 14:23).

Even in Gethsemane, where he battled furiously with the temptation to save his life, he placed himself apart to pray: "And he withdrew from them about a stone's throw, and knelt down and prayed ..."

The only exception is in John's Gospel, where the language suggests that the disciples were in his presence when he uttered the "High Priestly" prayer of John 17. In view of the powerful Truths contained in this prayer, it is likely that his motive was to make these words known to us through the disciples. He permitted them to hear him for this purpose. Had he gone completely out of earshot, we could never have understood the provisions that he made for us.

You may think that I have deliberately omitted the "Lord's Prayer" (Matthew 6:7-8; 9-13; Luke 11:2-4) which he gave as a model to his disciples, unless I include it somewhere here. This is not an exception to his rules, because he was not praying. He was only giving his followers some words to use whenever they should pray.

You have doubtless noticed that the "Lord's Prayer" is very short. This is consistent with his instructions as follows:

> *And in praying do not heap up empty phrases as the Gentiles do; for they think that they will be heard for their many words. Do not be like them, for your Father knows what you need before you ask him* (Matthew 6:7-8).

You see, it is like this: since the Father already knows everything about you, including absolutely all your needs, he doesn't need to hear your prayer to know what you need or wish to say to him. It is you who need the prayer, so that your dependence upon the Father may be realized more fully within yourself. Therefore a brief prayer is all that is necessary. If you prefer to use florid phrases and to extend your petitions endlessly, and especially if you are doing it publicly, something is terribly amiss in your heart. Of course, many in the congregation may go home saying, "Brother prays such wonderful prayers! How very close to the Father he must be!" You will have accomplished your real purpose, and you have your reward.

Now let's go to the root of the matter: what is the basic malady infecting those who love to show their piety, or who love to "wear their religion on their sleeves?" (or their "T" shirts). It is the same as the root of every other evil: such people are guilty of loving their lives in this world. Being thus in love with life, they seek ways of enriching it. Anything, therefore, that elicits the praise of others, and that is motivated to that end, adds to the luster of life, and thus comes from evil. Anything, absolutely anything, we may do to enhance our status among men springs from the love of life, which is the sole cause of condemnation. In all such cases, we have our reward. Our reward only, not our punishment; that comes later. It is the love of life that compels us to reach out for temporary rewards of every sort. It is the love of life that prevents our being obedient to the commandments of the Lord in every case.

If you are trying to reconcile the Sermon and its "hard sayings" with your outlook while you remain a captive to the love of life, you may as well forget it. It is a futile endeavor. But when you have learned to hate your life, consistent with the example and precept of Jesus, you will find that everything falls into place. It is the failure to realize this connection that has frustrated the many efforts of those who would interpret the Sermon on the Mount. Everyone who loves life will find it impossible to take the Sermon seriously. Everyone who hates life after the manner of Jesus will find it simple both to understand and to apply. The problem comes in making the transition from a lover to a hater. It is not easy, and Jesus always made the difficulty of it a prominent part of his message. He expressed it in the Sermon as follows:

Enter by the narrow gate; for the gate is wide and the way is easy, that leads to destruction, and those who enter by it are many. For the gate is narrow and the way is hard, that leads to life, and those who find it are few (Matthew 7:13-14).

A major part of the difficulty lies in the absolute cleavage that Jesus made between the two positions. That is, it is not possible to love both the temporal and the eternal life. Neither is it possible to make a slow and gradual transition from the one attitude to the other. Whoever loves this life, in any degree, will find that he has not qualified for life eternal. Whoever truly loves the life eternal, will find that he hates life in this world. One cannot love both a little. It is the nature of things. It is because of this feature that Jesus emphasized purity of heart and singleness of the eye. It was in the Sermon that he said:

Do not lay up for yourselves treasures on earth, where moth and rust consume and where thieves break in and steal, but lay up for yourselves treasures in heaven, where neither moth nor rust consumes and where thieves do not break in and steal. For where your treasure is, there will your heart be also (Matthew 6:19-21).

This passage has already received an extensive discussion, and I present it here to show Jesus' emphasis on the exclusiveness of the two positions. Where your treasure is, he said, there will your heart be also. Now the only way to maintain purity of heart is to have it all in one place, so that this saying underscores the beatitude:

Blessed are the pure in heart (Matthew 5: 8).

He then proceeded, in the Sermon, to make the same point about the eye:

The eye is the lamp of the body. So, if your eye is single, your whole body will be full of light; but if your eye is evil, your whole body will be full of darkness. If then the light in you is darkness, how great is the darkness! (Matthew 6:22-23).

The eye must focus upon a single object to be single, or sound. Jesus pressed this truth upon us yet again with his words on serving two masters:

No one can serve two masters; for either he will hate the one and love the other, or he will be devoted to the one and despise the other. You cannot serve God and mammon (Matthew 6:24; Luke 16:13).

So it is never both/and. Always it is either/or!

Jesus has told us that the Way is hard; that is certainly true. Yet the way of this world also can be very hard, and people often endure its hardness without realizing that it does nothing good for us, either here or hereafter. Anxiety is one form of the hardness of the world, but one who has effectively realized and applied the hatred of life is free of this experience. Jesus also spoke of this in the Sermon, and I include a portion of this utterance here:

Therefore I tell you, do not be anxious about your life, what you shall eat or what you shall drink, nor about your body, what you shall put on ... Therefore, do not be anxious, saying, "What shall we eat?" or "What shall we drink?" or "What shall we wear?" For the Gentiles seek all these things; and your heavenly Father knows that you need them all. But seek first his kingdom and his righteousness, and all these things shall be yours as well. Therefore do not be anxious about tomorrow, for tomorrow will be anxious for itself. Let the day's own trouble be sufficient for the day (Matthew 6: 31-34).

How is it that Jesus can command no anxiety? This seems not at all practical to us who have spent a great amount of time and energy on worry. The answer to this question is precisely the same as that of the prior similar questions: he does it because he expects us first to deal with the love of life. While we remain in love with life in this world, there is no possibility that we will get beyond all anxiety.

Only a little reflection will reveal the enabling power of a changed disposition. Once you have truly come to hate your life in the world, the causes of anxiety disappear, for anxiety is born of the love of life. We must keep in mind that the anxiety of which Jesus speaks looks to tomorrow, not to today. He is careful to assure us that the Father knows that we need these bare essentials, and that he will surely provide them according to our faith. Meanwhile, let today's troubles be sufficient for today! (Matthew 6:34). He assures us that the Father will provide the essentials if we first comply with the condition of seeking first His Kingdom and His Righteousness (Matthew 6:33). Now, we will find both the Kingdom and the Righteousness only through the hatred of life, so that the methodology becomes clear. When anyone seeks the Kingdom, that person finds it only through the conversion from the love of life to the hatred of life as exemplified by Jesus. Simultaneously, the new attitude to life relieves one, at the deepest level, of anxiety while the faith that empowers the new attitude trusts the Father to supply our needs.

Remember, his question is, "Why are you anxious about your life?" So, it is clear why your attitude to life determines your response. It is also important to recognize that Jesus does not counsel a careless and indifferent attitude concerning these provisions. If you are this day in want, hungry and thirsty and naked, you are in trouble and you should deal with it. You will even experience anxiety about your immediate circumstances, and Jesus has not forbidden such. All he has forbidden is anxiety about tomorrow. This leaves us free to deal with today's trouble without complicating it with worries about the future, provided we have faith to trust the Father to provide tomorrow's needs. When we do find ourselves in need of today's essentials, yesterday's faith may have been lacking, and that is a situation that calls for attention.

Another thing one must recognize is that Jesus is not commanding that we make no efforts to provide for ourselves. Even the birds, which he set before us as examples (Matthew 6:26), must get out and scratch for their worms! Also, if it were possible to obtain all one needs by doing nothing other than to trust God, lazy people would rush to take advantage. Jesus would be contradicting himself, having taught that the Way is hard while making it easy! The hardness of the Way demands that we at least scratch for our worms like everyone else. The only honorable means of obtaining them is the same for us as for others: that labor that makes a contribution to the needs of our neighbors. The nature of things is such that there can be no earthly advantage to becoming a follower of Jesus. The force of temptation must not be reversed to induce the lazy, the parasitical, the unproductive, and the irresponsible into the Kingdom for no good reason.

Those who commit themselves to the Way are under instructions from the Lord to be very careful about their attitudes toward others. The words of Jesus mediate his Spirit, and the ingesting of his words, those utterances from the Father, cannot fail to define the Spirit with which one approaches one's fellows. The temptation always is to be super-critical of others while being super-lenient with ourselves. This is a tendency that Jesus attacked most vigorously:

> *Judge not, that you be not judged. For with the judgment you pronounce you will be judged, and the measure you give will be the measure you get. Why do you see the speck that is in your brother's eye, but do not notice the log that is in your own eye? Or how can you say to your brother, 'Let me take the speck out of your eye,' when there is a log in your own eye? You hypocrite, first take the log out of your own eye, and then you will see clearly to take the speck out of your brother's eye* (Matthew 7:3-5; Luke 6:41, 42).

In this utterance, the key word is "first." "Take first the log out of your own eye." Thus, those who follow Jesus in the Way give primary consideration to their own character. They will be much more conscious of their failings than of their neighbor's failings. This specifically includes those neighbors who would do, or have done, them harm. Luke's Gospel expands this principle as follows:

Judge not, and you will not be judged; condemn not, and you will not be condemned; forgive, and you will be forgiven; give, and it will be given to you; good measure, pressed down, shaken together, running over, will be put into your lap. For the measure you give will be the measure you get back (Luke 6:37-38).

Here we face instructions about how to respond to our enemies, and what spirit to manifest to them. We all know how easy it is to pass judgment on those we simply dislike. How much more difficult it is to be charitable in our attitudes to those who actively seek our harm! But those who walk in the Way have this simple instruction: forgive and give. Again, how is this possible? As before, the answer is to be found in the acquisition of that hatred of life that Jesus has set before us. The love of life compels us to respond with harsh judgment to those who mistreat us. But when we see that their mistreatment of us harms them more than us, and that it does not touch the things we truly treasure, that is, the eternal treasures, the way opens for us to forgive. By that same means we realize our justification and promote our highest self interest, for

With what judgment you judge, shall you be judged (Mark 4:24; Luke 6:37).

The love of life causes us to be tempted to be lenient with ourselves and harsh with others. Jesus understood the dangers of this tendency, which results in disastrous self-deception, and he knew that the Fellowship of the Way would not be immune to it.

The result is that multitudes will stand before him on the Last Day in the confident, but mistaken, expectation that the Lord will approve them. A few will be standing fearfully to one side, in constant awareness of their tragic failures, who will hear instead those wonderful words of acceptance from on High:

Come, you blessed of my Father, inherit the kingdom prepared for you from the foundation of the world ... (Matthew 25:34).

Those who love their lives are compelled by their misapplied self-interest to justify themselves, but those who follow Jesus in the hatred of life wait in the hope of being justified by him. The Gospel of John reveals a Jesus who was intensely concerned with his Words, whether they would be heard in the world, and with the consequences of either hearing or not hearing them. The Synoptics go one step further in emphasizing not only the hearing, but also the doing of what we hear. This emphasis is especially prominent in the Sermon, which closes with the Parable of the Builders. Here, He showed that salvation and justification depend not only upon the hearing, but upon acting on what we hear. The parable begins in this manner:

> *Everyone then who hears these words of mine and does them will be like a wise man who built his house upon the rock: and the rain fell, and the floods came, and the winds blew and beat upon that house, but it did not fall, because it had been founded on the rock. And everyone who hears these words of mine and does not do them will be like a foolish man who built his house upon the sand; and the rain fell, and the floods came, and the winds blew and beat against that house, and it fell; and great was the fall of it* (Matthew 7: 24-27; Luke 6:48).

Luke's Gospel records the following rebuke:

> *Why do you call me 'Lord, Lord,' and not do what I tell you?* (Luke 6:46).

These are among the plainest words in all the Bible. Jesus stated them very precisely to prevent any effort to make them mean less than the obvious. My earliest frustration in the church grew out of fruitless efforts to bend these words to conform to the doctrine of justification by grace alone. I could never do it, because it simply cannot be done. Churchmen who promote this doctrine therefore never seriously apply them to life. I found it necessary to leave the church, mostly for this reason. I always felt alienated from a ministry that encouraged people to build their houses on sand, and I still do. Now, though, I can understand the failure of the churches. They fail to serve God because they have refused to deal with the change in attitude to life that Jesus has set before us. And then they betray him with a kiss!

"Lord, what must I do?" (Matthew 19:16; Mark 10:17; Luke 10:25; 18:18). This is the question put to Jesus by a young man disturbed by the complexity of determining right conduct in a world of many shades of gray. The Gospel of the Kingdom is wonderful good news to such persons. It disperses the fog of ecclesiastical obfuscation and enlightens a Way clearly defined, such that anyone who will can understand how to walk in this world. Only those who have faced and resolved the fundamental conflict of the will, as applied to life, can have the insight required to guide their conduct with confidence and hope.

One critical feature is the realization of the new set of values of the Kingdom. Obviously, one's values are highly determinative of conduct such that the doing of the Father's will remains an impossibility while we continue to treasure temporal life, possessions, and relationships. But those who give proper attention to the maintenance of the attitude to life counseled by Jesus will respond to God's will as commanded by our Lord. Jesus does not guide us into a new legalism that would bind us to the letter of the law. Far from it! He has given commandments, which he expects that we will obey, but the obedience comes naturally when we have put on Christ with his hatred of life. Then his commandments become, not rigorous codes, but firm guides, either affirming our faithfulness in the Way, or firmly rebuking us when we stray. He has liberated us from the heavy burden of legalistic righteousness, on the one hand, and the equally burdensome task of ferreting out the way through the maze of grays by pure faith, on the other hand, to stand approved of God solely because of the will's disposition to seek consummation in eternal glory. I do not mean that questions of conduct never trouble us, only that when we find ourselves so troubled, the difficulty is simple (but seldom easy) to resolve. We need only reinforce the right disposition of the will-to-life through abiding in the word of Christ. The sometimes seeming complexity of decisions about conduct never results from the character of the choices, which are in Truth clearly drawn. It is the result of confusion within ourselves. It signals that we have weakened in our resolve and have listened to the spirit that is of this world.

Permit me to illustrate: A young man lives in a country that is at war and in danger of being destroyed. He has received notification that he must report for service in the army. Should he, a lover of peace, respond? He is not afraid, but he loves his enemies in imitation of Christ and would do them no harm. On the other hand, his friends and kin may be greatly harmed by the enemy if he and other young men do not rush to the bastions of defense. Looking thus outwardly at the issue he becomes confused and uncertain. If he looks inwardly instead, to reinforce the heart's devotion to the Eternal Glory, he sees again that the only treasure is in heaven and that there is nothing in this world but losses. Then it is that he is free to respond to that word of our Lord:

Do not fear those who kill the body but cannot kill the soul (Matthew 10:28).

This statement of Truth clarifies the issue and he responds to his summons in the Spirit of Christ without concern for earthly consequences. He sees that it is a far greater service to his fellows to be thus a witness to Truth than to save their lives by the sword. Therefore, we do not need a "Christian Torah." We do not need a voluminous exegesis of scripture such as the preachers give, neither one of their "concise analyses of the issues." We do not need a host of counselors, because we have our "Wonderful Counselor" always with us. We do not need this book! We need only confront the dichotomy that knows no compromise and make our commitment to Eternity, not to time. Then, and only then, can we resolve the previously perplexing questions regarding conduct in this present age. We need only be aware of the Logos, the utterances of Jesus.

The world has many books purporting to give guidance in the will of God. We are writing more of them every day, including this one. Most of the writers know nothing of the way. They only confuse us, be they evangelists, missionaries, theologians, learned doctors, or anyone else. Those books that do not focus on the simple, though hard, utterances of Jesus are at best no more than sophisticated rubbish. Only the words of Jesus abide forever. I am not saying that it is easy to do God's will — only that it is easy to discern his will in the light of the Word. Of course this makes the doing easier, for how is a person to do the will of God if he cannot discern it? Still, the hardness remains; but the Way, though hard, is plainly marked. Jesus blazed a trail through the world so well defined that no follower need go astray for lack of guidance. The new attitude to life that issues from the commitment to Eternity clarifies all questions of behavior. What once seemed an impossible question has suddenly a simple answer, once the pure light of Truth disperses the fog of earthly mindedness.

The two eyes in our heads are generally so well coordinated that they move always in unison and focus upon the same scene. Otherwise, the single mind would be thrown into confusion by the constant input of disparate images. So it is as Jesus said,

> *If your eye is single, your whole body shall be full of light*
> (Matthew 6:22; Luke 11:34).

Sadly, people seldom profit from this object lesson built right into our heads. The tendency, instead, is to observe two vastly different scenes, the heavenly and the earthly, and to aspire to both. The result is a cross-eyed heart! Therefore, we can never correctly resolve questions of conduct apart from the prior attention to, and correction of, this malady of "double vision." It moves us always to strive after the impossible — to focus the eyes of the heart simultaneously on both spiritual and material aspirations. Jesus makes this unmistakable by his terse remark about serving God and mammon (Matthew 6:24; Luke 16:13). Why do people not heed him? Ah! The things of this world are so evident, so immediate!

What is the final significance of this refusal of an exclusive commitment? The word is this, a word without equivocation:

> *No man can serve two masters; he will hate the one and love the othe.* ... *(Matthew 6:24; Luke 16:13).*

The "God haters" pass by everyday on their way to get gain, totally in the service of mammon, and often under the inspiration of a morning devotional, betraying him with a kiss!

Jesus compels us to face the issue squarely with his categorical demand:

> *Except a man forsake all that he has, he cannot be my disciple* (Luke 14:33).

One must forsake all! Only this is adequate testimony to singleness of heart. If I withhold the smallest pittance — yea, one so small that it is worthless to anyone else — perhaps the memento of some precious event, a token of sentiment, one limited solely to sentimental value — if I hold back even so small a thing as that, can I be free of doublemindedness?

Nay — The last thing of this world to which I cling is in reality my most valued possession. It would be as though I were saying to the Father, "You may have everything else, but not this. No, not even for you will I forsake this!" Then I might console myself with a thought that is consistent with the appearance of the thing: that it is, after all, very small; surely God will not notice. In a manner of speaking, this would be true. He might not regard the pittance, but we may be very sure that he would notice my devotion to it — how I valued a pittance above him!

Behold the poor widow of the Gospels. They testify of her that she cast in only just such a pittance — two pennies, such worthless things! (Mark 12:42; Luke 21:2). But Jesus, and God her Father, noticed, because they were of great value to her, being all she had, even her whole living. In addition, she was a widow with no one to care for her! Perhaps they had some sentimental value. Her precious husband had earned them by hard labor in his old age and had denied himself, so that she might have something for her living following his departure. Now he has departed and the two pennies are all that remain of his legacy. How he loved her, and how she in turn valued his love and efforts for her! Although she bore him no children to comfort his old age, still he did everything for her! Now he is gone — and so is his legacy, all save these two small coins that he earned with his tired hands. But ... the priests (ah, the priests!) have convinced her that God's work goes begging; that God needs her two pennies more than she needs them. She, innocent and believing, pure of heart, out of her total love of the Father, casts in her all — yes, even her last two precious coins, her whole living! Ultimate devotion! Here is surely the perfect example of purity of heart that issues from genuine commitment to Eternity. (But as for the priests, well, that is altogether another matter.)

So what is her reward? Does she receive public acclaim? Does she get a front page write-up in the *Jerusalem Post*? Do friends call a meeting in her honor and praise her generosity? Do they praise her for her exemplary devotion? Does she go on to discover that, on that very day, her meager wealth was restored a thousand times over by another, totally unexpected bequest?

Absolutely not. What she gave was so small and insignificant that no one took notice. Or, if someone did, it was only to ridicule her: "Look how that foolish old woman has parted with her last penny!" No one took notice, that is, save Jesus. And what did he do? Did he go to her as God's representative and commend her devotion before all the world? Did he call her forward before all his followers and praise her? Did he, perhaps secretly, replenish her supply? No, he did no such thing. She never heard what he said about her. She heard only the derision of those who despised her devotion. Most likely she wandered thence out into the streets of Old Jerusalem to join the ranks of the old beggar-women, then soon sickened and died. What Jesus said of her he spoke quietly, from a distance, to only a few disciples, being careful not even to record her name.

"Do you see," he sa d, "that woman?"

Therefore she remains as nameless in the world as she was penniless. This is only as she wished, for in her singleness of mind and heart she did not give to receive the plaudits of men. Such a reward would only have brought sorrow to her. She would know that for some reason, perhaps the taint of doublemindedness, God had not accepted her gift. She was making a shrewd investment in her Eternity, not in her time. She does have a reward — that of having friends in heaven that she has made by means of the unrighteous mammon. And Jesus' commendation, made to others at a distance, in time — that she at length hears also — in Eternity.

Now, while we are looking at this nameless woman (from a distance), let us not fail to observe a thing that is characteristic of such persons. I mean that she was the only one of the givers who gave in singleness of heart; and so she cast in more than all the others. This suggests that the call comes to each of us as individuals and that each individually makes whatever response she (or he) chooses. In this matter of commitment to Eternity there is no "team effort," no "group decisions," no "commitment by committee." Each, as an individual standing alone in this world and before God, makes his or her solitary decision. If it is a true commitment to Eternity, each becomes, like that poor widow, a solitary individual in this world with little or no corporate support, for:

> *The way that leads to life is hard, and few there be that find it* (Matthew 7:14).

So it was that Jesus came to Simon Peter as to the solitary individual; not to all the twelve at once but to one only, in private. He came to that one person in particular who was called "Simon," and to that particular Simon who was also called "Son of Jonah," and said to him only,

> *Simon, son of Jonah, do you love me more than these?* (John 21:15).

And Simon wept bitterly, so bitterly, in great grief due to his doublemindedness! O, what a terrible grief it is — to be the solitary individual in the consciousness of God, and ... one's doublemindedness!

Jesus typically addressed himself to the solitary one. He said not, "If you all ...," but instead,

> *If any man would come after me, let him deny himself and take up his cross and follow me* (Matthew 16:24; Luke 9:23).

It was as a solitary individual that Jesus himself confirmed his commitment to Eternity — first in the wilderness, later in the Garden, and finally, on the cross. There is then absolutely no true comfort to be gained from a corporate relationship, for by itself it does nothing but deceive us. Yet throughout Christendom the multitudes, in ignorance of Truth, continue vainly to seek and to claim "innocence by association."

Typical is the position of a veteran of the Korean War who disclaimed any moral accountability for the blood he had shed. He said to me, "I only did what others compelled me to do. I acted only as an instrument of the state. It was not my wish to kill anyone. They gave me no choice in the matter — wherefore I am not responsible."

So it was that he would depersonalize himself. He is only an instrument, he lacks choice. Not so! When one solitary individual encounters another on the field of battle, each set to destroy the other, whether or not he acknowledges the truth makes no difference before God. Each is solely responsible for being there and armed in the first instance, and for acting as he does in the second. It is as the solitary individual that he makes his decision to press the trigger and to plunge the bayonet, and as such he bears accountability to God. His commitment is to time, not Eternity.

No one has to do such things. Every individual can and does decide for himself or herself whether to go to war. It is the individual who makes the decision, and when one decides not to go, then he does so as a solitary individual. This can be, and often is, a good decision motivated by singlemindedness, but even this is not always evidence of a firm commitment to Eternity. Often it signifies only a foolhardy commitment to relative temporal aspirations such as world peace — a love and vision not for Eternity, but for the world. The implications of doublemindedness, with an accurate definition of the singleness which one acquires through the commitment to eternity, has already been thoroughly examined and recorded by a brother of the past century and I refer you to him for further discussion. * The point here is that such singleness is essential to acquisition of the behavior of a true follower. Without it, there is no profit in considering the matter. Godly conduct is incomprehensible to the double minded, but is natural to those who, by the commitment to eternity, have acquired both singleness of mind and purity of heart.

The Way is hard. Yet it does not follow that it is hard from every perspective. For one whose eye is truly single, it is the easiest thing imaginable, like giving candy to a child. It is as when one acts fully in accord with one's true nature, with the Spirit that is within, so that the result is peace and contentment. Yet it is hard, and it is a hardness that knows no equal. It is the hardness of attaining and constantly maintaining this pure quality of singleness while under the constant bombardment of worldly influences. These seek to infect the heart with compromise, with the delusion that "there is no harm in it." Therein is the hard struggle — with one's old, crucified self, with the tearful pleas of the erring "loved ones," with the wider world of

----

* Soren Kierkegaard, *Purity of Heart Is To Will One Thing*. HarperTorch Books, translated by Douglas V. Steere

humanity, with Satan himself and the host of his demons, which all conspire to enslave the soul. Yet in Christ, in his Way, it is not only possible, it is inevitable!

Having discussed many aspects of the Way of Christ, let us now focus our attention upon that solitary individual who walks in the Way. Why does this person display such unique and peculiar behavior? How are we to account for the eccentricity?

First, it is a matter of value set, as previously discussed. Here, one's treasure is in heaven, distinct from that of the multitudes of this world. This is not a matter of relative evaluation, for such a one has learned to value only the heavenly. Things temporal and earthly concern such a person only as losses.

For the sake of illustration, consider the testimony of the Apostle Paul. "Whatever gain I had," he said, "I count as loss because of the surpassing worth of knowing Christ Jesus my Lord. For his sake I have suffered the loss of all things, and count them as dung in order that I may gain Christ and be found in him ... that, if possible, I may attain the resurrection from the dead. Brethren, I do not consider that I have made it my own; but one thing I do: forgetting what lies behind and straining forward to what lies ahead, I press on towards the prize of the upward call of God in Christ Jesus" (Philippians 3:13-14).

You see how, in Christ, there are but two categories? There is the "prize," consisting of the eternal verities associated with the resurrection from the dead. Then there is the "loss," consisting of everything. "I count," he said, "everything as loss." One must recognize the significance of the word "loss." We may easily miss it because of its similarity to the other word, "lost." He did not say "I count everything as lost." That might only signify the involuntary separation from things yet treasured, such as one might say in bemoaning a business failure, a burning home, or a broken marriage, "All is lost!" In such cases whatever is lost, being no more in one's possession, is yet highly valued. But if it has become a "loss" — that is another matter entirely! Although still in one's possession, it has lost all value, becoming nothing more than a dung-like thing about which one's only gain is to be rid of it forever. While it continues to be valued, it hinders and deadens true spirituality. What a "loss" it would be if there were no garbage disposal, no sewer of the spirit realm, no release from the lethal constipation of the heart! Then each of us would be doomed to bear for all one's days the accumulation of the dung of this life. How vile a burden it becomes in so short a time!

So, the multitudes have died to God from the malady of "constipation of the mind and heart." It is because they persist in bearing about with them, that is, in their hearts, the constant accumulation of dung-like, temporal things. If only they would partake of such a laxative as would open the bowels of the heart and purge their inner beings! Sadly, they refuse because, in their persuasion that happiness is a temporal state, they glut themselves with their refuse.

Second, that person who has made the total commitment to Eternity finds himself or herself in a blessed state in this world that one could not have imagined beforehand: nothing threatens! Such a one is wonderfully relieved of the fears and anxieties that attend life in the world. One is not afraid of thief, tyrant, famine, pestilence, or anything else in the whole creation. Above all, gone is the fear of death. Death, although a strait gate, becomes a blessed event to which one looks in eager anticipation in its appointed hour. There is a sadness in it, to be sure, but mixed with joy like that of a bride who, though joyful and happy, yet sheds tears when she embraces her parents, sisters, and brothers. She has lived with them all her lifetime, but she can live with them no more. Yet the joy is so overpowering that one is able quickly to put away the tears and rush ebulliently into the embrace of Eternity, just as the bride rushes into the embrace of matrimony.

The case is also like that of a student (we are called "disciples") who strains forward to a graduation that must await its time and the final examination. When at length it comes, it is a time of great joy for all. Yet again, there is a sadness in it that is fit and proper. It is the sadness that comes of separation from beloved and familiar friends. It is as when the graduates march across the stage to receive the diplomas, with joy and gladness in their hearts yet with ... tears in their eyes. Such sweet, mixed emotions! Yet again, it is with such a person in the Way as with that same bride, who later comes to bear her first child into the world. As there is a barrier of pain through which all pass to enter this world, just so, there is a pain barrier through which all pass to leave it behind. Yet, in spite of the pain, the young mother counts herself happy. She counts it as nothing in the ecstasy of the moment. So it is that the child of God counts every earthly pain as slight, even as nothing, in the ecstasy of the singular, everlasting moment of eternity!

There is no conclusion to be gleaned from the mere circumstances of one's death. A tyrant or a murderer may, or may not, pass painlessly in the night. The children of Eternity may, or may not, endure a long and painful terminal illness. There is not and cannot be any purely earthly advantage from the commitment to Eternity. Such would contaminate it with the care for time. Whatever one's lot in this world, the person in the Way neither fears nor embraces it, but passes victoriously over it into the Glory of the Father! It is only in the purity of this commitment that anyone can seriously consider the counsel of Jesus:

> *Do not fear those who kill the body, but cannot kill the soul!* (Matthew 10:28).

Why should we fear another, who can only extract from us our losses, but who cannot touch our gain? We can go even further: if we are in Truth not afraid of death, it follows that there is no fear of those things that threaten life, and no anxiety about the loss of those things that sustain it.

Since many human institutions exist to provide security in the face of threats, clearly the person walking in the Way of Christ needs no participation in them. This one fact is determinative of a broad spectrum of conduct, including the refusal of military service and political activities. Such a person lacks a mind for rationalizations about just wars, self-defense, and similar things. Clearly, even under the strongest justification, a "just war" remains, in its essence, a response to threats, the response of fear to him who is able to destroy the body.

Third, the child of God in the Way of Christ is in Truth no threat to anyone else. This is a state incomprehensible to the people of the world, so that they see only a strange, foreign, different person. They see a person who is to be viewed with suspicion and as a threat to them or to their "way of life." They say, "If he is not one of us, he must be one of them!"

So it was that Jesus was incomprehensible to the Jewish rulers, who mistakenly viewed him as a threat expressed by the words, "The Romans will come and take away both our Holy Place and our nation" (John 11:48). They ally such a person, irrationally and unreasonably, with all their worst enemies. They will not surprise him, then, if they heap calumny upon him, for, like those of old, "They know not what they do" (Luke 23:34).

There is never any good reason for anyone in the Way of Christ to express aggressive conduct toward the unbelievers. Such persons are, in this world, noncompetitors. This is the only reasonable position for one who, like the apostle, has counted everything as loss. In the realization of the blessed freedom from the bonds of the world and all its supposed threats, one finds the perfect freedom to respond to everyone in love. To seem vulnerable and defenseless in this world is a small thing, for it is in just such a state that one finds the assurance of heavenly security.

The Children of the Kingdom, living in the Way, are in this world nonthreatening noncompetitors whom nothing threatens. In the constant acknowledgment of this Truth lies the strength that gives stability and confidence. When the arch-prince of darkness tempts to doublemindedness, one need only take refuge in the Truth. If, for example, as an employee one is tempted to compete with fellow employees for a promotion in the world, then remember that this is only a loss, and the appropriate conduct will follow.

You see, then, how it is that God's children have a ready weapon always near in the struggle with evil. The Truth that we have in Christ Jesus, when oft acknowledged through deliberate recollection, makes us free. Its application confirms its power in every situation. So, if the devil does not flee at the first suggestion, one need only enforce the word with the acknowledgment of the victory of our leader. He was not and never is a competitor in this world. He does not in reality threaten anyone and was not and is never threatened by any earthly loss — including in particular the loss of his life. He did not fear those who could destroy the body but after that could do no more. His singleness of mind and purity of heart glorified him in his resurrection so that "every knee shall bow and every tongue confess that Christ is Lord." Whenever we bid the Truth to mind in this way, by meditation on the example of Him who is Truth, it will be for us as it was for that solitary individual in the wilderness: "Satan left him, and angels came and ministered to him." Therefore, to maintain godly conduct one needs only this singleness of mind; the rest will follow. The power to do this is Truth, constantly acknowledged. It can and will vanquish every demon so that in its light there is but one possibility: "Conduct yourselves becomingly, as in the day" (Romans 13:13).

One needs to guard against two widespread errors. The first is self-righteous Pharisaism, which supposes that righteousness resides in ourselves. It produces proud arrogance and condescension. Of ourselves we can do nothing but err. It is only by the power of Truth working in us that we manifest the righteousness of Christ. This enlightenment of the Holy Spirit that instructs us in Truth also reveals to our inner eyes our personal inadequacy to please God apart from the work and word of Christ. Yet, while we may be ashamed because of what we were before the hour of repentance, we dare not continue in a state of self denigration. We also see that God has accepted us as his sons and daughters so that we may with confidence approach the throne of Grace. We approach with neither shame nor pride, but in the blessed state of righteousness, peace, and joy that characterizes the Kingdom of God.

The second error to avoid is self-abasing evangelicalism. This proclaims that there is nothing good in man, even after Christ has redeemed him. This error ascribes every aspect of righteousness to another, wholly other person, Christ Jesus alone. Each lives out his time on earth in shame at this low estate, never realizing that God has exalted us beyond measure. This self-abasement depresses one mentally and spiritually. Also, it is positively evil in that it denigrates the work of God, namely ourselves, and calls that creation "evil" that our Father calls "good."

Both errors, self-righteousness and self-denigration, are attempts to obtain righteousness on the grounds of the same fundamental heresy: the belief that our "sins" are equivalent to our misdeeds. In the first case, the Pharisees suppose that they have lifted themselves by their bootstraps from bondage to sin and into a state of righteousness founded on deeds. In the second case, in foolish despair of self, they count such righteous deeds as impossible. Then they trust, just as foolishly, in the righteous deeds of another, Christ Jesus, as the grounds of their salvation and acceptability to God. In contrast, we know by the word of Christ that the righteousness of Christ, which has by God's grace become our righteousness also, consists in a disposition that deeds can only manifest. Any attempt to please God by focusing on deeds as the grounds of righteousness is futile to the utmost. There is but one disposition acceptable to the Father. Its word is near us, even in our hearts:

> *Whoever loves his life, loses it; and he who hates his life in this world, will keep it for life eternal* (John 12: 25).

This is the crucial word, full of both threat and promise, without equivocation or any other condition. First, whoever loves his life will lose it. This says nothing whatever about deeds, only about disposition — and it is the one and only essential condition. Second, whoever hates his life in this world will keep it for life eternal. Again, this says nothing about deeds. It only states, without exception or qualification, that whoever has this sole disposition will, without exception or qualification, enter our Father's glory.

This does not mean that deeds are unimportant. No, no! They become the telling evidence of our true disposition, raised in testimony for or against us on that day when He reveals every secret heart. Only, it is necessary to keep the horse before the cart through constantly cultivating the only godly disposition. That is the key, both to godly conduct and to the righteousness of Christ. It is so sad to hear the preachers — especially when they are delivering a funeral eulogy over the remains of a departed brother or sister. They say, "He loved life!" If they speak accurately, they are announcing his condemnation to all who hear, but they think they praise him! Apart from the accuracy of their speech, they always announce their own condemnation as those who suppose, contrary to the Word, that the love of life is righteousness. Those who say "Amen" also testify against themselves on that day. These errors are everywhere about us so that we must always be vigilant, knowing that they have had much influence. When temptation to sin confronts their pitiful victims, they think that they will be delivered by much praying. So they pray, "Father, deliver me from this great evil," without ever realizing Truth or cultivating the only acceptable disposition. Is it any wonder when they fall into sin, not having appropriated the power of Truth that alone overcomes evil? Instead, they call upon the Father to intervene for them in a mystery! This is like commanding the stones to become bread, while the true bread lies untouched in the cupboard. Let our prayers be recitations of Truth offered up to God through the Holy Spirit, and we will be strengthened. Thus it was that Jesus prayed and received strength in the wilderness, in Olivet, and on the cross. See how he calls to mind the Truth in the "High Priestly" prayer of John's Gospel (John 17:1-26), as one after another he related the facts of his work on earth.

There is no need for discussion of all the individual issues that we must decide during our sojourn in the Way of Christ. We settle every such issue with a single decision: the commitment to Eternity. While this commitment is secure, we will find the resolution to the particular issues to be clearly defined. Why should we smother the Truth in a sea of words about the issues, when all spring from a single root, and all have a single solution? Simple!

The "gray people" think of this as an oversimplification. These are those who arm themselves to confront each issue with an array of words about "gray areas," which can only mean that in their hearts, the shadow rules. Such talk constitutes a convenient refuge from the light. The Truth is simple. Their way, by contrast, is a bewildering complexity of truths, half-truths, and pure lies. It effectively insures against their ever realizing the childlike simplicity of the Way that leads to the only legitimate Father.

Now, "simple" does not mean "easy," and "complex" does not mean "hard." Any compromise can be justified by a complicated ideology, one that says both "yes" and "no" to everyone. Complexity is ideally suited to facilitate the choice of "the easy way" out of every moral dilemma. In the Way of Christ, it is always the either/or that rules, never the both/and. So, there is seldom any uncertainty about what is to be done to please the Father. Exactly here lies much of the sometimes terrible hardness of the Way — we can see it so clearly, and it always runs counter to the current of this world.

It also follows that the Way is contrary to the wishes of those who have been and are yet close to us in the bonds of purely natural affection. It is hard to maintain one's commitment, against the opposition of those "dear ones" who were once our close relatives but who now are strangers. One loves them much more than before, but in a different way that defines the Good in a different way, for them and for oneself. The Love of God has transcended every other love. It transforms every other love to that of the highest plain of eternal values that knows no discrimination. Yet, they also remain close in a natural way until those who walk in the Way of Christ have by The Father's grace attained to the perfection that is in Christ Jesus. Satan, in full knowledge of this, uses these purely natural affections as barbed spears to prevent our doing as we should. This has to do with the subject of our true relatives, about which I have already written at length showing how they are to be defined by the Lord Jesus. He never yielded for a moment to purely natural affection, not even to call Mary "Mother" or Joseph "Father." By examining the subject again, with this discussion of the Way, one can better understand both our relationships in Truth and their dominant influence on our actions.

We have seen how those who set their minds on earthly things are quickly threatened by others of a similar mind-set. We have also seen how, in consequence of the threat, they seek power in numbers by incorporating into local, national and supranational groupings. We can therefore classify such entities as "The Association of the Threatened Ones." Such associations inevitably become threats to others. These in turn feel compelled to respond by reinforcing their nationalism through parallel promotions of patriotism, civic duty, and the like things. Thus there is a snowballing process in the world in which the threatened threateners become ever more threatened and threatening, and they conduct themselves accordingly. Now, look sharply and you will see the solitary individuals who, in imitation of Christ, have set their affections exclusively on things above. Christ has delivered them from those earthly associations that exist solely for the sake of the threatened ones, because nothing threatens them. They no more belong to this world and are no longer related to it or to its children.

This quality of "not-of-ness" is an automatic status resulting from genuine repentance. It is a fact, not an ideal or elusive goal. The faithful practice of abiding in the Word constantly enforces it in the minds of the solitary individuals. In consequence there is an automatic response that brings our deeds into conformity with the singleness of our minds, and redefines our relationships and our relatives. This is fitting for all who have been born of God — not of the flesh or of the will of the flesh, but of the will of God.

Now it is also necessary to redefine the word "duty," and to give it a new significance. Is it to respond to the threats of the threatened, as though also threatened? Never! That may be their duty, but for those in the Way it is only hypocrisy. What patriotic, civic, or national duty can one have in any nation, when threats dictate such duties, and one is not threatened? When one is an alien to the state? When one's relationship is that of "not-of-ness?" No, it is none of these. It is instead the simplest thing imaginable: to respond to the will of the Father, and not to the contrary decrees of "The Fatherland." Yes, and what is the will of the Father? It is to set the mind on things above, and to love the Father himself with all the heart, mind, strength, and soul. Hard questions confront us, you say? How can you love your family, your friends, your neighbors, yet refuse to defend them from those who would do them bodily harm? Look carefully, and you will see that the guilt is in the mind of the questioner; for there is a dark duty, and there is an enlightened duty. The latter abides in the Truth and so sees only futility in efforts to preserve or protect an earthly status. It sees that very soon (oh, how soon!) one fate comes to all, both the victor and the vanquished, and all things thus pass away. Yes, even to the heavens and the earth! (Matthew 24:35; Mark 13:31; Luke 21:33).

There will always be defenders of the children of darkness, but God's children have the single duty to bear witness to the Truth in every circumstance. There is but one power that can deliver those who were once our relatives from the real enemy, the Prince of this world with his arsenal of threats. That is the Christ-witness, the consistent living testimony of the solitary individuals who hold steadfastly to the way of the cross, who thus can help others into the glorious freedom of the children of God.

Let both grow together
until the harvest . . .

Jesus, Matthew 13:30

13
THE FUTURE

The world's function dictates its future. Specifically, it functions as a place isolated from the Father's Glory. There, the children of God derive their being and resolve their willfulness. It also functions as a place of probation until the full number of them, having ceased their rebellion, have entered fully into the will of the Father. They will then have passed the critical tests associated with their probation. The essence of the matter is the willfulness of the children. Being in the likeness of the Father, they have ideas and the independence to assert them consistent with the freedom of the will.

Theirs would be an empty freedom, though, if they were without choices — that is, alternatives to the will of the Father. Therefore, the Father provided the world as a set of alternatives that gives reality to freedom. He also shared his creative qualities with the children so that they can create other alternatives using the raw material comprising the world-place. The Father's will for the children is one thing, and one thing only, absolutely exclusive of any other consideration. That one thing is his eternal Glory. Their reception into Glory, though, requires that they must first will it for themselves. If the Father were to take them in against their will, their contrary minds would spoil it, for themselves and for the Father. This is the particular willfulness for which the world serves as a place of resolution, and this is the essential goal of the probation of the children. The issue is the simple choice: the life of this world, or the life of eternal glory.

It follows that the world itself can never be glorious; therefore the glorification of the world is not a part of its future. We children evolve with eternal Glory in our hearts such that we can never realize fulfillment apart from Glory, but we must not find it here in the world. Then the Father's will for us would be frustrated, for it is his will that we share in *his* Glory. The withholding of glory is the sole limitation imposed on the world and on the life of the children in the world. This is the subjection of the world to futility mentioned by Paul (Romans 8:20) and defined by Jesus in terms of its "pass away-ness" (Matthew 24:35; Mark 13:31; Luke 21:33). Scientifically, this permanent futility of the world is expressed by and maintained by the Second Law of Thermodynamics. Therefore the world is and must always remain a futile place, a place of disappointments, of crushed hopes, of insecure possessions, of failed aspirations and doomed dreams. There will never be a glorious "millennial reign" of righteousness and peace on this earth. It is God's will.

The world has absolutely no purpose of its own, apart from the children. They are its sole reason-to-be. When all have qualified for glory, having successfully served their probation in the world, the world must end. The world is good, but only while it serves its essential function associated with the divine will. At its root, it is the fundamental manifestation of evil, being an alternative to the eternal Glory that is the will of the Father. So also it must have an end when it has fulfilled its purpose. Until then, it must remain bound by its chains of futility. *The continuation of this subjugation to futility is strong evidence of the reign of the Kingdom of God.*

Cosmology has now pretty well established that the world did have a beginning in the explosion of a primordial and infinitesimal singularity of infinite density — the Big Bang. According to current estimates, this explosion began some ten to fifteen billion years past. It isn't over yet. The material galaxies, flung outward from the primeval singularity with other forms of energy, continue to extend their vast trajectories at the frontier of the universe. The singular explosion also marked the birth of time, a rough intruder into eternity.

When we think of the end of the world, there appear to be two reasonable options. Scientists have shown that it will have one of two ends, depending on the unknown material density of the universe. Either it will burn out and grow cold as it expands forever (if the density is below a critical value), or gravity will turn it back upon itself. In the latter case it would compress itself into the primordial fireball from which it began, and ultimately, perhaps, to its birthing singularity. Its futility would then release it — into the "glorious liberty of the children of God."

Which of these two ends will be the lot of the world? This has been a subject of lively debate among scientists and philosophers. That the world will end by a gravitational contraction that reduces it to a fireball is not certain. Perhaps there is another route to an "end by fire" as described in Scripture; but why not? Why should not the Father from the beginning have invested the world with all the components necessary to bring itself to an end, once it has fulfilled its purpose? This would be an end by natural means: in a sense, nature committing suicide. The end of earth, and of earth-life, may also be accomplished naturally by the collision of the earth with a comet or some other astronomical body. According to Jesus:

> *Immediately after the tribulation of those days the sun will be darkened, and the moon will not give its light, and the stars will fall from heaven, and the powers of the heavens will be shaken; then will appear the sign of the Son of man in heaven, and then all the tribes of the earth will mourn, and they will see the Son of man coming on the clouds of heaven with power and great glory; and he will send out his angels with a loud trumpet call, and they will gather his elect from the four winds, from one end of heaven to the other* (Matthew 24:29-31)

Every one of the natural phenomena listed here: the darkened sun and moon, the falling stars, and the shaking powers of the heavens would be characteristic of a cometary collision with the earth. Such a collision could certainly destroy all life and render the earth uninhabitable. Vast clouds of dust and smoke would darken all heavenly bodies and render them invisible from the earth's surface, for anyone who might remain to look for them. The incoming cometary bodies would fulfill the prophecy of stars falling from the heavens.

There are at least two possible objections to this view of the end. First, Jesus seems to be speaking of something more cosmic than the end of life on a single planet. The end of life on earth may be the end of the world for us, but not necessarily for those children of God who have arisen on other planets throughout the cosmos. To this one might respond that Jesus was on the earth speaking to earthlings, and consequently he spoke in terms relevant only to us. Furthermore, our "cosmos" would certainly come to an end, which would justify the cosmic flavor of Jesus' prophecy. He did specify that "all the tribes of *the earth*" would mourn because of him.

The second objection to some such natural end as the cometary destruction of the earth comes from those who expect the world to end in consequence of supernatural action. The cosmos began super-naturally; perhaps it is to end supernaturally. The modern cos-mologists are in agreement here, for they admit that their natural laws cannot see back to the beginning closer than 10^{-12} seconds after the instant of the "big bang."* I see no reason to object to a supernatural end of all things, but I must acknowledge that I do not know how it will be, nor can I say with assurance whether Jesus spoke of the end of earth, or of the end of the cosmos. The important point here is to recognize that his words are consistent with either view.

There is only one sharp difference remaining between the biblicists and the cosmologists, and this time it is the biblicists who must compromise to effect a reconciliation. It is their turn, for most recently it was the cosmologists who acceded to the biblicists. That was when the cosmologists converted from the "steady state" theory of the Cosmos to agree with the biblicists that the world does, indeed, have both a beginning and an end. Einstein, for example, held long and tenaciously to the steady state, which led him to commit what he later called "the greatest blunder of my life." The major remaining differences are in the amount of time that has passed since the creation of the world, and in the amount remaining until the end. The biblicist must expand his thinking to conform to the known reality. He must turn from thinking "thousands" to thinking "billions." If he can accept that adjustment, he will have breached a major barrier to the reconciliation of science and religion.

Why should not these two disciplines have a reconciliation? They seek precisely the same goal: Truth, in all its glory. Since they have the same goal in view, and since each has made its own historic

---

* "Life In The Universe," by Stephen Weinberg in *Scientific American,* October 1994

contribution, why should they not now unite in the quest? The same Truth stands as the final goal; therefore there can be no contradiction between good science and good religion.

They use the same tool: the human mind. The difference is in their methods. Both are in quest of a revelation, and that the same one: the significance of the human experience. One seeks it through investigation and experiment coupled with the precisely logical method of mathematics. The other seeks it through divine revelation and experience coupled with the faith-based method of prayer and meditation. One seeks knowledge through observation, the other seeks knowledge through the eyes of faith, but both seek the same thing. One looks outwardly, at the world without; the other looks inwardly, at the world within. Yet in the end the differences are only quantitative — matters of emphasis, of degree and not of essence. Both have faith. Both exercise logic. Both listen attentively to the sources. Both are profound believers in the quest and in the reality of the Truth that is their common goal. In the end, they will be one.

I have said all this to introduce this one idea for subsequent discussion: the utterances of Jesus define a world view that is perfectly consistent with reality. From his perspective, only two primary stages of development pertain to the world experience, and these are implicit in his utterances. These two stages are defined by events that bracket them, which are also revealed in his utterances. A single human life has also these same two stages, which are: (1) the early period of growth and development, and (2) the longer period of mature experience that continues until the end. Historically, for the world, the first period is that before the crucifixion of Jesus and the coming of the Kingdom of God. The second, in which we now find ourselves, spans the time from the crucifixion until the end of the world. For the individual, the first ends when one "graduates" into adult responsibility and the second ends with one's death.

Now Jesus entered the world before his crucifixion, of course, so that his immediate perspective was near the end of the first period of the world. He was looking to future events that were to close the first period and inaugurate the second, and then to a second set of event that were to close the second. He also concerned himself with the circumstances that were to prevail during the brief time that remained until the end of the first period. Then, beyond that, he concerned himself with the circumstances that were to prevail during the second period. This, of course, includes our "today." His concerns therefore addressed two periods and two separate and distinct sets of demarcating events. Therefore we should expect his views to express a dualism growing out of the dual focus on two periods and two sets of events, and they do.

We also should exercise some care here to avoid two very common errors. First, we should acknowledge that Jesus' view of reality was from the perspective of eternity, where temporal distinctions are of no consequence. Therefore, the brevity of the time remaining until the end of the first period, at his crucifixion, is not relevant in evaluating the significance of that period. The much longer second and final period, in which we now live, may be much less significant in his view. Even if the second period should continue for billions of years, the length still is of no significance in evaluating the revelations of Jesus. His focus is upon the weight of events, not upon the measure of their times. When he expresses a sense of urgency, it is because of the gravity of the event to follow. It is the event that gives significance to the brevity of the time. Standing by itself, apart from the events, the time would be of no consequence. It is therefore conceivable that the events of the brief period remaining before the crucifixion carried, for Jesus, far more weight than all the rest of history and time. I do not say that they did, but they might, and we should be prepared to view them in this light. We should not evaluate them by their location (in our past), or by the brevity of their duration.

Second, it would be an error to allow ourselves to be influenced by the eschatological announcements of churchmen. Many of them form their confused views, involving millennial reigns and dispensations, without primary attention to the utterances of Jesus. Being captive to the love of life, they are loath to give it up to the reality that binds it. Therefore they conceive grandiose visions of a world where righteousness has triumphed. They little realize, in their darkness, that the vision is itself an evil delusion contrary to the will of the Father and to all reality. Their views tend to be complex and intricate and they present them with great authority. They buttress every point by chapter and verse. There is only one problem: they do not know what they are talking about, not having listened carefully to the utterances of Jesus. In contrast, the picture of the future that Jesus draws is simple and straightforward, as we shall see.

It is appropriate to introduce here a specific example of the confusion created by the preachers during their speculations about the future. One of their favorite themes is a thing they call "Armageddon." Notice first that Jesus never used the word, so that we should immediately question whether it justifies the attention given to it. The idea comes from the Revelation of John, where we read:

" The sixth angel poured his bowl on the great river Euphrates, and its water was dried up, to prepare the way for the kings from the east. And I saw, issuing from the mouth of the dragon and from the mouth of the beast and from the mouth of the false prophet, three foul spirits like frogs; for they are demonic spirits performing signs, who go abroad to the kings of the whole world, to assemble them for battle on the great day of God the Almighty. (Lo, I am coming like a thief! Blessed is he who is awake, keeping his garments that he may not go naked and be seen exposed!) And they assembled them at the place which is called in Hebrew, Armageddon [or 'Mount of Megiddo']" (Revelation 16:15, 16).

This passage comes in the midst of a longer one, in which angels are pouring the seven bowls full of the wrath of God out upon various unfortunate places. These include the earth, the sea, the rivers, the sun, the throne of the beast, the great river Euphrates, and the air. All this is highly allegorical language such that it is easy to err in seeking to understand it, as is true with the whole of Revelation. If we are to comprehend it aright, it will be necessary to relate it to the utterances of Jesus to establish its proper place in time. How will we do this?

We look for a clue; the Spirit always gives a clue, if we are open to receive it. It does not take long to find it: "Lo, I am coming like a thief!" Now, how does this relate to the utterances of the Lord? Both Matthew and Luke include utterances that are similar to this phrase. The following is from Matthew:

Watch therefore, for you do not know on what day your Lord is coming. But know this, that if the householder had known in what part of the night the thief was coming, he would have watched and would not have let his house be broken into.

Therefore you also must be ready; for the Son of man is coming at an hour you do not expect (Matthew 24: 42-44).

"The coming of the Son of Man" is Jesus' expression for his return at the end. Then he will receive the children of the Father and judge the righteous and the unrighteous as more fully described in Matthew 25. He will send no advanced notice. It is necessary to be ever watchful to respond properly to him when he comes to "break into the house." According to the Revelation, this is "the Great Day of God the Almighty" (Revelation 16:14), when the kings of the whole earth will be assembled for battle with the Son of man. This has already happened once, at a "mountain" called Golgotha. It was foretold by the Second Psalm and confirmed by the Apostles (Acts 4:24-31). Jesus also used similar language in interpreting his presence in the world. He explained how he could break into the house of the strong man and spoil his goods when he explained his ability to cast out demons:

Or how can one enter a strong man's house and plunder his goods, unless he first binds the strong man? Then indeed he may plunder his house (Matthew 12:29; Mark 3:27).

In both cases, he pictured himself as outside the house, about to break into it. In the first case he interpreted his ability to do this as a result of the "binding of the strong man," — that is, of Satan. In the second case, he interpreted his ability to do this as the result of thief-like stealth. He used the element of complete surprise, of coming totally unexpected, to keep the householder unprepared and asleep. Also, just as the Revelation describes a gathering of kings to do battle on "The Great Day of God the Almighty" when he comes like a thief, just so does the Second Psalm and the Acts present his first coming to do battle with the powers of this world, when "truly in this city there were gathered together against thy holy servant Jesus, whom thou didst anoint, both Herod and Pontius Pilate, with the Gentiles and the peoples of Israel, to do whatever thy hand and thy plan had predestined to take place."

There are then two events that follow the pattern laid out in the Revelation: The Battle of Mt. Calvary and the Battle of Mt. Megiddo or Armageddon. But are they really two separate events? The binding of Satan preceded the Battle of Mt. Calvary, as a thief first binds the householder, then enters the house to spoil his goods. Thus it involves a thief-like coming, and breaking into a house. It is associated with the gathering together of the kings of the earth, and it is also associated with a mountain. Also, the general language of the Revelation passage applies more aptly to the Battle of Mt. Calvary than to the end of the world. Armageddon is the outpouring of the bowl of the sixth angel. When the seventh angel pours out his bowl, there is a great voice out of the temple, and from the throne, saying, "It is done!" (Revelation 16:17). This is the language used by Jesus when speaking his last words from the cross: "It is finished!" (John 19:30). So, all the figures and events in the "Mount Meggido" passage in The Revelation are present at Mt. Calvary. Can the Revelation passage be only a figurative description of a past event? Perhaps, but Jesus also spoke of his next coming, the "Coming of the Son of man" as "like a thief," and that is the precise language of the Revelation. In addition, the words, "It is done," will be very appropriately spoken when the world ends. I conclude, therefore, that John in the Revelation spoke both historically and prophetically. He was looking back to the first coming and the Battle of Mt. Calvary, and projecting the same pattern of events to the future "coming of the Son of Man" and the Battle of Mt. Megiddo. The two are similar in that both involve powerful conflicts in the spiritual realm that have political ramifications. In the first case, Jesus overcame Satan and his subregents to establish the kingdom, or rule, of God on earth. In the second case, the Satanic powers will be released for one final rebellion against the divine authority. Their defeat will herald the end of the world and of what would have been their "political" domain had they been victorious.

Now, see how the gathering of the kings of the earth, with the gentiles and the peoples of Israel, was fulfilled at Mt. Calvary. Although the language of the Second Psalm seems aimed at fulfillment through the struggle of armies in a military conflict, that is not how it came about. Neither will it be so on the last day, that "Great Day of God the Almighty." These are metaphors only, intended to dramatize the cosmic dimensions of the struggle between the forces of Christ and of Satan. There will never be a literal "Battle of Armageddon" as portrayed here. Evil military forces will never battle with the armies of "righteous and God-fearing nations," in a struggle for the rule of the world. Jesus has already fought, and won, that battle at Mt. Calvary. You see, then, how the preachers err in failing to resort to the words of the Lord in their attempts at interpreting the other scriptures.

Jesus focused his ministry exclusively upon the Jews. This he made perfectly clear when he said:

> *I was sent only to the lost sheep of the house of Israel* (Matthew 15:24).

Not only was this the focus of his personal ministry, but he also made it the focus of the ministries of the disciples while he was with them. This he expressed just as clearly when he commissioned the twelve and sent them out to preach the Kingdom:

> *Go nowhere among the Gentiles, and enter no town of the Samaritans, but go rather to the lost sheep of the house of Israel* (Matthew 10: 5-6).

We do not conclude from this that he did not concern himself with the Gentiles. On the contrary, he never spurned an opportunity to manifest the outreach of his love to all persons everywhere. It was a matter of timing: the Jews first, the Gentiles later. It was because his concern was for all mankind that he made this one of the pillars of his message to the Jews ... so that those Jews who came to him could not fail to understand that they must, after his departure, reach out to all the world in his name. If the Jewish disciples should fail to broadcast his word to the world after his departure, then his mission would fail. It was therefore essential that they understand and accept this, and he expressed this very early in his preaching ministry — as early as his first sermon at the home synagogue in Nazareth. He seemed to know what the result was to be, for in his wisdom he lacked nothing in his understanding of the powerful national prejudices that are so common among men. The Jews are no exception. He prefaced his remarks at Nazareth with the words:

> *A prophet is not without honor, except in his own country,* *and among his own kin, and in his own house* (Mark 6:4).

The result of his speech was a disaster. They became enraged and rushed upon him so that he barely escaped. They had at first been very favorably impressed. It must have been a great temptation to him to say nothing offensive; but he did, and they were quick to turn against him! Yes, he knew well the power of their prejudice. He also knew that there must be no equivocation in this matter if he was to realize his purpose. The nearness of the Kingdom dictated his exclusively Jewish ministry and its urgency. After the coming of the Kingdom, the ministry must expand to include all the world. But in the short time remaining before the Kingdom's coming, the Jews, who were in some sense the exclusive possessors of the Kingdom, were to be gathered as lost sheep to the flock. They expected places of power and leadership in the Kingdom when it came. Thus it was that both Jesus and John called out to the nation to repent because of the nearness of the Kingdom (Matthew 3:2; 4:17; Mark 1:15). Thus it was that Jesus instructed the twelve, telling them to preach the Kingdom in every city where he himself was about to come (Matthew 10:7-23). Later he instructed the seventy messengers similarly, commanding them to tell everyone that the Kingdom of God had come near (Luke 10: 1-9). He promised the twelve that they were to sit on twelve thrones, judging the twelve tribes of Israel:

> *Truly, I say to you, in the new world, when the Son of man shall sit on his glorious throne, you who have followed me will also sit on twelve thrones, judging the twelve tribes of Israel* (Matthew 19:28).

When Jesus appeared after his resurrection, it was a return of the Son of man *in* his Kingdom. The Kingdom had come on earth, so that all power, in heaven and on earth, had already come to him (Matthew 28:18). Then it was that he recommissioned the disciples, saying to them:

> *All authority in heaven and on earth has been given to me. Go, therefore and make disciples of all nations, baptizing them in the name of the Father and of the Son and of the Holy Spirit, teaching them to observe all that I have commanded you; and lo, I am with you always, to the close of the age* (Matthew 28:18-20)

Do you see the clear implication? It was because he had received all authority, that is, because the Kingdom had come in power, that he then expanded the commission to include all the world. The limited ministry to the Jews therefore ended at the coming of the Kingdom. Since then, those Jews who survive have had to take their places in the midst of the other nations of the earth.

His feelings were ambivalent whenever he contemplated his people, Israel. On the one hand his great love and compassion caused him to see them as lost sheep without a shepherd, or as sheep whose shepherds had led them astray (Matthew 9:36). On the other hand, knowing that the multitudes of them would turn against him in rejection, he also saw them as wolves. I am thinking of when he sent the twelve out into the cities and villages of Israel, saying,

> *Behold, I send you out as sheep in the midst of wolves; so be wise as serpents and innocent as doves* (Matthew 10:16).

Yet his compassion was, and is, boundless. Though he knew the multitudes were wolves, "he had compassion on them, because they were harassed and helpless, like sheep without a shepherd." It was this emotion that moved him to say to the twelve, and later to the seventy also as he prepared to send them out on their preaching tours:

> *The harvest is plentiful, but the laborers are few; pray therefore the Lord of the harvest to send out laborers into his harvest* (Matthew 9:37-38; Luke 10:2).

John's Gospel expresses it as follows:

> *Do you not say, "There are yet four months, then comes the harvest?" I tell you, lift up your eyes, and see how the fields are already white for harvest. He who reaps receives wages, and gathers fruit for eternal life, so that sower and reaper may rejoice together. For here the saying holds true, "One sows and another reaps." I sent you to reap that for which you did not labor; others have labored, and you have entered into their labor* (John 4: 35-38).

In speaking of others who had labored, He spoke of the prophets before them whose labors were effective for the sowing of the word of Truth in the field of Israel. That seed had sprung up and grown white unto harvest. Jesus, "the Lord of the Harvest," is selecting and sending out laborers to gather in those who are to enter the Kingdom at its coming, and thus to have primary places therein.

He also expressed this view in parables, revealing how he looked, with the Father, to the nation of Israel for a harvest of fruit:

> *A man had a fig tree planted in his vineyard; and he came seeking fruit on it and found none. And he said to the vine dresser, "Lo, these three years I have come seeking fruit on this fig tree, and I find none. Cut it down; why should it use up the ground?" And he answered him, "Let it alone, sir, this year also, till I dig about it and put on manure. And if it bears fruit next year, well and good; but if not, you can cut it down"* (Luke 13:6-9).

Here Jesus is taking his cue from Isaiah, who described Israel in the same way: "My beloved had a vineyard on a very fertile hill. He dug it and cleared it of stones, and planted it with choice vines; he built a watchtower in the midst of it, and hewed out a wine vat in it; and he looked for it to yield grapes, but it yielded wild grapes. And now, O inhabitants of Jerusalem and men of Judah, judge, I pray you, between me and my vineyard. What more was there to do for my vineyard that I have not done in it? When I looked for it to yield grapes, why did it yield wild grapes? And now I will tell you what I will do to my vineyard. I will remove its hedge, and it shall be devoured; I will break down its wall, and it shall be trampled down. I will make it a waste; it shall not be pruned or hoed, and briers and thorns shall grow up; I will also command the clouds that they rain no rain upon it. For the vineyard of the Lord of hosts is the house of Israel, and the men of Judah are his pleasant planting; and he looked for justice, but behold, bloodshed; for righteousness, but behold, a cry!" (Isaiah 5:1-7).

Now going on to another of Jesus' parables, we find that he was fully as specific as Isaiah:

> *There was a householder who planted a vineyard, and set a hedge around it, and dug a wine press in it, and built a tower, and let it out to tenants, and went into another country. When the season of fruit drew near, he sent his servants to the tenants, to get his fruit; and the tenants took his servants*

*and beat one, killed another, and stoned another. Again he
sent other servants, more than the first; and they did the same
to them. Afterward he sent his son to them, saying, "They
will respect my son." But when the tenants saw the son, they
said to themselves, "This is the heir; come, let us kill him and
have his inheritance." And they took him and cast him out
of the vineyard, and killed him. When therefore the owner
of the vineyard comes, what will he do to those tenants? They
said to him, "He will put those wretches to a miserable death,
and let out the vineyard to other tenants who will give him
the fruits in their seasons"* (Matthew 21: 33-41).

Jesus also said to them,

*... have you never read in the scriptures: "The very stone
which the builders rejected has become the head of the
corner; this was the Lord's doing, and it is marvelous in our
eyes"? Therefore I tell you, the Kingdom of God will be taken
away from you and given to a nation producing the fruits of
it* (Matthew 21:42-43).

It was harvest time for Israel. The Father had invested everything
in this small nation; he had waited patiently for a very long time. He
had sent his prophets but they had killed them; and now he had sent
his son, whom they also would kill. Theirs was the Kingdom, and they
were the children of the Kingdom. Yet no fruit was forthcoming.
Jesus and his disciples would labor again in the Father's vineyard,
Judah and Jerusalem. This was their last chance. If they did not
produce this time, the tree would be cut down. The murderers of the
Son would be killed. The vineyard would be let out to others. The
Kingdom would be taken away from them and given to a nation
producing the fruit thereof.

Jesus therefore labored to bring forth fruit from the vineyard of
Israel as he and his disciples went forth to till and fertilize the
unfruitful fig tree. Yet he seemed to know all along that the effort
was largely in vain. The keepers of the vineyard would put the son to
death (Matthew 21:39). Then there would be a terrible judgment
against the nation — an outpouring of divine wrath such as the world
had never seen (Matthew 21:41). Jesus felt the force of this wrath as

it wrought a sorrow in his heart. Foreseeing its tragic end, he looked upon Jerusalem and lamented it as follows:

> *O Jerusalem, Jerusalem, killing the prophets and stoning those who are sent to you! How often would I have gathered your children together as a hen gathers her brood under her wings, and you would not! Behold, your house is forsaken. And I tell you, you will not see me until you say, "Blessed is he who comes in the name of the Lord"* (Matthew 23:37-39; Luke 13:34-35).

Finally, the end of the time of harvest had almost arrived. Only a handful had responded to him, and he foresaw the judgment of Jerusalem because of this lack of response. He approached the city from the descent of the Mount of Olives and looked upon the panorama grandly displayed across the Kidron valley. The tears flooded his eyes as he uttered the words of final judgment:

> *Would that even today you knew the things that make for peace! But now they are hid from your eyes. For the days shall come upon you, when your enemies will cast up a bank about you and surround you, and hem you in on every side, and dash you to the ground, you and your children within you, and they will not leave one stone upon another in you; because you did not know the time of your visitation* (Luke 19:41-44).

That very day he entered the city, cleansed the temple, and healed many blind persons. At evening he left, going to Bethany and lodging there for the night. The next day he again approached the city, hungry. Seeing a fig tree by the wayside he went to it and found nothing on it but leaves only. So he said to it:

> *May no fruit ever come from you again!* (Matthew 21:19; Mark 11:14).

The next day, as he approached the city again with his disciples, Peter said, "Master, look! The fig tree which you cursed has withered!" Jesus proceeded to use this as an object lesson on the power of the prayer of faith. But this was not his original reason for cursing the tree. In his disappointment at the fruitlessness of the fig tree of Israel, he chose to use this fruitless fig tree as an object lesson representing the nation. For as the fig tree withered and died, so was the nation to wither and die. The fig tree itself was not to be blamed for being fruitless. Mark informs us, " ... It was not the season for figs (Mark 11:13). Not so the nation; for that fig tree, it was the season for "figs," yet it was almost fruitless. There remained only the terrible judgment that Jesus had earlier foreseen and announced to his disciples:

> *Jesus left the temple and was going away, when his disciples came to point out to him the buildings of the temple. But he answered them, "You see all these, do you not? Truly, I say to you, there will not be left here one stone upon another, that will not be thrown down"* (Matthew 24:1-2; Mark 13:1-2; Luke 21:5-6).

The nation refused to respond. The desired harvest did not appear. Therefore, a time of judgment was foretold that would be the end of Israel as a nation, and of Jerusalem as a city of the people of God. The "fig tree" was to be "cut down."

We have, then, these major ideas woven into the tapestry of the future as revealed in the words of Jesus: A time of the harvest of Israel, but no harvest was forthcoming. Then a fierce judgment. John the Baptist initiated the time of harvest when he entered the scene proclaiming, "Repent for the Kingdom of God is at hand!" (Matthew 3:1-2). Jesus closed the time of the harvest of Israel when he departed with the cry,

> *It is finished!* (John 19:30)

The moment of that cry was the moment of the coming of the Kingdom of God in power upon the earth. Thereafter, for Israel and Jerusalem, there was the expectation of judgment that Jesus had announced to the unfruitful nation. Roman armies meted the judgment when, a few years later, they surrounded the city and laid siege to it. After a long and cruel time they overcame it and cast its stones to the ground as Jesus had prophesied. Even the die-hard remnant that later gathered at the Dead Sea fortress of Masada did not survive. They, too, fell to the sword of Rome that meted the wrath of God.

Yet the harvest had not been absolutely fruitless. Jesus had succeeded in calling out of the nation a small band of disciples through whom he expected to initiate a wider harvest of the world. In his prayer in John 17, he seems to focus upon these few persons as the key to the consummation of the work of the Father on the earth. They are the ones who will perpetuate the Word of Truth in the world. Others will believe through their word, and all believers will be as one. In the end, the believing remnant will enter the Glory of God (John 17:22, 24; Matthew 25:34).

What of the timing of these things? I remind you again that the Kingdom came when Jesus died on the cross, which was consistent with his utterance:

> *There be some standing here who shall not taste of death until the Kingdom of God be come* (Matthew 16:28; Mark 9:1; Luke 9:27).

Even if you have not perceived the coming of the Kingdom at Calvary, this saying still places it within the temporal bounds of that generation. Jesus repeatedly focused upon that generation of the Jews in his utterances, and this also gives knowledge about the timing of events. Not only the Kingdom, but also the final judgment of the nation of Israel was to come upon that generation. In the same context as that in which he pronounced the destruction of Jerusalem, he stated:

> *Truly, I tell you, all these things shall come upon this generation* (Matthew 23:36).

The most specific reference is from Matthew 24, where, after describing the awful judgment to be meted upon the Jews, he made it unmistakably plain that:

> *Truly I tell you, this generation shall not pass, till all these things be fulfilled* (Matthew 24:34).

We can conclude, then, that Jesus was speaking in the midst of the time of the harvest of Israel. The limited response of the nation was to result in its judgmental destruction before the end of that generation. The Kingdom of God was also to come within that same span of time. He labored in a field where others, the prophets, had labored before him, sowing the seed of the Word of God. Then followed a period of growing and of cultivation; but now the fields were white unto harvest (John 4:35), and the Father expected the harvest of the fruit of souls. The keepers of the vineyard had other plans. They wanted the harvest for themselves. Therefore they turned upon the Son and killed him, saying, "Now the inheritance will be ours!" (Luke 20:14). The result was that the Father mustered his sword, the armies of the Roman, Titus, and destroyed those villains. This took place about 70 A.D., after the coming of the Kingdom at the crucifixion, about 30 A.D.

Therefore the history of the Theocracy of the Jews embraced periods and events defined as (1) a sowing; (2) a growing; (3) a mowing; (4) the coming of the Kingdom; and (5) a final, destructive judgment upon that unrepentant generation. Items (1) and (2) were in Jesus' past. Item (3) was contemporary with him. Items (4) and (5) were in his future, with item (4) coming at his death. For us, in the end of the Twentieth Century, every one of these events is long past, and it is in the past that we will find them. They are not hidden in our future. Jesus foretold the coming of the Kingdom and the judgment of Israel exactly as they occurred. This fact gives confidence that his prophecies for the whole world are also being, and shall be, fulfilled.

The program for the world follows the same pattern as that for Israel. Jesus shows this in the Parable of the Tares:

> *The kingdom of heaven may be compared to a man who sowed good seed in his field; but while men were sleeping, his enemy came and sowed weeds among the wheat, and went away. So when the plants came up and bore grain, then the weeds appeared also. And the servants of the householder came and said to him, "Sir, did you not sow good seed in your field? How then has it weeds?" He said to them, "An enemy has done this." The servants said to him, "Then do you want us to go and gather them?" But he said, "No; lest in gathering the weeds you root up the wheat along with them. Let both grow together until the harvest; and at the harvest time I will tell the reapers, 'Gather the weeds first and bind them in bundles to be burned, but gather the wheat into my barn'" (Matthew 13:24-30).*

The disciples asked him to explain this parable and he replied:

He who sows the good seed is the Son of Man; the field is the world, and the good seed means the sons of the kingdom; the weeds are the sons of the evil one, and the enemy who sowed them is the devil; the harvest is the close of the age, and the reapers are angels. Just as the weeds are gathered and burned with fire, so will it be at the close of the age. The Son of Man will send his angels, and they will gather out of his kingdom all causes of sin and all evildoers, and throw them into the furnace of fire; there men will weep and gnash their teeth. Then the righteous will shine like the sun in the kingdom of their Father. He who has ears, let him hear (Matthew 13: 37-43).*

The same pattern is evident here, except that the field is the world, not just the nation of Israel. Everything else is self-explanatory.

The Parable of the Seed Growing Secretly also defines the processes proceeding in the world under the authority of the Kingdom of God. This is one of the "parables of the Kingdom," and describes the process prevailing at the present:

The Kingdom of God is as if a man should scatter seed upon the ground, and should sleep and rise night and day, and the seed should sprout and grow, he knows not how. The earth produces of itself, first the blade, then the ear, then the full grain in the ear. But when the grain is ripe, at once he puts in the sickle, because the harvest has come (Mark 4: 26-29).

Here is the obvious interpretation: Jesus has scattered the seed in the world, starting the process that ultimately issues in a harvest of souls for the Kingdom. Now the world is on its own while the process continues. There is no intervention from Jesus, the husbandman. He, as King, has all authority yet chooses not to interfere in the process that he has begun. He is the man who "sleeps and rises night and day" while the world produces, of itself, first the blade, then the ear, then the full grain in the ear. After the grain is ripe, that is, after all nations have heard the Gospel of the Kingdom and the full number has responded, then he will again spring into action. At once he puts in the sickle, because the harvest is ripe. Not only are we forbidden to root out the tares, or otherwise to interfere in the operation of the world, but even the King does not interfere! The Word is here, the Spirit is here, the Kingdom is here ... yet all leave the world to produce "of itself!"

Summarizing the program for the world at large, it includes: (1) The sowing of the seed, which Jesus and his disciples did. He who sows the good seed is the Son of man (Matthew 13:37). The good seed is the Word (Luke 8:11), which consists of the utterances of Jesus. The word enters the hearts of the sons of the Kingdom. They are the visible manifestations of the sowing, and are identified with the seed. The sons of the evil one (the devil) are also at work in the world, sowing the seeds of evil. (Matthew 13:25). They also produce their healthy offspring.

(2) Next, there is the period of growing together. "Let both grow together." This is our period. The most important thing to acknowledge is that the owner of the field has forbidden any effort to root out the evil from the world (our world) (Matthew 13:28-29). Jesus specifically acknowledged that both the sons of the evil one and sons of the Kingdom are to coexist throughout the growing period (Matthew 13:29). Any effort to root out the evil will be equally hazardous to the sons of the Kingdom and to the evil ones. Here he has said to everyone who would change the world, "Don't do it!" "Let both grow together!" Yet the clergymen continually bombard us with their calls to dedicate our lives to the task of "changing the world." This is totally contradictory to the Word of Christ.

(3) Next is the mowing of the world. This is when he "puts in the sickle." The harvest of the world will come, and will correspond exactly with the earlier harvest of Israel. This is the Second Resurrection, the ultimate fulfillment of the will of God.

(4) Then is the Parousia, the Second Coming, the Coming of the Son of man, when "every eye shall see him," when there will be no "Lo, here" or "Lo, there!" This corresponds with the first coming and more particularly with the "Coming of the Kingdom" at the first Resurrection, that is, the resurrection of Jesus from the tomb.

(5) Finally, there is the end of the world, the end of the age, the final consummation of all things together with the final Judgment — and yes, Armageddon!

Jesus has two sowings, two growings, two mowings (harvests), two comings, and two judgments in his schedule. Everything comes in twos, because he dealt first with Israel, then with the world, and the pattern for his dealings with both is the same. Even the same metaphors apply!

In the Synoptic passages, or "Olivet Discourse," Matthew 24, Mark 13, and Luke 21, we see how these two sets of ideas come together in the mind of Jesus. We also see how the disciples often confuse them. These passages describe events on a day when Jesus and the disciples were in the temple area of Jerusalem. Let us focus on Matthew 24, where we read:

> *Jesus left the temple and was going away, when his disciples came to point out to him the buildings of the temple. But he answered them, "You see all these, do you not? Truly, I say to you, there will not be left here one stone upon another, that will not be thrown down"* (Matthew 24:1-2; Mark 13:1-2; Luke 19:40-44; 21:5-6).

Later, as he sat on the Mount of Olives over against the panoramic view of the Temple Mount and all its great buildings, the disciples came to him and asked him this question: "Tell us, when will this be, and what will be the sign of your coming and of the close of the age?" (Matthew 24:3). This question, which the disciples supposed begged a single answer, was really two questions in one, with two different answers. Jesus proceeded to provide the two answers, one to each question.

Impressed as they were by the seeming permanence of the structures on the Temple Mount, the disciples supposed that they must stand forever. Therefore they identified the destruction of the Temple and related structures with the "close of the age." Jesus, of course, knew better. He was careful to provide an answer intended to clarify for them this distinction. He also told them, and us, all we need to know about the time of the two events, the destruction of the Temple and the end of the world. Jesus' answer makes the distinction clear enough, but for some reason the disciples did not grasp it. Neither did whoever first recorded the words as we now have them. They mixed his answers to the two questions, (1) When is the destruction of the Temple?, and (2) What will be the sign of your coming and of the close of the age? We will be confused if we read the verses consecutively. The two answers need first to be sorted. Then they will be seen to make perfect sense and to be the answers to two questions, not one, as the disciples supposed. Jesus' answers follow, appropriately sorted from Matthew 24.

The answer to the first question is in the following two segments: verses 15-22, and 32-35. Remembering now that the question is: "When will this be?" (i.e., the destruction of the great buildings of the Temple Mount), here is Jesus' answer:

When you see the desolating sacrilege spoken of by the prophet Daniel, standing in the holy place (Let the reader understand), then let those who are in Judea flee to the mountains; let him who is on the house top not go down to take what is in his house; and let him who is in the field not turn back to take his mantel. And alas for those who are with child and for those who give suck in those days! Pray that your flight may not be in winter or on a sabbath. For then there will be great tribulation such as has not been from the beginning of the world until now, no, and never will be. And if those days had not been shortened, no human being would be saved; but for the sake of the elect those days will be shortened. From the fig tree learn its lesson: as soon as its branch becomes tender and puts forth its leaves, you know that summer is near. So also, when you see all these things, you know that he is near, at the very gates. Truly, I say to you, this generation will not pass away till all these things take place. Heaven and earth will pass away, but my words will not pass away

Daniel's "abomination of desolation" (Daniel 9:27) is in a context that describes the profanation of the Temple by Gentiles. The events related to the destruction of the temple by Titus about 70 A.D. fit the prophesy well. This was surely the fulfillment of Daniel's prophecy of the "abomination that makes desolate." The second segment also must speak of the same, since it was particularly stated that "this generation will not pass away until all these things take place." 70 A.D. fits this well, coming about 40 years after Jesus spoke, designating "this generation."

There is yet another good reason to relate the first segment to Titus' destruction of the Temple. Jesus would not have instructed the disciples to flee for their lives at the end of the world. On that day, whoever would save his life will lose it (Matthew 16:25; Mark 8:35; Luke 9:24; 17:33). But in 70 A.D., it served the agenda of the Kingdom of God for the disciples to save themselves so that they would be preserved to propagate the Gospel of the Kingdom to all the world. Jesus likewise saved his life from danger in Nazareth, and elsewhere, so that he might fulfill his purpose upon earth. It will be helpful to refer to Luke 17, to a passage where Jesus responds to the Pharisees' question about the coming of the Kingdom. Here he used similar language but with a totally different meaning:

> ... *so will it be on the day when the Son of Man is revealed. On that day, let him who is on the housetop, with his goods in the house, not come down to take them away; and likewise let him who is in the field not turn back. Remember Lot's wife. Whoever seeks to gain his life will lose it, but whoever loses his life will preserve it* (Luke 17: 30-33).

The distinction is plain. In Matthew 24, Jesus provided instructions to insure that the lives of the disciples would be saved from the disaster to come upon the nation and the city of Jerusalem. In Luke 17, his instructions were to insure that the disciples do not try to save anything, including their very lives. For, if they try to save themselves, they will lose life eternal.

The second question, about the signs of the close of the age, has three segments as follows: verses 4-14, 23-31, and 36-44.

> *Take heed that no one leads you astray. For many will come in my name, saying, "I am the Christ," and they will lead many astray. And you will hear of wars and rumors of wars; see that you are not alarmed; for this must take place, but the end is not yet. For nation will rise against nation, and kingdom against kingdom, and there will be famines and earthquakes in various places: this is but the beginning of the sufferings. Then they will deliver you up to tribulation, and put you to death; and you will be hated by all nations for my name's sake. And then many will fall away, and betray one another, and hate one another. And many false*

prophets will arise and lead many astray. And because wickedness is multiplied, most men's love will grow cold. But he who endures to the end will be saved. And this gospel of the kingdom will be preached throughout the whole world, as a testimony to all nations; and then the end will come.

Then if anyone says to you, "Lo, here is the Christ!" or "There he is!" do not believe it. For false Christs and false prophets will arise and show great signs and wonders, so as to lead astray, if possible, even the elect. Lo, I have told you beforehand. So, if they say to you, "Lo, he is in the wilderness," do not go out; if they say, "Lo, he is in the inner rooms," do not believe it. For as the lightning comes from the east and shines as far as the west, so will be the coming of the Son of Man. Wherever the body is, there the eagles will be gathered together. Immediately after the tribulation of those days the sun will be darkened, and the moon will not give its light, and the stars will fall from heaven, and the powers of the heavens will be shaken; then will appear the sign of the Son of Man in heaven, and then all the tribes of the earth will mourn, and they will see the Son of Man coming on the clouds of heaven with power and great glory; and he will send out his angels with a loud trumpet call, and they will gather his elect from the four winds, from one end of heaven to the other.

But of that day and hour no one knows, not even the angels of heaven, nor the Son, but the Father only. As were the days of Noah so will be the coming of the Son of man. For as in those days before the flood they were eating and drinking, marrying and giving in marriage, until the day when Noah entered the ark, and they did not know until the flood came and swept them all away, so will be the coming of the Son of man. Then two men will be in the field; one is taken and one is left. Two women will be grinding at the mill; one is taken and one is left. Watch therefore, for you do not know on what day your Lord is coming. But know this, that if the householder had known in what part of the night the thief was coming, he would have watched and would not have let

his house be broken into. Therefore you also must be ready;
for the Son of man is coming at an hour you do not expect.

This plainly describes events that cannot have transpired as of the time of the present writing. Here is not the destruction of a city; here is nothing less than the end of the world. When the Romans destroyed Jerusalem, the disciple who was in the field fled to the mountains. He or she also survived to preach the Gospel to the nations. It will be different at the close of the age. Then, the disciple who is in the field "will be taken." The cosmic happenings defining this event clearly speak of the end of the world, for here is a darkened sun, falling stars, darkness, and the sign of the Son of man in heaven.

Jesus did not know the time of the end of the world, and he said so. What he did was (1) describe the kinds of events that would occur in the interval preceding the end, and caution us not to be deceived and think the end is nigh, and (2) describe events near the end. He did caution us to be ready always, because his return and the close of the age is to be at a time we do not expect. Paul expressed it this way:

When men are saying "Peace and safety," then comes sud-
den destruction upon them" (1 Thessalonians 5:3).

Curious, isn't it? When times are dark and doomsayers abound, that is not the time of doom. But some day when things are bright and peace and safety prevail, comes the end — catastrophically, unexpectedly, finally.

The full span of history, from the moment Jesus died on the cross until the moment you are reading this, belongs to the interval preceding the end. Review the history of this time and see how accurately he spoke: nations and kingdoms have been continually rising against one another, and they are still doing so (Matthew 24:7; Mark 13:8; Luke 21:10). There has been no secure peace, nor will there be. The faithful ones have suffered tribulation in the world, and they will continue to suffer (John 16:33). The world has never been hospitable to the children of the Kingdom, nor will it be. False prophets of every stripe have arisen, and they will continue to do so. They have led many, many people astray, and will continue to do so. There have been famines and earthquakes in many places, and there continues to be such. Wickedness is multiplied, and most men's love has grown cold, and so it will continue. The most precise description given of the conditions that are to prevail in the world until the end is this:

Wickedness is multiplied (Matthew 24:12).

This world is not a perfect place, and it cannot be so. It has peaked and now is in decline, becoming more imperfect as the centuries pass. This is true though the Kingdom of God has fully come on the earth! Far from securing the perfection of the world, as the preachers think, the operation of the Kingdom perpetuates its bondage to futility.

In another utterance Jesus said, "The poor you have always with you" Matthew 26:11; Mark 14:7; John 12:8). Why, then, do some disciples dedicate themselves to the proposition that poverty must be eliminated from the earth? Poverty, war, famine, pestilence, the multiplication of evil, the deceitfulness of false prophets — Jesus foretold them all, and history has confirmed him. It will continue to do so, even until the end, just as he prophesied.

Yes, the Kingdom has already come, long ago at the crucifixion, at the moment of Jesus' death, after he partook of the fruit of the vine. All authority, in heaven and on earth, has been given to him, and he is reigning from the right hand of the Father in Glory. These things therefore exist according to the will of the King. He could purify the earth if he would, whenever he would, so great is his power in his Kingdom. That he does not do so says something very important about the function the world is fulfilling — that it is and must forever remain an alternative to glory. As an alternative, it must never become glorious.

In Christendom there is a common conviction that the Kingdom of God has not yet come, but when it comes it will usher in a worldwide, utopian reign of peace. This would be the fulfillment of one of man's oldest dreams. Sadly, this conviction is in diametric opposition to the reality with which we have to deal.

The facts are (1) the Kingdom of God has come. It is on earth in its consummate form. And (2) It operates in a way that prevents the Golden Age. That the world has not found secure peace among men and nations is powerful evidence of the rule of God in his Kingdom. I remind you how it was in the Roman Empire of the first century. It was a time of relative peace in the world, enforced by the Pax

Romana. Then the Kingdom came, and he who now rules from the right hand of God has dashed them in pieces like a potter's vessel, fulfilling the Second Psalm.

The language of Jesus suggests that at the time of the end, the world may be permitted again to unite and have peace, for then men will be saying "peace and safety" (Matthew 24:37-39; 1 Thessalonians 5:3). The breakup of the Roman Empire was not the first intervention of the Father in human affairs. That is exactly what happened at the primeval Tower of Babel. There he confused the language of a united humanity and scattered them abroad over the face of the earth. The end of the world is to follow a similar pattern.

I have shown how the prophecy of Jesus in Matthew 24 must be sorted. There are two separate prophecies, one pointing to the end of the Jewish nation and of Jerusalem before the passing of that generation. The other points to the end of the world. The parallel passages in Mark 13 and Luke 21 also must be sorted. I will not quote them here, but the proper sorting is as follows: Judgment on the Jewish nation: Mark 13:14-23, 28-31; Luke 21:20-24, 28-33; Judgment on the world: Mark 13:5-13, 24-27, 32-37; Luke 21:8-19, 25-27, 34-36.

Now let us return to Matthew 24 to examine in greater detail the events prophesied for the present and for the end of the world. Verses 9-14 describe the tribulation that is the lot of true disciples in every age while the world stands. There is no basis in the utterances of Jesus for a special "tribulation" at the end time, seeing that the world has always been, and will always be, hostile to the Truth. This describes the normal condition of legitimate discipleship throughout history. The earlier passage, Matthew 10:17-21, describes a similar tribulation that was the lot of the early disciples as they went out to witness to the nation of Israel. This is only another aspect of the duality of the future in the utterances of Jesus. He foresaw both the tribulation of the first disciples in Israel, and the tribulation of later disciples throughout the world until the end, and described both tribulations similarly. Verse 14 reads as follows:

And this gospel of the kingdom will be preached throughout the whole world, as a testimony to all nations; and then the end will come (Matthew 24:14).

This tells us the prime condition for the end of the world — the Gospel of the Kingdom must first be preached to all nations!

It duplicates the prime condition for the destruction of the nation of Israel. Then, the Gospel of the Kingdom consisted of the proclamation of its nearness, and Jesus urged the disciples on to their preaching mission to the cities and towns of Israel:

> *When they persecute you in one town, flee to the next; for truly, I say to you, you will not have gone through all the towns of Israel, before the Son of Man comes* (Matthew 10:23).

Here the coming of the Son of Man refers not to his coming at the end of the world, but to his coming "in his Kingdom" after the resurrection. Therefore, that the world has not yet ended strongly suggests that the particular gospel, called by Jesus the "Gospel of the Kingdom" has not yet been preached to all nations. Has it been yet been preached to any nation,? We hear little or nothing of the good news, that the Kingdom is consummated on the earth, having fully come. How very much one hears from the preachers about how it is yet to come! That, of course, is not good news at all. It is bad news that tells us that the kingdom is yet to come, and therefore is not yet come!

I do not deduce from this that the world will end the instant the last nation hears the Gospel of the Kingdom. There may be other conditions that will delay its coming beyond that. One thing is certain — it will not end before the last nation hears it.

How long will it take now for the last nation to receive the proclamation of the Gospel of the Kingdom? Many would suppose that this has already occurred, since they identify the Gospel of the Kingdom with what the preachers are busily spreading around the globe. Or, if it has not, they think that it must happen in this generation. They point to the development of electronic communications worldwide, and to the plethora of electronic evangelists. They are mistaken. What they are seeing and hearing must be only the fulfillment of Jesus' prophecy from verse 24:

> *For false Christs and false prophets will arise and show great*

signs and wonders, so as to lead astray, if possible, even the elect (Matthew 24:24; Mark 13:22).

Or, that from verses 11 and 12:

And many false prophets will arise and lead many astray. And because wickedness is multiplied, most men's love will grow cold (Matthew 24:11-12).

These two verses describe the exact condition of the world today. So it is not surprising that the world has not yet heard the Gospel of the Kingdom. Considering the little progress since the introduction of this gospel two thousand years ago, many more millennia may pass before all nations hear. If the years should stretch out into the billions? Even that is conceivable, given the little progress to date.

Jesus prophesied two separate "comings" in the passages listed above and in others not yet mentioned. One was the coming of the Kingdom, fulfilled at the crucifixion; the other is the coming of the Son of Man, which is not yet fulfilled. The coming of the Kingdom coincided with the first coming of the messiah, whereas the coming of the Son of Man will coincide with the Second Coming. The first one is long past, the second is not yet, but Jesus spoke of them in similar fashion.

The Kingdom of God is not coming with signs to be observed; nor will they say, "Lo, here it is!" or "There!" for behold, the Kingdom of God is in the midst of you (Luke 17:20, 21).

And he said to the disciples, "The days are coming when you will desire to see one of the days of the Son of man, and you will not see it. And they will say to you, 'Lo, there!' or 'Lo, here!' Do not go, do not follow them. For as the lightning flashes and lights up the sky from one side to the other, so will the Son of man be in his day" (Luke 17:22-24).

Do you see the titillating similarities and differences? The coming of the Kingdom is invisible ("comes not with observation"). No one saw it, and so no one is aware of it, except through the revelation of the Word. Therefore no one said, "Lo, here it is!" or "There!" Why, it was already in the midst of them! The coming of the Son of Man is different, in that it will be universally visible. No one will be unaware of it, and so, again, no one will cry out, "Lo, here it is!," or "There!" Meanwhile, if someone cries out to you that the Son of Man is here, or there, do not believe it. When it happens, you will know it! It will take place precisely as Jesus described it in Matthew 24, Mark 13, and Luke 21. His angels will be sent out to gather the elect from every corner of the earth and from one end of heaven to the other, that

> *Wherever the body is, there will the vultures be gathered together* (Luke 17:37).

That this gathering will not be on the earth is clear, for he will gather the elect "from the ends of the earth to the ends of heaven" (Matthew 24:31; Mark 13:27). Paul agrees. In the letter to the Thessalonians he writes:

"For the Lord himself will descend from heaven with a cry of command, with the archangel's call, and with the sound of the trumpet of God. And the dead in Christ will rise first; then we who are alive, who are left, shall be caught up together with them in the clouds to meet the Lord in the air; and so we shall always be with the Lord" (1 Thessalonians 4:16-17).

Therefore there is no place in the future for any kind of renovation of the world or of human society. The earth will continue into the future as it has in the past, perfectly consistent with the prophecies of Jesus. Then, sometime near or distant, the Son of Man will appear like lightning and will gather his elect from the earth, including those he must first resurrect.

These are the only end-time events in the prophetic utterances of our Lord. There is no yet-coming Kingdom, no end-time tribulation, no future millennial reign of righteousness on earth, no restoration of the Jews to Palestine. Modern Israel is an anachronism, not a fulfillment of biblical prophesy. The Father is through with the Jews as a nation, and has been through with them since the final desecration of their Temple by Titus in 70 A.D. The fig tree has been cut down!

What, then, does John in Revelation mean by "Over such the second death has no power, but they shall be priests of God and of Christ, and they shall reign with him a thousand years" (Revelation 20:6)? When the Kingdom of God came at the death of Jesus on the cross, his milleneal reign began. Every witness in the New Testament agrees that his reign began at or near that time. Jesus himself said,

All authority in heaven and on earth has been given to me (Matthew 28:18).

Paul wrote, "... you have come to fullness of life in him who is the head of all rule and authority (Colossians 2:10). And also he recorded these glorious words: " ... when he raised him from the dead and made him sit at his right hand in the heavenly places, far above all rule and authority and name that is named, not only in this age but also in that which is to come; and has made him the head over all things for the church, which is his body, the fullness of him who fills all in all" (Ephesians 1:20-23).

Peter wrote of Christ: " ... who has gone into heaven and is at the right hand of God with angels, authorities, and powers subject to him" (1 Peter 3:22).

But perhaps John said it best: "The kingdom of the world has become the kingdom of our Lord and of his Christ, and he shall reign for ever and ever" (Revelation 11:15).

There can be no doubt. He is reigning now! He is reigning together with all those who have been raised to newness of life in him (the First Resurrection). He will reign with them forever and ever. We are in the midst of the Millenium, and you are missing out on it if you do not believe. But, you ask, what about the 1000 years? It has been nearly two thousand years since his resurrection.

The thousand years means one thing and one thing only: a very long time. It could end tomorrow (a thousand, but not thousands, as some have foolishly thought). It may last for thousands or millions or billions of years longer. The numbers mean absolutely nothing to the Absolute One. His realm is the infinite and the eternal, and it is from that perspective that Jesus looked upon the world. What are numbers, anyway? Are they not merely marks on the meter stick or the yard stick, marks on the measuring cup, marks on the balance, marks on the face of the clock? Devices by which we attempt to measure the finite physical reality with which we have to deal and by which we are accustomed to think? But the eternal one, the Lord Jesus who rules from the right hand of the Father, has no need of such devices, for no numbers can comprehend the width, height, or length of the Eternal Glory. There is no measure by which we can measure him. It is foolish even to think of such a thing. So when Jesus, as the Son of God, the eternal one, came into the world, he had very little use for numbers. He utilized them very seldom, and then only as an accomodation to our mode of thinking. The only numbers important to him were, perhaps, two or three, as when he said,

> *Wherever two or three are gathered together, there I am in the midst of them* (Matthew 18:20).

The only really important number was the number "one." He loved this number more than any other, and spoke of it often, for in eternity it alone has significance. See how he looked to it and utilized it in so many ways in the following example:

> *The glory which thou hast given me I have given to them, that they may be one even as we are one, I in them, and thou in me, that they may become perfectly one, so that the world may know that thou hast sent me and hast loved them even as thou hast loved me* (John 17:22, 23).

But what of the earth, you ask? Is it not to be purged of evil? Foolish person, why do you ask? Have you not heard the word of our Lord:

> *Where your treasure is, there will your heart be also?* (Matthew 6:21).

So why are you concerned about the earth if you do not treasure it? Seek those things that are above! Here is your problem: you love your life, this earth experience, and you cannot give it up to its ultimate futility.

Turning now to Matthew 25, one learns that not only the elect ones, but also the wicked, will be raised to stand before him on that day. They will stand in a different group, separated from the elect as the shepherd separates the goats from the sheep. Then comes the judgment — a day of surprises for all. The wicked:

> *... will go away into eternal punishment, but the righteous into eternal life* (Matthew 25:46).

Also consider this: because no one could see the first coming, the coming of the Kingdom, we now have a commission to go into all the world and proclaim the Gospel of the Kingdom to every nation. It came, but not with observation; therefore no one will know of it unless we tell them. The second coming, the coming of the Son of man, will be universally visible. Therefore absolutely no one will or can have any commission to proclaim it to others. There will be no need. So when they say, "Lo, here it is!" or "There!" do not believe it! (Matthew 24:23; Mark 13:21).

I am the way . . .

Jesus, John 14:6

14

THE APPLICATION

The precepts of Jesus apply to every disciple, in every situation, time, and place. They are not confined to him and the early apostles. He is the leader who, by precept, commandment, and example, has mandated the Way, the only Way, to life. It is the only route to his kingdom and glory. He is the way and the door, and *everyone* who would enter must follow. There is no other way to God. There is no other way to inherit eternal life.

The Way is hard. It was hard for him; it is hard for us who follow. Hard, yes — but possible. We have his footsteps to trace, like a trail blazed through the wilderness of this world, because he has gone before us. If we abide in him, that is, in his Word, he strengthens us with his presence. He will never leave or forsake us. Still, it is hard. He said it, and made no apology for it. It is hard, because it means to take up the cross in the world. This must inevitably have radical effects that we would prefer to avoid. I have found, though, that the application is not always so radical as it first appears, nor the effect of the application always so severe as one might suppose. This final chapter seeks to clarify some points of application. The principles are so simply and concisely stated, though, that their application should not require much clarification.

I also offer this word of caution: this is the application as I see and experience it. It may differ for you, though the principles are unvarying. I am not offering myself as an example. Only Jesus is uniquely qualified to exemplify the Way, and he alone is our leader.

It is easy to make mistakes. I illustrate here by describing two of mine. Joining a church was the first great mistake of which I am aware.

This exposed me to a multitude of errors masquerading as the Truth, which I eagerly accepted. With many others, I kissed him in the midst of betrayal. The result was some twenty-five years of heartache and perplexity of mind as I sought to blend church loyalty with loyalty to Christ. This is not possible. I know it now; if only I could have known it then! Still, all was not lost — I learned from it. It was a learning experience from which our Lord finally extracted me. I tell you this: I am glad it is over!

Another mistake came after I left the church. Having lost there a ready congregation, I was ill prepared for having no one eager to hear what I had to say. I felt compelled to reach out for converts and fellowship, and Jesus' words were ever near me:

> ... *whosoever does not forsake ... cannot be my disciple* (Luke 14:33).

The words are plain enough, so I finally forsook my employment and my family and went out into the world to make disciples. There was nothing right about it. I never felt that I was in the Lord's will. I tried many places, people, and things. Nothing worked. There was little fruit and less gratification as I moved from place to place. Finally, like the prodigal, I "came to myself" in the realization that I was still confused and uncertain about the implications of the Gospel. There were many questions and few answers. I could not accept a commission to go into all the world and preach the Gospel unless I understood it. I realized eventually that I should return to my family and to secular employment, which I did.

Later yet, I came to see that it was a need to do something great in the world that had at least partially motivated me. I wanted to get a little worldly glory for myself. That motivation is the kiss of death to true discipleship. I had thought I was only being obedient to Christ, but my motives were impure and confusion reigned in my heart. Through this and other experiences I came to realize that the motive is crucial, because it has it's origin in the will, which is the prime focus of both righteousness and salvation.

These are not my only serious mistakes. I mention them because each illustrates opposite extremes of error in the application of the principles of Christ to life in this world. On one hand stands the temptation to go with the crowd, to defer to the wisdom of the elders, to follow the easy way. On the other hand there is the overemphasis of radicalism, the taking of extreme positions in the seeming literal application of every aspect of the Word. This can sometimes be pure folly. It may be folly even when it appears to be the obvious response to the Word. Whatever we do, the motive must be pure! The heart must be single!

I could have avoided such mistakes by carefully examining the life of Jesus. He stands in an exclusive relationship to us as a leader and example. No one else is able legitimately to occupy that position. It is for this reason that I do not offer myself as a leader. He said:

> *Neither be called leaders, for one is your leader, the Christ* (Matthew 23:8-10).

Churchmen offer lip service to this principle, but in practice they ignore it. This has contributed to a fragmented religious establishment. Some follow the Pope as leader, some the Patriarch, some Calvin, some Wesley, some Luther, some Campbell, some Rutherford, some Smith, some Eddy, and only a few, Christ. It was no different during the Apostolic Era, nor is there any prospect of change in the future. Jesus called us to follow him. It is imperative that we do so, exclusively, if we are to be pleasing to God. Let us therefore study his example and apply it to our lives.

What can we learn from one so long crucified? There is a paucity of information about Jesus. Except for the last three years of his life, we know very little. Is this the only period when he served as an example? I do not think so. His uniqueness sprang from his beginnings in the world. Therefore the early, and longer, portions of his life also must have been exemplary.

He acknowledged his uniqueness as early as the age of twelve when, speaking to Joseph and Mary in the Temple he said:

> *How is it that you sought me? Did you not know that I must be in my Father's house?* (Luke 2:49).

Yet in many ways I think he was not unique. He returned with his parents to Nazareth, where he remained with them for many years. He was subject to them, as is normal with young children. I infer from scripture that Joseph died while Jesus was still very young, about fourteen. There were many siblings. There is specific mention of

James, Joses, Judas and Simon, together with a plurality of sisters (Mark 6:3). I infer therefore that his siblings had come along about every two years during this early period of his life. There would have been, at Joseph's passing, at least six of them, of whom the eldest was about twelve, the next ten, the next eight, the next six, the next four, and the last, two. You may object that average birth intervals of two years are unrealistic during an age that knew little of birth control. Perhaps so; there may have been more than two sisters. Some may have died in early childhood. Anyhow, Joseph at his passing left Mary with a large brood of at least seven young children of whom Jesus was the eldest. As such, it fell to him to take on the primary responsibility of family breadwinner. He would logically have done so by continuing Joseph's practice of carpentry. We also can infer that he continued in this capacity until about the age of thirty, when all knew him as "the carpenter" (Mark 6:3). He then forsook his trade and his family, and began to fulfill his mission.

So, for perhaps sixteen years, he labored as an ordinary carpenter — until the youngest children had reached maturity and could fend for themselves. His mother did not remarry. It would have been very difficult for her to find a husband, burdened as she was with the dual disadvantages of poverty and many children. Had she remarried, she would have relieved Jesus of his bread winning responsibility earlier. He would have begun earlier to pursue his mission. These inferences account for his townspeople knowing him as "the carpenter," and for their making no reference to Joseph in identifying him. Jesus served as our example during this ordinary period of his life, as he did later when his uniqueness again prevailed. By working as a carpenter and fulfilling family responsibilities for many years, he showed that we who follow can also be breadwinners. We, too, can engage in a skilled occupation. We likewise can support ourselves and our families.

Was he a wage earner, an independent contractor, a shopkeeper or a businessman? It is no matter. As a carpenter he could have been all of them. If Jesus could follow this type of activity in the world, so can we. Therefore, no man has followed the example of Jesus until he has earned a living. No one has followed the example of Jesus apart from fulfilling family responsibilities. There is no "free ride" in the Kingdom of God.

His stance toward the world was not so radical that it interfered with success in earning a living. As a person of unparalleled honesty who treasured neither material wealth nor time, he would have provided full value for goods and services sold, and a full days work for a full days pay. These characteristics contribute to a successful career. They might present a temptation, to one so engaged, to commit his life to this success and to become a wealthy man. This is a temptation to which Jesus never yielded. He was, after all, not of this world (John 8:23), and to that non-relationship he tenaciously and consistently adhered.

Since it is true that he was not of the world, he would not have identified himself as a citizen of Israel, a nation of this world. His basic stance must, then, have been that of an alien. As such, he would not have participated in the civic, political, and national activities of his home country. Neither would he have been a party to the revolutionary movements that were common among the Jews. He would have accepted the circumstances of his people, doing nothing either to alter, to end, or perpetuate them. He had a unique mission in the world, and a unique agenda for fulfilling it. With this as his compelling interest and commitment, he lacked any inclination to involve himself in local, national, and world affairs.

Jesus' stance as an alien in the world is the most radical position imaginable. Yet the world does not recognize it as such until one reaches out for converts and succeeds in winning them. Until then it poses no evident threat. This contrasts with the effect produced by most radicals, who gain their laurels by efforts to effect changes in society, thus making many enemies. Therefore Jesus would have incited no animosity while he pursued the mundane chores of a carpenter. I think he would have had much respect from the community for his hard work, skill, honesty, and fulfillment of family responsibilities. It was a different story, though, after Jesus won adherents and gained influence. It made no difference then that he was not seeking to change the world. All who are threatened by new ideas will suppose that change is in the offing, and will react, in a hostile manner, with misguided efforts to protect their worldly interests. The love of life compels them. Look at the Pharisees, whose antipathy toward Jesus was fueled by the thought that his growing movement would result in the coming of the Romans to "destroy both our holy place and our nation" (John 11:48).

Some may have thought him strange due to his lack of interest in public issues, but this would not have generated hostility. His neighbors could have perceived no threats to themselves. I believe, therefore, that we can follow the example of Jesus and live a normal life in the world until we become militant witnesses. On the positive side, we work as Jesus worked, earn our living, maintain our integrity, love our neighbors, and show mercy. On the negative side, we do nothing in disobedience to his commandments. This means that we do not take oaths or seek wealth. We do not go to war. We do not, we cannot, divorce. We do not engage in the public display of piety. We do not seek our living through appointment to religious posts, since our religion teaches that "whoever seeks to find his life shall lose it" (Matthew 10:39). We, who seek only the glory of God, do not engage in or support seditious activity. We do not involve ourselves in either revolutionary or counter-revolutionary movements, or in either national, political, cultural, or racial initiatives. I must add, though, that Jesus is, in Truth, the paramount revolutionary and the ultimate radical. His movement has already sealed the fate of the nations and of the whole world. That is one reason we seek no other revolution. But do not suppose that Jesus manifested a normal life for many years because he sought such a life. Such a motive would have been a gross inconsistency for one who hated his life in the world, as Jesus surely did. No, it simply turned out that way as Jesus moved in an exemplary fashion to earn his wages and fulfill responsibilities to those who depended on him. It was the will of his Father in heaven, and the ensuing circumstances of life were incidental.

What of his personal relationships? How did he relate to those closest to him — his immediate family? His rapport with his brothers was not good. They hated him with passion, and nursed strong resentments. Their familiarity with him bred contempt to the point of seeking his death. I refer to this account in John's Gospel: "After these things Jesus walked in Galilee, ... because the Jews sought to kill him. Now the Jews feast of tabernacles was at hand. His brethren therefore said unto him, 'Depart hence and go into Judea ...' For neither did his brethren believe in him (John 7:1-5). Then Jesus said to them:

My time is not yet come; but your time is always ready (John 7:6).

They were urging him to go into a territory where they knew the Jews were seeking to kill him. They did not believe in him. We therefore draw the conclusion that they hated him to the point of seeking his death. I infer therefore that anyone who imitates Jesus can expect to be the object of animosity, even from close relatives. The True Faith is no prescription for good relationships with one's neighbors and relatives. Loving our neighbors after the manner of Jesus does not solve our relationship problems. It may add to them. The Gospel is no free ticket to a smooth ride in the world. We will have all the problems that others have, and sometimes, depending upon the nature of our calling and the state of world affairs, there will be additional ones.

The above incident in the life of Jesus also reveals an important key to his actions: he did everything in its time. When it was time to abide with Mary and help to raise his siblings, he did so. When it was time to forsake his family and pursue his mission, he did so. When it was time to lay down his life in Jerusalem, he did so, but he did nothing before its time.

The early period with his family in Nazareth is therefore very revealing, just because of its existence. He could live with his family and pursue a normal occupation for many years without gaining any reputation other than as the carpenter, the son of Mary (Mark 6:3). There is no evidence that Jesus manifested radical ideas and activities during this period. To the contrary, the evidence, sparse as it is, strongly suggests that it was a very ordinary life. It was filled with responsibilities, work, and sibling resentment and rivalry.

From all this I conclude that it is not essential that everyone take on a radical lifestyle to follow Jesus. Lifestyle is irrelevant to one who hates life in this world, as Jesus did. The lifestyle we happen to experience will be incidental to whom and what we are. It is never an object for consideration within itself. It is only the life that becomes ours because of Christian discipleship. I can think of no circumstance that would cause us to make lifestyle one of our goals. Jesus does not compel a radical response from his followers. He only asks for obedience. Whatever life results from that is the one we must lead. The life, or lifestyle, is not a consideration as we contemplate the will of the Father. Can one find other evidence from the gospels to sustain this?

Yes. Here are some examples: There was a Roman centurion in Capernaum who sought help from Jesus. He did not seek it for himself, but for his sick and dying slave. When Jesus responded by approaching his house, the latter objected saying, "I am not worthy to have you come under my roof; but only say the word, and my servant will be healed. For I am a man under authority with soldiers under me; and I say to one, 'Go.' and he goes, and to another 'Come.' and he comes, and to my slave, 'Do this.' and he does it." And Jesus replied:

> *Truly I say to you, not even in Israel have I found such faith. I tell you, many will come from east and west and sit at table with Abraham, Isaac, and Jacob in the Kingdom of heaven, while the sons of the kingdom will be thrown into the outer darkness; there men will weep and gnash their teeth* (Matthew 8:10-12).

This man was a Roman officer and the commander of soldiers in the army of occupation. He maintained a house and owned slaves according to the custom of the times. Yet Jesus gave him high praise, with words that made him a strong candidate for the Kingdom. Significantly absent from Jesus' response was any command to resign his post or commission, free his slaves, or forsake his house, family, and Roman associations. Instead, Jesus granted his request and healed his slave, while giving him high praise for his great faith.

There was a man in Jericho named Zacchaeus. He was a chief tax collector (a publican) and he was rich. Being also short of stature, he climbed a tree to view Jesus above the crowds. Jesus commanded him to come down and invited himself into the man's house. Zacchaeus received him joyfully and said, "Behold, Lord, the half of my goods I give to the poor; and if I have defrauded anyone of anything, I restore it fourfold."

Then Jesus replied:

> *Today salvation has come to this house, since he also is a son of Abraham. For the Son of Man is come to seek and to save the lost* (Luke 19:9-10).

Jesus granted salvation to this man who had resolved to give up only half his wealth. Nor did he say anything to him about abandoning his house, or resigning his office as a tax collector.

Again, a young lawyer (scribe) once stood up in the crowd to put Jesus to the test. He said, "Teacher, what shall I do to inherit eternal life?" Jesus replied:

What is written in the law? (Luke 10:26).

He answered, "You shall love the Lord your God with all your heart, and with all your soul, and with all your strength, and with all your mind, and your neighbor as yourself."

And Jesus said to him,

You have answered right. Do this and you will live (Luke 10:28).

Here, as before, Jesus promised eternal life with no evident radical qualifying demands. We now know that the love of God entails the radical hatred of life, yet Jesus did not see fit to press this lawyer on the details. He did not command him to alter his occupation or other functions in the world. Perhaps Jesus, knowing the man was hostile, chose not to waste words. We know that he would not "cast his pearls before swine." Yet Jesus' complete prescription for life here is simple obedience to two commandments, which the man himself enunciated.

Finally, we have the very different case of the rich young man who came to Jesus asking, "Teacher, what good deed must I do to have eternal life?" Jesus replied,

Why do you ask me about what is good? One there is who is good. If you would enter into life, keep the commandments (Matthew 19:17).

Then Jesus quoted certain of the Ten Commandments and the young man replied, "All these I have observed. What do I still lack?"

Jesus answered,

If you would be perfect, go sell what you possess and give to the poor, and you will have treasure in heaven; and come, follow me (Matthew 19:21).

Then the young man went away sorrowfully, for he had great possessions.

Now here, for a change, is a radical demand! Why require so much from this man, and so little from the others? I think the answer is implicit in the mood of the young man as he went away, sorrowfully. His possessions possessed him. They had infected his heart and molded his character. He could not part with them. Jesus, knowing his heart, knew this also — and with Jesus, the heart is critical. This man's love of money was in the same category as an alcoholic's love for alcohol. The cure for both is the same — abstinence! He was not free to embrace the love of God until he had dealt with his love of money — therefore he could not enter eternal life. On the other hand, the centurion, a commander in the hateful army of occupation, was a good man who was mercifully attentive to the needs of the Jews. He had built their synagogue! His heart was open to the love of God in Christ. His office did not possess him. If Jesus had required him to resign his commission, he would doubtless have done so. Therefore Jesus did not require it. This man could have maintained his position in the world without guilt or qualms of conscience while circumstances permitted him to use the office to express love. This tells us that guilt comes not solely by association. It is the heart that is determinative, not the uniform!

But changing circumstances can make a vast difference. A generation later, when the Roman army brutally suppressed rebellion and purged the land of Jews, this centurion would certainly have resigned his commission before ordering his men to kill. Jesus' command to love the enemy (Matthew 5:44; Luke 6:27, 35) would have taken precedence over any order to muster his troops and march on Jerusalem.

It would be an unnecessarily radical response to the Lord for one to resign every worldly association. We will continue to be "in the world" until death, which is our most obvious association. Jesus also was in the world, and his Father did not condemn him. How could he? He came only because the Father sent him. One thing is needful — that we love the Lord and keep his commandments (John 14:15). While the association permits this, there is no need to sever it. If, however, the association compels one to disobey the Lord, a severance is in order. *This includes our association with life itself.* The associations in which we find ourselves when we come to Christ, of themselves, bring condemnation to no one. If it were otherwise, we would end our association with this world in the moment of our conversion.

Understanding the application of the Gospel can be a tricky business. It is important to recognize that the Centurion, from the moment of his commitment to Christ, ceased to be "of" the Roman army, though he may have remained "in" it. When you have committed your heart to Christ, you cease to be "of" anything that is of the world (John 15:19).

There are some associations in the world that do not permit this detachment while allowing a continued involvement. Then it is necessary to make a clean break. If one does not, compromises will destroy the faith. So the rich young man went away with his wealth rather than break that association to follow Jesus.

I made a similar decision when I resigned a commission in the Navy in 1951, during the Korean war. Before the war, I wore my uniform without guilt or qualms of conscience. Then the war came, and I realized a responsibility, as a Reserve officer, to enter active duty. No one compelled me to enter, but they encouraged me, a seminary student, to go into the Chaplaincy. They did not call me to active duty, due to my status as a ministerial student, but this was a problem for me. Why should I be free, while others were not? I carefully considered becoming a chaplain, but I could not do so as that compelled an intimate association with a military that was killing its enemies. In the end, I found peace only by resigning my commission. I think the Centurion, if he were still in the Roman army, would have done the same when his army began its genocidal war with the Jewish rebels.

Jesus' response to Zacchaeus implies that it is possible to be a disciple and retain the possession of wealth if it does not possess our hearts. Zacchaeus' readiness to give half his wealth to the poor while restoring four-fold any fraudulently obtained funds probably would have left him penniless anyway. Whatever the details, it was his willingness to begin such a divestiture that was his salvation, for it revealed that his heart was pure.

The application of the way of Christ to life in the world has powerful liberating effects. For one thing, we find ourselves freed from any compulsion to effect changes in the world, no matter how adverse the circumstances of birth. If our circumstances happen to be painful, and we find it possible to relieve them, we do so. No one enjoys pain, nor do pain and suffering in themselves have any redemptive effects. We do not, however, feel compelled to spend our energies in efforts to change what strongly resists change. We are free from the evil Crusades!

Second, we are free to accept ourselves, just as we are free to accept our circumstances. We can feel good about ourselves. We do not condemn ourselves, but if we have bad characteristics, we change them. A liar can feel good about himself only by lying to himself. The ability to make such changes is part of the liberation. However, we are able gracefully to accept our natural limitations in the knowledge that we are not to be condemned for them. If God does not condemn us, why should we condemn ourselves? This is the freedom found in Paul's counsel to the disciples who were slaves: "Were you a slave when called? Never mind. Nevertheless, if you can gain your freedom, do so" (1 Corinthians 7:21). So, a slave need have no compulsion to change either himself or his circumstances. Neither must he remain a slave, should the opportunity for freedom come.

Third, we are free to accept others. That means that we have no compulsion to condemn them because of their associations, circumstances, or natural characteristics. While I was unable to maintain my association with the military during a time of war, I have no right to judge others who followed a different course. Only God knows what is in their hearts! Besides all this, we have the commandment of the Lord:

> *Judge not, that you be not judged. For with what judgment you judge shall you be judged* (Matthew 7:1, 2).

Fourth and lastly, we are free to be or to become anything that is in accord with the will of God. There are no compelling worldly allegiances or loyalties, such as family or nation, that can dictate the course of our lives, or that can continue to hold us contrary to the will of God. The essence of this, of course, is the hold that life itself would continue to place upon us. These things are crucial to the freedom that Jesus promised when he said,

If the son of man shall make you free, you shall be free indeed (John 8:36).

The application of the principles of Christ to life in the world is so simple that a child can understand, provided one has once realized that our only purpose here is to qualify for hereafter. Having realized the Truth, having found the Kingdom of God, we hate life in this world and do not any longer wish to remain here. The Father also does not want us to remain, but wants only that we share with him his eternal Glory.

There are therefore only two reasons for our remaining — to confirm our faith and to witness that others also may see and enter the light. These two purposes mandate two functions that must be fulfilled — discipleship and witnessing. We can serve no other legitimate functions in this world. Any effort to do so testifies to our continued attachment to one or more facets of life in the world, and therefore to our condemnation.

As disciples, we commit ourselves to study in the School of Christ, who alone is our Schoolmaster and Teacher. We apply ourselves to the task of learning from him, so that we may be confirmed in the faith. The instantaneous point of conversion, when we decided to look at things from a different point of view, does not immediately purge all worldly affection from our hearts. That takes time. It takes more time for some than for others. Our Lord mercifully provides this time to purge our hearts of attachments to the world. Then, we may appear before him without spot or blemish or any such thing. It is not that we do this in our own strength. Never! Christ gives us the needed strength, as Lord, Teacher, Example, Wayshower, Savior, and Divine Word. As we yield to him and learn from him, we become like him. We strain forward eagerly to our graduation from this School, hoping only to pass the final examination and enter the Glory of our Father. It is therefore a time for growing in faith and knowledge and for purging our hearts of every taint of defilement, which is affection for life in the world.

As students of Christ, we have no grounds for glorying in ourselves. Our frequent failures must inevitably humble us and purge our hearts of false pride, leaving us with no worldly ambitions. Our inevitable learning to value only the eternal while despising the temporal treasures leaves us no earthly treasure, tangible or intangible, for which to seek. When he has fully taught us, no material wealth, no temporal relationship, and no earthly position will have any value in our hearts. The world will have no value and no hold upon us. We will be perfectly free, precisely as our Lord and Teacher promised.

As witnesses, we operate on the authority of our Lord's commission, which he expressed as follows,

> *Thus it is written, and thus it behooved Christ to suffer, and to rise from the dead the third day: and that repentance and remission of sins should be preached in his name among all nations, beginning at Jerusalem. And ye are witnesses of these things* (Luke 24:46-48).

FACING THE THREAT TO LIFE

Some persons face the threat to life repeatedly, yet without dying. Everyone must face it at least once, that is, when death comes. This threat comes in many different forms, yet when all is said, they remain the same. Each is a threat to life in this world; this, and nothing more.

There is the threat presented by another person. The enemy on the field of battle, the armed robber, an enemy intent on murder, a state executioner (as with Jesus) — all are examples of this threat. Here, the distinguishing feature is that another person moves with violence, deliberately perhaps, but not necessarily with premeditation, to threaten one's life.

There is the threat presented by accident. Traffic accidents, industrial accidents, accidents in the home and on the farm and at work, are appropriate examples. Here, while another person may be involved, there is no intent to harm. That is the distinguishing characteristic. Yet circumstances still combine to create a danger.

There is the threat presented by physical afflictions. Disease, physical malfunctions such as aneurysms, kidney failure, and infections exemplify this threat. These are the threats that hospitals and physicians combat.

There is the threat of old age, which will finally claim us if the others do not. The body and the brain, shackled to the futility of this age, inevitably wear out and at some point can no longer sustain life.

There is the threat arising from natural disasters. Famine, flood, tornado, and earthquake are prime examples. These are the so called "acts of God," and they claim many, many lives.

I could continue categorizing threats to life, for this is not all. These are sufficient, though, to illustrate the point, which is that while the threats may in themselves exhibit differences, they are ultimately all the same. They threaten the end of each life they approach. This overrides all differences and compels a common strategy for dealing with them. It also greatly simplifies the analysis of this topic, for it means that our responses to these threats are similar, although there will be differences in the details.

To yield or to resist? This is the question. The answer does not depend upon the nature of the threat. It is entirely dependent upon subjective features of the heart of the individual. Therefore, only the individual can properly judge whether to yield or resist. No one can make this judgment for us, and we can make it for no one else.

There is an utterance of Jesus that is applicable to every threat. He said:

> *Whoever would save his life shall lose it. And he who loses his life for my sake, will save it* (Matthew 16:25; Mark 8:35; Luke 9:24; 17:33).

This reduces all considerations to the root level of the will of the individual. It is "whoever would" (wishes to, wills to, wants to, desires to, aims to) save his life, who will lose it. One may save one's life for other reasons without coming under condemnation, but one must not save it because one *desires* to save it. So it was that Jesus rescued his life from the threat of death at the hands of the citizens of Nazareth when they sought to cast him off the precipice. He remained in this life only to fulfill his mission in the world, and not because he wanted to save his life. His desire was — first, last and always — to go to the Father in Glory.

We must not judge others who have saved their lives. We cannot know the desires of their hearts. With ourselves it is generally a different matter. If we respond to the threat-to-life in fear of death, desiring from the heart to save the life in this world, we will generally know it. Remember that the love of life is your ticket to hell, and pray that the Father will leave you here only while necessary to cleanse your heart of this defilement.

Since it is the will of the individual (the desire of the heart) that is crucial, let us examine the threat-to-life as it relates to the will. First, one's life is wholly dependent on the beating of the purely physical organ known as the heart, but the heart begins and goes on beating with absolutely no reference to the will of the individual. Your will does not start its action, does not maintain its operation, and cannot stop it as a mere act of the will. While men call it a natural function, we know that, in its essence, it is the act of divine will that operates it. Your will can stop it only by putting a bullet through it, or by committing some other form of suicide. I have already shown how suicide is an act of despair, and is not the will of God. Or else, it is putting God to the test, tempting him with the presentation of yourself at the gates of Glory to test his willingness to receive you. In either case, it is not the will of the Father.

Second, one's life requires the continued action of breathing, the constant operation of the diaphragm, chest muscles, and lungs to inhale and expel air. Like the beating of the heart, this is an automatic action having no reference to the will. It started without the operation of the will, and it continues thus. Also, you cannot will the cessation of breathing, except very temporarily. If you hold your breath until unconsciousness, then you lose control and resume breathing again, contrary to the will that held the breath during consciousness. What you can do is remove the air (as in drowning), or introduce some poisonous substance into it. Then, though you continue to breathe, it does not sustain life. But this, again, is an act contrary to nature and to God. It is suicide.

Third, the maintenance of life requires the ingestion of food and drink. As with breathing, one can willfully refuse food and drink, and for a much longer period. If the will is strong enough, one can fast to unconsciousness and death. It is done with great suffering and difficulty, and against all the natural inclinations of the body. Hunger and thirst have driven people to madness before death arrived. For those who persist until death, the result is the same as for those who breath poisonous gas or put a bullet through their hearts. It is suicide, and therefore forbidden by Him who long ago proclaimed,

You shall not tempt the Lord your God (Matthew 4:7; Luke 4:12).

The food requirement introduces a new dimension to the picture, not found in the other two. The heart beats without willful effort and requires no special provisions. The air that the lungs require is everywhere. Food is different. It must be provided and prepared. It must be wrestled from the earth or sea by hard labor, and stored up for the off-season. Now, if a person in isolation, knowing the necessity of providing food for himself for the winter to come, decides not to do so and perishes from hunger — that person also commits a form of suicide.

Fourth, the maintenance of life requires the provision of protection from exposure. Here, the threat to life is not so obvious and immediately evident as in the other cases, yet it is there. Therefore, at the most basic level, people build houses to shelter them from the extremes of heat and cold. They prepare garments to protect them from the cold and rain when they must be in the elements. Failure to make the necessary provisions, when possible, is tantamount to insuring one's own death. This also is suicide. It is as if a person, despairing of life, should go naked out into the winter storm with the expectation of freezing to death.

Fifth, the maintenance of life requires the provision of safety measures when circumstances are hazardous. When crossing the street, one looks both ways. When repairing electrical equipment, one turns off the power. When driving, one observes safe driving practices. The failure to approach such hazards safely is a form of Russian roulette. It is pure folly at best, and at worst, may expose a death wish. In the latter case, when it results in death, it is, again, suicide. It is the will operating to take one's own life.

Sixth, we often require medical care for the maintenance of life. How does the hatred of life apply to this? It usually makes no difference, but there are special circumstances where it interdicts any recourse to medical care. You are hurting; you get care as required to control the pain. You are injured and bleeding profusely; you get care to stop the bleeding and bind up your wounds. There is no divine calling to bear pain needlessly, or to fail to repair the injuries to the body to minimize the damage. You have accidentally ingested poison; you seek an antidote. You have an attack of appendicitis; you have an appendectomy. You have influenza; you apply appropriate remedies. You have cancer; you seek remedies.

The difference lies in the motive for doing these things, for if you are doing them solely to save your life, you are under condemnation. Instead, you do these things because you act in the faith that the Father has placed you here and has given you this time to be a witness, and to confirm your faith in the life to come. You do them reluctantly (except measures specifically applied to control pain) because, if your faith is firm, you prefer not to do them and go quickly to the Father in Glory. Thus it was that Jesus acted always to preserve and maintain his life until his crucifixion. As you are doing these things it will be evident to you, if your faith is firm, that there is no fear of death in your heart. A proper testimony mandates that this also should be the impression you impart to others. The time will come, though, when we know we witness much more effectively by dying than by living. Jesus knew this when Golgotha approached. No one can tell us this time, nor can anyone decide for others. Therefore we can make no judgments about others who are acting to preserve their lives.

Seventh, and last, the maintenance of life may require protection from the enemy. If my city comes under aerial bombardment, I would seek sanctuary in the bomb shelter with others. If the shelter becomes full so that others could not enter, my only recourse would be to yield my place to someone else. This would not be a form of heroism. I would only be going according to my heart's leading if I consequently lost my life. I would not be making a sacrifice of my life when, as Paul aptly declared, "To die is to gain" (Philippians 1:21).

Now, let me speak for myself. It seems to me, as I contemplate my departure from this world, that there are certain circumstances that would dictate my prompt departure. If my condition is incurable, and leaves me no energy to witness, then my only witness is to go joyfully to the Father. If it comes to the use of extreme measures, it is time for me to go. If I engage in futile efforts to extend my life, without any other purpose, I have stayed too long. Every day longer under these conditions only detracts from whatever testimony I may have previously made. I should have called a halt at some earlier time, before damaging my testimony. Again, if I should be persecuted for the faith, and threatened with death unless I recant, I go gladly to that fate. I do it in gratitude because the Father will have called me to the most glorious witness, martyrdom. Thus it was that Jesus went to the cross without hesitation. Know your own heart, and neither judge others nor be afraid of the critical judgments of others. Do everything according to the will of the Father, who places us here and wills that we remain until he calls us to his Glory. He sets the time, but we will know when it comes. This should provide each of us with the precious opportunity to use the hour of death as a powerful witness to the hatred of life. We endure it, like Jesus, for "the joy set before us." Let us therefore go joyfully and gladly. That is our marvelous freedom in the Lord.

In summary, one who follows Christ confronts every threat to life wanting to go to the Father, yet reconciled to remaining according to his plan and purpose. Like Jesus, one appropriates all natural and normal means of preserving the earth-life, yet without willing to save that life for its own sake. We recognize that the Father has so ordered reality that we preserve our lives without any operation of the will by respiration and heartbeat. We also recognize that he has ordered the body so as to require food, shelter, and certain kinds of care for its preservation. We therefore accede to the will of the Creator until our time comes to go to Him. We must not seek death before our time. We must not seek to preserve our lives beyond our time, which testifies to the love of life, and therefore to condemnation.

Jesus showed how to apply the hatred of life to the living of it. His Truth has liberated us from the bonds of this world, to live out the rest of our time in joyful anticipation of the glory of God. We approach the hour of death filled with gladness and hope. We are glad he has blessed us to find the purpose of this life in its fulfillment in the life to come. It was, you see, for the "joy set before him" that he endured the cross (Hebrews 12:2).

Come unto me, all ye that
labour and are heavy laden,
and I will give you rest.

Jesus, Matthew 11:28